# ROCKEFELLER PHILANTHROPY AND MODERN SOCIAL SCIENCE

T0330567

# Studies in Business History

# ROCKEFELLER PHILANTHROPY AND MODERN SOCIAL SCIENCE

BY

David L. Seim

LONDON AND NEW YORK

First published 2013 by Pickering & Chatto (Publishers) Limited

Published 2016 by Routledge
2 Park Square, Milton Park, Abingdon, Oxfordshire OX14 4RN
711 Third Avenue, New York, NY 10017, USA

First issued in paperback 2015

*Routledge is an imprint of the Taylor & Francis Group, an informa business*

BRITISH LIBRARY CATALOGUING IN PUBLICATION DATA

Seim, David L.
Rockefeller philanthropy and modern social science. – (Studies in business history)
1. Rockefeller family. 2. Rockefeller Foundation. 3. Laura Spelman Rockefeller
Memorial. 4. Philanthropists – United States – Case studies. 5. Endowment of
research – History – 20th century. 6. Social sciences – Research – Finance – Case
studies. 7. Business and education – United States – History – 20th century.
I. Title II. Series
361.7'632-dc23

ISBN-13: 978-1-138-66220-9 (pbk)
ISBN-13: 978-1-8489-3391-0 (hbk)
Typeset by Pickering & Chatto (Publishers) Limited

# CONTENTS

# ACKNOWLEDGEMENTS

This book is based on research at the Rockefeller Archive Centre (RAC). I am grateful to the RAC, which makes available an extraordinary quantity of materials on the history of Rockefeller philanthropy. In June 2005, I had the good fortune to visit the RAC, located just north of New York City. I gain a greater sense of appreciation every year since then, partly because of vivid fond memories of those intensive days 'in the archive'. I wrote a dissertation based on that research, and I thank my dissertation committee for their hard and caring work during that stage of the project. I appreciate many friends and family who helped me, and I shall offer appreciative words in person. I am grateful to my father, a social scientist with insights that I treasure; this book would be much less than it is, had he and I never had our conversations before this project was even imagined.

I acknowledge permission to publish extracts from materials at the RAC (abbreviated in all notes as 'RAC'). I confirmed quotations in Allan Nevins's *Study in Power* during a visit to the Allan Nevins Papers (abbreviated 'ANP') at Columbia University. Any use that I make of any person's unique expression of ideas is intended to be true to all original intent. Any errors herein are the responsibility of the author.

# NOTE ON THE TEXT

John D. Rockefeller is referred to herein as 'Rockefeller' or 'Rockefeller, Sr', depending upon the context. John D. Rockefeller, Jr is always 'Rockefeller, Jr'. The Rockefeller Foundation is often referred to as the 'Foundation'. The Laura Spelman Rockefeller Memorial is often referred to as the 'Memorial'.

# INTRODUCTION

*Rockefeller Philanthropy and Modern Social Science* studies a forty-year period of efforts to provide financial support to social scientists. The period is from the late 1880s to the late 1920s. Historical studies have tended to conclude either that Rockefeller philanthropy aimed to guide the directions of social science or that it did not. Some historians see the relationship between Rockefeller philanthropy and social science as compatible with the autonomy of social scientists. Others conclude that Rockefeller financial support conflicted with scientific freedom. I reconsider how and why Rockefeller donations were made to social scientists. By looking at what these donations aimed to do and what these donations accomplished, I conclude that each of two opposing camps among historians is partly correct. I bring to the conversation much archival research, which I employ to understand discussions and bargaining procedures between social scientists and foundation personnel. I find that the Rockefellers and their foundation officials developed many protective strategies to enable uncontroversial support of social scientists.[1]

This book is also about the Rockefellers – John D. Rockefeller and John D. Rockefeller, Jr – and what they did when they understood that the American people expect business activities and business profits to serve 'the public interest'. A key underlying issue throughout the book is that 'the public interest' was a changing concept over time. John D. Rockefeller was very wealthy. He made more money than perhaps anyone in history, and he gave away more money than perhaps anyone in history. He lived nearly one hundred years, amassing his fortune over some eighty of those years. In his lifetime, Rockefeller witnessed some extraordinary shifts in public opinion about the responsibilities of business.

Rockefeller did not simply hand out money. He cared how it was used. He saw his wealth as hard earned, and he believed the bar should be kept high for any money given away. Just as there was a method to his business success, so there was to his philanthropic work. Rockefeller started many philanthropic organizations during his life. His son, John D. Rockefeller, Jr, became an outstanding philanthropist as well.

This book aims to understand how Rockefeller philanthropy made the world a better place. Fine historical studies have been made about Rockefeller philanthropy.

Many of them focus on Rockefeller support of medical research and public health. Some studies explore Rockefeller support of education. Historians increasingly study how Rockefeller philanthropy helped to establish the modern social sciences.

The two established ways of understanding relationships between Rockefeller philanthropy and social science can be wrapped into a single explanation. The explanation is developed by considering a history of ideas about relationships between business and society. As developed by business leaders and scholars, by the first decades of the twentieth century some clarity was achieved concerning ideas about business interests and the public interest.

A history of ideas about social responsibilities of business can begin at various points in the nineteenth century. Much importance must be placed on the appearance of the concept of 'stewardship', by the 1880s. A decade later, the popular phrase was 'civic duty', as represented by civic clubs, the Civic Federation and then the Chamber of Commerce movement. In the business schools, conversation spoke of a 'modern economy', with some emphasis on the concept of a business' need to earn 'good will'. Business 'profit sharing' plans became popular (yet also criticized), and there was a shift in phrasing from 'uplift work' to 'welfare work' – the beginnings of welfare capitalism. By 1910, the argument was well made that when society developed its institutions to enable big business, society placed a 'trust' in big business. On the business side, it became popular to hire 'public relations' experts to distribute the right information to show that business activities serve the public trust. Throughout this period from the 1880s through the 1910s, a line of argument consistently coming from business leaders was that good behaviour is good business – i.e. that when a company shows good behaviour, consumers will like the company, workers will be healthy and the economy will be stable.[2]

John D. Rockefeller, who got his first job in 1855, lived through every one of these transitions in thought about business and the public interest. Rockefeller and later his son, John D. Rockefeller, Jr, gave away their fortune in the ways that they did in part because they developed ideas about the social responsibilities of business.

The Rockefellers donated a great deal of money to social scientists. In principle, social scientists can serve private interests such as business, or they can serve the public interest. This is a distinction much discussed in the history of social science. A long-running goal held by Rockefeller philanthropy was to promote a neutral relationship between financial support of social science and research results that come from social science. One way to define a 'neutral result' is that research findings can help foster the discovery of the best arrangement of institutions for a productive industrialized society that serves all interests. The open question was what would be this best arrangement of institutions?

To discover the best arrangement of institutions in society, leaders in Rockefeller philanthropy employed a variety of methods to help build an essential piece within the institutional framework of modern society. This piece was a community of social scientists who would focus on guiding business and government to best serve the public interest. Such a community of social scientists needed to be built without any assertion of business or government control over the social scientists. Social scientists needed to be free to discover whatever they would discover about how business and government perform in serving the public interest.

Disagreement exists about how to best understand John D. Rockefeller and his goals. Historians scrutinize Rockefeller's career as 'oil titan' for evidence of aggressive business behaviour. There is also a focus on seeing Rockefeller as a giant among philanthropists. When these two areas of inquiry are taken together, Rockefeller can be seen as something of a contradiction. He was a very aggressive monopolist. He was also a highly generous philanthropist. Most common among historians is to understand Rockefeller's religious views as a way through any seeming contradiction; yet other historians are not sure that this works. I suggest that the two sides of Rockefeller can be brought together when we include ample consideration of business beliefs of his time.[3]

If there was any single event of greatest importance in the life of John D. Rockefeller, it was in May 1911 when the United States Supreme Court ordered the dismantling of the Standard Oil 'Trust'. The American public received the Court's decision as confirming what they already believed: that Rockefeller's business practices were unfair, and even criminal. For some four decades since its creation, Standard Oil had shown a history of persistently forceful tactics, which kept the company's extraordinary profit-making ahead of slowly reacting laws of the day.

Severe competitive practices of Standard Oil were often the subject of complaint. Two great names among the critics, without question, were Henry Demarest Lloyd and Ida M. Tarbell. In 1894, Lloyd described Rockefeller's apparent manipulation of government officials, particularly those responsible for regulatory oversight of the nation's first oil fields in western Pennsylvania. 'The Standard Oil Company', as Lloyd put it, 'has done everything with the Pennsylvania legislature except to refine it'. Between 1902 and 1904, Tarbell produced a multi-year series of articles revealing a litany of violations of the public trust, which she published as the 'History of the Standard Oil Company'. Released as serial installments in *McClure's Magazine*, Tarbell's investigative piece compelled people to look critically at a range of Rockefeller's activities. Also in 1903, when the US Congress discussed whether to toughen the nation's enforcement of its anti-monopoly laws, newspaper revelations introduced the so-called 'Rockefeller telegrams', supposedly aimed at influencing the votes of lawmakers. As one news reporter described the matter, these contacts with US Senators were a strong-arm effort potentially representing 'the most brazen attempt in the history of lobbying'.[4]

And this was not all. Many reasons were found to criticize Rockefeller. It can be difficult to imagine all the kinds of bad press that were once aimed at Rockefeller and Standard Oil. Some stories through the 1890s discussed Rockefeller's supposed attempts to suppress academic freedom at the University of Chicago, a school that he contributed immensely to help establish. In the 1900s, some words of disapproval focused on methods of animal research (including vivisection) supported by the Rockefeller Institute for Medical Research. In 1905, religious leaders grabbed headlines when they accused Rockefeller of donating 'tainted money' to a religious group. The legal decision to dismantle Standard Oil was big news in 1911. Rockefeller and Rockefeller, Jr both went into the news cycle in 1914 for their reported neglect of workers at a Rockefeller-owned mining company, where many workers, and some women and children, went to their deaths during a labour strike. Many times through the years Rockefeller got into the news for saying things like, 'God gave me my money'. All told, there was a time when John D. Rockefeller was looked upon with such distain that even the President of the United States, Theodore Roosevelt, took time in 1906 to label him as an 'evil' and a 'sinister' man.[5]

All of this is harsh. But to remind ourselves, there was another side of the story. John D. Rockefeller sometimes did great things with his money. His first major works of philanthropy were to establish and support seminaries, colleges and universities, including one for Native Americans, and two schools for African Americans. In 1892 he helped found the University of Chicago. In 1901 he established the Rockefeller Institute for Medical Research (today's Rockefeller University). Two years later he established the General Education Board, to support schools for black and white communities in the American South. In 1909, he established the Sanitary Commission to help cure people of hookworm. Rockefeller's son, John D. Rockefeller, Jr, established a philanthropic organization of his own, the Bureau of Social Hygiene, between 1911 and 1913. In May 1913, Rockefeller, Sr established the Rockefeller Foundation, which he endowed with $100 million. Various ideas pertinent to the social sciences appeared in all of these organizations.

In October 1918, Rockefeller established his last major philanthropy, to honour his wife; he named it the Laura Spelman Rockefeller Memorial. The initial purpose of the Memorial was to promote the welfare of mothers and children, which were two great concerns of Laura Rockefeller. During the first few years of the Memorial, the philanthropy was operated out of the office of Rockefeller, Jr; but during 1921, after distributing much of the Memorial's original $13 million, leaders in Rockefeller philanthropy decided to try an experiment. Rockefeller donated a great amount of money to the Memorial in January 1921, and a plan was developed to support the broad development of the social sciences.

Between 1922 and 1929, the Memorial intensively developed a major programme to support the advancement of social and behavioural knowledge. Director Beardsley Ruml and the Memorial officers implemented the programme by various means, including fellowships for individual social scientists, project grants for teams of scientists, block grants to university-based research centres, endowments for independent research organizations and a very substantial endowment for a Social Science Research Council (which in turn dispensed money to social scientists). The Memorial's project represented a novel experiment in the history of social science. It was an experiment to discover what level of success might be attained by getting a great amount of financial support to social scientists. The work of the Memorial was ultimately about solving an ethical dilemma: how to financially support social scientists without manipulating or distorting the direction of advancements in the social sciences. The Memorial ended its programme in January 1929, when the programme was merged into the Rockefeller Foundation.

Historians ask direct questions about Rockefeller philanthropy: why did Rockefeller donate such vast sums of money to build his great philanthropic foundations? Were his reasons primarily pure, stemming from a genuine giving spirit? Were his gifts a result of emergent feelings of personal guilt over ill-gotten gains? Or, potentially even a bit sinister, were his grand acts of philanthropy a design to control the uses of the social sciences to obtain policies promoting his own capitalist success?

In donating such great sums of money, Rockefeller and (later) Rockefeller, Jr were not motivated from ulterior motives first and foremost; yet neither did they possess a strictly charitable mindset. Their overriding goal was to help discover remedies for social and economic problems, and the approach that they decided was best was to help build a community of public-serving social scientists who could make these discoveries. Over the period of forty years covered in this book, the Rockefellers refined their understanding that business enterprise has responsibilities to help support the process of assessing what the public should expect of business. Business enterprise is, above all, to serve the public interest, and social scientists needed to continually identify what is in the public interest. Social scientists therefore needed to be objectively discovering facts about the condition of people and groups in a modern industrial society.

The Rockefellers acted on a belief that more social science would achieve more accurate understanding of all social and economic problems that arise from the capitalist system.

Through many of the years in this study, the United States was in the 'Progressive era', when politicians and other social leaders held great confidence in the potential to achieve 'social control' over a whole variety of problems in society. Among supporters of the idea of social control were many of the nation's industrialists, who were concerned about the nation's levels of immorality, poverty and suffering. America's upper class sometimes wondered what a widely lowered level of economic well-being might do to the viability of capitalism itself. Industrialist families often decided to assume leadership roles by becoming philanthropists in order to share in the dream of establishing a more progressive society.

Great optimism abounded – shared by industrialists, politicians and academics – that social science could provide the knowledge to guide the necessary social and economic reforms. One optimistic family was the Rockefellers.

# 1 BUSINESS AND PHILANTHROPY

Between 1855 and 1900, John D. Rockefeller was an extraordinary business success. He got his first job in 1855, and by 1900 he was ready to retire from leadership of the Standard Oil Company. For his work as president and majority owner of Standard Oil, Rockefeller became the person who remains considered the single richest individual who ever lived. Rockefeller also learned how to give away more money than perhaps anyone who has ever lived.[1]

## Young Rockefeller

John Davison Rockefeller was born 8 July 1839, the second of six children, to William Avery and Eliza (Davison) Rockefeller. Young John grew up in modest economic circumstances, beginning life in a rural home near the village of Richford, New York. By the age of fourteen, Rockefeller moved three times with his family. They went to Moravia, New York, then to Oswego and then out of the state entirely. Rockefeller's early years likely had some feelings of insecurity to them.

In the summer of 1853, the Rockefellers established a home in the small community of Strongsville, Ohio, near Cleveland. Yet John moved again, this time into the city to attend Cleveland's Central High School. He joined the Erie Street Baptist Church, located in a new red-brick building, with a fine cathedral. He became active in church affairs. After just two years of high school, Rockefeller enrolled in a six-month business programme at Folsom Mercantile College, which he completed in three months.

In late 1855, Rockefeller gained his first job as an assistant bookkeeper for Hewitt & Tuttle, a small firm of commission merchants and produce shippers. He did not get paid for three months. But when he received his pay, the company paid him not only his $50 for work performed, but awarded him a raise of $25 a month, and soon a position as bookkeeper and cashier. When he received that first payment of wages, Rockefeller started a record of his personal giving. He tithed to his church, to which he provided a percentage of every pay cheque. He would always care greatly to donate money, and to do it wisely from every pay cheque or profit distribution that he received. Rockefeller contributed money in accordance with his Baptist faith, and he perceived that for every dollar earned as a blessing for hard work, he was called to donate a percentage of it with equally disciplined effort.

By 1859 Rockefeller had $1,000 saved. He asked to borrow what his father could spare, and his father came up with $1,000 as well. Rockefeller joined with an acquaintance, Maurice Clark, to establish a partnership in the commission business. This was the same year that drillers struck oil in western Pennsylvania, and as it happened, railroad routes passing through Pennsylvania picked up the crude and transported it to Cleveland, where a large immigrant population was available for work in the refineries. Rockefeller and Clark began doing some accounting work for the crude transporters and refiners, and Rockefeller built a good level of savings by the time that the Civil War began. With his financial stability he paid a substitute to fight for him. His commission business expanded during the war, most remarkably through his access to the product of an Ohio whisky distillery. Rockefeller received a tip that a heavy excise tax was about to be imposed on the whisky, and he participated in a move to buy up all the barrels. He then sold the whisky at a price just below the government's price, by which he made tremendous profit selling it to the Union army. In 1863, with much capital on hand, Rockefeller and Clark entered the refinery business. They brought in a third partner, Samuel Andrews, a chemist with refining experience, and their new company was Andrews, Clark & Co.

In his personal life Rockefeller became increasingly active in his church. He also met his love, Laura Celestia Spelman. Laura, born in Massachusetts on 9 September 1839, and often called 'Cettie', was one of two bright and educated sisters who grew up near Cleveland. John and Laura became high-school sweethearts, and on 8 September 1864, they married. Laura was from a family of reformers and abolitionists, and she became a Cleveland schoolteacher. John and Laura had five children over the next ten years: four daughters (three surviving through infancy), and a son, John Davison Rockefeller, Jr, born in 1874.

By the time of his marriage, on the business side of his life, Rockefeller's company was succeeding royally in the refining business. But the partners in the company, five in number by 1865, began experiencing disagreements. They decided to sell the company to whoever among them could bid the highest. Rockefeller paid $72,500. Retaining one of the partners, he formed Rockefeller & Andrews. The company performed well, aided by the nation's expanding railroads and a booming market for kerosene. Rockefeller and Andrews joined with Henry M. Flagler and John's brother, William, and in 1870 they formed the Standard Oil Company of Ohio.

From the time of its creation, with a capital valuation of $1 million, the history of growth and conquest by 'The Standard' is stunning. Within some twenty months of the company's creation they controlled nearly all of Cleveland's refining capacity. The major episode in this growth was known as the 'Cleveland Massacre'. The episode was during 1872, when dozens of small oil producers across Ohio and western Pennsylvania were pushed hard to sell their businesses to Rockefeller, under the threat that if they tried to compete they would face ruin. Rockefeller employed intimidating tactics to push competitors into selling their holdings at approximately 40 per cent of asset value, which he accomplished on the declaration that anyone refusing his offer would be pushed into bankruptcy anyway (since all that Rockefeller needed to do was sell below cost and obtain agreements from the railroads to charge any resisting company double or triple the usual shipping costs).

The company made a strong expansion eastward, and with two new refineries near New York City by 1873, the company could refine nearly 30,000 barrels of crude oil a day. They had their own manufactory of storage barrels, they owned and operated warehousing facilities and they built plants to manufacture a wide range of petroleum products, from kerosene, to machine oil, to paints and glues. There was a market crash in September 1873, and Standard Oil took advantage of the situation by absorbing refineries from Pittsburgh, through Philadelphia, all the way to New York. Within five more years of further consolidation of this rapid expansion, Standard Oil controlled nearly 90 per cent of the oil refined in the United States. Some observers saw the Standard Oil Company as a wise and frugal outfit. Others perceived it as an outright violator of the law. Any way that one looked at things, the company was driven to succeed; and it made extraordinary profits for Rockefeller.

Rockefeller also needed to continue donating money, and his strategies for giving changed over time. He remained a committed churchgoer, and he served his congregation through tithing as well as with other charitable gifts. He supported reform organizations through his church, including the temperance movement and the YMCA. As his wealth became sufficient for heightened levels of giving, Rockefeller gave to church friends, to the widowed and the disabled, and to the poor and the needy. The ties to bind all of this together remained his personal religious tenets and the financial needs of his church. Rockefeller's trusted sounding board during his first decades of giving remained his friends among Cleveland's Baptist leaders.

By the 1880s Rockefeller made even greater amounts of money. Still he required himself to donate a portion of every dollar that he earned, and any standard means for donating money could no longer keep up. He was also receiving great numbers of hard-luck letters. He was often in the news, generally for being one supremely rich fellow. In many news stories would appear the detail that he gave money away, and so more appeals kept on arriving. He tried to make more small gifts. He tried giving more to his church. Indeed, his church soon came to rely on him very greatly; it is said that by about 1880 he covered nearly half the annual budget of his church, which had moved into a fine new building and become Euclid Avenue Baptist Church.

## Lifting through Individual Donations

In 1882 and 1883, Rockefeller began a period of introspection into how and why he gave money. Many of his thoughts are preserved in letters. In one letter, to family friend Mrs Laura M. Irvine, he shared his impression of the Five Points missions in New York City. He decided that he disapproved of simply handing out meals, as a better strategy would be to find ways to provide work. When he contemplated donating $1,000 annually to a missionary chapel, Rockefeller added: 'I am not willing to be a party to a failure in this undertaking'. In a letter written to another friend, a Mr Dowling, Rockefeller again described the Thanksgiving Day visit to the Five Points House of Industry soup kitchen, and how he and his family 'were much interested' by what they saw:

> One feature ... we decidedly objected to, but I have not had sufficient time to confer with the Managers and get their idea of the policy of feeding all the tramps that come. My impression is they only do it once a year. I would give them work and make them earn their food.

What was needed, in other words, was to promote a fundamental lift by 'giving work'.[2]

On another occasion in 1882 Rockefeller replied to an appeal from a friend. 'I want to know surely in giving', he explained, 'that I am putting money where it will do most good'. Rockefeller preferred believing that carefully targeted assistance can help to 'lift' people.[3]

And again he wrote in 1882, this time to a Mr Duncan of Steubenville, Ohio, from whom he had received a letter. Rockefeller responded with his 'rejoice to hear of the good work being done in the region. I wish I had enough money to give to all the good objects presented. It would be a most delightful occupation'. Rockefeller felt he could give $1,000 for present needs. 'I am sure there will be others just as important and I fear the money will not hold out. If, however, you cannot get through with this I will lift again'.[4]

Rockefeller was recognizing the need to think about his principles for effective giving. He was also thinking about how to select recipients. This first phase in his experiments in giving lasted for a few years. A letter in 1886 shows Rockefeller's sense of responsibility to do his best work with limited funds: 'I haven't a farthing to give to this or any other interest unless I am perfectly satisfied it is the very best I can do with the money'. That same year, in March, Rockefeller shared his concern to see donated money produce long-term benefits. He wrote to a friend in Cleveland, seeking an impression of a potential recipient: 'Is it a feeble interest, that cannot hope to succeed'? On the specific subject of supporting Baptist churches and schools, Rockefeller added: 'I think mistakes are made by organizing too many feeble institutions – rather consolidate and have good, strong working church organizations'.[5]

There is another fine example of Rockefeller's thought about how to give money without wasting it. In April 1885, he wrote to his friend Louis Severance, a founding member of the Standard Oil Trust. Rockefeller offered thoughts on a proposed Music Hall and Tabernacle for Cleveland. 'I don't want to put the money into a sinking ship', he stated. 'Do you think others will join? Can the money be raised? Is there a good feeling in respect to this undertaking?' We see Rockefeller exploring possibilities for some sort of a 'matching funds' approach.[6]

Rockefeller was still in his phase of struggling with his desire to help people when, in December 1886, he shared some thoughts with his brother Frank. Rockefeller described how he did 'not want to encourage a horde of irresponsible, adventuresome fellows to call on me at sight for money every time fancy seizes them'. He soon expressed an added thought to Frank, as he described how his energy was becoming exhausted: 'I have been overwhelmed with this sort of thing of late and want to shut down brakes a little until I can catch breath'.[7]

Indeed by 1886 and even increasing over the next few years, the volume of mail asking for Rockefeller's help was stunning. He could receive 2,000 letters in a day. Regarding this period of inundation by supplicants' appeals, Rockefeller put it this way by December 1888: his personal time was gone, 'taken up with the consideration of petitions from many sources'. 'I have never known them so numerous', he added.[8]

And even when he gave money to an individual, Rockefeller could discover an experience that further drained him. He would tell of the sadness of seeing recipients squander away their opportunities. 'I have lent and given people money', he once told his son, 'and then seen them cross the street so that they would not have to speak to me'.[9]

Rockefeller developed a sense of the inadequacy of small, one-time donations. He shared a more crystallized view with the Rev. Edward W. Oakes, in New York City. '[A]s I have often expressed to you', Rockefeller wrote in 1885,

> I am very anxious that people once committed to good work should be placed in the harness and educated in taking up responsibilities – trained for increased usefulness. To do this in the best way, I think it quite desirable for the shepherd to abide with them.

Writing again to Oakes, in that same year, Rockefeller believed that Oakes could do well to be 'in the midst of the multitudes thronging up and down the Bowery or thereabouts, and settle and stay right there with them, establish a church'. The scale of problems was immense, and Rockefeller realized that an institution needed to take the lead.[10]

## Lifting through his Church

As Rockefeller recognized the scale of what would be needed to genuinely address problems of poverty and suffering in industrial society, he began donating more money through his church. He built a relationship of confidence especially with Rev. George O. King of Cleveland. King was a friend of Rockefeller, and Rockefeller was happy to assist anyone recommended by King. But one day Rockefeller hesitated to make some donations that King recommended. King asked about this, and in March 1881 Rockefeller opened up: 'I have been holding back answer[ing] in part from the fact that I had so many obligations for benevolent objects that I was almost overwhelmed'. Rockefeller lamented having 'no time to investigate all these calls from different churches throughout the country', and he added a request for an opinion about a particular Ohio minister who wanted money. Rockefeller wondered if he could manage so many demands on his 'missionary work', and not just 'pass them by'.[11]

Rockefeller and King corresponded often. It was a friendship strong enough for the Rockefellers to invite the King family to accompany them on a vacation, or that the Kings might occasionally send flowers to the Rockefellers. This was a friendship that emerged when Rockefeller needed it, for his business was going well, and he could hardly stop accumulating profits. He therefore could not stop donating money. And above all, as he expressed in November 1885 to King, he wanted to continue 'my lifting'.[12]

At some point King began making requests beyond church matters. He asked for money for jobs for some people and he requested tuition money for others. Rockefeller helped King purchase some personal clothing, and even pay for minor travel expenses. Rockefeller typically came through for King, and he learned to trust King's advice, which was most valued when visitors came to Cleveland as missionary educators on fundraising tours.[13]

One visitor was Almone C. Bacone, who was establishing a school for Native Americans in Oklahoma. Located near the eastern edge of Oklahoma's Cherokee Territory, 'Indian University' was established in 1880 under Bacone's leadership, and with the support of the American Baptist Home Mission Society (ABHMS). Bacone visited Cleveland in 1880, and Rockefeller offered support. Indian University's trustees then named their first building Rockefeller Hall, or simply, 'The Rock'. By the end of the subsequent decade, Rockefeller personally contributed over $12,000 to Bacone's work, most of it to finance building construction. The school proved to be a success, and renamed Bacone College, it stands today as Oklahoma's oldest continuing centre of higher education.[14]

Also visiting Cleveland were Sophia Packard and Harriet Giles, who hoped to establish a female seminary for the education of African-American women in the South. Following the American Civil War, freed slaves and their descendants were greatly in need of education. In 1877, Packard helped establish the Women's American Baptist Home Mission Society, with a goal to assist in this. Representing her mission society, Packard visited the South to assess the conditions of freed slaves. During her tour, Packard recruited a teaching acquaintance, Harriet Giles, to join her.[15]

The two northerners travelled together for nearly two months during the spring of 1880, and then returned home to Boston and shared what they had seen. Bolstered by expressions of support, Packard and Giles gained a determination to open an institution of higher learning for African-American women in the South. They asked their mission society's leadership to help support the school, and with additional assistance from black ministers around Atlanta, in April 1881 Packard and Giles opened the Atlanta Baptist Female Seminary, serving eleven students in a church basement. The school's numbers rose and soon the seminary had some 200 students – more than one basement could hold.

In June 1882, Packard and Giles's fundraising efforts brought them to a Sunday-morning introduction at Cleveland's largest Baptist church. In attendance that morning was Rockefeller. He awarded them some $81 that he had on hand, and he pledged $250 more. The additional pledge soon arrived for the school's building fund, and it was supplemented with $250 more for furniture. Packard and Giles moved the school into some former Army barracks, where faculty and students could now excel, including their creation of an experimental, 'model school' approach to training teachers.

Rockefeller's support of the Atlanta Seminary fit well with his interests at the time. Baptist concerns mattered to him, as did the needs of persons for whom targeted assistance could be most uplifting. He felt secure when his philanthropic work involved personal interaction, and the money provided to Packard and Giles was directed through the mission society, and this also helped in keeping track of the overall progress of the institution.[16]

As Packard once phrased an overall view of the work to establish the seminary, 'to elevate the women is the only salvation of our country'. For in turn, women can purify the home, and a purified home 'is the solution of the greatest problem before the American people today'.[17]

## Rockefeller and the American Baptist Home Mission Society

Rockefeller was familiar with the ABHMS, to which Rev. King belonged. The society's focus was to support Baptist missionary and education work. One frequent visitor to Cleveland was Henry L. Morehouse, the society's corresponding secretary. Rockefeller began regular correspondence with Morehouse by the spring of 1881, and he learned of the financial needs of many Baptist schools that fit the society's focus on supporting 'Freedmen and Indians'.

While Rockefeller himself was educated only slightly past high school, he believed in promoting greater access to education, and he believed that the more recipients of higher education there were, the more people could help elevate the human condition. Or, as he once expressed it, great achievements with one's education are valued as they 'minister to the wants of all people'.[18]

Morehouse brought to Rockefeller's attention a particular school in need. At the end of the Civil War, the US federal government established a National Theological Institute. School sites were in the two national capitals during the war: Washington, DC and Richmond, Virginia. But the branch in Richmond fell on tough times, and was soon a run-down building in financial distress. Virginia's lawmakers decided to try again. In 1876, they established a new Richmond Institute, naming as its president Dr Charles Henry Corey, a Canadian minister who had gone to South Carolina to help out after the Civil War. But the school again was on a downward slide. A conference of the ABHMS was held in New York City, on 4 June 1879, where interests of the Richmond Institute were considered.[19]

Morehouse initiated more intensive inquiry when he wrote to the Richmond Institute in January 1880. He described the mission society's desire to assist the school in improving its facilities to admit female students. This soon was done. Morehouse wrote again to the school, that April, and he offered the mission society's assistance in purchasing a small land parcel on which new buildings could be 'judiciously planned and located'.[20]

Time went by, then in June 1882 a large conference of the mission society was again held in New York City. At the conference, after some discussion it was voted, 'that, in their opinion, a higher Theological School ought to be developed at Richmond'. Communications began with the school's trustees, another year and a half went by, and in November 1883 the mission society's board resolved that 'the time has arrived for the establishment of a distinctively Theological Institution of a higher order for the education of coloured students for the ministry, and that Richmond is a suitable location for such an institution'.[21]

This had been a long road. The Richmond Theological Institute was going to be supported. At the following month's meeting of the mission society, they further recorded their belief 'that the increasing intelligence of the coloured people in America, and the need of well-qualified missionaries for Africa, imperatively demand that immediate measures be taken for the establishment of a distinctively Theological Institution at Richmond, Virginia'. In addition to that, the board added a practical view of a plan which 'contemplates the permanent establishment of a theological institution that shall be for the coloured Baptists what theological institutions in other sections are for their white brethren'. The board finally announced their earnest appeal to persons of means who have at heart the welfare of the coloured people here, and the evangelization of Africa, to do for this institution what has been done for others – namely, to endow two or more professorships in the sum of not less than twenty thousand dollars each.[22]

This was the context of an extended interaction that, in January 1884, brought Morehouse to pen an announcement. 'I have good news for you' were his simple words; a special gift of $25,000 had come from John D. Rockefeller, and it was a matching gift. The gift was for a Professorship of Theology, contingent upon the raising of the equivalent sum for a second professorship. 'So you see', added Morehouse, 'we have not been too fast in deciding to make this our first high grade theological school'. In September, two weeks before the fundraising deadline, Morehouse could write excitedly once more. The matching funds were received. 'Hallelujah!', he exclaimed. Morehouse reported a pledge of $25,000 by J. B. Hoyt, of Rochester, NY. Hoyt had a long-standing interest in the welfare of the South, and in fact immediately after the war, he had visited ruined Charleston. The donation was for a fully endowed second professorship. Thus the two gifts created two named chairs: 'The John D. Rockefeller Fund, Chair of Biblical Theology' and 'The J. B. Hoyt Fund, Chair of Church History'. While the first endowed chair was focused on theology, the chair supported by the matching funds that met Rockefeller's requirement created a position effectively in a social science. Soon the school began to offer a Bachelor of Divinity.[23]

On Christmas Eve 1883, while early successes with the Atlanta Seminary were being realized, and while work with the Richmond Institute was ongoing, Rockefeller wrote a nice letter to Morehouse. Rockefeller considered opening a new phase in his giving. He was weary of the constant appeals to rescue people, and he shared with Morehouse his wish 'to avoid having all these people from every part of the country calling on me'. Rockefeller asked 'whether it is not much better for the cause ... to give all through the Home Mission Society'. Rockefeller, trusting Morehouse's wisdom, asked if Morehouse might know of 'other more important calls'.[24]

Morehouse replied enthusiastically and arranged a meeting. On the first Saturday morning of the New Year, the two met at New York City's Buckingham Hotel. They set plans to meet again, three weeks later. Following the second meeting Morehouse obtained some pledges from Rockefeller. Especially important were new details about the situation of the Atlanta Seminary.

But already Sophia Packard was quick to contact Rockefeller, doing so directly. In her letter sent only a few days after Morehouse received the Christmas Eve letter from Rockefeller, Packard drew attention to the school's need to pay off a mortgage debt of nearly $5,000.[25]

A financial crisis had hit the Atlanta Seminary. They had taken their concern to the women's mission society, and an expectation had been set (some months earlier) that if supporters of the school could raise enough money to pay $9,000 of a remaining $11,500 mortgage on the land, then Rockefeller would pledge the other $2,500. But as the year came toward its close, prospects dimmed for obtaining all of the required money. And so it was that Packard wrote to Rockefeller on 29 December:

> Can it be that for the lack of a few thousand dollars the Baptist denomination will suffer this school to be given up! Can you not come to our relief and give of your abundance as God has prospered you?

Packard also offered a new idea: 'Give it a name; let it if you please be called Rockefeller College, or, if you prefer let it take your good wife's maiden name or any other which best suits you.'[26]

It so happened that the deadline for paying the mortgage was extended. Rockefeller then engaged in those two January meetings with Morehouse, and soon after this, he contributed the remainder of what was needed. On the next anniversary of the school's opening, the school changed its name to Spelman Seminary, thereby honouring the abolitionist parents of Rockefeller's wife. In 1886, Spelman Seminary also dedicated a new building, their first true permanent structure, as Rockefeller Hall – or, 'the Rock'.[27]

## Business, the Courts and New York City

In 1882, Rockefeller and his company's attorneys created the Standard Oil Trust, chartered in Ohio, and capitalized at $70 million. The company's major innovation was a legal manoeuvre designed to merge all of its properties into a single business formation. A 'trust' was formed by placing a majority of the shares of stock of a corporation in the control of persons called 'trustees'. Stockholders could then own a group of companies by transferring their shares to the single group of trustees, who would control all of the companies. The trustees could see to it that all the companies functioned in unison. All profits from all the companies would then be sent to the trustees, who decided the dividends. A trust was a legal instrument suited for creating a highly aggressive system of internal and external financial controls, capable of achieving monopolization over an entire industry.

Standard Oil's trustees also happened to have connections with financial institutions. A new Rockefeller tactic emerged by 1883. It was his willingness to push hard to borrow great amounts of money to expand Standard Oil's operations. Certainly this was a tactic capable of testing one's nerve; indeed there was enough of a recklessness to the practice that at least one close partner balked. The prime example of Rockefeller's willingness to accept a high risk with borrowed money was his decision to buy up great quantities of oil fields discovered in western Ohio, in a region locally known as 'the sulfur springs'. The crude in the area was low grade, 'skunked' with sulphur, and the price it fetched was rock-bottom. But Rockefeller kept buying these fields. He had confidence that a way would be discovered to 'sweeten' the crude, and sure enough, Standard's chemists discovered a new means of refining it. By 1888 the company could sell the Ohio crude for seven to eight times what they originally got for it, and the company turned a massive profit.[28]

There were legal challenges to the new business formation. While Standard Oil was by no means the only 'trust' coming into existence, it seems clear that 'The Standard' always drew special attention; it was, after all, the first of the trusts. And so Rockefeller, as the company's president, was the one in the news for always dodging the legal challenges. But in 1892, after some four years of persistent charges filed by Ohio's attorney general, a state court dissolved the trust; it was an illegal monopoly, in violation of a new federal bill called the Sherman Antitrust Act. At the time of its dissolution in Ohio, Standard Oil controlled somewhere around 85 per cent of the petroleum business in the United States.

With such an immense size and ability to pay taxes, the Standard Oil Company of course reestablished itself, in the state of New Jersey. With some slight organizational changes, Standard Oil was now a 'holding company' – which meant that a parent company could hold ownership in stocks of other companies. Rockefeller and his lawyers had again created a business formation well-suited for maximizing profit in an age of extreme capital accumulation and expanding markets.

Since the early 1880s, Rockefeller lived in New York City, at least for much of the year. In 1884 the Rockefellers bought a large brownstone house at 4 West 54th Street. Soon after that the family began acquiring substantial plots of prime acreage in the Pocantico Hills, along the east side of the Hudson River some 25 miles north of Manhattan. New Yorkers knew that Rockefeller lived there. Columbia University certainly did, and in 1883 the school – a non-Baptist institution – asked him for money. The school was then called Columbia College, and their proposal was interesting. It may have been that from Columbia's perspective they contacted Rockefeller because he was becoming a New Yorker; this seems logical enough. Looked at from Rockefeller's position, he may have seen Columbia's request as an opportunity to apply some thought toward the matter of helping to build an institution of higher education.

On 2 May 1883, Columbia's Professor Charles Sprague Smith made the appeal to Rockefeller. 'Dear Sir', Smith opened his letter. 'I would ask but a moment of your leisure'. Smith noted how a movement was underway 'to establish here a national university', and he provided some accompanying papers describing it all.

> Will you from the start identify yourself with this movement? Believe me Sir it is bound to succeed since an historical necessity demands it and determined enthusiastic convictions are impelling it forward. From the true strong men of New York we confidently expect sympathy and support.[29]

Smith, a professor of modern languages and foreign literature, was actually a logical choice for the person to contact Rockefeller. There is ample evidence that Smith was one of Columbia's finer thinkers on questions about how to plan a great university. But Rockefeller did not jump at the chance to support the initiative. Potentially he could have been influenced by the fact that Columbia's administration had already vetoed Smith's plan. Either way, Rockefeller now had in his thoughts the idea to build some kind of a 'national university'.[30]

## Ideas about Building Colleges and Universities

The inquiry that came from Columbia College in 1883 may indeed have given Rockefeller a new avenue of thinking. There were many wealthy individuals at the time who were getting involved in creating new colleges and universities. The idea for a single individual to create a great school was not a new idea. One early American donor to a variety of charitable and municipal organizations was Stephen Girard, of Philadelphia. Girard, a banker and investor, is still today measured as one of the half dozen wealthiest Americans who ever lived. In 1832 he bequeathed money to create a school in Philadelphia for children of coal miners – a school that became the renowned boarding institution, Girard College.

Peter Cooper, the builder of America's first steam locomotive and an investor in iron and real estate, in 1853 established in New York City the Cooper Union for the Advancement of Science and Art. The idea then began to really catch on. Asa Packard provided a half-million gift in 1865 to establish Lehigh University. Ezra Cornell co-founded Cornell University in 1865. Sophia Smith willed most of her wealth in 1870 to establish Smith College. A gift of $1 million from Cornelius Vanderbilt, the rail tycoon, established Vanderbilt University in 1873. In 1876, Johns Hopkins, also a rail tycoon, opened his great research university in his name. Five years later, Francis Drake opened his fine school, Drake University, and in 1886 Pratt Institute was established with an endowment from Charles Pratt. Jonas C. Clark had a project underway by the mid-1880s, which opened in 1887 as Clark University. Leland Stanford, another rail tycoon, had a project underway by 1886 to establish his great university to honour his son by the same name; the school opened in 1891.

However nothing could quite compare to the scale of the project that Rockefeller was about to undertake. One story much told is that of John D. Rockefeller's founding of the University of Chicago. Yet there are certain aspects of the story more rarely mentioned. Rockefeller's work to create the school was a major event in his maturation as a philanthropist. The story begins, as much as at any date, on 20 March 1885. This was the day that Rockefeller sent to Morehouse some questions. The two had gained each other's trust, and Rockefeller needed advice. He asked about donating to church projects in Wheeling, West

Virginia and in New York City. He asked for news about Spelman Seminary, and he inquired how things were with Indian University. Upon seeing that so many different projects were of interest to Rockefeller, Morehouse responded with his shared pleasure at having formed with Rockefeller a relationship that was not so focused on any 'High-pressure, cork-screw methods to obtain benevolent contributions from some who hold on to every dollar as if they expected to take it to glory with them'.[31]

Morehouse knew about one particular grand project. There were members in the mission society who pushed for a broader scope for the society. And one leader in the society was Augustus H. Strong, of the Rochester Theological Seminary in New York. Strong hoped to see a new university established for all of the nation's Baptists, and he wanted it in New York City. Also being explored, with some small level of advocacy, was a possibility of putting such a school in the nation's capital, Washington, DC. There were also persons who believed that a great Baptist institution should be established somewhere to better serve 'the West'. And this was where it all got interesting. One plausible location was Chicago.

Rockefeller was aware of the discussion. After all he was the nation's supreme donor among Baptists. Rockefeller had already provided small amounts of support for the Baptist Union Theological Seminary, located in the Morgan Park section of Chicago, and he had made small contributions to another Baptist school in the city, known as Chicago University. But as to whether Rockefeller might have any preference for any of the candidate cities, the fact was that he lived in New York City.

Two months prior to Rockefeller's letter to Morehouse, however, in January 1885, an Illinois court announced the impending bankruptcy of Chicago University. The event was a foreclosure, as the school had failed to make payments on its $100,000 mortgage. The school was to operate only through the summer of 1886. Following the court's decree, the school's trustees held a few final meetings to plan the closure, and at one meeting in 1890 (convened actually a few years after the school's demise) the trustees did something important: they amended the school's legal name to the 'Old University of Chicago'. Legally this cleared a path for another institution to become the University of Chicago, if ever any such school should so desire.

The Old University of Chicago was never a bad idea. Established during 1856 and 1857, by Illinois Senator Stephen A. Douglas among others, the school was established just as the railroads first came through town. Douglas donated ten acres near 31ˢᵗ Street on Chicago's near South Side, a location not far from the stockyards and packing houses, as well as the board of trade. After about a dozen years the school connected itself with a new school of theology, the Baptist Union Theological Seminary in Morgan Park, established in 1865 some 100 blocks south of the Chicago Loop. Rockefeller, about some dozen years after that, provided small bits of financial help to both schools.[32]

It would have been no surprise in 1886 that Rockefeller heard from Baptist supporters of both the New York and Chicago plans. The tone of communications could be earnest; after all there were a lot of Baptists who really wanted this new school. But neither group of supporters was able to convince Rockefeller of a preferred location, let alone whether to even support such a school.

We come then to the year 1888, when Baptist leaders across the nation grew increasingly concerned about the state of the nation's Baptist colleges and universities. They decided to create a new organization to raise funds for Baptist higher education in general. Much good work had been done by the mission society, but the mission society's official empowerment was to assist only schools for Native Americans and African Americans. Secretary Morehouse and others suggested creating a new organization to support all Baptist institutions. The American Baptist Education Society (ABES) was established in May 1888, with a purpose to promote 'Christian education under Baptist auspices in North America'. But Morehouse soon discovered that not all Baptists supported a major fundraising effort. Easterners tended to accept the status quo, whereas Baptists elsewhere, especially in the West, were more enthusiastic about an idea to establish a new school.

But a deepening divide now emerged. The issue remained the question of location. One person who favoured such a school for New York City remained Strong, just recently the author of *Systematic Theology* and a renowned teacher at the Rochester Theological Seminary. Also not to be overlooked was the fact that Rockefeller and Strong knew each other, for Rockefeller's daughter Bessie was engaged to be married to Strong's son, Charles (they married in March 1889). Yet there were also strong voices coming from the West. One person who knew Rockefeller was Thomas W. Goodspeed, the preeminent professor at the Morgan Park Seminary. Rockefeller was vice president of the Theological Union of Chicago, a body which supported the Morgan Park Seminary.

Finally there was William Rainey Harper. Rockefeller knew about Harper. While Harper may not have been as established as Strong, he was an extraordinarily promising young teacher and scholar. As an 1875 PhD recipient from Yale University (at age eighteen), and then as a respected teacher of Hebrew at Denison College in Ohio during the late 1870s (when Rockefeller was on the school's board of trustees), Harper was hired by the Morgan Park Seminary in 1879, where he taught Hebrew and the Old Testament.

All of this made for an interesting mix. Many respected Baptist scholars wished to see the new Baptist school created, and each wanted it in a location of their choice. Back in 1886, when news broke that Chicago University was bankrupt, Goodspeed contacted Rockefeller. He shared the news that he would land on his feet, for he had been offered the presidency of Kalamazoo College in Michigan. Goodspeed and Rockefeller were also aware that Harper had just departed for Yale University, to be a professor of Semitic languages. With mixed sentiments of surprise and realism, Rockefeller could only respond to Goodspeed to admit that he had somehow pretended that Harper and Goodspeed would be permanent fixtures at Morgan Park, 'and that in contributing to the Theological Seminary I was placing money where it would remain doing good for ages'. This was an important learning experience for Rockefeller. Goodspeed, later reflecting on Rockefeller's response, recognized a fine example of 'skill in balanced phrasing'. Goodspeed had in mind a section within Rockefeller's reply which offered:

> I cannot advise you, I do not know what is best, but I am anxious in respect to the future of the Seminary and by no means unmindful of yours. I have felt great confidence in you and will take some time to adjust myself to any change.[33]

So by 1888 a campaign process was in the works. Solid cases could be made for both New York and Chicago. The situation came down to who was first to say the wrong thing to Rockefeller. Throughout the process it was Goodspeed who said the right things, and it was Strong who was the first to make a misstep. Just months earlier, Strong had travelled abroad with the Rockefellers, doing so as a future in-law. But would such a personal acquaintanceship put Strong's views into any sort of a favoured status? Or, if Rockefeller already perhaps favoured Chicago, would such familial relations only slow Rockefeller in finding a way to eventually announce his preference for Chicago? A situation now unfolded to show that Strong had difficulties with holding his patience.

The infraction came when Strong composed a letter calculated to stir things. He played to what he presumed were Rockefeller's motives. Strong opened his letter with a somewhat harsh suggestion:

> Very many people do not understand you and they very unjustly accuse you. Your friends love and admire you, but very many are not your friends. Your present gifts, to education and to the churches, do not stem the tide of aspersion as would the establishment of an institution for the public good, so great that it has manifestly cost a large self-sacrifice to build it.

Strong suggested that Rockefeller recall how another businessman, once also disliked, saved his reputation as he 'changed in his later days; began to make benevolence and not money-making his principal aim in life; immediately got a name for charity and public spirit; now he is remembered for nothing else'. Strong concluded that Rockefeller could now have 'the opportunity of turning the unfavorable judgments of the world at large into favorable judgments – and not only that – of going down to history as one of the world's greatest benefactors'.[34]

But Rockefeller never felt he needed to correct anyone's views of him. Any person who might hold an unfavourable judgment of Rockefeller was misinformed. As to what the effect of Strong's approach was: in a phrase, Rockefeller did not go for it. Rockefeller's response to Strong shows the usual restraint. He measured back any expression of resentment, and resorted to mere curtness in tone: 'I have decided to indefinitely postpone the consideration of the question of the university or the theological seminary in New York'.[35]

Rockefeller was in fact working to make up his mind. And the infraction by Strong was of such a nature that Rockefeller effectively did not have to make any close decision anymore.

Many others were also trying to pick a location. One founding member of the ABES was Dr Frederick T. Gates, a Minneapolis minister. When the society held its inaugural meeting in Washington, DC, in May 1888, some 427 delegates attended. The majority of them hailed from what were then considered Western states – roughly from Ohio westward. At that meeting, Morehouse nominated Gates for executive secretary. Gates already advocated for a new Baptist university, and his personal opinion favoured placing it in the Midwest.[36]

One of Gates's first tasks as executive secretary was to deliver a presentation to a Baptist convention in Chicago, on 15 October 1888. He titled his paper, 'The Need for Baptist University in Chicago, as Illustrated by a Study of Baptist College Education in the West'. Shortly before the meeting, Gates shared with Morehouse how he intended to communicate 'A scheme so vast, so continental, so orderly, so comprehensive, so detailed; it will in my view capture a mind so constituted as Mr. Rockefeller is'.[37]

Gates's paper stayed a safe distance from any sharp emotions, as he stuck to the facts and introduced a researched and reasoned argument: the evidence supported Chicago. Gates looked at multiple denominations and compared their student numbers and monetary investments in higher education. There were eleven Baptist schools in the region that offered at least some college coursework, but only 300 to 400 Baptist students actively took such courses. This was by far the smallest number of the denominations. Gates introduced a comparative conclusion: that on a per member basis, the Presbyterians owned nine times as much educational property as the Baptists and had four times as many students; the Congregationalists owned five times more educational property and enrolled four times as many students; and the Methodists had more than six times the educational property and five times the students.[38]

Gates's argument was solid. He also described the situations at each of eleven Baptist schools in the West. All were poorly located, with few Baptist students living within any easy reach of them. All eleven schools were poorly financed, and all had low faculty salaries. The solution was clear: it was for Baptists 'to found a great college, ultimately to be a university, in Chicago'. Chicago was the heart of the West – it was 'the fountain of western life'. With phrasing a bit fluorescent, Gates declared that Chicago alone could 'lift so far aloft a Baptist college as an intellectual and religious luminary, that its light would illuminate every state and penetrate every home from Lake Erie to the Rocky Mountains'.[39]

Soon after he presented his report, Gates introduced it to the society's executive board, which unanimously endorsed it by December.

One person who responded most positively was Yale's professor of Semitic languages, Harper, who shared his encouraged sense of things in a letter to Goodspeed. Writing in January 1889, Harper noted a personal visit he just held with Rockefeller ('Mr. R'), who was in an 'affable mood'. Harper described Rockefeller as 'never so kind; nor so interested; nor so anxious to just do the right thing', and that he 'seemed certain now to do something for Chicago'.[40]

Responding as well to Gates's paper was Rockefeller himself, who began to interact with Gates. He shared with Gates his feeling that 'I am more and more disposed to give only through organized institutions'.[41]

Who then was Frederick T. Gates? What did people think of him, and what sense of the workings of philanthropy did he possess?

When Gates was elected executive secretary of ABES, the election was unopposed. He was clearly the outstanding choice. Gates was from the East, like Morehouse, and he had graduated from the Rochester Theological Seminary, like Morehouse. Gates became a pastor in Minneapolis in 1880, and in 1888 he was fresh from a successful campaign to raise $50,000 for the endowment of a new school, in Owatonna, Minnesota. That effort was an important test for Gates. In 1874 a Committee on Education for the Minnesota Baptist State Convention had proposed to establish a new school. Three local pastors announced the idea, and they received three proposals. They selected the town of Owatonna and determined that $50,000 was needed as an initial endowment. They also announced that any donor of at least $20,000 could name the school. In February 1878 the Minnesota Academy was established, with its future name to be determined. Seven years later, a donation came from George A. Pillsbury, a 62-year-old former mayor of Minneapolis, and father of the founders of the Pillsbury Flour and Milling Co. His donation was $27,000, enough to immediately build a women's dormitory, named as Pillsbury Hall. In 1887, the school changed its name to Pillsbury Academy.

Pillsbury was in weakening health by then, and he decided he wished to prepare a donation of fully a quarter million dollars to the school. He decided first to donate $50,000, and he hoped to see the people in the area give the same amount to show their support for the school. He hired Gates to help make this happen. Gates developed a two-part approach, involving a matching grant that was first necessary for the academy to receive the $50,000. This was a success.

The school then needed to show a level of responsible use of that money, so that Pillsbury could leave the remaining $200,000 upon his death.[42]

Gates then found himself chosen as executive secretary of ABES. He interacted various times with Rockefeller during spring 1889, and by early May, Rockefeller was ready to make a major pledge. It was to be a donation toward creating a Baptist school in Chicago. He informed Gates that his figure was $400,000, but through some discussion with Gates, including a morning stroll on 17 May, Rockefeller began questioning such an amount – not for the worse, but for the better. Rockefeller decided to elevate his contribution to $600,000. He also requested that his pledge be kept a secret until such time as ABES's leadership independently decided to raise at least $1 million for the school.

The next day, in Boston, before the general meeting of ABES, Gates sat near the front of the room, and he waited. He kept his word that first the society must independently commit to raising the $1 million. When the society reached this agreement, Gates stood and reported that in his hand rested 'a letter from our great patron of education, Mr. John D. Rockefeller'. Gates announced that Rockefeller 'promises that he will give six hundred thousand dollars' toward the initial endowment for the school. Cheers broke out.[43]

But this meant that $400,000 needed to be raised from other sources, and that was a lot of money. Gates committed to overseeing the effort, and he soon accomplished it. A year and a half following the Boston announcement, the new university was incorporated as the University of Chicago. In February 1891, William Rainey Harper accepted the presidency of the school, and he began his work within the month.

What did Harper understand needed to be done, and was he up to the task? Who was William Rainey Harper? Born in 1856 in a rural Ohio log cabin, Harper received home schooling and was reading by the age of three. By the age of fourteen he had a college degree. Four years later, he had his doctorate. He taught Greek, Latin and Hebrew for two years at Masonic College in Tennessee, and he then received Denison University's professorship of Hebrew and biblical studies. In 1879 he moved to the Baptist Union Theological Seminary, where in a single year he attained full professorship. He was an administrative innovator, who in 1881 introduced a summer school programme as well as a programme of correspondence courses. But Harper left in 1886 for a professorship of Semitic languages at Yale. During his first summer in the north-east, Harper became active in the Chautauqua events in upper-state New York, and it was there that he visited with Rockefeller.

## Lessons in Giving

In those two years between Rockefeller's donation in May 1889 and Harper's taking office in March 1891, a new topic of discussion emerged in the worlds of business and philanthropy.

In June and December 1889, Andrew Carnegie announced a rigorously considered method for giving. His statement, published as a two-part article in the *North American Review*, was soon dubbed the 'Gospel of Wealth'.[44]

Many Americans at the time were asking questions about how and why to give to people in need. The famous response to the question was Carnegie's. He said that successful business leaders have a duty to find the best ways to assist people in need, and that the very best way is to assist people to better help themselves. Carnegie offered a philosophy of the 'stewardship' of wealth. He wrote about how America's industrialists attained their success because the American system made it possible, and that a successful industrialist is therefore expected to be a 'trustee and agent for his poorer brethren, bringing to their service his superior wisdom, experience, and ability to administer, doing for them better than they would or could do for themselves'. An industrialist is to innovate better ways of production, and will accrue financial rewards for doing so. But these rewards are not for the industrialist alone; they are for all of society. Carnegie also recognized that vastly greater needs exist than there is money available. Thus he explained how a 'practical philanthropy' will focus on finding target points where donations can best avoid wastage while helping to reduce social problems. One main target point must be education, where the goal should be to encourage habits of self-help. A prime focus for Carnegie was to support local libraries. However, even such facilities might not be for everyone, as Carnegie also asserted his distinguishing – and perhaps social Darwinian – judgment: 'It is better to reach and touch the sentiment for beauty in the naturally bright minds ... than to pander to those incapable of being so touched'.[45]

Carnegie began his donations to support schools and libraries, as well as cultural centres and museums. With some preference for publicity, Carnegie proceeded – over many years – to establish over 2,500 'Carnegie Libraries' worldwide. With this system of libraries, Carnegie identified a kind of lever mechanism that potentially could help lift all people. He also pursued one very high-end project, and on 5 May 1891, Carnegie opened Carnegie Hall in New York City. John D. Rockefeller was there. As Rockefeller once expressed to Carnegie regarding this method of lifting, 'be assured, your example will bear fruits, and the time will come when men of wealth will more generally be willing to use it for the good of others'. Rockefeller undoubtedly learned some things from Carnegie.[46]

Something else happened in 1889 in addition to Carnegie's announcement of a philanthropic method; in November of that year a meeting was held of the board of trustees of Denison University in Ohio. The result of the meeting seemed to leave Rockefeller shaken a bit. The trustees discussed and elected a new president for the school; Rockefeller, a major donor, and a trustee, was not present at the meeting.[47]

This story might best begin with work that was done over many years to endow this Baptist school in central Ohio. In 1831, Baptist leaders established in the town of Granville a school called the Granville Literary and Theological Institution. It was later renamed Denison University, and in 1874, Rockefeller became a trustee of the school. Rockefeller first donated money to Denison in 1868. Then, between 1872 and 1874, Denison undertook two fundraising initiatives, and Rockefeller donated to both. One campaign was a 'twenty-five thousand dollar subscription', and it was met by six donors, with Rockefeller contributing $5,000 of it. Denison also aimed to raise a special fund of $100,000 for the support of faculty, and to this Rockefeller donated a small amount ($535) as well. About a half a decade later, once he was a trustee, Rockefeller donated $1,000 to the school during the spring 1878 meeting of the trustees, and he donated another $1,000 at the next meeting, that autumn. In 1882, when Denison needed to complete another $100,000 campaign, they did so, with Rockefeller donating $20,000 of it.[48]

So, in November 1889 the trustees of Denison named Daniel B. Purinton as their new president. Rockefeller learned about this major decision only afterwards, even though he was a trustee. At the time, Rockefeller had another major donation outstanding, as a matching pledge with a deadline of 1 January 1890. His track record, to that point at least, was that he evidently never failed to extend a pledge deadline if needed. But in this case, upon his learning that Denison had hired the new president without consulting him, Rockefeller took it hard. He wrote about what was on his mind, in a New Year's Eve letter to his friend King: 'My pledge to Denison University expires January 1st, 1890, and I do not recall any promise to renew the same'. Rockefeller noted that he was aware of 'the new President of Denison', and then he got nearly to the point: 'I have not the pleasure of knowing him, and had no knowledge whatever in respect to his being chosen for the position, until I chanced to hear of his appointment'. Of course Rockefeller had already made his point, which was his uncommon statement that a deadline for matching funds would not be extended.

Eventually Rockefeller got over it. In 1891 he offered 'a considerable sum' to the school, and with Rockefeller's continuing generosity, Denison University became an outstanding educational institution – the oldest continuous Baptist college or university west of the Appalachians.[49]

Rockefeller learned something from the Denison experience. He learned what can happen when one donates money to a school. He at least initially interpreted the situation as one in which an institutional recipient failed to provide him with enough of a voice in guiding the direction of the institution.

From his variety of experiences through the 1880s, Rockefeller learned that scattershot methods of giving money generally fail; that little bits of help here and there will never be enough to achieve the greatest success from donated money. We can appreciate what Rockefeller expressed in November 1892, to his friend Rev. Edward Judson of New York City's Berean Church. He opened up with candour and admitted spending a great deal of time thinking about things: 'I was up until eleven o'clock last night and the night before on this general character of work trying to help to devise ways and means'. Rockefeller, to be clear, was trying to figure out better principles for giving.[50]

## Rockefeller hires Gates

Following the initial fundraising campaign for the University of Chicago, Rockefeller hired Gates as a personal advisor. Rockefeller needed help to organize his philanthropic activities, and his foremost expectation was that Gates should deal with all of those 'begging letters'. Above all Gates was to permit nothing to reach Rockefeller directly. Gates was to be a wall. In addition, Rockefeller needed help managing his personal investments. He had been trying to diversify his holdings, and in addition to shares in Standard Oil, Rockefeller owned timberland and iron mines, holdings in manufacturing companies and financial stakes in transportation.

When Gates accepted the job, he came into a situation that might stand as a novel one in the history of capitalism. Rockefeller's amassing of wealth was virtually unstoppable, and he was in the newspapers more than ever for this. Everyone knew that he had more money than he could handle, and so he remained swamped by letters pleading for help. Desperate times had hit. There was a depression on, and numerous friends had fallen hard. Gates described many letters by 1893 as being urgent appeals 'to save old friends'. 'Mr. Rockefeller', as Gates reported, 'was constantly hunted, stalked and hounded almost like a wild animal'. Rockefeller had no privacy, not at the office, not at home, and not at church. It seemed there was nowhere he could go 'secure from insistent appeal'.[51]

Gates did good work for Rockefeller. He learned how to shield him, and he guided and advised him. Most important, Gates listened to him. Gates researched Rockefeller's personal investments and found troubles galore. Rockefeller had made his own decisions about where to place his wealth, and often he invested large amounts of money without verifying details provided by friends. Too often he was manipulated or deceived. Gates recommended that Rockefeller institute new oversight procedures for his investments, and Gates established a small committee to oversee investment decisions. Gates helped Rockefeller improve his ideas about philanthropy as well.[52]

## Controversies at Chicago

Gates also served as Rockefeller's communication channel to the University of Chicago. The university opened in the fall of 1892. Rockefeller and Harper had seen eye to eye quite well on the need to attract world-class educators. By the school's opening, between 100 and 120 outstanding faculty members were needed. Harper in effect took to raiding other colleges and universities for the best minds in the country. He offered more money than other administrators could match, and within less than two years he brought in the necessary talent, enticed as they were by high pay, reduced teaching loads and an expectation of academic freedom. Harper and Rockefeller were not popular around the nation's other colleges and universities for this.

Rockefeller soon gained more of an education in how not to behave – particularly in how to not try and guide the general direction of an institution that he was building. Words exist to show Rockefeller's willingness to suggest how the school's administrators might handle certain situations that came up.

In late autumn of 1892, toward the end of the school's first term, a section appears in a letter from Harper to Rockefeller that potentially reveals how Rockefeller played an active role in some of the affairs of the school. Harper, who wanted to stay in Rockefeller's good graces, addressed matters in a way that shows how Rockefeller came across as religiously motivated. Harper catered a bit to Rockefeller's wants. 'We were glad to learn anew of your deep personal interest in the religious condition of the university', Harper wrote. 'From the very beginning ... every possible effort has been made ... to emphasize the fact that the institution is a Christian institution'. Harper saw some value in emphasizing that the school's first faculty meeting was opened with a prayer, that the school's first service was a chapel service and that the first general lecture at the school was a Bible lecture. Presumably such a tally of activities would please Rockefeller.[53]

There were occasions when Gates contacted Harper to request that a particular action be taken with respect to an admissions decision. Gates sent one such letter suggesting a personal favour in February 1893. He noted for Harper that the parents of a prospective student were recently assured by Rockefeller that the president of the school will 'do anything at my request that lies in his power'. Another letter from Gates to Harper told of a family friend of the Rockefellers who Rockefeller personally wanted to see receive admission and a fellowship, and Gates told Harper directly: 'It would be a favor to him'.[54]

A year later, Gates asked for another favour. He described a young man who hoped to attend the school, and he indicated that 'The family are friends of Mr. Rockefeller's family'. While Gates knew nothing of the student's qualifications, he explained that Rockefeller, 'as a kindness to the family, directs me to say that he would be grateful if the young man should be found worthy of a position in the university'.[55]

But these examples were requests. In no way were they orders.

Finally there were a few conflicts at the university that brought some public attention to the question of whether Rockefeller's money might itself restrain academic freedom. All three cases involved professors and their moral, social or political values.

During the first few years of the university there was one particular controversy that must have influenced Rockefeller's views about how to financially support an institution that supports social scientists. In 1892, in the school's first year in existence, President Harper hired Edward W. Bemis, a well-regarded teacher and scholar, as the school's first tenure-track extension economist. Bemis, who came from Vanderbilt University, practised a kind of economics called 'historical' economics, and he was known for holding anti-capitalist leanings. As he taught about the need to deal with real-world facts about complex problems and potential policies for fixing them, Bemis's publications focused especially on monopolies known as 'gas trusts'. During his recruitment period Bemis sought and gained reassurance that Harper understood that his approach to economics differed from the views of the chair of Chicago's department of political economy, J. Laurence Laughlin, as well as the school's founder, Rockefeller.[56]

Bemis's dismissal from Chicago, three years later, received much news attention. The university said he was fired for incompetence; that he simply did not teach well. The press argued that Bemis was fired for his economic views, and in particular for his criticism of the Standard Oil-controlled United Gas Improvement Company, located in Chicago.

Historians have studied the Bemis Controversy, and they agree that Bemis's first 'infraction' likely was his expressed critical stance toward Chicago's gas trust. Gas industry complaints against Bemis probably arrived at the school, and perhaps local donor money was withheld from the school until something was done about Bemis. Also a possibility is that Chicago's gas companies decided to withhold any favourable rates from the school until Bemis's dismissal.[57]

On 15 January 1894, fifteen months after Bemis started at Chicago, President Harper informed him that he would not be reappointed. Bemis did not see this coming. His quality teaching and research had attained for him a tenured status at Vanderbilt, and he brought this status with him to Chicago. Bemis is on record as drawing respectable attendance numbers for his extension lectures, even though the university would claim otherwise.

Harper's letter could not announce a dismissal, but could only request a resignation. He offered that if Bemis did this, there should be no difficulty finding another fine job for Bemis, with Harper's support. But Bemis decided not to resign. The burden thus fell upon the university to create pressures enough to obtain Bemis's resignation, or perhaps even to produce a basis for firing a tenured professor. This is where the big controversy took place – and it can be traced through what the press communicated about their feelings for Rockefeller.[58]

On 30 June 1894, some six months after Harper's private request for Bemis's resignation, the *Chicago Tribune* announced that Bemis planned to leave the school upon completion of the school year. The writer for the *Tribune* tended to distrust the school and emphasized that Bemis was getting a cold shoulder; indeed that 'the differences of opinion which separated Profs. Laughlin and Bemis were so decided that the former refused to recognize the latter on the streets'. It even 'has frequently been told that Prof. Laughlin openly advised students in economics not to take Bemis' courses if they desired to do scientific work'. This particular article tended to see the issue as a methodological disagreement: Laughlin's free-market theories versus Bemis's real-world case studies.

The *Tribune* continued with the story over time, as did the *Chicago Daily News*, doing so with at least five articles by August of the following year. In the *Daily News* on 7 August 1895, for example, it was written how 'it is generally conceded that the professor's study of economics is not prolific of agreeable results to the "authorities" at Mr. Rockefeller's fane of learning'. So it was not so much Laughlin disliking Bemis, as it was that the school was Rockefeller's school. Which person would the press end up deciding was ultimately trying to control economic doctrine at Chicago?

Many news outlets covered the story by the summer of 1895. In New York, the new home city of Rockefeller, the *World* covered it (14 August), as did the *Voice* (17 August). The *New York Evening Post* (12 August) impugned Rockefeller:

> Any suggestion that capital in the form of a university is oppressing labour in the person of a professor is capable of indefinite expansion. It happens that Mr. John D. Rockefeller has given a large sum of money to this university, and the conclusion is obvious that the Standard Oil Company has built up an institution of learning to promote its own theories of political economy.

In Great Britain, the *Bath Times* (8 August) covered the story by arguing that maybe truths attained by the social sciences differ from truths attained by other sciences. The story added this:

> The removal of Prof. Bemis, of the Chicago University, for teaching his students the truth in political economy is not surprising. Every institution of learning dependent for its existence on the bounty of millionaire monopolists is in constant liability to similar calamities. It is quite natural that Mr. Rockefeller should not relish having a teacher, paid with his money, expose the essentially unjust and iniquitous way in which that money was obtained.

Looking westward from Chicago, the *San Francisco Bulletin* (19 August) suggested the problem was Bemis's opposition to the monopolists:

One particular object of his hostility was the Chicago Gas Company, a corporation which makes gas at 6 cents a thousand feet and sells it at $1.10. The Chicago Gas Company's stock was known to be inflated, and it was also known that enormous dividends were paid on this inflated capital. Professor Bemis thought that some method should be devised by which the profits of making gas should be distributed among the people.

'The inference', the *San Francisco Bulletin* concluded, 'is that Mr. Rockefeller did not approve of the position Professor Bemis took and tenaciously held'.

In response to this turn of opinion against Rockefeller, on 20 August the University of Chicago released a statement expressing that any matter between the university and Bemis had nothing to do with Rockefeller. Also it was to be known that the university does not violate academic freedom.

The *Boston Herald* (22 August) still figured that it was Rockefeller who had Bemis removed:

> In all the letters sent out from this institution the heading reads that Mr. John D. Rockefeller is the founder, and it is impossible at the present knowledge to avoid the inference that Prof. Bemis has been discharged at his instigation.

The *Philadelphia Inquirer* (26 August) agreed that Bemis's 'scalp now dangles at the breast of monopoly'. But this was fine somehow, in that Rockefeller's money had left their own state, and so it was 'just as well after all that the Standard Oil Money made in Pennsylvania went to no Pennsylvania College'. The *Ft. Worth Gazette* (31 August) – in the midst of the great 1895 Texas oil rush – also saw Bemis as the one on the side of truth. 'The institution was chiefly endowed by John D. Rockafeller [*sic*], assisted by Charles T. Yerkes – the Standard Oil magnate of the continent, and the street railway potentate of Chicago', the writer observed, and then added that Bemis's 'conclusions as to the danger from natural monopolies passing into private control are derived from scientific and historic study'. Yet the *Montreal Witness* (3 September), citing also an article in the *New York Recorder*, opined differently and said that Rockefeller should be able to have his views supported by any social scientist at the institution supported by his money:

> Mr. Rockefeller and his associates have a perfect right to employ professors and pay them roundly for teaching the Rockefeller views of political economy, and if they do not get the views they pay for they have also a clear right to stop the teaching and discharge the teacher.

In September 1895, University of Chicago sociologist Albion Small used the school's *American Journal of Sociology* to try and stop those who expressed support for Bemis. Small understood that the issue was largely about what people thought of Rockefeller. He reprinted a letter said to be typical of many letters. The letter had a supposed flaw in its logic for supporting Bemis. Small quoted the letter as describing a university 'founded by the arch-robber of America and which already, by its treatment of Professor Bemis, exhibits a determination to throttle free investigation of sociological or economic subjects wherever there is any danger of running counter to plutocratic interests'. Small proceeded to try and destroy such a view.[59]

But more press coverage came. The *Voice* (1 October) aligned itself with Bemis, who was respected for his efforts which have 'contributed more than the efforts of any other individual to the municipalization of gas and cognate commodities in this country'. The *Chicago Daily Tribune* (3 October) distrusted the university's continued silence. The *Chicago Daily News* (9 October) published Bemis's challenge to Harper to explain what he meant in the original letter on 15 January 1894, when Harper allowed that 'peculiar circumstances' existed at the school which would make it tough for Bemis to remain there. The *Kingdom* (11 October) supported Bemis and asked what kind of social science Rockefeller's university might allow.

News outlets soon also had new material to consider. On 18 October the university released its press statement explaining why Bemis was being let go, and it was not because of any expressed viewpoint, but because of his poor teaching. According to the school, Bemis was dismissed for 'incompetence'. The university's press release, which included a statement by Harper, was published in multiple papers.

After that, the news story slowly trickled away. It seems that the press either accepted the university's explanation, or they simply did not speak out against the school any more.

An interesting opinion piece came in October 1895, in the journal *Social Economist*. 'The University of Chicago is a private, not a socialistic, institution'. The article added a question quoted from the *New York Times*: 'Why should an institution pay a professor to teach social doctrines which are contrary to the consensus of opinions of the faculty, the supporters of the institution, and of the general community'? Thus there was no reason for any further explanation from the University of Chicago. In seeing capitalism and socialism as competing systems of faith, so incompatible with each other as to preclude their coexistence, the writer – George Gunton – added his analogy:

> There is no more reason why those who believe in the present industrial institutions should be surreptitiously made to support teachers of Socialism than there is that Catholics should employ Protestants as priests or Jews install Christians to preside in their synagogues.

Capitalism was sacred. As to Bemis, within about a year of his departure he was hired by Kansas State Agricultural College, renowned at the time as the leading progressive state university in the nation; Bemis was viewed as a social scientist who stood up against money interests.

But overall the whole Bemis Controversy was just awful stuff for the reputations of Rockefeller and the University of Chicago, and it must have jarred Rockefeller. The University of Chicago was the first great institution that he built as a philanthropist, and many persons had really hammered him for it.

But just a few months after Gunton's final word on the Bemis Controversy, another episode unfolded, this one more privately. Yet it was still a situation that involved Rockefeller's continuing self-education in how to support an institution that might produce viewpoints different from his own. That year the University of Chicago prepared to publish one of its new scholarly journals, a religious organ called the *American Journal of Theology*. On 10 February 1896, Gates informed Harper that Rockefeller had received letters asking how religious the university's overall attitude really was. Gates explained, on Rockefeller's behalf, that no publication of the theology journal was allowed without 'full conference' between Harper, Gates and Rockefeller.[60]

Gates followed up with Harper the next month. He reported that Rockefeller 'has no objection' to publishing the journal, so long as this is done by 'the Divinity School as distinguished from the University'. Rockefeller, it seems, saw a separation between where objective secular inquiry should take place and where inquiry into values should take place. Rockefeller also considered the Divinity School to be an institution over which he had no sense of personal responsibility.

> The University, on the other hand, is a peculiar creation of Mr. Rockefeller himself. He has given nearly all its pertinent funds and he has received many letters from many parts of the country complaining of the attitude which the university has seemed to take regarding the Bible.

Rockefeller was being held responsible 'for what is a real or fancied injury to religion'. Rockefeller, in response, wanted it made clear that the theology journal must 'be launched exclusively under the auspices of the Divinity School'. Gates emphasized Rockefeller's concerns:[61]

> He founded in Chicago a peculiar institution of learning. He had no thought of the institution entering the theological area. He would prefer that the great power and prestige ... of the university should not be thrown into the theological scale on either side. The sphere of theology should be delegated to the Divinity School and the denomination may hold the Divinity School responsible.

Rockefeller believed that the university's aim should be to explore the world strictly to attain greater knowledge of it.

But Harper went ahead and published the inaugural installment of the *American Journal of Theology*, with the 'University of Chicago Press' indicia placed upon it. The first volume was dated 1 January 1897. In a letter dated 2 January, Gates expressed stern anger. 'I am in receipt of the first number of the

*American Journal of Theology*', he reported. 'You will remember that Mr. Rockefeller was opposed to this magazine being put forth by the University of Chicago ... I presented his view in extensor to you'. It had been the clear understanding of Rockefeller that the journal 'should not be put forth by the University of Chicago'. Gates insisted that a letter of correction must be forthcoming, to express that the Divinity School is responsible for the publication. But no such letter it seems was produced.[62]

Three years later there was another situation that emerged at the university, and this one went public. President Harper found himself in the news for supposedly pressuring the school's faculty to conform to Rockefeller's views about capitalism. In October 1900, Oscar Lovell Triggs, a professor in the English department and a published commentator on the critical social thought of Walt Whitman, discussed an intriguing comparison during two of his classroom lectures. In the first lecture he explored whether the business genius of Rockefeller might be compared, in any way, to the genius of Shakespeare. According to the *New York Times*, 'a storm of protests' erupted from admirers of Shakespeare across the country; for how dare Triggs make such a blasphemous comparison between the monopolist Rockefeller and someone as truly great as Shakespeare?[63]

In response to the cries of objection to such a comparison, Triggs returned to the topic in a second lecture. He wondered once more whether Rockefeller could seem 'superior in creative genius to Shakespeare, Homer, and Dante'. Triggs offered a guided comparison: 'To the ordinary commercial mind, the mystery of play-making is as great as is the wonder of making money to the ordinary academic mind'. At some length, Triggs answered the mystery:

> Genius of life assumes many and diverse forms. The test is the quality of the mind. It is measured by what it does, not by what it works with. The contemplation of American life reads as great as the reading of our greatest literary compositions. To me, the city of Chicago is more marvelous than 'Hamlet'.

Triggs concluded that 'the new, profound and far-reaching questions are industrial'. But cleverly he did a bit of a manoeuvre with respect to the good and bad sides of the trust builders. 'Trusts are to grow upon themselves to higher and fairer forms of their own life. And these forms will be as fair and worthy of humanity as the achievement of older civilization'. Triggs spoke of the 'robber baron' as the 'type' that can resemble Shakespeare, in that Shakespeare had lain hands on so many experiences and stories not his own. Shakespeare resembled Rockefeller in that Shakespeare 'has tyrannized over every dramatic writer since his own day. He has driven out of business every playwright who has had less intellectual capital when it came to competition'.[64]

Leave it to the creativity of a professor of literature to take such a path to a point of comparison.

There were responses to Triggs. One letter writer, a defender of Shakespeare, happened to try a rough estimate of the amount of support that Rockefeller had provided to the school over the years, and said: '$90,000,000 is to 30 cents as Rockefeller's intellect is to Trigg's mentality'.[65]

And so it was, at about this point, that Harper stepped in. Some ten days following the original news item in the *New York Times*, an article appeared in the *New York Herald*, under the title, 'Must Not Talk of Mr. Rockefeller'. It was reported that the Chicago faculty were informed that they said too many controversial things.

> In the faculty room of the University of Chicago, President William Rainey Harper took members of the faculty into his confidence last night, and the result of his talk is that less notoriety in the future is expected from utterances of the professors.

Harper commented on the need to restrain from 'pyrotechnical, irrational and sensational statements'. Then, said the news story: 'From the inner recesses of his coat the president produced a sheet of letter paper which was said to bear the monogram, "J. D. R"'. While holding Rockefeller's letter aloft, Harper continued to say that in 'mentioning this matter, I might also add that instructors are employed in this university to teach and not to express personal opinions'. Harper added that the faculty members were henceforth to avoid comparing any contemporary persons of commercial success to historical figures of any notoriety, positive or negative.[66]

Triggs left the University of Chicago two years later, at the age of thirty-seven.

## Conclusion

Between 1855 and 1900, Rockefeller gathered valuable learning experiences in how to give money, and how to behave after giving money. He was often heavily criticized in the public sphere for his business behaviour, and more of that was yet to come. As to his work as a philanthropist, Rockefeller was generally admired for it, although there were mixed opinions overall.

# 2 TWO ROCKEFELLERS

By about 1900, John D. Rockefeller had outstanding success in both business and philanthropy. But he was under broad attack, in both areas of his life. The attacks continued for the next fifteen years. Yet all the while there were people who wanted to find reasons to like Rockefeller; and indeed there were reasons for doing so. During the first dozen years of the twentieth century, Rockefeller became a great philanthropist. This is also when he became the wealthiest single individual in recorded world history.[1]

## Bad Rockefeller

In September 1894, two years after the opening of the University of Chicago, an investigative news reporter, Henry Demarest Lloyd, published *Wealth against Commonwealth*. Lloyd's book was some thirteen years in the making. He had published a short piece in 1881, titled 'Story of a Great Monopoly', but that early account only initiated Lloyd's interest. He set to work meticulously researching his subject, and in *Wealth* he revealed what he uncovered: Rockefeller employed a range of aggressive tactics to increase his company's profits, including the elimination of competition by employing trade agreements called rebates. Lloyd's attitude was influenced by Rockefeller's own testimony before the newly established Interstate Commerce Commission. Lloyd read Rockefeller's wording and decided that Rockefeller 'will never sacrifice any of his plans for the restraints of law or patriotism or philanthropy'. Rockefeller's greed was rapacious. 'He will stop when he is stopped – not before'. Lloyd said that a public mission must begin, as it was up to the American people to stop Rockefeller.[2]

Lloyd's book provoked deepened distrust of Rockefeller. One comment, offered by novelist William Dean Howells, might be typical of the level of anger:

> To think that the monstrous iniquity whose story you tell so powerfully, accomplished itself in our time, is so astounding, so infuriating, that I have to stop from chapter to chapter, and take breath. It is like a tale of some remote corruption, some ancient oppression, far from us, and merely masquerading in the terms of civilization.[3]

Lloyd's book was not even the first major publication to lambast Rockefeller and Standard Oil. In 1892, Roger Sherman published *The Standard Oil Trust: The Gospel of Greed*. The title would have struck the public as an unmistakable contrast to Carnegie's well received 'Gospel of Wealth'. Sherman began his account at around the year 1862, when the price of petroleum began to skyrocket. Rockefeller had been at this for thirty years, and no one had figured out how to stop him.[4]

Many news pieces showed an interest in Rockefeller during the 1890s. Anyone reading Lloyd's book, or perhaps hearing new reports from the University of Chicago, could decide that they had their sense of 'the real Rockefeller', who was a bad person. But there was always more to Rockefeller than what the public believed they knew.

## Good Rockefeller

By the end of the 1890s, the new Baptist school in Chicago was going strong. Rockefeller thought highly of President Harper, even if he disapproved of Harper's view that a university is not a profit-making (or even budget-balancing) institution.[5]

Rockefeller made one visit to the University of Chicago, in spring 1896. He spoke briefly at commencement ceremonies. At the podium he shared some thoughts on what his donations had accomplished, and he did so somewhat in terms of returns on the dollar. 'It is the best investment I ever made ... It is but a beginning, and you will do the rest. You have the privilege to complete it'. He added: 'I am profoundly thankful that I have had something to do with this great work. The good Lord gave me my money, and how could I withhold it from the University of Chicago'?[6]

Of course Rockefeller got criticized. One response in the campus newspaper described how Rockefeller had 'modestly announced that Divine Providence is keeping a special watch over him and his monetary affairs'. Rockefeller, who had been so generous to their school, was depicted as a person who could not perceive his own doings: '"The good Lord gave me my money!" Let the ruined refiners, the impoverished producers, the corrupted legislators of the oil belt stand as an answer to the blasphemy'. But another writer, in the *Independent*, could simultaneously believe that 'No benefaction has ever flowed from a purer Christian source'.[7]

It was not long before Rockefeller began to contemplate completing the project.

In 1906 he donated $100,000 for a new library, to be named in the memory of Harper – who died that year. He dropped the requirement that the school and a majority of its trustees must be Baptist, and he stated his expectation that the university's activities be 'conducted in a spirit of the widest liberality'. Discussions turned toward finding a plan to separate the Rockefeller family from the school. Rockefeller, Jr suggested one last major gift to the school, and Gates concurred: 'It will conclusively demonstrate the fact which the public has not been able to grasp – the fact of your entire disinterestedness'. Rockefeller, Jr, who was thinking in terms of how to 'round out the institution', added in a letter to his father:

> your motives in founding the institution are solely to bless and benefit your fellow men; that you have not been seeking through it to increase your personal power, to propagate your political views, to help your cause, or to glorify your name.[8]

Rockefeller thought it over, and in December 1910 he made the final payment of $10 million – bringing to $35 million his total gifts to the University of Chicago.[9]

Rockefeller learned important lessons from his experiences building the University of Chicago. He learned that it can be easier to begin a philanthropic involvement than to end it. He learned more about how to employ methods of conditional giving. He learned that the time can come for a built institution to become an ongoing concern. Rockefeller shared a thought with Chicago's trustees when he made his culminating gift: 'I am acting on an early and permanent conviction that this great institution, being the property of the people, should be controlled, conducted and supported by the people'. The school would keep going financially only with wise management, and with many persons contributing to it. 'In the uplifting influence of the University as a whole upon education throughout the West, my highest hopes have been far exceeded'.[10]

## From the World of Business to the World of Philanthropy

In 1896, Rockefeller made an important decision on the business side of his life. He decided to retire from active leadership of Standard Oil. It was time to focus on philanthropic work.

As he made his transition, Rockefeller closed his last refinery in Cleveland, thus completing a full move of the world's oil capital to New York City. After having been disallowed by the Ohio Supreme Court, Standard Oil's attorneys created a new corporate structure, a holding company, and their new headquarters was in New Jersey. He and his family now lived north of New York City, on substantial acreage purchased in New York's Pocantico Hills, overlooking the Hudson River between the villages of Tarrytown and Sleepy Hollow.

Rockefeller's son, John D. Rockefeller, Jr, graduated from Brown University in May 1897. The timing of Rockefeller's transition out of Standard Oil made some added sense then. Rockefeller cared greatly for his son, and had always looked out for him. On 1 October 1897, Rockefeller, Jr moved into an office at the Standard Oil Building at 26 Broadway. 'Junior' came into his father's office initially as something of an apprentice. He learned about each department and all interests of the company, and he soon took his place at a fine roll-top desk in an office suite dedicated to philanthropic and 'outside' interests.

Rockefeller, Jr gained from a period of tutelage under Frederick Gates, and he travelled with Gates to tour some investment interests. They visited the Minnesota iron range and they travelled through Rockefeller-owned timberlands in the Pacific Northwest. Rockefeller, Jr also joined the University of Chicago's board of trustees. In his own words, as he shared with his mother at the time:

> I feel but little confidence in my ability to fill the position which is before me, but know that I am not afraid to work or do whatever is required of me, and with God's help I will do my best.[11]

Just as Rockefeller, Sr announced his retirement from business, and in the same year that Rockefeller, Jr joined the work at 26 Broadway, things were about to change in terms of what the older Rockefeller wanted to do with his money. In the summer of 1897, Gates took a vacation. He carried with him a book, and a new turn of direction was about to begin for Rockefeller philanthropy. The book was no light reading. It was William Osler's *Principles and Practice of Medicine* (1892), and evidently Gates read all 1,000 pages or so. Gates described the book as an 'intensely interesting' experience, and one that rendered him stunned by the backwardness of medical knowledge.

Osler, a professor of medicine at Johns Hopkins University, said that much progress should soon be possible in medical research, and especially in the field of endemic diseases. Gates knew about new European laboratories, where breakthroughs were being made with the germ theory of disease, and he wondered if it might be possible to discover a whole host of vaccines to control infectious diseases. Gates approached Rockefeller with his idea, and the two began envisioning a new kind of medical research facility.[12]

A first step for Rockefeller was to gather opinions. By 1898 he and Gates enlisted the skills of Starr Murphy, Rockefeller's 'personal investigator'. Born in Connecticut and a graduate of the Columbia Law School, Murphy had for some years headed a legal firm in Montclair, New Jersey. Rockefeller evidently had gone to Murphy for legal advice once or twice. Murphy's task was to help assemble an understanding of best opinions on the state of medical research, and he produced a preliminary report.[13]

Discussions over the next year created a comfort zone for believing that creation of a medical research institute should be uncontroversial in nature, which had become important to the Rockefellers. But how can outstanding medical scientists be recruited to a research institute? And, what level of success would be possible by implementing 'institutionalized innovation', in which increased financial support should directly correlate with an increased rate of scientific discovery? Gates soon expressed his optimism in a letter to Dr Osler: 'This line of philanthropy, now almost wholly neglected in this country, is the most needed and the most promising of any field of philanthropic endeavor'.[14]

Gates and Rockefeller, Jr sought advice from physicians and scientists, particularly as to whether they believed that more money would lead to better medical science. It seemed that all were agreed that the great barrier to advancing basic medical knowledge was the lack of research funds. But also there was the problem that too few persons were even trained to succeed in such research positions. The goal was to find some sort of a 'lifting' or a 'jumping' mechanism to get everything going at once. Rockefeller, Rockefeller, Jr and Gates put much of their monetary thinking into a single question: What amount of support for additional training might be required for medical researchers to be ready to do outstanding fundamental research?

In June 1901, Rockefeller decided to establish the Rockefeller Institute for Medical Research (RIMR). The goal, simply put, was to discover causes and preventions of and cures for disease. The project also was to build a research community from scratch. Rockefeller launched the RIMR with no initial endowment; instead he pledged $200,000 over ten years. In 1902 he added a promise of an additional $1 million over ten years. The money, he said, 'will have value for mankind only as we can find able men with ideas, imagination and courage to put it into productive use'.[15]

The first step was to award grants to promising researchers. Next, two years later, it was time to rent and equip some laboratories. Next the focus turned to acquiring land and planning some buildings suitable for a medical research complex. A dedicated structure was begun in 1903, and it opened in May 1906. The facility was a grand one, situated on thirteen acres of farmland leading up to a stony bluff overlooking the East River on Manhattan's Upper East Side. A small number of researchers moved into the facility, and they began their pursuit of knowledge in medicine and public health. Among a number of noteworthy medical scientists recruited to the RIMR was Simon Flexner, a tenured pathology professor at the University of Pennsylvania. Flexner, appointed as director of the RIMR's board of directors, was a talent scout who recruited many outstanding medical scientists for the institute's core staff.[16]

These outstanding scientists were freed from financial constraints, as the RIMR was designed to hold a researcher's attention on tangible goals. The kinds of research they did also required patients, and so the institute needed to include a hospital for the observation and treatment of cases. All of this was done well, and by 1910 the RIMR could be considered 'probably the best equipped institution for the study of the causes and cure of disease to be found anywhere in the world'.[17]

Rockefeller, Sr never set foot in the halls of the RIMR. In fact he consistently declined even to drive past the grounds, which apparently he did just once. His chief concern was to keep the scientists motivated and pursuing success. The

RIMR proved to be an outstanding success for Rockefeller as a philanthropist. The institution was his first major philanthropic undertaking that was wholly non-denominational in nature.

Another institution in New York City, Columbia University, also asked for Rockefeller's money, seventeen years after they asked him the last time. In January 1900, Rockefeller decided to donate $100,000 for a new professorship in psychology. But there was criticism of this. One media response in the *World* stated that 'we naturally expect important light on this science from the Rockefeller endowment. One of the obscure problems of psychology is the problem of telepathy'.[18]

But what was this; what did such a comment mean? The news magazine had actually thrown a barb at Rockefeller. Their accusation was that Rockefeller could seem to possess knowledge of all things just by sitting at a desk in a New York high-rise, since all he needed to know were the favours being purchased from distant legislatures.

Of course there was more bad press still to come. One new cause for such treatment came in 1905, as a result of Rockefeller's decision to support a religious organization of Congregationalists. But it seems the whole situation really began with a book by Ida Tarbell the year before that. It was a book which had the effect of convincing a lot of people that Rockefeller was a really bad person.

## From Bad Press to the Idea of 'Two Rockefellers'

In November 1902, Tarbell began publishing one of the most famous serialized works of all time, perhaps rivalling even Harriet Beecher Stowe's *Uncle Tom's Cabin*. Having already authored a number of articles on 'The Life of Lincoln' for *McClure's Magazine*, Tarbell began what became her 'History of Standard Oil', published as installments in the same magazine. She produced an article every month or so, for nearly two years. Her research efforts were extensive, as she filled her writing with interview excerpts joined with numerous details collected during years of investigating all doings of the Standard Oil Company.

The American people had been interested in Rockefeller's business practices for years. They were very interested in what Tarbell found. But before we look into what Tarbell introduced, let us consider what information the public generally had prior to Tarbell's book.

On the business side of his life, Rockefeller sometimes was required to testify under oath. From the point of view of his critics, here at last was where he would have to put the truth on record.

In December 1900 and January 1901, Rockefeller testified before the United States Congress. He was called upon by a special commission, and he appeared with written responses to their questions. In response to what it was that originally induced the aggressive movement toward combination in the oil business,

Rockefeller said it was all about a 'desire to unite our skill and capital' toward achieving efficiency and providing consumers with the most affordable product. And when the industry grew, and new markets opened at home and abroad, the object was 'always the same – to extend our business by furnishing the best and cheapest product'. Standard Oil's profits were earned simply by wise service to the public. He stated in full:

> I ascribe the success of The Standard to its consistent policy to make the volume of its business large through the merits and cheapness of its products. It has spared no expense in finding, securing and utilizing the best and cheapest methods of manufacture. It has sought for the best superintendents and workmen, and paid the best wages. It has not hesitated to sacrifice old machinery and old plants for new and better ones. It has placed its manufactories at the points where they could supply markets at the least expense. It has not only sought markets for its principal products, but for all possible by-products, sparing no expense in introducing them to the public. It has not hesitated to invest millions of dollars in methods for cheapening the gathering and distribution of oil, by pipe lines, special cars, tank steamers and tank wagons. It has erected tank stations at every important railroad station to cheapen the storage and delivery of its products.[19]

The success of Standard Oil was all about good and responsible behaviour. It was a company that looked out for the people. There was a natural law of economics and it had revealed the 'advantages of individual combinations'.[20]

Yes, 'the powers conferred by combinations may be abused'. This Rockefeller admitted. So there is a role for government to step in and control the danger of abuse. 'These abuses are possible to a greater or less[er] extent in all combinations, large or small, but this fact is no more of an argument against combinations than the fact that steam may explode is an argument against steam'. Steam is necessary. So is business combination. That, in a way, was the logic.[21]

From time to time the nation was introduced to Rockefeller more formally in the courtroom – and not just with canned answers to Congress. Although he was no intellectual, Rockefeller had a fine mind, and this is greatly an understatement. Rockefeller had to be smart with abstract thinking, what with all that he accomplished. One kind of an occasion in which observers could come to understand the logic horizon within Rockefeller's mind was when he ended up required, by legal procedures and sworn oath, to break his silence and actually say things. Historians are, to this day, amazed at how many questions ahead Rockefeller could anticipate an attorney's line of questioning.

In May 1897, Rockefeller was called to testify in the case of the New York merchant banking house, Ladenburg, Thalmann & Co., against the Pennsylvania Railroad. The bankers sued to recover damages – $178,150 in overcharges – from allegedly discriminatory rates. The case began with an accusation that Standard Oil shipped its crude oil at lower rates than what its competitors paid.

A line of questioning unfolded that revealed that, when under oath, Rockefeller did procedurally what the law required of him, and he did nothing more. He maximized what could be achieved within the framework of the law.[22]

With Rockefeller seated as the witness, the attorney for the banking house began the examination:

> You are connected with the Standard Oil Company?
>
> I am president of the Standard Oil Company of Ohio.
>
> Were you connected, between 1884 and 1887, with the Standard Oil Trust, then in existence, or with any of its affiliated corporations?
>
> I was.
>
> Was the National Transit Company one of these corporations?
>
> It was.
>
> Was the trust agreement made in January, 1882?
>
> I couldn't state.
>
> Was it about that time?
>
> I decline to answer on the advice of counsel.
>
> You were examined before a legislative committee of this State in 1883 as to the manipulation of freight rates by the Standard Oil Company?
>
> I do not recall that I was.

And so the questioning proceeded, with no real information forthcoming. The attorney decided at some point, perhaps in frustration, to pause for small talk. The attorney asked Rockefeller if he was bothered by an open door to the courtroom: 'Does the draught bother you?'

Rockefeller found his moment to take control of the situation: 'Oh, no; the draught is not from the door. It is here', as Rockefeller seemed to point beyond where the lawyer stood. 'From the window?' asked the lawyer. 'No', replied Rockefeller with a smile. Placing his finger upon the lawyer's suit jacket, Rockefeller explained: 'The draught is right here'.

'Pretty hot one, isn't it?' the lawyer offered, playing along.

'Oh, a regular cyclone', said Rockefeller.[23]

It turns out that while he was finding his responses to challenging questions, Rockefeller could take a moment to taunt.

Rockefeller was able to go year after year, dragging along a process that the public, the press and lawmakers all figured would eventually pin guilt on him – if only they could get him onto a witness stand. The strategies that were employed simply to find Rockefeller, somewhere, anywhere, a backdoor or an alley, and 'serve notice' are legendary. But what happened when the American legal system finally got him to answer questions for the record is legendary too. Rockefeller was a shrewd leader of an amazing and aggressive company. He was confident, he was smart, and he was clever. He was always thinking about how to win each day. Consistently he interpreted his and his company's doings as legal and moral.

We can look back and sympathize that in odd ways Rockefeller was constrained to having to be as aggressive as the law allowed. This was his obligation, to the principles of business and the law and – by default, he would have figured – to the public. For what if Rockefeller ever decided to push less hard to make profits for the company? In such a case he would have failed in his responsibilities to the company's stockholders, and thus he would have failed in his responsibilities to the modern economic system. This is how Rockefeller saw things. And, because such a person in such a position could never know exactly how much push the law could take, Rockefeller was ultimately constrained into always pushing. Whenever the law managed to get him under oath, Rockefeller found some way to provide something that was legal, or at least allowable, in response to every question.

All of this surely represented the kind of testimony that got under Tarbell's skin. As much as it may have gotten to her that Rockefeller seemed to get away with so much on a witness stand, it seems it also got to her that Rockefeller could stay so calm through it all.

We should consider then what Tarbell put before the American people in her book, published in 1905. She recorded abuse after abuse by the company, seemingly without end. She revealed to the world the litany of Standard Oil tricks over the years: using their large volume of oil shipments to negotiate pacts with the railroads, compelling the railroads to grant to Standard Oil secret 'rebates' on shipping prices; temporarily undercutting the prices of competitors until they were bankrupted; buying up all the components needed to make oil barrels so that only Standard Oil could ship oil for a time; secretly creating oil-related supply companies (such as for barrels, pipelines or engineering expertise) and having these companies charge higher prices to Standard Oil's competitors; and, when all else failed, hiring thugs to threaten physical violence against competitors who refused to sell their companies.

Tarbell's book presented a very different story from what Rockefeller told in assorted hearings and testimony.

Rockefeller was not happy with the book. Yet he never said anything publically about it, for in his mind, Tarbell simply misunderstood. When he was once asked how he believed Standard Oil ought to respond to Tarbell's accusations, he replied to a friend: 'Not a word! Not a word about that misguided woman'. The Rockefeller approach was simply to put no words on record.[24]

Tarbell's brutal portrayal of Rockefeller as a person waited until the end of her series, and came in her two-part 'Character Study', published in *McClure's* in July and August 1905. Simultaneous with the release of her book, this final chapter in Tarbell's exposé was dramatic with descriptive language. She portrayed Rockefeller as 'indefinably repulsive', and a 'living mummy'. He was a monster with 'unclean flesh' and a 'thin slit of a mouth'. He was a guilt-ridden paranoid who scrutinized every room for his would-be assassin. 'For what good this undoubted power of achievement, for what good this towering wealth', she concluded, 'if one must be forever peering to see what is behind!' Rockefeller came across, in the end, as almost an embodiment of evil.[25]

Many other people were now digging for some sort of an incontrovertible piece of evidence with which to pin the guilt, not just on Rockefeller, but on a whole generation of America's magnates and tycoons.

In April 1906, President Theodore Roosevelt made a speech. While discussing a proposed railroad bill, he cited a character in John Bunyan's seventeenth-century essay, *The Pilgrim's Progress*. The character was a 'man who could look no way but downward with the muckrake in his hand' – a man who was willing to 'rake to himself the filth of the floor'. The image, Roosevelt believed, might well describe a movement among journalists. He intended his allusion as a light jab at those journalists who were into the routine of uncovering the graft of American business and politics. An idea soon caught on that such journalists were 'muckrakers'. The *Atlantic Monthly* also identified a journalistic style, which it called a 'literature of exposure'. Henry Demarest Lloyd's *Wealth Against Commonwealth* was looked back upon as perhaps the first such writing – a work of muckraking and an exposé.[26]

In the wake of Tarbell's articles on Standard Oil, a wave of studies emerged. Silas Hubbard, in 1904, agreed that 'Rockefeller's career is a subject, not for admiration, but for criticism'. But Marcus Brown published *A Study of John D. Rockefeller* in 1905, and he decided that 'It is not surprising that Mr. Rockefeller suffers a good deal of criticism, and even worse, from poisonous seed sown in the popular mind by persons craving notoriety, or actuated by the unconscious motive of envy or unkindness'. Rockefeller's Standard Oil was doing fine things for the world; and the world had the gall to respond with such ingratitude? 'This is only what the best and truest characters have always suffered'. John Spargo, in that same year, published a socialist critique of Rockefeller. He saw two sides. 'Mr. Rockefeller represents in his person, so to say, the transition from competitive industry to monopoly. He personified in a remarkable measure the greatest economic problem of our time'.[27]

The magazine the *Outlook* tried, in 1905, to understand the decent side of Rockefeller. The magazine quoted Rockefeller speaking to citizens in Cleveland, and offering some guidance to think about 'the higher things in life':

Let your question be, 'What shall be the fruitage of my career? Shall it be the endowment of hospitals, churches, schools, and asylums'? Do everything you can for the
betterment of your fellow-men, and in doing this you will enjoy life the better.

The writer added that while we might question whether Rockefeller always prac-
tises what he preaches, 'there is no room for questioning that he preaches sound
doctrine'.[28]

That same year, at Christmas time, the *Woman's Home Companion* decided
to humanize Rockefeller. It was here that a much-quoted thought emerged from
Rockefeller, as his faith led him to say, 'God gave me my money'.[29]

When he soon tried to clarify this one, in a 1906 interview with the *New
York American*, Rockefeller explained what he meant to convey in the Christmas
interview: 'I believe the power to make money is a gift from God ... to be developed and used to the best of our ability for the good of mankind'.[30]

The *New York Times* got hold of a short interview, conducted in 1907, in
which Rockefeller reflected on what he once heard a minister say: 'Get money;
get it honestly and then give it wisely'. Rockefeller added that he kept those
words with him, written 'in a little book'.[31]

But all the while that journalistic chatter explored how Rockefeller believed
he became so rich, a new episode unfolded with respect to how Rockefeller gave
money away.

## 'Tainted Money' and an Understanding Press

In 1905, seemingly out of nowhere, some of the nation's religious leaders decided
to attack Rockefeller for his giving. The episode really must have stung him, even
though he never said so. The situation is the 'tainted money' controversy.

Early that March, Rockefeller donated $100,000 to the American Board of
Commissioners of Foreign Affairs, a Congregational group also known as the
Board of Missions. On 30 March, the periodical the *Advance* published words
from a sermon delivered a few days earlier by Congregational minister Washington Gladden, of Columbus, Ohio. Gladden described Rockefeller's large
donation as having been 'proffered' to the board. Clearly informed by Tarbell's
writings, Gladden described the money as gained by business practices displaying 'the most relentless rapacity known to modern commercial history'. The
Standard Oil Company had attained 'colossal' wealth 'largely due to unlawful
and outrageous manipulations of railway rates. The whole country is now up in
arms against this species of robbery. It has a right to be'. Gladden added that it
was time to stop Rockefeller: 'The man from whom our missionary society pro-
poses to accept the gift is the great organizer of this system of plunder'.[32]

Articles, letters and commentaries soon abounded. An interesting question
came from Dr H. C. Applegarth, pastor of Cleveland's Euclid Avenue Baptist

Church. Applegarth asked if by donating money from business profits to a religious concern, that potentially Rockefeller 'has laid it on the alter and thus sanctified it'. There was a letter in the *New York Tribune* that offered the phrase 'tainted money of Judas' to suggest that sometimes money simply needed 'to be taken out of its evil path', and that this was appropriate for a religious organization to do.[33]

The *Outlook*, on 1 April 1905, published 'Mr. Rockefeller and the American Board'. Could anyone who would 'condemn all questionable methods of money-getting' ever, in practice, 'attempt the impossible task of determining whether and to what degree money offered for benevolent work is tainted by the method in which it is believed to have been acquired'? A resolution, passed by the 'commendable' Congregational ministers of Boston and vicinity, had stated a 'protest against the acceptance by the American Board of the gift of $100,000 proffered to the Board, for its work, by Mr. John D. Rockefeller'.[34]

A few days later, on 6 April, the *Independent* reported on Gladden's accusation and responses to it. The title of the story was most concise: 'Tainted Money'. The article quoted Gladden, who had submitted his protest demanding the board's rejection of Rockefeller's gift:

> The good that is done by lowering our ethical standards might best be left undone. Shall the young men and women of the missionary colleges be taught to regard Mr. Rockefeller as a great benefactor? The colleges might better be closed.

Yet the writer of the article also opined that maybe it was best to accept the money:

> Above all take it from a bad man, a gambler, a thief, if with his wickedness he has a weakness for doing good. Let the taint in some of his money be cleansed. Let the gold as well as the worth of a bad man prove the good.[35]

Published the next week, in the *Christian Work and the Evangelist*, was a news piece titled 'The Tainted-Money Question'. The article emphasized and supplemented some wording taken from the *Independent*, which was catching on as something of an encapsulating quote about the whole controversy:

> Take money, for a good cause, from anybody, if there be no conditions or implications that you will approve a wrong. Take it from the Unspeakable Turk; take it from the Devil himself. Above all, take it from a bad man, a gambler, a thief, if, with his wickedness, he has some weakness for doing good. Let him have that little honest pleasure to relieve his sin. Let the taint in some of his money be cleansed.[36]

But the controversy was only just beginning. A news item in the *Missionary Review* asked: how could the ministers have decided to accept money from a company under indictment for business methods so 'morally iniquitous and socially destructive'? Yet how much practical effort can ever go to investigating the means of moneymaking behind a gift? 'If this is true, the Rockefeller case does not stand by itself. Every dollar thrown upon the plate must be scrutinized, and its pedigree searched out by the administrators of church and benevolent funds'.[37]

Discussion of that question went on for a while. The *Congregationalist and Christian World* published an editorial, a few months later in August, which phrased the question clearly:

> Whose gifts may honorably be sought, and when received by Christians as trustees may be honorably used for benevolent purposes? This question, which has been pressed on the attention of the people during recent months, must be answered sooner or later by those who administer any kind of benevolent enterprises.[38]

In point of fact the gift had been announced in secret. This was in Boston, at a meeting of the American Board of Commissioners of Foreign Missions. Great debate broke out at the meeting. Some ministers questioned whether

> acceptance of such a gift involves the constituents of the board in a relation implying honor to the donor and subjects the board to the charge of ignoring ... the repeated and formidable indictments in specific terms for methods which are morally iniquitous and socially destructive.[39]

But was the money ever 'proffered'?

The answer to that was no. Unfortunately the consistent response by the Prudential Committee of the Congregational Church was anything but to come clean. They announced that Rockefeller's donation was an 'unsolicited' gift. It was therefore Christian of them to accept it.

Frederick Gates decided it was time to confront them on this. He explained that he was prepared to produce the correspondence that showed it was the ministers who solicited Rockefeller's money. Only then did the ministers admit what the truth was. The reality of the situation ended up being this: one late-winter Sunday in 1905, Dr James L. Barton, a Congregational minister, visited Gates's residence in New Jersey. Rockefeller's personal investigator and advisor, Starr Murphy, was also there. Barton asked Gates to ask Rockefeller for a major donation. So, on Barton's behalf, Gates spoke with Rockefeller and recommended a $100,000 contribution to the board. Gates shared with Rockefeller an impression that not only would the money serve well in terms of 'persons converted', but that there should be a bit of commercial value as well: 'Our export trade is growing by leaps and bounds. Such growth would have been utterly impossible but for the commercial conquest of foreign lands under the lead of missionary endeavor. What a boon to home industry and manufacture!'[40]

Rockefeller, trusting Gates, did not ruminate long over the idea, and he sent the cheque. The understanding was that the Board of Missions would announce receipt of the gift, with Rockefeller garnering a brief statement of recognition. But the group offered no such statement. They embedded a short notice within their newsletter, to state how it was 'with surprise' that Rockefeller gave them the money.[41]

The Board of Missions announced publicly that they really had contacted Rockefeller first, and public discussion of the matter began to fade. One side still believed that somehow the church had been bought. Another side tended to see that there was no big deal about accepting the money. In Washington, DC, a progressive senator from Wisconsin, Robert M. La Follette, contemplated how Rockefeller could one day defend Standard Oil in court, the next day give money to a college, and the day after that attend a prayer meeting. 'He gives with two hands, but he robs with many. If he should live a thousand years he could not expiate the crime he has committed'. Rockefeller, La Follette added, 'is the greatest criminal of the age'.[42]

But as an overall sort of collective public assessment of it all, it could actually now be easier to believe that Rockefeller was the one who was 'abused'.

From about the time of the 'tainted money' controversy there comes another quote from Rockefeller. Speaking to a Bible class in 1905, Rockefeller lamented for a moment: 'It is wrong to assume that men of immense wealth are always happy'. He was interviewed the following year by his old hometown newspaper, the *Cleveland Plain Dealer*. He reflected on the situation spanning the last thirty years when so many good people asked for money, and again he was candid:

> There was only one of me and they were a crowd – a crowd increasing in numbers every day. I wanted to retain personal supervision of what little I did in the way of giving, but I also wanted to avoid a breakdown.[43]

But the press stayed mixed. There was some good press in the aftermath of the 1906 San Francisco earthquake and fire, when Rockefeller instructed California Standard Oil to apply company resources to relief efforts. Standard Oil operations in all states donated money and even company tankers as shelters. Rockefeller provided $100,000 of his own money.[44]

Noticed as well, at least by informed people, was the help that Standard Oil provided during a stock market panic and recession in 1907, when just about every major company laid off workers and cut wages. Rockefeller instructed Standard Oil to increase its hiring by undertaking new construction. This was a move with enough of an impact to help the federal government restore public confidence just a bit.[45]

But continuing on the attack was Joseph Pulitzer, publisher of the *New York World*. Pulitzer wanted to learn about Rockefeller's childhood, and so he decided to offer a prize of $8,000 for any information leading to the whereabouts of Rockefeller's disreputable father – a man reported to have been a horse thief and nearly always on the run. In 1908, two years after Rockefeller's father died in anonymity (buried under a pseudonym) in rural north-western Illinois, Pulitzer ran a story to chronicle 'the sins and flim-flams' of William Rockefeller. Potentially this published story hurt, but again Rockefeller never said so. The public at least believed that it had, and Rockefeller gained even a bit more public sympathy.[46]

There was also a downside episode that emerged within the story of Rockefeller's newest project, the Rockefeller Institute for Medical Research. The episode unfolded between 1907 and 1909 when antivivisection activists criticized experiments at the institute. The disapproval began when the institute purchased and operated a farm for the production of laboratory animals. Some of the institute's researchers performed experiments on these animals, and antivivisection societies placed information booths near the institute. In the midst of the protests, in a meeting with a few of the RIMR scientists in February 1909, something of an absolute position was stated, that 'any restriction on vivisection, no matter how slight, would seriously hamper scientific research'. The vivisection issue was not an easy one to solve.[47]

## The General Education Board and the Sanitary Commission

A remarkable little ten-day journey took place in April 1901. It was a journey that involved a group of north-easterners on a chartered train through the American South. The journey involved not Rockefeller, but Rockefeller, Jr, twenty-seven years old at the time. The group of travellers had an aim to learn about the conditions of Southern higher education. Organized by business leader Robert Curtis Ogden, and with participants hailing mostly from New York, the group rode to Birmingham and back, in a chain of Pullman cars dubbed the 'Millionaires' Special'. They visited black institutions of higher learning, including Hampton Institute in Virginia, Spelman Seminary in Atlanta and Tuskegee Institute in Alabama. While heading south, the group attended a conference in Winston-Salem, North Carolina, on the topic of southern education. Rockefeller, Jr was affected by the whole journey, which left him always recalling the trip as 'the most instructive experience of my life'.[48]

Rockefeller, Jr paid special attention when the train readied to leave one particular depot and Washington and Lee University's president Henry St George Tucker stepped on board. Tucker nearly chastised them all:

> If it is your idea to educate the Negro you must have the white of the South with you. If the poor white sees the son of a Negro neighbour enjoying [education] through your munificence and benefits denied to his boy, it raises in him a feeling that will render futile all your work. You must lift up the 'poor white' and the Negro together if you would ever approach success.[49]

Once back home, Rockefeller, Jr took it upon himself to further investigate problems of black education in the South. He consulted with his father, and he discussed ideas with friends. He arranged a meeting with Booker T. Washington, of Tuskegee, and the meeting went well. In a press release, Rockefeller, Jr opined that Washington 'is a truly remarkable man. His school is doing a wonder for the race'.

Rockefeller, Jr found that his father could relate to his concerns as well. For not only had Rockefeller, Sr provided outstanding financial assistance to Spelman Seminary and the Richmond Institute, but on numerous occasions he attended black Southern Baptist churches. He once saw to it that all of the Rockefeller children were matched to an African-American scholarship recipient, whose education was paid for by the Rockefellers.[50]

In 1901, it was Rockefeller who held the purse strings, but Rockefeller, Jr who was working on the ideas. Rockefeller, Jr was interested when his friend Ogden convened a group called the Southern Education Board, and he might well have been present the day that the executive secretary of the organization, Edgar G. Murphy, spoke of how blacks and whites 'must be schooled apart', and even 'must live apart'.[51]

Rockefeller, Jr probably learned some things by reflecting on the attitude of his friend Gates, who removed his children from public schooling in New Jersey, because 'some of the coloured and of the foreign-born children were ill mannered, filthy, and unsanitary'. Gates, back in 1891, even once described how

> Latin, Greek and metaphysics form a kind of knowledge that I fear with our coloured brethren tend even more than with us to puff up rather than to build up. The coloured race is not ready it seems to me for high culture.[52]

Rockefeller, Jr, however, was one to develop his own views. He worked with his father to get some details in order, and by early 1902, work was underway to establish a new philanthropy. Rockefeller, Jr considered Ogden's proposed name of Southern Education Board, and he also contemplated naming it the Negro Education Board. When it was officially created, in January 1903, with a $1 million gift from Rockefeller, Sr, the new philanthropy was the General Education Board (GEB) – a name which, in the context of the other options, says a lot. The federal charter stated an aim to promote 'education within the United States of America without the distinction of race, sex or creed'. The GEB distributed money to improve education at all levels, but with special emphasis on higher education.[53]

Rockefeller, Sr generally stayed some distance from the GEB, and he used the strategy of making a slow rate of money distribution, which was done over ten years. One of the first priorities for the GEB was to create new high schools in the South. They needed to forge contacts with state universities, which included paying salaries of a few professors who would travel their states to identify potential best locations for high schools. Eight hundred new southern high schools were built, and many colleges and universities were also supported. An essential element in the strategy to maximize the lifting power of donated dollars was to use the GEB's resources to stimulate matching grants to bolster college and university endowments.[54]

But the GEB's leadership soon understood that the quality of southern education might not be so easily lifted, at least not until something more fundamental received attention. What was needed was to build a regional economy. Gates joined with Dr Wallace Buttrick, executive secretary of the GEB, and in 1905, they set out on their own train excursion to the South. While looking out of a train window, Gates is recorded to have stated:

> This is a favored section of the world. It has a superb climate, an abundance of fertile soil, and no end of labour. It must be enriched so that it can properly tax itself if it is to support education and public health.

The idea was to employ limited funds to best lift an entire productive economy.[55]

Gates and Buttrick visited the United States Department of Agriculture. There, in the spring of 1906, they introduced their interest to learn whether Rockefeller funds might be used to assist the advancement of southern agriculture – which, it might be noted, was suffering from quite a disastrous boll-weevil infestation at that time. The GEB and the US Department of Agriculture soon reached an agreement to jointly support 'demonstration work' in the South. From that time onward, the GEB brought Rockefeller philanthropy into increasingly close familiarity with the living conditions of southerners.[56]

In October 1909, informed by the work of the GEB, and officially established as a spin-off group from the RIMR, John D. Rockefeller created the Rockefeller Sanitary Commission for the Eradication of Hookworm Disease. This story actually begins about a decade earlier, when a US army surgeon stationed in Puerto Rico observed that many poor people suffered acute lethargy. He believed their ailment was malaria, but soon discovered the cause was hookworm. At about the same time, Dr Charles Wardell Stiles of the US Public Health Service was busy investigating health and living conditions in impoverished regions in the American South. In September 1902, when news spread of the hookworm discovery in Puerto Rico, Stiles looked through a microscope to examine human faecal matter of southern African-Americans who suffered from lethargy, and were often slandered for their 'indolence'. Stiles found hookworm eggs, everywhere. He surmised that hookworm infections were contracted by barefooted persons, through the soles of their feet. A person could harbour as many as 5,000 of these worms in their intestinal walls at once. Yet, a person could also be cured of hookworm with relative ease, with simply a mixed protocol of thymol and Epsom salts. Stiles sought financial support to apply his findings and he met with persons at the RIMR. The RIMR's board voted for a programme to eradicate hookworm from the American South, and Rockefeller allocated $1 million to establish the Rockefeller Sanitary Commission.[57]

The Sanitary Commission, based in Washington, DC, and directed by Dr Wickliffe Rose, a native Tennessean, had an expressed purpose 'to bring about a cooperative movement of the medical profession, public health officials, boards of trade, churches, schools, the press, and other agencies for the cure and prevention of hookworm disease'. The commission intensively mobilized in eleven states to educate and medicate populations suffering from hookworm. Director Rose developed a technique similar to the GEB's strategy of focusing targeted funds as catalysts for promoting greater action, including from the government. 'Health Trains' travelled the South as dispensaries, and some half a million southerners were cured of the disease by 1914.[58]

## Random Reminiscences and the Idea of a 'Rockefeller Foundation'

In addition to creating the Sanitary Commission, three other noteworthy events happened in 1909: Rockefeller published a book, he appointed a publicity agent for Standard Oil and he announced plans to establish a major philanthropy, the Rockefeller Foundation.

Walter H. Page, editor of the *World's Work*, was the one who in 1908 got Rockefeller to agree to write his memoirs, which were published serially beginning in October 1908. The whole work was published together in 1909 as *Random Reminiscences of Men and Events*. There Rockefeller introduced his crystallized view that 'The best philanthropy is constantly in search of the finalities – a search for a cause, an attempt to cure evils at their source'. He stated how one of his chief objectives over many years was to address a shortcoming, that 'Today the whole machinery of benevolence is conducted upon more or less haphazard principles'. He also indicated his intention to establish the Rockefeller Foundation. Rockefeller thought back at some length to how Gates helped him define his philanthropic priorities to seek improvements in '(1) material comforts, (2) government and law, (3) language and literature, (4) science and philosophy (5) art and refinement (6) morality and religion'.[59]

In 1909, Rockefeller designated a trust fund for the Rockefeller Foundation. He began the work to obtain a federal charter for a charitable trust to be endowed with $100 million. The Foundation's mission would be most direct: to promote 'the well-being of mankind throughout the world'.

The press tried once again to understand Rockefeller. Who was this person who ran such an aggressive company, who just published his autobiography, and who aimed to establish a great philanthropy? *Harper's Weekly* showed Rockefeller relaxed and 'at play'. A booklet in St Louis attempted to understand all angles of 'public opinion' about Rockefeller. An article in *Current Literature* conveyed a sense of the 'simplicity of Rockefeller', while a story in the *World's Work* wondered if Rockefeller was really just a 'modest and friendly man', whose harsh treatment owed solely to 'mob judgment'.[60]

An article in *Current Literature* was titled 'Two John D. Rockefellers'. The writer asked if the business and philanthropic sides of Rockefeller might be two parts of a single, integrated whole:

> The few pictures of John D. Rockefeller which have been exhibited in public for many years represent two distinct personalities: a Mr. Hyde Rockefeller who became 'money mad' in his early twenties and went on his evil course through life sucking the life-blood of myriads, avid of power and joying in but one thing – the piling up of golden dividends; and the Dr. Jekyll Rockefeller, simple, kindly, courteous, beneficent and broad minded. In the last few years we have seen the process in Stevenson's story exactly reversed. It is the picture of the diabolical Mr. Rockefeller that has been gradually fading from view and losing its clearness of outline, while that of the simple and human Mr. Rockefeller has been growing clearer and more distinct to the public eye.[61]

But an opposing writer decided that the two beings could not merge into one. The article, in *The Living Age*, offered that Rockefeller's *Random Reminiscences* revealed a calm and contented person, even if he was 'two Rockefellers':

> [A] person kindly, tranquil in mind and soul, at ease in his relation towards the Universe and the general scheme of things. But his success as a man of action does not spring from this source. It is due to his expertness in a difficult art – the art of financial adventure – in which he would probably have failed if he had not kept it sternly apart from his religious ideals.[62]

Another writer, in the *Independent*, saw the proposed Rockefeller Foundation as 'a magnificent scheme, and most admirably designed'. Especially pleasing was the Foundation's breadth of purpose.

> The charter makes no limit to it, save that it shall be for the benefit of humanity. It is tied to no present notion, religious, political, sociological, educational, which happens to prevail in this decade. When the times change the service may change also.

The Foundation was to be a great act of public service.[63]

## The United States Supreme Court

Back in the autumn of 1906, Rockefeller believed it was time to make an important change in his life. In secret he dictated a letter to the board of directors of Standard Oil. The letter was his resignation as president of the company. However, the approval took a few years, as the board resisted the resignation.[64]

In 1909 Rockefeller's resignation was official. Rockefeller, Jr also considered resigning as a director of the company, and after applying some thought to it, he did so in January 1910. Public announcement of these resignations went widespread that March, during some congressional hearings over a proposed bill to incorporate the Rockefeller Foundation.

In March 1910, two important events took place for the Rockefellers, separated from each other by five days. On 4 March, the US Congress introduced a bill for a charter for the Rockefeller Foundation, with an endowment of $100 million to be held in perpetuity, in a tax-exempt manner, for the 'acquisition of knowledge, the prevention and relief of suffering, and the promotion of any and all the elements of human progress'. On 9 March, Standard Oil's attorneys filed their defence briefs against the US federal government's case to dissolve the Standard Oil trust.[65]

Two branches of the US federal government were called upon, in the same week, to decide how Rockefeller would be permitted to make money and how he would be permitted to give money away. The US Congress was to consider one of the greatest single gifts in the history of philanthropy, while the US Supreme Court was to consider the legality of the very business formation which had enabled all of this money to be amassed.[66]

One government process moved faster than the other. The bill to create the Rockefeller Foundation got sidetracked. Within the month, the bill went to the Senate for discussion, but it was withdrawn. While a potential legislative act for the Rockefeller Foundation also languished in Congressional committee, the Supreme Court moved ahead. On 15 May 1911, the Court announced its decision to dissolve the Standard Oil Trust. The Court ordered Standard Oil to divest itself of all thirty-three of its subsidiaries. Using its newly established 'rule of reason', the Court found that Standard Oil used illegal methods to attain a monopolistic market share. The Court announced: 'For the safety of the Republic we now decree that the dangerous conspiracy must be ended by Nov. 15, 1911'.[67]

But a funny thing happened upon the dissolution of Standard Oil: Rockefeller's wealth skyrocketed. When the Supreme Court split the company into thirty-four parts, the end result was a gift of some $200 million to Rockefeller and his associates. The dissolution was, as *McClure's Magazine* expressed it, 'the greatest killing in one stock that Wall Street has ever seen'. And as to the leaders of the Standard Oil Company, they had their usual strategy: 'They kept their mouths shut'.[68]

'Immediately a great noise of talking ran across the continent and over the wide world. The greatest secret power of Wall Street had been smashed!' But from one place and one place alone, 'no sound emerged'. Throughout that first day, and then for many weeks to come, 'nothing was heard from the office of the Standard Oil Company'. As *McClure's* described it:

> For twenty-five years the strange rectangular building that harbored the Trust stood there, always the same. Above its entrance lies plainly as if painted its old motto:

'Hush! Hush!' There is no directory of its tenants in its entrance corridors; its halls are dark, quiet and subdued.

The writer of the piece described the six persons at the head of the trust (Rockefeller, his brother William, and four others), all in unflattering terms: 'These aging men in the Standard Oil building bowed slightly to the decree of the court. "There is nothing to say", they reiterated sadly, "we will carry out the decision of the Supreme Court". They were grieved and polite'. And, they said nothing else – and this meant that still no one knew anything about the actual state of affairs of the company. Standard Oil had never released a single report, to any of the 6,000 stockholders who owned it.[69]

It took until 31 July for Standard Oil's press agent to announce, in the briefest manner, that the company would give to each stockholder his or her fraction of shares in thirty-three distinct companies, to be added to their portion of stock in Standard Oil of New Jersey. And that was all. In accordance with the letter of the law, nothing needed to be executed until the very hour that the company was required to act. As reported in similar wording in multiple news magazines of the day:

> On November 15, the last day of legal grace, the second announcement came. The stockholders were notified that on December 1st they would be given their fractions. And then on that first day of December came the deluge. Each and all of the six thousand received their fractions – their little nine hundred and eighty-three thousand three hundred and eighty thirds.[70]

Disillusionment set in. What had happened, people asked. What response had Standard Oil innovated in its technical observance of the law?

During subsequent days some 6,000 shareholders discovered the reality of it all. Mailed to each of them, over a period of a few weeks, were thirty-four engraved certificates. These certificates the recipients carried to their brokers, where they found no help; for as it happened there were only two or three specialists in Standard Oil stocks. As if any further unexpected disincentive were needed, evidently it cost $4.39 to make just one transfer of the thirty-four different fractions of stock that were contained in one original share of Standard Oil. 'Meanwhile', in the words of a contemporary journalist, 'the time of dividends came on. Certificates for seven cents were insane enough; but declaring dividends on them rose to the mathematical height of idiocy'. One of the thirty-four companies, the Chesebrough Manufacturing Company, sent out dividends per share in three-cent cheques. Another, the Galena Signal Oil Company, sent 1,200 separate cheques of less than ten cents each, and 600 of them for three cents. Meanwhile it cost a two-cent stamp and an envelope for Galena just to mail each of these. The end result was frustration and shock. The company had studied the language of the decision, and they had thought through it all. The result, as *McClure's* again put it, was that 'The three-cent dividend checks were not cashed; their holders tore them up or tacked them on the wall as souvenirs'. The small stockholders, seeing the financial losses that would come if they tried to locate a broker to help them reconsolidate any sort of practical aggregations of stock, simply let their holdings go.[71]

Of course some stock firms were happy enough to receive the Standard Oil 'splinters', as they were called. These firms knew how to piece these things back together again. It was during this process that the value of the new stocks began fluctuating wildly. Stock swings began due to the fact that the managers in each of these companies were still not required to distribute any information about their companies. Standard Oil of Indiana decided to multiply their stocks by 30 to 1. Most of the other companies behaved similarly. In the case of Standard Oil of Indiana, its stock price rose from $1,400 to $4,000 per share. It went onward to around $7,000. But then it dropped, precipitously. As to Standard Oil of Nebraska, their stock went from $115 to $350 a share in three months. Standard Oil of Kentucky had their stock go from $150 to $1,000, but then it dropped to $400 – and all of this in 1912 dollars. Who had any useful information with which to make any decisions as to what might be an accurate valuation of any of these stocks? Only the company's management did.

## The Rockefeller Foundation

In 1912, the bill was reintroduced for a federal charter for the Rockefeller Foundation. But this time there was a great level of protest. The Rockefellers tried offering concessions. They suggested that the Foundation might be placed in the nation's capital. They offered to limit the Rockefeller family and their close employees to 20 per cent of the board. They allowed that Congress could, at any time, decide to limit the activities of the Foundation. They even allowed that any new members of the Foundation's board must be approved, simultaneously, by the President of the United States, the Vice President of the United States, the Chief Justice of the Supreme Court, the Speaker of the House, and presidents of five major universities. But all efforts to obtain the federal charter were to no avail.

The Rockefellers decided they did not need a federal charter. On 14 May 1913, the State of New York granted a charter for the creation of the Rockefeller Foundation, established with slightly more than $100 million in gifts of securities. The Rockefeller Foundation would have a charter to perpetuity. Rockefeller and Rockefeller, Jr worked with a small group of advisors to legally establish the Foundation, and Gates wrote the finalized motto, which was to serve 'The Well-being of Mankind Throughout the World', with the specific goal to advance the civilization of the United States and its territories and possessions and of foreign lands in the acquisition and dissemination of knowledge, in the prevention and relief of suffering, and in the promotion of any and all the elements of human progress.[72]

This has been a highly regarded mission statement ever since. Yet at the same time there could be public outcry against the mission statement. Some persons decided to see its breadth as a potential instrument of control, or even to see the Foundation itself as a sanitizing instrument for Rockefeller's 'tainted' money. Critics also did not like the Foundation because it shielded a large portion of Rockefeller's wealth from inheritance taxes.[73]

## Conclusion

In 1913 there were people who did not like it that Rockefeller established one of the greatest philanthropic foundations in history. Rockefeller had attained extraordinary success in the worlds of business and philanthropy, and during all of those years that he was attaining such levels of success, there were many people who did not know what to think of him. There had never been a person quite like Rockefeller. And, Rockefeller would live for nearly another quarter of a century.

# 3 EARLY PHILANTHROPIC SUPPORT OF SOCIAL SCIENCE

## Introduction

The first great philanthropic foundations were the Carnegie Institution, the Russell Sage Foundation and the Rockefeller Foundation. All three were established in the United States between 1902 and 1913. Early in their development, each of these foundations looked for opportunities to support social science. A crucial question began to be asked: could philanthropists legitimately support social scientists whose research findings may favour the personal views of the philanthropists? These first foundations – along with numerous smaller organizations during the same period – developed approaches to assessing problems that could arise from supporting social scientists.[1]

## The Carnegie Institution and the Russell Sage Foundation

In 1902, Andrew Carnegie established the Carnegie Institution (CI) of Washington. Two years later he and his advisors established, within the CI, a department of economics and sociology. The focus for the department was labour issues. Leadership at the CI appointed industrial economist Carroll D. Wright to direct the division, and Wright's official responsibility was 'to encourage, in the broadest and most liberal manner, investigation, research, and discovery, and the application of knowledge to the improvement of mankind'. Wright received support for a team of some fifteen researchers, who comprehensively assessed the social and economic consequences of state-level labour legislation. The project – ultimately an effort to produce a detailed labour history – required seven years to be brought near to completion in 1909, the year of Wright's untimely death.[2]

The CI's report on the history of labour was an impressive achievement. Yet the CI's department of economics and sociology never transformed into anything more than one group of economists appointed to work on one project. The CI soon closed this department, and Wright's research team pushed to produce a finalized, multi-volume report, *History of Labour in the United States* (1918).[3]

The Russell Sage Foundation (RSF) was chartered in April 1907, with a $10 million gift from Margaret Olivia Slocum Sage (known as Olivia), the widow of industrialist Russell Sage. The RSF had a goal to promote 'the improvement of social and living conditions in the United States of America'. Within a month of the charter, the RSF's board of trustees named John M. Glenn as director, and Glenn and the trustees agreed that the foundation should pioneer in the fields of social work, housing, public health, working conditions, education and welfare. The RSF also devoted substantial efforts to improve the quality of statistical investigation.[4]

A number of projects were supported by the RSF. One early project was to assess relief efforts following the San Francisco earthquake and fire. Another project, headed in 1908 by Ethel Dodge Wilcox, was 'An Investigation of the Housing Question for Working Women'. Also in 1908, the RSF's executive committee authorized a study by Mary Van Kleeck of the Alliance Employment Bureau, to investigate the working conditions of women in New York City's bookbinding trade. As a result of the investigation the New York State Legislature soon passed a law to ban factory night shifts for women. In 1911, the RSF formalized some of their focus by creating a Division of Statistics.[5]

One prime interest of the RSF's Division of Statistics was to serve municipalities in need of research services. Municipal research was often done by implementing 'social surveys', a basic goal of which was to gather social and economic data useful as evidence for guiding reform efforts. Surveys began largely with the settlement-house movement over the preceding quarter of a century, which focused on recording data in America's cities, including making maps of the incidence of crime, poverty and illness. Another kind of institution doing surveys was state universities, mostly in rural regions of the country. Several state universities with 'extension services' were particularly known for sending teams of experts to make 'a diagnosis' of any community desiring it. Persons did so especially from schools in Wisconsin, Kansas, Southern California, Chicago, Iowa and Minnesota.[6]

When the RSF developed its dual interest in survey methods and statistical analysis, the foundation also formed a Department for Surveys. The department's full-time director, Shelby M. Harrison, undertook as his first project to make a study to account for all surveys carried out in the United States by 1912 – he identified 154 general surveys and 2,621 surveys in special fields (such as crime, health and recreation).[7]

But above all the RSF focused on data collection and analysis in two particular major studies, in two different industrialized areas capable of serving as 'demonstration cities' for the power of the survey method. The locations were Springfield, Illinois, and Pittsburgh, Pennsylvania, and the projects were the 'Springfield Survey' and the 'Pittsburgh Survey'.

The attention paid to Springfield came in light of some serious race riots in the city during August 1908, which in fact also contributed to the formation of the National Association for the Advancement of Coloured People (NAACP). In Pittsburgh the focus was to understand the impact of intense factory environments on the overall living conditions of working-class families. Each of these surveys looked at such things as schools, recreation, housing, public health, correctional systems, industrial conditions, city and county administration, sanitariums for alcoholics and institutions for the insane.[8]

The Pittsburgh Survey is the legendary one. Already conceived by 1907, and executed under the leadership of Paul U. Kellogg, a former newspaper editor and a leader in the New York Charity Organization Society, the survey was completed and published between 1909 and 1914. The survey's detailed statistical tabulations represented the first such completed study of a major city. Kellogg directed several dozen researchers to categorize and measure all relevant conditions of life and labour in Pittsburgh's steel district, which was among the nation's most intensively industrialized regions. Much attention also focused on a nearby milling and textile centre, the company town of Homestead. The Pittsburgh Survey's six published volumes came to symbolize the severity of America's urban–industrial crisis. The survey was designed to gather data as a preliminary to reform, and the published data and interpretations contributed to establishing minimum-age laws for women workers, as well as industrial accident insurance. Yet the Pittsburgh Survey and the Springfield Survey (ten published volumes itself) recorded primarily conditions, and did not aim to take any major step toward a controlled scientific study. The RSF's two major surveys positively impacted the development of the social sciences, particularly through the work of University of Chicago sociologist Robert E. Park. And in 1916, following the success of the two major surveys, the RSF created a Division of Industrial Studies.[9]

## Other Early Approaches – Urban, Rural, Public and Private

A variety of other similar projects also got underway in the first dozen years or so of the twentieth century. These projects each tended to be directed toward specific areas of concern.

One new organization, established in 1907, was the New York Bureau of Municipal Research (BMR). The BMR, which was wholly privately supported, focused on developing 'sound administrative' techniques. One supporter of the BMR was R. Fulton Cutting, a New York civic leader and advocate for charity reform. Cutting helped to obtain funding from the likes of Andrew Carnegie and John D. Rockefeller, and from other New York families as well.[10]

The BMR was part of a broader 'municipal research movement' at the time. Leaders in the movement, according to historian Jane S. Dahlberg, 'made an extraordinary and permanent contribution to American government, civic life, education, and management practice and theory'. In its earliest years an identified basis for the movement was Woodrow Wilson's 1887 essay, 'The Study of Public Administration'. During a sort of middle period of the movement, a touchstone accomplishment was New York City's 'Tenement House Exhibition' of 1899, a two-week display that showed over 1,000 photographs designed to communicate a fifty-year history of New York's tenements in decline. The exhibit included a model or 'demonstration' tenement that remains considered important in the history of Progressive-era fact-gathering, as well as in learning how to communicate science to the public. The exhibition contributed to New York City's Tenement House Act of 1901.[11]

In later years the movement tended to identify especially with Charles A. Beard's *American City Government* (1912). The goal of many leaders in the movement was to achieve greater 'administrative efficiency' as a centrepiece to municipal reform. In the pursuit of this, the BMR focused on using such methods as surveys, legal analysis and budget studies. The BMR also supported programmes to train people for public service.[12]

Other directions were also taken by reform-oriented social science during the 1900s and 1910s. One kind of experiment was known as 'the company town'. Beyond just Pittsburgh and Springfield, new kinds of company towns dotted the landscape across America. Well-known especially were the steel city of Gary, Indiana, and the mining encampments around Ludlow, Colorado. Perhaps a challenge to recollect today, but Gary was once promoted as US Steel's 'model city'. However, the company's management overseeing the creation of Gary unfortunately ignored many of the latest ideas and recommendations of urban planners in their focus on 'bending nature to the needs of steel', as it was nicely expressed in 1903.[13]

At Ludlow, Colorado, the Colorado Fuel and Iron Company pursued a venture in community welfare. The Rockefellers – both father and son – were significant owners in the company, although they were not quite majority owners. The CFI Co. created at Ludlow a store, a library and other useful facilities to assist migrant workers and their families. To help monitor it all they established a 'Sociological Department', which was headed by Clarence Hicks, formerly the international secretary of the YMCA's Railroad Department. The project to establish the company's Ludlow Valley mining camp as a progressive community reached an apex by about 1911; soon after that a workers' campaign of collective bargaining was begun.[14]

The best-known sociological department, without question, was the one that Henry Ford established in 1913, to oversee the lives of Ford employees working for their 'Five Dollar Day'. Ford's workers lived in single-family homes surrounding the Highland Park plant, and later, the River Rouge plant. Ford believed that the needs of industry ought to help determine the conduct of the household. When Ford and his engineers implemented their assembly line between 1909 and 1913, they were already knowledgeable about Frederick Taylor's principles of 'scientific management'. Ford's sociological department was, in part, an experiment in carrying some of Taylor's doctrine out of the factory and into the community and the home. One problem that concerned Ford was that many workers received his company's training but proved unable to keep up on the job. The assembly line moved fast. So it helped if all the workers understood each other. But Ford's workers came from all over, many in fact from other nations and cultures entirely. Ford came to conclude, 'I am more a manufacturer of men than of automobiles'. Ford's sociological department aimed, at least in some sense, to 'manufacture' people. He employed social scientists to help shape migrants and immigrants into productive workers, who were to become a unified group with only minor differences retained within the group.[15]

The President of the United States, Theodore Roosevelt, was at the same time pursuing yet another approach to researching the needs of people. During late 1908 and early 1909, Roosevelt appointed a group of experts to his 'Country Life Commission' (CLC), with an assigned task to report on the social and economic conditions in rural communities around the eastern half of the nation. Agricultural land needed to be made more productive, and rural waste needed to be cut. Social scientists appointed to the CLC identified rural communities as in bad need of restoration, both economically and culturally. These experts tended to believe that there were two main categories of rural problems, each susceptible to solution with the right policy tools. One category of problems stemmed from economic failures, while the other stemmed from some deeper lack of 'vitality' in rural life. Any complete solution would need to involve both economic adjustment and spiritual uplift. To some social scientists there was also a third supposed problem, which was a notion that a better genetic 'stock' of people had already migrated out of rural America, thereby leaving behind only a lower grade of people. The CLC remained active through much of the subsequent decade, and the commission's members learned to do social surveys of their own, often with organizational assistance of Progressive Protestant reformers. Some of their surveys led to interpretations of the causes of moral decay in rural society, and their policy ideas included providing rural communities with better social services, transportation, communication infrastructures and education. Emphasized most of all was a call for new rural leadership. But where all of the money would come from was not actually identified.[16]

There was also the Taft Commission, in the political world of Washington. With William Howard Taft's victory in the 1908 US presidential election, ideas emerged to pursue greater administrative efficiency through all levels of government, and especially at the federal level. Taft's concerns were impacted by the financial panic of 1907 and the recession that followed, to which he responded by creating a Commission on Economy and Efficiency – or, simply, the Taft Commission. The commission's task in the spring of 1909 was to critically study efficiency in government. The commission presented some findings to the US Congress in 1912, and one proposal was for an 'executive budget system' that in effect would give greater power to the president. Reformers advocated this as a way past various legislative roadblocks of the day. But the shift in power would be at the expense of Congress, and Congress saw to it that the plan went nowhere.

One impact of both the Country Life Commission and the Taft Commission was the Progressive Service, an organization created in 1913 by the Progressive Party. It was a short-lived organization with the purpose of working on social reform, particularly with an aim to focus on problems at a national level.[17]

Still another approach to employing social science as applied science was something known as 'Americanization studies'. This approach had more of an urban concern. The goal was to better assimilate immigrants, and one financial supporter was the Carnegie Corporation (CC) of New York. The CC was founded in 1911 with an extraordinary financial endowment of $125 million, and a main purpose to support education. This new philanthropic foundation soon (in 1913) outspent even the federal government in the support of education, doing so by $5.6 million to $5.0 million. The CC decided to support research into the enculturation of American values, a programme which was officially called the 'Study of Methods of Americanization or Fusion of Native and Foreign Born'.[18]

In 1906, sociologist Grover Huebner had described a process that he called 'the Americanization of the Immigrant'. The term preexisted even Huebner's description, as it was the first word in his article, and his focus was on defining it more clearly than had yet been done: 'It is that process by which immigrants are transformed into Americans'. It was a process that could either run its natural course, or could be intentionally pressed upon people.[19]

A decade later, the second of these two processes was the predominant focus, especially by sociologists at the University of Chicago. At the centre of their work was a series of ten commissioned projects, supported by the CC, executed between 1918 and 1922, and directed by Robert Park and William I. Thomas. Research in Americanization studies had an intellectual aim to better understand the processes through which immigrants become socialized as 'Americans'. There was a policy objective as well, which was to help urban regions better handle their burgeoning populations, including an assortment of problems potentially associated with immigrants. The idea of an American 'melting pot' became something of a media focal point during the 1900s and 1910s.[20]

## Social Science and the Rockefeller Foundation

The Rockefeller Foundation was chartered in New York State. The first gathering of the Foundation was on 19 May 1913, at the Rockefeller offices at 26 Broadway in New York City. While Rockefeller did not attend, Rockefeller, Jr and Frederick Gates were there, and they were named as two of the Foundation's nine trustees. The trustees elected Rockefeller, Jr as president, and they named Rockefeller, Sr as a trustee with special veto power.[21]

Three days later, the Foundation trustees convened their first meeting. They began their work by searching for projects likely to produce no major controversies. They focused especially on medicine, a field, according to Rockefeller, Jr, 'in which there can be no controversy'. Their first major project was agreed upon, and it was to support the Rockefeller Sanitary Commission's ongoing hookworm campaign. Eradication of the disease would have not only health but also great social and economic benefits, and the trustees resolved 'that the advancement of public health through medical research and education, including the demonstration of known methods of treatment and prevention of disease afforded the surest prospect of such usefulness'.[22]

The trustees voted to bring the Sanitary Commission into the Foundation, and so they established an International Health Division to focus on a worldwide campaign of hookworm eradication. Projects remained under the guidance of Wickliffe Rose, and would now also include efforts to control and eradicate malaria, scarlet fever, yellow fever and tuberculosis.[23]

A second interesting conversation that got underway at the Foundation was one that can be traced to the work of the Taft Commission. A proposal in 1913 was made to establish an Institute for Government Research (IGR). Frederick Cleveland, formerly a member of the Taft Commission, introduced a proposal for an independently funded research organization. The proposal found its way to the desk of Jerome D. Greene, secretary at the Rockefeller Foundation, who studied it. Greene responded by writing in March 1914, that 'due to political conditions an independent citizen agency is at present the only effective means in developing a public interest and demand for harnessing the government to a constructive welfare program'.[24]

A turn of events three months later is recorded in a brief memorandum. Written by Greene, the memorandum introduced an idea to identify $100,000 at the Foundation to establish an Institute for Government Research. The aim was 'to do for our Federal Government what the Bureau of Municipal Research has done for the City of New York'. Greene recognized the delicate nature of contributing any financial support to establish a research organization to pursue 'scientific inquiry into government problems and practices with a view to making the results available for the Federal Government'. The year 1914 was a time of heightened levels of hostility toward the Rockefellers, especially for their supposed shenanigans in trying to 'buy politicians'. The year 1914 was also a time of a horrible event in Colorado, at the Ludlow miner's camp (as will be discussed).[25]

The Foundation voted, and in November 1914 they provided $25,000 to the IGR. The IGR's organizers kept themselves aware of the public's perception of things; Greene especially did so. Greene understood that the work of the IGR was 'intelligence and energy applied to the Federal Government'. With respect to the purposes of the IGR and the possibility that the IGR would use Rockefeller support to apply scientific intelligence to studying government, Greene added that, with respect to certain high-level government officials, including President Woodrow Wilson, '[t]hey need not know of this'.[26]

Nevertheless the news went public. The press announced that the Rockefellers financially supported the IGR. The word broke when Congress, just recently so critical of Taft's efforts at budget reform, reacted to the revival of such an inquiry into government budgets and expenditures by directing their criticism toward the Rockefellers. Journalists labelled the IGR the 'Rockefeller Inquiry'. Some critics interpreted the Foundation's support of the IGR as an attempted revenge for the 1911 *Standard Oil* decision.[27]

Creation of the IGR would not be easy. But Greene continued to recognize a particular field of social science that might be ready for greater financial support. When would it be the right time to help create an independent organization to undertake scientific studies of federal and state government?

It took until March 1916 for the IGR to gain a federal charter. The organization, headquartered in Washington, DC, received a pool of funds when Greene and the Foundation's trustees approved a grant of $50,000 for an exploratory committee, which was responsible for helping to design the organization, and to help identify initial projects. The exploratory committee concurred with the recommendations of others, that a private research organization was needed to study the efficiency of government. Such an area of research ideally should be uncontroversial; after all, whatever government was doing, should it not at least do it more efficiently? There was a place for social scientists to try and determine the attainable level of government efficiency, and any specific political or policy goals were not to be assessed.[28]

Under Greene's guidance, and with help from Cleveland, the Foundation's exploratory committee developed a preliminary research programme for the IGR. The committee also crafted a mission statement: 'to make investigations on problems of governmental administration and advise legislators and administrators upon request'. Robert S. Brookings, a respected businessman, economist and public servant, was appointed to direct the institute in its work to bring 'scientific efficiency' to the federal budget process.[29]

The IGR, as it happened, was established during the years that the 'Great War' broke out in Europe. Leadership at the IGR recognized that a nation's transformation from a peacetime to a wartime economy would fit well with their interest in influencing government to achieve greater efficiencies. The First World War indeed had a strong impact on the IGR, as economists and other researchers there increased their emphasis on studying the formation of budgets and policies. Over time the IGR would help to elevate the level of efficiency in many areas of government, including budget analysis, civil service methods, retirement programmes and various statistical operations.[30]

## Elevating the Level of Discussion

There was at least one other major conversation that got started at the Foundation in 1913. From the first months of the Foundation, an idea shared among the trustees was the possibility of creating a division that would focus on supporting social science. The conversation focused on a possible Institute of Economic Research (IER).

The Foundation's leadership helped to organize conferences aimed at exploring whether the time was right to create such an institute. A common notion among business leaders was that opponents of big business thrived on peddling 'misinformation', and that the best way to counter inaccuracy was to provide more accuracy. Early conferences in 1913 were organized in large measure by Theodore N. Vail, president of AT&T, and they were attended by such university leaders as Edwin F. Gay (dean of the Harvard Business School) and Harry Pratt Judson (president of the University of Chicago). Also attending was Foundation secretary Greene. Conference participants tended to blame manipulative 'agitators' and 'demagogues' for dispensing lies about American business. Greene listened to the conversation, and he identified a common goal 'to see whether something might be done to relieve the general unrest' so prevalent between management and labour. Conference participants agreed on a goal to promote better communication of accurate information about the contributions of business to society. 'What was needed', Greene took note,

> was a constant chain of correct information, put before the public by a sort of publicity bureau, with the special idea of reaching not so much the better educated members of the community, as the middle and lower classes upon which the demagogues chiefly preyed.[31]

Greene shared with the Rockefellers the perceived need for such an institute. He explained how it should benefit both business and the public, and in particular he said that 'the business interests of the country as a whole have everything to gain and nothing to lose by the dissemination of accurate information as the starting point for intelligent public opinion and wise legislation'. Conference participants understood that Americans viewed big business differently than they had just a decade or two earlier. Industrial conflicts were fairly common, and such violence seemed irrational. The US Congress created a 'Commission on Industrial Relations', with a goal to better understand such conflicts, and among those who testified before the commission was John D. Rockefeller, Sr.[32]

Over the upcoming year the Foundation held a series of meetings to discuss a potential institute of economic research. These conversations ultimately explored two basic possibilities, which were to better dispense existing information, or to support efforts to discover new information about the economy. Those who supported the latter aim expected that any new information would likely help big business. But most participants tended to believe that the state of economic knowledge was sufficient already, and that better distribution of existing information was what was needed. Greene wanted to think more about this. One who joined Greene in considering possible goals for such an institute was Frederick Gates, whose initial inclination was to focus on discovering new facts about forces that drove social and economic progress. But the question was how to do this?[33]

Gates held high optimism that all of society's problems could be solved with a direct and constant level of persistence, which to him meant that well-placed financial assistance should produce a predictable rate of scientific progress, in each and every field. Gates especially espoused such a belief for research done by medical scientists, and he believed that a common source of a great many of society's social and economic problems was physical disease, which he considered to be the 'prolific root of every conceivable ill'.[34]

Discussion about a possible Institute of Economic Research really got going near the end of 1913. Greene believed such an institute should be created, and by October he introduced his ideas to the board of trustees. On 22 October 1913, the trustees approved a plan for an intensive round of discussion with a small 'Committee of Leading Economists and Business Men'. Gates believed that a chief goal for these discussions should be 'to invite suggestions as to the desirability of establishing an organization for the study of important social and economic questions vitally affecting the welfare of society at the present time'. Five group interviews were arranged over six weeks, and by December Greene recorded a conclusion that committee members 'were favorable to the establishment of some sort of an agency for the scientific investigation of economic subjects'. Greene shared the information with the trustees, who recommended an additional conference. Greene arranged for the group conference, led by Columbia University's Wesley C. Mitchell, to convene and to prepare a preliminary proposal for such an institute by January 1914.[35]

Greene assembled the group, and most of them were agreed that better fundamental research would be needed, especially given that many of society's more urgent problems seemed fundamentally economic in nature. Group feedback came in the form of multiple reports that were produced in March and April 1914, where the group concluded that significant value should exist in establishing a new institute to do basic economic research; for it would be through better science that the paths to social and economic reform would be made clearer. Greene's economist friend, Edwin Gay of Harvard, described the need for money to support more than dispensing information: 'The work now done in the universities is almost entirely the work of individual students writing theses for their doctorates, necessarily circumscribed in scope, usually far from thorough, and by the very nature of things apt to be scattered'. The economics work in the universities was low-grade science at best. Gay suspected that any first projects for an institute would be unlikely 'to be comprehensive and thorough investigations of large subjects'. But something at least needed to be tried. 'There is a real need for such an institute', he emphasized. Gay, in a follow-up statement, recommended that the Foundation ought to 'insist' at the outset that 'the primary purpose is the discovery of truth', and that any investment in disseminating economic information was to be 'only incidental'.[36]

Greene appreciated the work of economists, and he was pleased that they understood the importance in maintaining political neutrality alongside scholarly integrity. As Mitchell explained, any potential relevance for such an institute 'would depend primarily upon the impartiality of its management and the strictly scientific character of its productivity ... [I]n the long run', he added, 'the practical benefits of science can be secured more quickly following the natural growth of knowledge than in following the natural growth of popular issues'. Mitchell favoured a primary focus on fundamental research, for it was necessary first to expand knowledge before applying it to 'improving the practice of social regulation'.[37]

Greene began to consider potential projects. Rather than focus on just one or two projects, he wondered about undertaking a comprehensive research programme. A few scattered projects, as he suggested back in January, held little promise of getting 'to the very foundations of the great economic and social problems of the day'. He believed that a programme of economic research should operate in ways that resemble the proven success of the programme of medical research at the RIMR.[38]

Another person interested in the matter was Rockefeller, Jr. He asked for advice from Edwin Gay. 'For several years I have been discussing with various people the desirability and possibility of establishing an Institute of Economic Research', said Gay. What was needed before anything else was 'to create a saner attitude on economic and social problems by providing a centre for scientific examination of questions of the day uninfluenced by politics or business gain'. The primary focus should be 'to make accessible in popular form the results of scientific study, to stimulate understanding of economics, and attract the ablest young men to find careers in that field'. Rockefeller, Jr responded that he was willing to consider helping to establish such an institute.[39]

By March 1914, the trustees approved a next step of creating an exploratory committee. Such a committee would 'make a selection of problems of economic importance which could be advantageously studied'. The committee met on 18 March 1914, at the home office of the Rockefeller Foundation. Attendees included Charles Elliot and Edwin Gay of Harvard University, J. Lawrence Laughlin and Leon Marshall of the University of Chicago, Wesley Mitchell and John Bates Clark of Columbia University, Henry C. Emery and Arthur Hadley of Yale University, and John Koren of the American Statistical Association. Representing the Rockefeller Foundation were Gates, Greene and Rockefeller, Jr. The committee's collective recommendation was that the new institute should focus on studying such problems 'as would require the accumulation of a large body of statistics or the extension of research in different parts of the world'. They considered whether any new discoveries were likely in the near-term, or whether new discoveries were more likely only as a long-term prospect. There was also great interest in comparing the two basic goals: a focus on science versus a focus on publicity. But Greene and Gates were beginning suddenly to develop more opposed viewpoints; whereas Greene supported a focus on science, Gates preferred a focus primarily on public persuasion. Rockefeller, Jr, it seems, was beginning to tend more to the latter view as well.[40]

As to the economists, increasingly they supported a focus on strengthening the scientific status of their field. They wanted a focus on promoting 'better conditions for the cultivation of the social sciences than were possible under any university or government auspices'. They wanted an institute that 'would have the necessary funds to provide investigators whose whole time would be given uninterruptedly to the work' of advancing science.[41]

Some conference participants shared more specific thoughts as well. Koren believed that the primary purpose for a new institute 'was necessarily the collection of facts to perform the same service in the field of economics and sociology as an institution for medical research in the domain of public health'. Mitchell saw industrial progress as generally 'proceeding by an extremely crude method of trial and error, sadly wasteful of money, time and human strength'; what was needed to prevent more 'blundering experiments' was 'to acquire and to disseminate genuine knowledge in the field of economics and other social sciences'. To J. Laurence Laughlin, one priority was to deflect any interpretations that a new institute was attempting to rival university-based research, for avoiding any such a perception would minimize the chances of university economists rejecting research findings by the institute. Laughlin added an analogy to help distinguish discovery of knowledge from dispensing of knowledge: 'The carp must be caught before it can be cooked; investigative results and new ones yet to come must be had before any distribution can take place'.[42]

What was needed, all were agreed, was better factual understanding of complex problems of a modern industrial economy. Creation of an institute of economic research was to be officially recommended. As the Foundation had stated back in January, the objective was to move by March to a final assessment of

> the desirability of establishing an Institute of Economic Research, to make a selection of such problems of economic importance as would in their judgment be advantageously studied through such an agency, to recommend a method of organization, and to present an estimate of the approximate cost of initiating and carrying on the work to be first proposed.[43]

But on 19 March 1914, the day after the exploratory committee met, Gates introduced his own view. If the main purpose was to pursue new research, then the Foundation should not get involved. A place remained only for supporting a focus on problems that are actively discussed in society, for in most cases such problems seemed to stem from an incomplete distribution of information. The need was to decrease 'all the violence and the strikes around the country'. Gates had decided that economic research was different from medical research, in that basic economic research was actually unnecessary. 'Life is short; time is fleeting', he said. 'We cannot do everything, we can do only a few things. The selection of the things we undertake to do is therefore of the first importance'. If the Foundation were to support any economic studies with its limited resources, then 'we ought to select, if we can, that department which is most urgent and of most practical importance' – and that which was most urgent was to better distribute existing knowledge. Any new knowledge 'will have no immediate and perhaps not even a distant practical value'. Again he emphasized: 'What is urgent in economics is not research, but a clearer apprehension by the masses of the people and the voters of the United States of the simpler and more fundamental economic laws'. And as if all that were not enough, Gates continued, businesses were unlikely to relinquish their current data, and any large quantity of data 'valuable yesterday is useless today'.[44]

The Foundation's trustees met in mid-April 1914. They invited Harvard's Edwin Gay to join them. Some of their discussion focused on contemplating potential first research projects for the institute, and the trustees worked to include a full mix of views. Gay remained positioned at one end of the spectrum, where he advocated for an institute to do science. In opposition stood Victor A. Morawetz, a New York attorney, and a friend of the Rockefellers. Morawetz was there to represent the position that an institute should focus solely on a 'propagandistic point of view'. Morawetz had previously contacted Rockefeller, Jr to express some preference for establishing a 'bureau of economic publicity', so he was well-suited to articulate the opposing argument.[45]

The exploratory committee also held a meeting, and on 4 August 1914 the committee recommended creating an institute. They advised undertaking a single project for one year. Four members of the committee wanted a somewhat large study of price stability. One committee member, Morawetz, in a second report, recommended studying a small and more 'concrete' problem that the public cared about, such as profit-sharing. All were at least agreed that no person at the Rockefeller Foundation should directly do any of the work. The committee members were also agreed that what was needed was to consider 'the general character of the work to be undertaken by a proposed Institute of Economic Research and, if possible, to recommend a subject or subjects appropriate for its initial investigation'.[46]

The exploratory committee decided that the institute's first project should be a study of prices. This was a research field that governments tended not to be involved in, and it was a field too big for any university's resources. Problems associated with price levels represented a clear public interest, and as Gay put it, a study of prices would produce results 'singularly adapted to the use of methods that are in the strictest sense scientific'. Most important, from a scientific study of prices, 'results of great value could be obtained without arousing suspicions that the study was carried on for selfish or for class interests'. The economists concluded:

> [I]t is expedient that the proposed Institute should address itself primarily to the full and dispassionate investigation of problems of fundamental scientific interest, and that the work it does should be of such solidity as to establish firmly its repute as a competent and indispensable organ of research.[47]

Along with the majority report from the committee, Morawetz was invited to submit his statement for an alternative project, which would focus on distributing information with an aim to better explain to the public the nature of profit-sharing. Such a problem seemed urgent, and to Morawetz it seemed more likely to succeed than any study of prices.[48]

Gates considered the two reports, and he sent a communication to Rockefeller, Jr to ask directly: what does the Rockefeller Foundation believe economics to be? To Gates economics was not yet a science. And unlike medical research on disease, Gates knew of no particular problem in economics that 'urgently needs solution'. No institute was needed to do basic research. 'Beware of an institute of economic research. It is the last thing needed. But create if you can a bureau of economic publicity that for once shall be really popular and efficient and do not count the cost'.[49]

Rockefeller, Jr decided to leave open the option of pursuing a little bit of both kinds of activities: some science and some publicity. 'Perhaps we can hit upon some medium of course', he expressed to Gates on 24 August 1914, 'which will give us the things most desirable from each point of view'.[50]

But while the Foundation held all of this discussion in the spring and summer of 1914, an urgent matter unfolded in the western United States. The matter was an upwelling of labour frustration and violence at various locations, and most of all at a Rockefeller-owned mining camp in Colorado. One impact of the violence would be to disrupt the Foundation's plans for an Institute of Economic Research.

## Ludlow

A tragedy happened on 20 April 1914. It was a tragedy in which many people died. And not just workers died, but their families did too. It was a tragedy that started on an awful day, and which took months for the American people to really process. The tragedy was called the Ludlow Massacre.

There was a background to the events at Ludlow. Miners had worked and set camp in the area for a couple of decades by that time. There was a brief little spat of disruption back in 1903 and 1904, but all parties had restored order. Then, between about 1910 and 1914, wage cuts coupled with price inflation led to labour conflicts in increasing numbers, in a variety of industries across the nation. Many workers were unhappy with their work environments and their pay, and the American public regularly heard about labour conflicts. One particular media focal point was unrest at Colorado's mining camps, and the Rockefellers were the largest owners (although not quite majority owners) of the largest of the companies operating the camps: the Colorado Fuel and Iron Company.[51]

The CFI Co. had some twenty-four mines around a region in southern Colorado called Ludlow Valley, located twenty miles north of Trinidad. A tent camp was in the valley, and it was run as something of a company town. It was a unique sort of a town, designed to suit the particular industry. The conditions of things at Ludlow first really soured about a year before the tragedy. In August 1913, miners for the CFI Co. requested some reforms. They asked for such things as a miner-elected weighman, the right to trade at any store and an eight-hour workday. They also asked for union recognition. But none of their demands brought even a reply; and so, following a meeting of the miners, on 23 September they called a strike. The company's mine officials still refused to meet with the miners, and the miners (with their families) walked away from the company town. They headed into a mountain meadow just beyond the company's property line. It was there that they pitched their tents.[52]

How would the company respond?

In October, managers of the company went to the local Sheriff Tarr who sent in 326 deputy sheriffs to be stationed around the perimeter of the company's property. Clashes occurred nearly every day. Striking miners periodically tried to enter company property, usually for small bits of wood or coal for a camp fire. Possibly once in a while a guard or two might walk into the strikers' encampment area, maybe just to make mischief. As the frequency of small skirmishes escalated by the end of a long and frustrating autumn, Colorado's governor sent in the state militia. Things quieted down, and a long winter set in. On any given day, the militia might mistreat or arrest a striker, and the strikers might harass the militia.

By April 1914, the inhabitants of the tent colony around Ludlow were greatly reduced in number. But one enthusiastic leader among the miners was a man named John Tikas, who became the target of a number of the militiamen still stationed in the field. Some of the soldiers decided to 'get him', and on 20 April they captured Tikas. Some of the miners detonated a signal explosion to alert other miners to run and rescue Tikas. Meanwhile, one of the militiamen was beating Tikas to death with the butt of a gun. Some of the militia decided to burn what they may have believed was an abandoned tent village. The next morning, burned bodies of two women and eleven children were found beneath some of the tents. Shocked and grieved, the remaining strikers rampaged through the mining district, destroying everything they could find. Three mine guards were killed in one battle, nine miners died in another – and so on it went. US federal troops were called in and 163 miners were arrested on murder charges. The nation was shocked. The press slammed the Rockefellers once more. The American people again saw the Rockefellers as the enemy.

The Ludlow tragedy infuriated workers and sympathizers nationwide. US President Woodrow Wilson signed off on sending federal troops to Colorado; while they were ostensibly not to take sides, the troops evidently were soon persuaded – once in the West – to defeat the miners. The press continued to report that the militiamen and troops were recruited by the Rockefellers, and so the Rockefellers were now vilified in the press.

Just when it might have seemed that matters could not get worse, they actually did. It was soon learned by the public that on 6 April, two weeks prior to the Ludlow tragedy, Rockefeller, Jr had testified before a US House of Representatives Subcommittee on Mines and Mining. Rockefeller, Jr was on record as giving a vigorous defence of the CFI Co. and its management practices. Rockefeller, Jr had conversed about how he saw nothing seriously wrong with the way the Rockefeller-owned mine camps were operated.[53]

At least that was how Rockefeller, Jr's views were conveyed in the newspapers. But what Rockefeller, Jr had actually intended to communicate to Congress was that he cared. His fuller words were clear enough. He was worried. Yet he also believed that the Rockefellers were constrained in their actions, essentially by the workings of a modern understanding of the responsibilities of a stockholder. The model of stockholder responsibilities was, in the mind of Rockefeller, Jr, the key issue. It served as a basis for what he believed about the appropriate procedures for handling industrial disagreements. When the Congressional subcommittee asked whether he believed that a director of a public company 'should take the responsibility for the conduct of the company', Rockefeller, Jr answered the question based on a modern business principle: 'No'.

> [I]t would be impossible for any man to be personally responsible for all of the management of the various concerns in which he might be a larger or small stockholder. It would be simply impossible to do that, and all that any man can do is to find the ablest men that he can find, and put the responsibility squarely on them.

And as to whether any particular minority stockholder of a company should be responsible for the actions of a single manager in the company, the answer was clearly no.[54]

Rockefeller, Jr also reported to the subcommittee that he had attended no meetings of the CFI Co. board of directors since the strike began in September 1913; neither had his father. The American people surely did not like learning this, for such a lack of personal engagement was despite many months of ongoing media reports concerning the crisis at Ludlow. What this indicated to Congress and the public was that Rockefeller, Jr had not even cared enough to confirm whether reports of intimidation and violence against the workers were true.[55]

It was concluded, in the end, that the Rockefellers had little knowledge of the conditions in the Colorado mine camps. Historians believe this is true. Neither Rockefeller had visited the place. As to Rockefeller, Jr, who was the one who testified, in his business way of thinking it was the responsibility of managers on site to know what was happening there. Perhaps some responsibility was incumbent upon the CFI board to try and gather information about what was happening, and two of the board members were John D. Rockefeller, Jr and Frederick T. Gates. Both were busy people, and two seats on just one of many company boards represented only the slightest sliver of their attention. It was a tough situation all around.

Rockefeller, Jr definitely tried to make appropriate responses after the tragedy. But many persons saw him coming off as a bit bumbling and out-of-touch. Some historians have focused, for example, on Rockefeller, Jr saying simply (and naively) before the Commission: 'Our office staff is a sort of family affair. We talk over all kinds of matters of a common interest. We have not drawn sharp lines between business and philanthropic interests'. Perhaps Rockefeller, Jr was, for just a moment, trying to be his father.[56]

But Rockefeller, Jr persisted, and he decided to take the lead. After the disaster, among the Rockefellers, it was John D. Rockefeller, Jr who decided to make a genuine effort to figure it all out. He made plans to go to Colorado and meet with the miners, and he did so. He also spoke with many people around the state. In contrast, Rockefeller – then seventy-five years old – seems likely to have stuck with an older, paternalist view. For an informative illustration, which dates from about the same time, there was an occasion when Rockefeller declined to allow even the workers on his own estates to take holiday time for Labour Day. He explained this by saying that he knew better than they did what was good for them. 'Instead of spending money on amusements my employees will have an opportunity of adding to their savings. Had they been given a holiday, money would have been spent foolishly'.[57]

Obviously in the aftermath of Ludlow somebody would have to testify in detail. That person was Rockefeller, Jr. The testimony began on 27 January 1915, as Rockefeller, Jr answered questions for a special US Congressional Commission convened in New York City. Originally the Commission had scheduled their New York hearing for a general investigation of large philanthropic institutions, but they changed their focus. The atmosphere, as Rockefeller, Jr entered, was hostile. Yet he maintained an outstanding calmness through the proceedings. He stayed composed, and it seems all the nation was willing to listen to whatever words a Rockefeller might at last offer. Rockefeller, Jr really did quite well. The *New York Times* admired that he 'never waivered from his entire self-possession and courteous humour'. The socialist magazine *Masses*, while seeing Rockefeller, Jr start out a bit like his father as a 'master of evasion', also saw Rockefeller, Jr come into his own as a person both 'gentle' and 'apparently frank'.[58]

## Whether to Support Social Science?

At the Rockefeller Foundation, there were two series of conversations during 1914 about the possibility of supporting social scientists. One dialogue focused on the idea to help create an Institute for Government Research. The other focused on the idea to establish an Institute of Economic Research. The first of these was to be outside of the Foundation, and the institute only asked for money. And, as we saw, some money was awarded in a low-profile manner. That was in November 1914 – after Ludlow – with Jerome Greene adding his view that people 'need not know of this'.

The Institute of Economic Research was envisioned to be an actual division of the Foundation. The debate was whether the institute should focus on science or publicity. But could either of these directions still be taken after Ludlow?

After Ludlow, some attention certainly turned to the need for better publicity. The Rockefellers now recognized the importance of public opinion, and Rockefeller, Jr guided the family to hire a professional advisor, Ivy Lee, who was already known as an outstanding 'publicity man', most of all for the Pennsylvania Railroad. As he came to work for the Rockefellers, Lee emphasized a new bottom-line goal in addition to any profit-sheet objectives. This new measure needed to be the value in 'shaping the affairs of the corporation so that when placed before the public they will be approved'. Lee came in and oversaw a publicity campaign funded directly by the Rockefellers. His task was to attempt to diminish what the Rockefellers interpreted as the main problem in all of this: the widespread prevalence of misunderstanding. Lee proved to be a tremendous asset for the Rockefellers.[59]

## Conclusion

By the time that 1914 came around, quite a number of private and governmental organizations were experimenting with supporting social science. It seems the basic idea of this had been new in the 1880s and 1890s, when the Settlement House movement enlisted the services of social scientists to walk the city and gather data on the condition of the city. By 1914, the idea to support social scientists had really turned quite popular among philanthropists and politicians. However the Rockefellers, technically speaking, had not yet decided in an institutional manner to support any specific research projects to be undertaken by social scientists. Or, had they?

# 4 EARLY ROCKEFELLER SUPPORT OF SOCIAL SCIENCE

## Introduction

Rockefeller philanthropy began supporting social scientists with a few small-scale efforts. These efforts were overseen not so much by Rockefeller, but by Rockefeller, Jr, and they typically began with some careful sharing of ideas about whether and how to financially support social scientists. The main experiments were the Bureau of Social Hygiene (1913), the Rockefeller Foundation's Division of Industrial Relations (1914) and an Institute of Economics (1922). Various additional thoughts and discussions were woven through this exciting period of change within Rockefeller philanthropy.

## Ludlow and William Lyon Mackenzie King

The tragedy at Ludlow in April 1914 was simply awful. In the months that followed, the Rockefeller New York office made real efforts to provide for injured employees and their families. They asked for assistance from neutral mediators, and they requested that a special adjudication board be appointed by the Chief Justice of the US Supreme Court.

At the same time, however, the Rockefeller Foundation needed to keep moving ahead. The Foundation continued to discuss the idea to establish some kind of an institute or division that could focus on social science. Perhaps an initial project for the division could be to develop a comprehensive study of the causes of industrial conflict. The scale of the study somewhat resembled the Russell Sage Foundation's project to survey urban working and living conditions. It also rivalled in scale the Carnegie Institution's project to survey the history of labour. But the Foundation's planned project would be headed by a single individual, who would study one concrete problem.

Rockefeller, Jr took some initiative in committing to the idea that a single outstanding social scientist could execute a single detailed study. Jerome Greene, as Foundation secretary, was asked to contact an old friend, William Lyon Mackenzie King, a labour unions expert. King, a Canadian, had graduate training at the University of Chicago and Harvard University, and had field experience working with Jane Addams at Chicago's Hull House. Through the months of June and July 1914 Greene contacted King on behalf of the Foundation's exploratory committee that was interested in establishing an Institute of Economic Research. Greene asked King if he believed that enough separation from partisan engagement could be achieved so as to 'permit you to advise large interests I represent in regard to present labour difficulties and probable far-reaching studies looking toward the future'. In Greene's estimation there was one very urgent problem: it was not prices (as many economists on the committee believed) and was not profit-sharing (as one of them suggested); the single problem was labour difficulties in general. A study of such difficulties could potentially meet Rockefeller, Jr's hope of identifying an acceptable 'middle course' between the goals of science and publicity.[1]

King responded positively to the idea. On 1 August he paid a visit to New York City. In a meeting with Rockefeller, Jr the two agreed that problems of industrial relations represented an urgent concern. Rockefeller, Jr had Gates draft a one-year contract to state that King would be paid by the Foundation to research causes of labour violence and potential paths to improved labour–management relations. King agreed to investigate the 'great problems of industrial relations' through a research effort that was 'to be intensive study rather than extensive investigation'. Stated in King's job title was that he headed not an Institute of Economic Research, but a Division of Industrial Relations.[2]

King began his work on 1 October 1914, with a clear statement of what kind of a project he was to conduct. It was to be

> an investigation of the great problem of industrial relations, with a special view to the discovery of some mutual relationship of labour and capital which would afford labour the protection it needs against oppression and exploitation, while at the same time promoting its efficiency as an instrument of economic production.

His research would help improve conditions for workers as well as improve productive efficiency, thereby contributing in two ways to the public interest. King was to inform the Foundation of his planned research methods. 'It is our desire', the Foundation indicated,

> that the scope should be as broad and comprehensive as possible, for only as a result of such an intensive investigation can we hope to be in a position to make helpful suggestions looking toward the improvement in industrial relations.[3]

King began his project by describing an objective to study labour issues in ways that would meet 'the desire to make an important contribution toward our knowledge of the causes of the prevailing unrest'. He aimed to employ scientific methods to explain why there was so much violence in a modern, industrial economy, and the Foundation's trustees supported King's plan. They too favoured a project to discover 'if any substantial improvement in the relations between capital and labour could be worked out on a basis compatible with sound economics'. Secretary Greene approved the project as a starting point toward a 'far-reaching study of the labour question in America'.[4]

King's relationship to the Rockefellers was also something to be clear about. The public distrusted the Rockefellers. Therefore King officially worked for the Foundation. But the public still perceived King as working for the Rockefellers. They tended to see his research as added evidence of the Rockefellers' willingness to commit acts of wrongdoing; they interpreted King as likely to make some 'scientific' argument designed to support Rockefeller interests.

King's research continued within the context of tough times. The US Congress directed the Rockefellers to answer questions in December 1914 and January 1915. It was Rockefeller, Jr who showed up. For the first hearings, in December, his submitted materials consisted simply of written responses to twenty-nine questions. It was clear that Congress wanted to learn about the Foundation's sudden creation of a Division of Industrial Relations, and the Congressional commission asked the question straight up: 'What were the facts, reasons and considerations which led to the establishment of the Industrial Relations Division of the Foundation?' Rockefeller, Jr responded by saying that labour violence was an urgent problem, and that King's task was to employ scientific methods to discover the 'causes' of such violence. Rockefeller, Jr described in some detail the work that the Foundation asked King to perform. He emphasized that King's project fitted with the mission statement of the Foundation, and that the Foundation hoped that a study of the subject 'could work out sound and substantial improvements in the relation of capital and labour' – indeed that 'it could hardly do anything better calculated "to promote the well-being of mankind", for which purpose the Foundation was created'.[5]

Rockefeller, Jr described the requirement that King's work be impartial and objective, and that in no way should his research 'be local or restricted, or carried on with particular reference to any existing situation, or to the conditions in any one country'. The research was to be general in its execution, and all research matters were 'left to Mr. King to decide'. The Foundation's hope was 'that by careful study of world experience there may be disclosed methods of adjusting individual relations which if applied will prove of permanent value'. King's research,

in spirit and in method, will be akin to that of the Rockefeller Institute for Medical Research ... the attitude will be that of a physician who investigates the nature and causes of the pathological conditions with which he has to deal, with a view, if possible, to the discovery of effective remedies.[6]

By early January 1915, a Congressional subcommittee again called on Rockefeller, Jr to testify. This was the first occasion in which he was asked to respond on the spot – including responding to some questions about Ludlow that made it into the press's reporting. Rockefeller, Jr was asked if King had stated anything specific about his research methods and goals. Rockefeller, Jr described how King was 'surveying a special field of work', and that by applying a thoughtful method, King was 'ascertaining in the first instance how far investigation of the great problem of Industrial Relations has been already profitably carried out by others, and determining as to wherein further investigation may be made to advantage'. Worth reiterating was that no attempt would be made by anyone to influence King in 'the questions he may wish to ask or the course he may wish to follow'. No interim progress reports would be asked for. King would be fully autonomous throughout the project.[7]

A little over two weeks later, Rockefeller, Jr was brought back to testify. This time there was much more focus on the CFI Co. and the events at Ludlow. Rockefeller, Jr prepared an eleven-page statement. He had been asked 'to what extent the stockholders and directors of a corporation are responsible for the labour conditions which are produced', and in his responses he was a bit more detailed than before. He explained that in any publicly owned business there are many different responsibilities 'to be divided and vested' in many different groups, including stockholders, directors, officers, managers, workers and perhaps others. One thing that a large stockholder can do is exercise 'moral influence' over those who run the daily operations of a company. Such influence was what the Rockefellers had tried to exert. Rockefeller, Jr personally emphasized his 'deepest concern' about so much suffering among workers and their families. Yet he added that with respect to labour conditions in general, they 'are a matter for which the officers of the corporation are primarily responsible and with which they, by reason of their experience and their first-hand acquaintance with the facts, are best qualified to deal'. There was a division of knowledge and a division of experience in connection with 'the facts'. When asked if he personally believed that workers had a right to strike, Rockefeller, Jr replied in a fair enough manner: 'I believe it to be just as proper and advantageous for labour to associate itself into organized groups for the advancement of its legitimate interests, as for capital to combine for the same objects'. Only by allowing that every group can try to advance their interests can collective bargaining accomplish the fairest results for all.[8]

Rockefeller, Jr was invited back to the Commission yet again. By May 1915 much media reaction focused on Rockefeller, Jr's supposed declaration that the Rockefellers had 'no knowledge' of the conditions at Ludlow before all the violence. Rockefeller, Jr thus took this occasion to emphasize that he really had kept himself informed. 'I have sought to inform myself and have not hesitated to make suggestions looking towards more adequate representation on the part of the employees and participation by them in the determining of matters pertaining to their working conditions'. He emphasized how he had 'studiously avoided' doing anything that could allow for any appearance of 'dictating a policy or to arbitrarily control any situation'. It needed to be set clear, on record, that all of the CFI Co. policies in Colorado prior to and during the strike 'were decided upon and carried out by the executive officers at Denver without asking our advice'.[9]

All of this Congressional testimony between December 1914 and May 1915 can be assessed as a piece. There is no question that the Commission on Industrial Relations directed tough questions to Rockefeller, Jr. Also clear is that he answered their questions. The Commission investigated business as well as philanthropic motives, and the Commission was clear about its concern over the relationship between the Rockefellers and King.

Testimony also came from others. The New York Bureau of Municipal Research reported that they had received direct support from the Rockefellers, from as early as 1907. The original director of the BMR, Frederick A. Cleveland, suggested before the Commission that his own dismissal came, at least in part, from his disagreeing with certain conditions attached to the money received from Rockefeller, Sr. Such a statement – true or not – could never sit well with the press. Also introduced to the Commission was a reminder of Rockefeller Sr's offers to support publication activities by the United States Chamber of Commerce. That offer, even though it was declined, became further 'evidence' that the Rockefellers intended to gain control over any government oversight of business.[10]

Some elements of the truth existed, in some of this. The Rockefellers had given money to the Bureau of Municipal Research. Both Rockefeller and Rockefeller, Jr had considered supporting the US Chamber of Commerce, specifically to help in publishing some economic data. And so some lessons were learned by the Rockefellers, again.[11]

The public developed an opinion along the way. The Commission's summary reports were open records, and the American people could now question the relationship between the Rockefellers and King. News writers admired Rockefeller, Jr's willingness to answer questions, however they disapproved of his claim that in no way was the Foundation trying to buy any scientific conclusions that would favour the Rockefellers. In his testimony, Rockefeller, Jr had actually cited the committee of economists that were consulted by the Foundation. This part of his testimony revealed much optimism that the problem of industrial violence was something for which it should be possible to discover ready solutions.

The public also learned that Rockefeller, Jr told the Commission why he hired King. 'I determined that insofar as lay within my power I would seek means of avoiding the possibility of similar conflicts arising elsewhere.' This was how it happened 'that I came to recommend to my colleagues in the Rockefeller Foundation the instituting of a series of studies into the fundamental problems arising out of industrial relations'. Rockefeller, Jr hired King according to his great confidence in what scientists can accomplish. The only real problem to overcome was that prescriptions from social scientists lagged behind the rate of change in the industrial economy. Rockefeller, Jr thought that 'there was something fundamentally wrong in the condition of affairs which rendered possible the loss of human lives, engendered hatred and bitterness and brought suffering and privation upon hundreds of human beings'.[12]

## Revisiting the Idea of an Institute of Economics

The decision to bring King on-board technically still allowed for creation of an Institute of Economic Research. When the discussions were left off in August 1914, no decisions were made. Persons at the Foundation were willing to go another round of discussions to try and figure this out. Secretary Greene definitely wanted to press onward and assess the possibility of it. Others did too. But what remained of greatest importance was to continue 'keeping clear of controversial issues'. Greene wrote to Gay concerning 'the close relationship which [King's] work may have to the subjects in which an Institute of Economic Research will be interested', and he looked forward to 'any report that Mr. King may make within the next year or two'. It could be possible that King's research will be 'of the kind that an Institute of Economic Research would most appropriately father'.[13]

Back on 4 August 1914, at that moment when the two reports came from Gay and Morawetz, Greene still had thoughts about an institute that might focus on data collection and analysis. We saw in the last chapter that both Gates and Rockefeller, Jr decided to chime in at the point when these two reports – the 'majority report' and the 'minority report' – were submitted. Greene also decided to write his own brief statement, aimed at reiterating, for the Foundation's Executive Committee, that the existence of King's research did not preclude supporting other economic research. A broader research programme could even likely assist King.

> The great undertaking Mr. King is about to enter will require a large amount of data; we will need an instrument for research and for the proper collection of material such as a properly organized Institute of Economic Research could furnish.[14]

Greene also shared thoughts directly with Gay. He interpreted his view as generally agreeing with Gay's majority report that suggested studying prices, which could be most useful given that research into price problems would 'be fundamental to almost all other possible or profitable studies'. Greene wanted to know about any thoughts concerning the form of a possible directorship for the institute. The majority report suggested perhaps three economists. Yet Greene also heard that Gay might prefer appointing a single director. There was also the minority report by Victor Morawetz, which recommended something more like a rotating directorship. Greene asked Gay: 'Will you consider the advisability of writing me a letter which will serve both as a rejoinder to Mr. Morawetz's proposition and an elaboration of the argument in favor of the majority report'.[15]

Gates still supported a propaganda approach, and in a letter to Rockefeller, Jr he opined that the only truly urgent objective was to 'get before all reading and thinking people', from the lowest demagogues to the finest ministers, 'a few of the elemental principles of economics'. But by September and October 1914, all persons associated with Rockefeller philanthropy had to know that the horrible events at Ludlow were having a deepening impact on the public's perception of the Rockefellers; the US Congress was calling for those hearings at which Rockefeller, Jr would testify. The Foundation trustees met on 21 October 1914, and they decided that no immediate action should be taken. Their main recorded reason was 'the fact that since the question of establishing an Institute for Economic Research had been under consideration, an Investigation of Industrial Relations had been instituted under the direction of Mr. W. L. Mackenzie King'. Gates and Rockefeller, Jr stated their agreement with the decision. Greene accepted it too, even though he received it as 'a disappointment', partly out of his personal confidence that 'King's work will demonstrate the need for the Institute' – King had just been hired that month.[16]

## King's Project

King worked hard on his research, and no matter what anyone – Rockefeller, Rockefeller, Jr, or any other person – might think of its worth, King would always believe that his contribution was 'a good piece of work'.[17]

Receiving various typewritten chapters of King's report were both Rockefeller, Jr and George E. Vincent, president of the Foundation. Writing to Rockefeller, Jr at one point, in December 1917, Vincent opined 'that practical people who want concrete programs and definite suggestions as to social policy will be disappointed because the book deals in general and abstract statements'. There could also be a problem that 'the persons who are interested in theory, the economists, sociologists and social philosophers, will be likely to question the validity of Mr. King's methods and the nature of his reasoning'. Two months later, after looking over another draft chapter, Rockefeller, Jr agreed with Vincent in holding 'disappointment that it was not more practical – that it was too philosophical'. King began to feel that Vincent and Rockefeller, Jr quite missed the importance of what he was doing.[18]

All the while that King worked on compiling his research results, Rockefeller, Jr needed to prepare for his trip to Ludlow. King was there for him. In fact, King even made his own trip to Ludlow, during 1915, to form some first-hand understanding of local conditions. King worked quickly to develop a kind of preparation sheet for Rockefeller, Jr, which was ready in time to inform him before he visited Denver in October 1915.[19]

King progressed onward in his search for causes of labour problems. He realized the need to adapt to unfolding events in the world, and he reacted to what he learned was or was not possible with the current methods of social science. In October 1915 the Foundation decided to clarify King's role. He was appointed solely for his objective science, and not to serve as any advisor. His one-year budget was emphasized as being entirely within the Division of Industrial Relations, and his duty was to produce a general study with no special focus on any particular situation, for this was the way of true science.[20]

King pressed onward to complete his project, and he did so by the end of the following year. He created a somewhat unique method of scientific presentation. In some ways he extended what he learned while apprenticing at Hull House in Chicago, where he learned the method of social surveys. He blended together an extensive quantity of data, often in summarized form, with many descriptive personal observations. Overall his strategy was to produce one solid volume of observations and conclusions with a genuine tone of objectivity to it. Numerous tables and charts can seem designed to put a kind of official seal upon the whole project as being solid science. But it also had proven difficult for one person, in a little over two years' time, to meet the level of scientific achievement that the Foundation expected.

Many persons at the Foundation were dissatisfied with the end result of King's work. They had funded it to see where it would go, and they decided they preferred to free King to publish the report without any stamp of the Rockefeller Foundation on it. And with that, King ceased his work for the Foundation.[21]

King, working with an independent press, published *Industry and Humanity: A Study of the Principles Underlying Industrial Reconstruction* (1918). The book aimed to identify realistic solutions to ongoing failures in labour–capital relations. King stayed true to an overall emphasis on the 'public interest', as he opined that the greatest need was to better understand one particular 'party to industry', which is the party that 'furnishes opportunity to all the others, and without whose implied sanction and cooperation the other parties could effect nothing. That party is the Community'. King defined the community partly with an economic interpretation, which saw a community as a comprehensive group of people entitled to a 'fair return' on all of their collective contributions to industry. Possibly as a scientific way to conceptualize 'the community interest', King described how any business or industry will interact with the entire community as a 'social service', which means that any business or industry must be accountable for all of its impacts. A core problem for social scientists could now be stated: it was to create mechanisms to achieve the community's 'right to representation in the control of industry'. Mechanisms were needed, for example, for better worker representation on corporate directorships. Yet King also ran into the limitation presented by free-market attitudes, which was that such representation would need to be a volitional granting of a degree of voice and empowerment to workers.[22]

The Foundation was left wondering whether scientific research on social and economic problems might somehow face fundamental limits for practical execution. Yet perhaps the whole thing would have succeeded if the Foundation had imposed tighter controls over their expectations. If leaders within Rockefeller philanthropy really wanted to support scientific study of human and societal behaviours, then some careful thinking was needed. How might specific projects in the social sciences be evaluated for financial support without needing to worry about any potential research results, applications or policies?

## The Bureau of Social Hygiene

Back in time, in about 1909, Rockefeller, Jr was thinking about establishing his own philanthropy. One geographical dimension in America that was having its bout with social and economic problems was urban life, and Rockefeller, Jr saw this, nearly every day, when he travelled into New York City. Many American cities were destinations for great numbers of immigrants arriving with dreams of merging into American life, if sometimes only at its urban margins.[23]

Rockefeller, Jr thought about problems in the cities, and he began to consider strategies for supporting applicable social science. With great interest he followed the efforts of the Carnegie Institution and Russell Sage Foundation, and Rockefeller, Jr decided to try and support some of his own social science. This decision stemmed from his appointment, in 1910, as chairman of New York City's special grand jury to investigate an alleged 'white slave traffic' in the city. This worrisome problem was rumoured to include the kidnapping of respectable young women who were forced into prostitution. While the jury's investigation revealed that no such traffic substantially existed in the city, the hearings confirmed the existence of other serious problems, including those associated with alcohol, prostitution and police corruption.[24]

Rockefeller, Jr decided to create his own small philanthropy, which he incorporated in 1913 as the Bureau of Social Hygiene. The Bureau set out to investigate the 'prostitution problem' from a scientific perspective, and did so with an expressed general purpose to undertake 'the study, amelioration, and prevention of those social conditions, crimes, and diseases which adversely affect the well-being of society, with special reference to prostitution and the evils associated therewith'. In May 1913, Rockefeller, Jr hired Raymond B. Fosdick, a Princeton graduate and former student of Woodrow Wilson, just as Wilson was starting his US presidency. Fosdick was a trained attorney working for the New York City mayor's office to study tenements and settlement houses. His assignment for Rockefeller, Jr's Bureau was to study European police handling of such problems as alcoholism, prostitution and pauperism. Rockefeller, Jr also recruited Abraham Flexner (brother of Simon Flexner) to identify any useful data that might be collected on prostitution activities in these same European cities. By combining the information produced by Fosdick and Flexner, Rockefeller, Jr hoped to identify what sorts of policy reforms might be useful. Although the Bureau remained small, it sponsored some important investigations, including studies of venereal disease and other consequences of prostitution.[25]

One organization that received the Bureau's support was the Eugenics Record Office (ERO), located at idyllic Cold Spring Harbor, Long Island. Established in 1904 with an aim to introduce methods and policies for encouraging more births by certain groups while discouraging childbirth among other groups, the ERO did well at making connections with wealthy donors. Some of the ways in which money donated to the ERO could innocently enough support the eugenics movement included training of office and field workers, awarding of student scholarships and support of summer training meetings.[26]

But in 1913, just as the Bureau of Social Hygiene was gaining a bit of positive recognition, British sociologist Henry Havelock Ellis published *The Task of Social Hygiene*. Ellis argued strongly about some possible causes for an individual's moral and behavioural 'failings', and he defined the term 'social hygiene' not with the usual connotation of trying to clean up one or a few social problems at a time, but instead described a comprehensive effort to 'purify' society of all things that cause social problems. In sweeping language he declared his fundamental point of intervention: 'It is the control of reproduction of the race which renders possible the new conception of Social Hygiene'. This was a doctrine that would soon be labeled race hygiene. Ellis's book produced some public attention, and Rockefeller, Jr decided that any support of eugenics research was now more likely to be controversial.[27]

Then after Ludlow, in April 1914, the Rockefellers decided to emphasize their dissociation between personal and philanthropic interests. Their public relations expert, Ivy Lee, and Foundation secretary, Jerome Greene, helped to draw clearer lines between the family and their philanthropies. As far as the Foundation was concerned, it needed to tighten its understanding of what it would mean to be an 'operating' institution focused on its own research, versus what it would mean to be an exclusively grant-awarding institution. As regarded the Bureau, Rockefeller, Jr decided to keep it without any permanent endowment, which actually meant that he personally would always ultimately make every decision, which was at least one way to try and avoid falling victim to bad decisions by others.[28]

Rockefeller, Jr was a friend of Margaret Sanger. Sanger is well known for her work to found a birth control and family planning organization, now called Planned Parenthood. In 1914 Sanger visited Ellis, in England, and returned to New York and did some writing. Influenced by her reading of Sigmund Freud's works, Sanger believed that a 'sex force' at the core of our being represents 'one of the strongest forces in Nature – an instinct by no means less powerful than the instinct of Hunger'. This was an instinct not to be suppressed, but to be guided through applied social science and policy. Sanger began her work to help establish the American Birth Control League (ABCL), which was officially founded in 1921. Her greatest concern was to support policies that would help get birth control and planning options to the lower economic classes, who very often were immigrants. Over a number of years Rockefeller, Jr made personal yearly donations to Sanger, and then to the ABCL.[29]

Rockefeller, Jr was interested in using his Bureau to explore ways of doing objective social science. In his 1913 introduction to Flexner's *Prostitution in Europe*, Rockefeller, Jr explained the level of thought and care that went into ensuring truly objective social science. The problem of prostitution 'is a highly controversial one', he offered:

> For this reason, its investigation was assigned to one who had, on the one hand, previously given it no critical thought or attention, but whose studies of education in this country and abroad had demonstrated his competency to deal with a complicated topic of this nature. Mr. Flexner was absolutely without prejudice or preconception, just as he was absolutely unfettered by instructions. He had no previous opinion to sustain; he was given no thesis to prove or disprove. He was asked to make a thorough and impartial examination of the subject and to report his observations and conclusions.[30]

Flexner's objectivity stemmed from the fact that he came to the project with no preconceptions, that no instructions were stated to guide him, and that he had no specific thesis to test. The method of such 'Baconian' objectivity in fact gathering relied largely on trust: Flexner was well trained, he was respected and he was capable of the self-discipline necessary to be impartial.[31]

There was to be a series of volumes in the Bureau's planned scientific studies. Already published by the time that Rockefeller, Jr offered his thoughts on objectivity was a study by George J. Kneeland, director of the Chicago Vice Commission, on conditions of vice in New York City. Kneeland hired a number of assistants to make a comprehensive survey of the conditions of vice, and he published what Rockefeller, Jr described as a 'systematically corroborated' and 'dispassionate' account of things. The second volume in the series was Flexner's study. A study by Raymond Fosdick on European police systems was forthcoming, and was published in 1915. There was also a planned study to deal with prostitution in the United States, but this project did not get done.[32]

Through the decade of the 1910s, Rockefeller, Jr handled many challenges and displayed great levels of responsibility in doing so. He rose to the occasion time and again, including during that most severe of trials, the Ludlow tragedy and its aftermath. Coming out of all of this was a kind of final elevation of Rockefeller, Jr in the estimation of his father. Rockefeller, Sr decided that the time was right to bequeath a substantial portion of his wealth to his son, and in a series of moves beginning in 1917, he transferred to all of his children nearly half a billion dollars of stock ownership. Yet the vast majority of it went to Rockefeller, Jr, whose net worth went from about $20 million in 1917 to about $500 million just five years later. Rockefeller, Jr now had enough money to truly begin doing great works of his own. As he later recorded, he recognized that it was his father's financial generosity that enabled him to 'carry on his philanthropic and charitable work in the same spirit which had activated' his father.[33]

## War and Peace

The First World War was an extraordinary event, for just about everyone. It was something to which the Rockefellers – as well as other businesspersons and philanthropists – paid great attention. The war definitely diverted the Foundation's focus, primarily to humanitarian aid and war relief.

Through the war years Rockefeller, Sr behaved with mixed motives that were humanitarian and pragmatic. He purchased liberty bonds to support the nation. He donated money to the YMCA and the Red Cross, as well as to nursing schools. He donated much assistance to the Belgian and French relief efforts. His personal contributions during the war are estimated to tally to around $70 million. The Rockefeller Foundation also released some $10 million of its own funds to support wartime relief programmes.[34]

Yet there was also the factor that by the time that the war came, Standard Oil had a business structure firmly in place in Europe. The collapse of all of Europe into war threatened the stability of American companies, and this very much included Standard Oil. Perhaps it was also for public relations that Rockefeller donated money to help in the war causes.

But Rockefeller was not alone in his concerns. During the war years, many American businesses donated money and resources, including much to war relief. Business leaders could argue that such donations were in the business interest and the public interest. Wartime production pressures also provided new incentives to improve work conditions and employee morale.

Toward the end of the war years, an important project was to figure out how to truly make this 'the war to end all wars'. One noteworthy person who got involved was Raymond B. Fosdick, Rockefeller, Jr's friend from the Bureau of Social Hygiene. Fosdick, as a former student of Woodrow Wilson at Princeton, escorted the president in Paris during the Versailles peace talks. Fosdick remained active after the war, through his work to help build American support for participation in the League of Nations. Rockefeller, Jr, even though he was in the political party that vigorously opposed Wilson's plan for US membership in the League of Nations, himself quite strongly favoured US participation in the League. Rockefeller, Jr went further than simply stating his view, as he financially supported the League, especially its health organization and its new library.[35]

Back at home after the war, the US economy hit the skids badly. Factories were slow to convert operations back to peacetime production. Many more people lived in the cities than before the war, and cities were where the idle factories were. Soldiers deserved jobs when they returned home. Women and African-Americans who had gone into factory work during the war deserved to keep their jobs. Labour unions had gained strength during the war, and the labour movement reflected on its wartime gains and disliked the prospect of losing these gains. There simply were not enough jobs to go around. Labour violence broke out just about everywhere. Some violence stemmed from strikes. Some violence was along race lines. Something needed to be done.[36]

President Wilson, in 1919 and 1920, convened his Industrial Conferences. One of these conferences, in September 1919, was focused on a need to settle an impending nationwide steel strike. A more continuous phase of discussions followed the initial conference by trying to understand broader problems in general. Rockefeller, Jr contributed a significant amount of money to help arrange and sustain these conferences. And although in historical accounts the conferences are said to have failed, what is striking is that Wilson added the representation of a third party alongside management and labour: the general public.[37]

As the war in Europe came to a close, Rockefeller, Jr became personally interested in the value of international projects. He helped in 1921 to build support for the founding of a Council on Foreign Relations, and he helped finance the construction of grand-scale 'International Houses' at Columbia University (in 1921) and the University of Chicago (in 1932).

When the war ended, there were also shortages of manpower in some fields of work, as businesses recruited more scientists into the private sector. Even though they mostly recruited physical scientists and engineers, many businesses needed social scientists as well. In turn, one potential response to the recruitment of social scientists into the private sector (as well as into government) was to encourage greater incentives for partnership between philanthropists and science departments in universities. With universities having their status increasingly judged on the basis of their research production, they recognized their need for money, especially to boost the supply of science graduates willing to stay at the universities. One of the first persons in a position to recognize and work with this new demand factor was Wickliffe Rose at the Foundation. Rose believed that scientists inherently bring with them a progressive way of thinking.[38]

## New Principles and Methods

During 1916 and extending through the war years, Rockefeller, Jr worked to develop his own system of social and economic thought. He produced quite a number of papers between about 1916 and 1920, and he published many of them. He began his process of developing a systematic point of view in October 1915, when he prepared a talk for his personal visit to Colorado, where he met with managers and employees of the CFI Co. Speaking with company officials and miners and their representatives, Rockefeller, Jr outlined his vision for what he believed was 'the best thing for us all'. The core principle in his thinking was 'profit sharing'. Speaking in terms of group cooperation, he offered a notion that workers, managers and company officials are all 'in our own family'. All groups must work together to make capitalism work. Workers have appropriate roles to play, as do managers and owners. Rockefeller, Jr reasoned that the miners do receive fair pay. He focused on the fact that the Rockefellers often got nothing from operating the company, and very often this was because the company made sure to pay the workers first.[39]

Rockefeller, Jr did more than offer words. It was really quite an interesting visit that he made to the mining camps. He made every genuine effort to get to know all parties well, even sleeping in the miners' camp, and showering with them, as he said jokingly. In other words, he experienced their lives – and they, in turn, appreciated this.[40]

The best-known result of the whole matter of the CFI Co. was that Rockefeller, Jr followed up his visit to Colorado with something wholly tangible: his 'representation plan', which was passed by the workers. The miners received some concessions in the end, which could be interpreted as a granting of workers' rights. They could meet once a year, hold meetings on company property, elect their own chairman and secretary, select their own representatives with respect to working and living conditions, employ their own weighman, buy items in any stores that they wished and once a year elect representatives to a joint conference on conciliation, safety and accidents, sanitation, health, housing, education and recreation.[41]

At the Foundation, Jerome Greene did not wait long after the debates in 1914 to take a lead in trying to find new guiding principles for how to support social scientists. One prominent figure with whom he interacted was Edward C. Pickering, a leading physicist and astronomer, and a national leader in the 'endowment of research' movement. Greene wanted to assess whether any long-term partnership could work between philanthropists and social scientists. To get such a partnership underway, the partnership would need to serve the interests of both parties. It was through his communications with Pickering during 1915 and 1916 that Greene hoped to better understand how to achieve mutual benefits while still maintaining a clear separation between financial support of research and any research results.[42]

The conversation between Greene and Pickering got going when Pickering asked the Foundation for $50,000 to disperse into the physics community as grants-in-aid to persons identifiable as 'men of genius'. Pickering proposed that such a programme could be administered by a committee of scientists from multiple fields. Even though Greene respected Pickering, he had to decline Pickering's request for money; it would be in poor judgment to begin 'diverting a great Foundation from its true function of experiment, discovery, initiative, and demonstration, to being a mere bag of money'. Nevertheless, Greene saw Pickering's proposal as an opportunity to explore a concrete example. The potential solution of providing money strictly to great scientists was cast aside, for the Foundation could not react to every important research problem simply by handing over money to a small number of the most accomplished and honest scientists. But if some selection between scientists and scientific fields needed to be done, then how much involvement should the Foundation want to have? Would they ever want to directly oversee any of the activities undertaken with the granted money? The problem remained, namely to find a middle path between no control and complete control over the content and applications of supported research.[43]

Of course this particular conversation was not directly focused on the social sciences, but on what could be learned from supporting research in the physical sciences. One example of the support of research in the physical sciences was recent work to establish the independent research laboratories associated with the Rockefeller Institute for Medical Research. Also worth learning about was how the Carnegie Institution developed research programmes in the physical sciences.

Once Greene began his communications with Pickering, Pickering in turn brought geneticist Thomas Hunt Morgan into the discussion. Like Pickering, Morgan was a scientist supported by the Rockefeller Foundation. The two scientists guided some discussion of potential guidelines for the philanthropic support of science. In particular they discussed possible frameworks that might allow Rockefeller money to be distributed as grants to individuals. Pickering emphasized that such grants could help improve education in the physical sciences, while Morgan focused on the idea that grants can assist specific scientists to develop new research methods that can in turn help entire scientific communities do better science. Pickering and Morgan may or may not have shared any particular one of their numerous thoughts with Greene, but many of their ideas were communicated to him.[44]

Greene also considered an approach at the Carnegie Corporation, where a goal was 'to promote the advancement and diffusion of knowledge and understanding'. Greene gained some awareness of strategies employed by the CC, whose aim was to support specific scientific communities. Similar in ways to the

CC's approach, Greene contemplated whether a true measure of philanthropic success might be the amount of stimulation achieved within a scientific community. Greene hoped to avoid having the Foundation support undistinguished research, and he feared it would be flawed to try and measure success by some quantity of nondescript research projects. An alternative measure could somehow involve tracking of outcomes from initial grants, through expanded graduate training, all the way to the building of entire research programmes. Grants could be targeted toward particular research areas, which would grow over time.

Greene also considered the views of George Vincent and Wickliffe Rose. Vincent was not yet keenly interested in establishing a programme for directing aid to universities, at least not of the kind that was being done at the CC. Vincent, a sociologist trained at the University of Chicago, certainly knew things about the social sciences. In addition, he was familiar with a new experiment in committee structures at the National Research Council (NRC, established 1916), which he approved of as a way to minimize any troubled involvements for philanthropists. Vincent directed the Foundation to begin providing money to the NRC, which used committee decisions to decide on support to selected universities.[45]

The creation of the NRC opened new possibilities. An important fact was that the founding documents for the organization included a goal to better reconcile private science and public purpose. The first chairman of the NRC was James Rowland Angell, a Chicago-trained social scientist (a psychologist), and under his leadership the organization quickly proved its worth. Angell worked with Pickering and others to help the NRC be considered worthy of philanthropic support, which it received in 1919 from both the CC and the Foundation. A particular concern within Rockefeller philanthropy was to learn how to administer fellowships, and the Foundation proposed supporting NRC-administered fellowships in the physical sciences.[46]

Leadership at the NRC aimed to persuade philanthropists that scientists serve humankind. Between 1916 and 1919, Angell helped the NRC show that scientists can accept other peoples' money yet pursue research to serve the public interest. The NRC established some successful mechanisms by working according to a committee structure with different committees designed to organize cooperative projects in different research fields. Each committee selected its own grant recipients, and any philanthropist who gave money to the NRC learned that the NRC could be trusted to direct funds to useful research areas.[47]

Also connected with Rockefeller philanthropy was Wickliffe Rose, a philosophy PhD from Harvard, who was interested in using Rockefeller funds to build research communities. Born in 1862 as the son of an itinerant Tennessee preacher, and later a professor of social ethics, Rose was a rising leader at the Foundation. He joined the Foundation in 1914, as director of the International

Health Board (IHB), and he soon travelled around the world visiting numerous countries whose people experienced hookworm epidemics. Under Rose's leadership, efforts to eradicate hookworm produced outstanding results, which resulted in much positive recognition for the Foundation. Rose was respected to a point that he could experiment with a new giving strategy which resembled certain aspects of what Angell instituted at the NRC, and which the CC was experimenting with as well.[48]

From the hookworm project Rose learned about a global shortage of public health administrators. He worked to set up a system of public health agencies, designed to implement rigorous standards for health officials. The IHB also established certificate and degree programmes in public health at a few selected universities. Rose recruited Simon Flexner (who was still connected with the Rockefeller Institute for Medical Research) to help establish a fellowships programme designed to recruit talented medical scientists into the new university programmes.[49]

Following the success of the IHB at establishing schools and programmes in public health, in 1919 Rockefeller, Jr selected Rose to guide the General Education Board (GEB). There Rose introduced a programme to provide general endowment funds to American colleges and universities. At the GEB Rose implemented the new strategy to build 'regional centres'. He began by using the available money to select only a few of the best universities, including some elite schools and a few regional stars.[50]

Rose's accomplishments for Rockefeller philanthropy during the 1910s represented a fine example of innovating ways to distribute financial support. Rose helped form a vision for all of Rockefeller philanthropy. He helped craft an important central principle, which was to focus on a limited number of researchers and research groups as grant recipients. Grants went to those persons who were best prepared to promote 'community development' through their scientific leadership. Rose's goal, as he phrased his approach to lifting, was to first 'make the peaks higher'. The goal, when it came to developing scientific communities, was to find ways to develop a collective ability of scientists without having to give money to everyone across an entire scientific community.[51]

The 'community development' approach – for Rose, for Greene and for others – was based on an idea that the benefits will ultimately far outpace any initial investment, even perhaps by an exponential effect.[52]

## The National Bureau of Economic Research

There had once been exciting discussion at the Foundation about establishing an Institute of Economic Research. Participants in that discussion remained interested in the idea. Harvard economist Edwin Gay, who had been an enthusiastic supporter, continued his interactions with persons in industry and at the

Foundation. During 1919, Gay initiated a new appeal for an economics institute, and he proposed a need for a specific study of income distribution in the United States. Gay believed that income distribution was a problem for the nation, and that the problem was worsening. In communication with Malcolm C. Rorty, a vice president at AT&T, Gay argued that a study of income distribution was urgently needed, and that it would be in the public's interest to achieve an income distribution that could better promote improved performance for the entire economy. Another goal, already of interest to Rorty, was to try and achieve a 'greater degree of political stability than exists now', which he believed 'could be brought about if certain of the fundamental facts of industry and business were determined with accuracy or within reasonable limits of error'. Rorty thus joined Gay in advocating that support of social science could help to stabilize government and grow the economy. Rorty offered AT&T's company data, and he asked Gay if the Harvard Business School might be a home base for the envisioned institute. But Gay, lacking confidence that Harvard's resources were up to the task, put Rorty in contact with Columbia University economist Wesley C. Mitchell, who along with Gay had already participated in earlier discussions. Mitchell shared some ideas about what was needed for institutional support for such an institute, and Gay recommended Mitchell as the institute's director. Gay, Rorty and Mitchell discussed matters, and they moved to establish the new institute, based at least loosely out of Columbia University.[53]

Initially the institute was the 'Committee on National Income' (CNI). Mitchell established some working rules and he encouraged a belief that the 'character of economics is such as to require co-operation' between many researchers. The CNI needed to be at least somewhat sizeable, so as to support enough personnel to represent a range of emerging subfields in economics. Such size should also help neutralize any differences of ideology or political opinion between the researchers. In contrast to what was tried earlier in the decade when the Foundation appointed King to go alone into the research field of labour relations, founders of this new committee were agreed that in light of the increased complexity of a post-war world, more research was needed than any single researcher could ever hope to accomplish by focusing on a single problem.[54]

In early winter 1920, from out of the CNI was born the National Bureau of Economic Research. In their commitment to establishing the National Bureau (today known as the NBER), Mitchell and Gay worked with an aim to obtain data and provide data analysis for policymakers. Consistent with an idea to pursue fundamental knowledge about both individual economic behaviour and the behaviour of a national economy, the National Bureau's mission was 'to encourage in the broadest and most liberal manner investigations, research and discovery and the application of knowledge to the well-being of Mankind'.[55]

Procedures were established to ensure objectivity in the National Bureau's research. They stated their goal, which was 'to conduct, or assist in [the] making of, exact and impartial investigations in the field of economics, social and industrial science, and to this end co-operate with governments, universities, learned societies and individuals'. Mitchell hoped to help achieve social and economic progress with better results than so many 'jerky' reform movements in past decades. He wanted careful, scientific planning for social change. 'Are we not intelligent enough to devise a steadier and more certain method of progress?' The National Bureau was to be an organization that would assist with the 'intelligent experimenting and detailed planning' that modern society needs. The founders of the National Bureau were agreed that their organization should maintain no direct connections to any business, governmental or philanthropic organization. They needed to be truly independent as a research organization. Mitchell emphasized that a blend of statistical and empirical methods was to be practiced, including careful interplay between the two. It was time to transform economics from a field based on dusty books and theories to one founded on tangible facts; indeed this was what the National Bureau needed do if it was to merit financial support.[56]

Still to be proven was whether the National Bureau could succeed as a non-ideological, non-partisan research organization. One of their first projects, guided by Mitchell, was *Income in the United States: Its Amount and Distribution, 1909–1919*, a 1921 report that was valuable for its content. The report showed that economists could execute objective and neutral research, and the organization soon received its first major endowment, from the CC, now directed by James Angell. A smaller bit of support came from the Foundation. Additional projects soon followed. The National Bureau's researchers explored new strategies for dealing with large quantities of data in order to obtain accurate measures of total national income, income distribution, rates of unemployment and patterns of business cycles over time. Some of the CC's funds were earmarked for specific projects, including one that was recommended by Secretary of Commerce Herbert Hoover.[57]

In December 1921, Hoover asked for a study of labour unemployment during business cycles. He requested research results in less than six months, for presentation to President Warren G. Harding. The National Bureau undertook the project, on the understanding that their work was fact-finding, with no policy recommendations to be made. Mitchell believed that business cycles were complex phenomena resulting from many interdependent supply and demand factors in the economy. Many simple factors could, because of principles of interdependence, result in potentially unpredictable events at an aggregate level. Such an idea had been relatively absent in economics prior to the 1910s. Economists had previously focused on a concept of market 'panics', which led them to interpret economic downturns as stemming from large aggregations of irrational fear. The National Bureau completed the study on time.[58]

Another commissioned project during the National Bureau's early years was an investigation of immigration. Immigration was already a focus for sociologists; the economists, however, focused not immigrants socialized into 'Americans', but on a data-driven study that focused on the nature of things as they happened to be. Still another new line of research, initiated by Hoover in 1923, was to deliver to President Calvin Coolidge a study that would focus on recent changes in the US economy. While this latter study took some time, it was completed and released in 1929, under the title *Recent Economic Changes*.[59]

The important point about all of these early accomplishments by the National Bureau was that social scientists were able to show that an independent organization could achieve a respected status as a group of scientists who neutrally serve the public interest.

Comforted, no doubt, by what was happening at the National Bureau, in February 1922 the CC began its financial support of another new organization, which was also interested in economic research. The organization, which began to receive the support of Rockefeller philanthropy in 1923, was the Institute of Economics (IE). The IE was largely the brainchild of Robert S. Brookings. During 1916, Brookings had played a central role in helping to establish the Institute for Government Research (IGR), which was financially supported by the Foundation. Brookings's guiding framework for the IE drew upon that earlier experience, as he proposed that the new institute should be structured not as small teams of economists working on one or two projects at a time (as the National Bureau was doing), but should be a loose-knit collection of economists undertaking many projects at once. The main research objective should be to gather data useful to civil servants and policymakers.

Established in 1922, the IE was directed by Harold Glenn Moulton, a professor of political economy at the University of Chicago. Moulton placed some nice phrasing about scientific neutrality into the IE's by-laws, which stated that 'the primary function' of persons at the leadership level within the IE 'is not to express their views on the scientific investigations conducted by the Institute, but only to make it possible for such scientific work to be done under the most favorable auspices'. Brookings and Moulton worked with Henry S. Pritchett, president of the Carnegie Foundation, to assure that the IE could be established as an organization wholly independent from other organizations.[60]

Director Moulton placed the IE's economists into four research groups: agricultural economics; international commerce; industrial and labour issues; and economic reconstruction. He recruited Edwin G. Nourse, a professor of agricultural economics at Iowa State College, to direct the agricultural economics section. Thomas Walter Page, a University of Virginia economist, and a former member of President Taft's US Tariff Commission, was placed in charge of research in international commerce. Isador Lubin, a young Michigan-trained PhD, with experience on the War Industries Board, was deemed well-suited to guide research on industrial and labour issues. Moulton directed the research in economic reconstruction. In 1923 Moulton's research group produced a study of *Germany's Capacity to Pay*, which argued quite strongly (more so than J. M. Keynes four years earlier) that to expect successful reconstruction in Germany along with war reparations payments was a scientific impracticality; when evaluated rigorously, the only possible conclusion was that Germany could not afford to do what other nations had ordered it to do in the peace treaty. A thin line existed between data analysis, scientific conclusions and policy advocacy in the study, but at least any offering of such a policy conclusion would be relatively uncontroversial at the time. In 1924 Charles Dawes, Director of the US Bureau of the Budget, drew upon the IE's (Foundation-supported) research, worked similar calculations and a year later won the Nobel Peace Prize for this work.[61]

## His Wife's Passing and 'the Business of Philanthropy'

The morning of 12 March 1915, John D. Rockefeller's wife, Laura Spelman Rockefeller, passed away at Kykuit, the family estate in the hills overlooking the Hudson River. When he received the telegram, Rockefeller was at Ormond Beach, Florida. As he travelled home by train, escorted by Rockefeller, Jr and his wife, Abby, a great many people surprised Rockefeller by lining the route in a show of sympathy. Something in the tide of opinion had turned just a bit.

Within a couple of years of his wife's passing, Rockefeller announced his plans for his last major philanthropic organization. The project would approach closer than ever to certain fields of activity that the Rockefellers had learned to be wary of. These were fields that were favoured by Rockefeller's wife. Planned by the end of 1917 and formalized through much of the following year, in October 1918 the Laura Spelman Rockefeller Memorial began operations. The initial mission of the Memorial was to promote the welfare of women and children.

By 1915 Rockefeller was known, mostly, as a great philanthropist – even if it had been only four years since the *Standard Oil* decision. The creation of modern philanthropy was much discussed in the press, and Rockefeller was getting a lot of credit for it. He had over many years concluded that simply handing money to a person in need was generally a failed strategy. He sometimes expressed the idea directly: 'To give is an art. To give to everybody who asks is an injustice'. What he meant was that a gift to one who squanders it will only have the effect of 'tak[ing] from a more deserving one'. As Frederick Gates once reflected upon Rockefeller's innovations in philanthropic methods, he offered that Rockefeller's focus was often on achieving greater cause-and-effect efficiency, and that Rockefeller 'came to have hardly less pleasure in the organization of his philanthropy than in the efficiency of his business'. Rockefeller had long ago concluded that it was best to direct his resources toward discovering causes of human suffering.[62]

Rockefeller openly shared his views a number of times in the years following his wife's passing. He did so in 1917, in an interview in *Forbes*, where he spoke essentially of the principle of lifting:

> That has been our guiding principle, to benefit as many people as possible. Instead of giving alms to beggars, if anything can be done to remove causes which lead to the existence of beggars, then something deeper and broader and more worthwhile will have been accomplished.

And as he offered in another 1917 interview: 'It is a great problem to learn how to give without weakening the moral backbone of the beneficiary'.[63]

Yet, in another 1917 interview, Rockefeller let himself believe that an individual's level of success or failure in life was largely predetermined; that 'the failures that a man makes in his life are due almost always to some defect in his personality, some weakness of body, mind or character, will or temperament'. Rockefeller added how it was his 'personal belief that the principal cause for the economic differences between people is their difference in personality'. Yet even here there was something that he believed a philanthropist could focus on: 'that it is only as we can assist in the wider distribution of those qualities that go to make up a strong personality that we can assist in the wider distribution of wealth'.[64]

Another series of interviews, also conducted in 1917, were with newspaperman William O. Inglis, who planned to write a book. During his many hours with Inglis, at one point Rockefeller stated a thought on what he called 'the business of philanthropy': 'All of those in the business today are doing business along the modern lines, following the plans which we were the first to propose'.[65]

## Conclusion

At a certain level of inquiry, today's historians are not able to decide if there was 'one' John D. Rockefeller, or if there were 'two'. This chapter looked at an overall learning path for both Rockefeller and Rockefeller, Jr as they sought ways to expand their philanthropic support of science to include support of the social sciences. In October 1918, Rockefeller, Sr established the Laura Spelman Rockefeller Memorial. But even though the money for the Memorial came from Rockefeller, the basic approach of what the Memorial would end up doing was much more in line with the world view of Rockefeller, Jr.

# 5 THE LAURA SPELMAN ROCKEFELLER MEMORIAL

## Introduction

In October 1918 John D. Rockefeller established the Laura Spelman Rockefeller Memorial. For its first four years the Memorial focused on providing resources to assist the well-being of women and children. In January 1921 Rockefeller supplemented the Memorial's original endowment of over $13 million with an additional roughly $60 million, which would be used for a programme to support fundamental research in the social sciences. This programme represented a radical redirection of Rockefeller philanthropy, and was a profound event in the history of social science. For its next eight years, until January 1929, the Memorial focused on providing resources to social scientists in an effort to promote the broad advancement of knowledge, methods and applications in the social sciences. This chapter looks at the creation of the Memorial and at the transition phase between 1921 and 1923.

## The Laura Spelman Rockefeller Memorial

John D. Rockefeller established the Laura Spelman Rockefeller Memorial in honour of his late wife. The charter purpose of the Memorial was to assist women and children. Through its first three years in existence, the Memorial focused on its charter purpose, which it pursued mostly through religious organizations.[1]

The Memorial initially was operated out of the office of John D. Rockefeller, Jr, and the main executive overseeing the Memorial was Willard S. Richardson. Between 1918 and 1921, recipients of the Memorial's support included local organizations such as the East Harlem Health Centre and the Maternity Centre Association of Manhattan, and national organizations such as the YMCA, the YWCA, the Boy Scouts of America, the Girl Scouts of America, the Salvation Army and the American Child Health Association. Donations went to famine relief in Asia, to emergency needs in post-war Europe and to Baptist churches around the world. The main goal, in all cases, was to promote the physical, intellectual and moral well-being of women and children.[2]

Early work at the Memorial aimed to address multiple 'fields' of concern. One field was religious organizations, which could serve as effective channels for getting aid to the needy. Roughly one-third of total dispersed funds between 1918 and 1921 went to religious organizations, primarily to Baptist churches in the United States and Canada. Another field, receiving approximately 16 per cent of all allocated funds, was emergency relief, particularly in post-war Europe and famine-struck China, where food and shelter were primary concerns. Some 7 per cent of funds went to public health, mostly to treat infants and younger children, while the field of educational work accounted for 9 per cent of funds, mostly to Christian educational organizations in Asia and the Near East. The remaining field was child development. While the ultimate purpose of all projects was the well-being of women and children, leadership of the Memorial decided that parent education should also be supported. But the question was: how far should such an extended focus go, i.e. what kinds of programmes could be interpreted as supporting successful parenting?[3]

By 1921, some uncertainty had set in at the Memorial. An ideal goal for many social workers and social scientists was to move beyond addressing symptoms of social ills, to discover ways to diminish and even prevent the kinds of social and economic problems that can make quality parenting difficult to achieve. Even though such an ultimate goal was true from the beginning of the Memorial, many early efforts were found to have too little connection to any understanding of the fundamental causes of social ills. Increased dissatisfaction existed over the quality of the Memorial's performance. In all branches of Rockefeller philanthropy, a feeling was gathering that the Memorial lacked direction.[4]

In November 1921, the new secretary of the Rockefeller Foundation, Edwin Embree, assessed the Memorial's goals. Embree observed that certain areas of science, such as child nutrition and pre-natal care, could fit well with the Memorial's expressed purpose. The Memorial might also consider supporting research on infant and maternal illness and mortality, and perhaps could study impacts of housing conditions on infant and maternal health. These were all new and interesting possibilities. And if impacts of housing conditions could be studied according to the original expressed purpose of the Memorial, then would it be possible to look at all the causes of differing housing conditions across society? There were many new possibilities here.[5]

Rockefeller, Jr was still a leader within Rockefeller philanthropy. In early 1922, he chimed in with his views concerning the Memorial's undistinguished performance to date: 'It is becoming more and more clearly recognized that unless means are found of meeting the complex social problems that are so rapidly developing, our increasing control of the physical forces may prove increasingly destructive of human values'. Rockefeller, Jr's point – which was a frequent topic of interest at the time – was that scientific understanding of social forces and institutions needed to stop lagging so far behind the forces of technological progress. Leadership across Rockefeller philanthropy decided to search for a full-time director for the Memorial.[6]

## Beardsley Ruml

In quick time, Beardsley Ruml was selected as the preferred candidate for director of the Memorial. Rockefeller, Jr had recently employed Ruml to make assessments of the New York Public Library, the American Museum of Natural History and the Metropolitan Museum of Art – all as prospective grant recipients for Rockefeller, Jr's personal funds. But Ruml was actually trained as a social scientist. A graduate of Dartmouth College in 1915, Ruml earned his PhD in psychology from the University of Chicago in two years, with a dissertation on mental testing, advised by James R. Angell. Ruml then worked alongside Angell on personnel selection for the War Department, followed by a brief period during the early 1920s assisting Angell at the Carnegie Corporation. While working under Angell's guidance, Ruml saw how Carnegie funds were employed to build science programmes.[7]

In addition to Rockefeller, Jr, among Ruml's other strong supporters were George Vincent, president of the Foundation, and Raymond Fosdick, a Memorial trustee. Also supporting Ruml was, of course, Angell – now president of Yale University. These were all fine people to have in one's corner. In addition, numerous respected social scientists supported Ruml, including Abraham Flexner. Fosdick contacted Rockefeller, Jr in December 1921, and made the official recommendation. In the letter that made the recommendation, Fosdick expressed some ideas for an expanded programme for the Memorial. He advocated Ruml's ability to emphasize a more scientific focus while finding ways to remain true enough to the Memorial's original charter. Fosdick specifically cited the potential for increased attention to such fields as pre-natal care, child nutrition and nurse training.[8]

In the spring of 1922, Ruml was hired as director of the Memorial. He came in recognized as a proponent for scientific approaches to solving all sorts of social and economic problems, and he was hired to develop plans to employ the better part of nearly $74 million in total endowment toward developing such scientific approaches. Serious discussion was already underway on how to redirect the Memorial's activities; the ideas of Embree and Rockefeller, Jr had already been noted. Raymond Fosdick, building on Embree's ideas, tried a distinction between two kinds of programmes that could go beyond focusing solely on mothers and children. One would be an 'education and food program', designed to focus on projects aimed at improving the 'conditions of life of backward peoples'; the other would be a 'social science program', with the aim to improve the 'conditions of life of the most "advanced" peoples'. Success of the social science programme, Fosdick said, 'must depend not on the application of methods now known, but on methods yet to be discovered'. This would be a dramatic shift in focus to begin supporting the development of new scientific methods. Another early idea to help maintain continuity with the Memorial's original purpose came from Leonard Outhwaite, a newly hired assistant to Ruml. Outhwaite explored potential new areas of research to identify which were relatively more in line with the Memorial's traditional focus, and he added an emphasis on promoting 'the status of the social sciences and the development of scientific studies in the social science field'. More study was needed with respect to contact points between 'social science' and 'social technology', which was Outhwaite's way of referring to the discovery of knowledge and the application of knowledge.[9]

Ruml thus joined the Memorial at a time when new ideas were rich and plentiful. Yet these ideas were not fully worked out. Another sense of things might also have been in the works – this being a recognition that the Memorial might not last very long. From the beginning of Ruml's tenure, the likely direction for the Memorial's new emphasis was that it would be an intense programme focused on quickly distributing an incredible amount of money with a goal to discover whether a philanthropic foundation can support a broad level of advancement in the social sciences. Unlike the objective at the Foundation, which was to sustainably manage a great endowment, the Memorial's remarkable task was to use its great endowment. But although a permission slip may have been granted for the Memorial's leadership to rapidly deploy millions of dollars, also recognized was the imperative to use money wisely.[10]

One thing that was quite clear by 1922 was that the First World War was a watershed event in many ways. Among the many historical turning points that the war represented, one of these was its impact on the social sciences. Much attention was paid to psychological testing, especially in the United States, where psychology PhDs worked on recruiting and selecting soldiers. Research work to develop selection tests arrived at a stunning discovery, which was that many potential soldiers needed to be rejected based on their supposed 'psychological inadequacies'.[11]

Economists were also important, as they helped to formulate various logistical tactics for winning the war. Most notably the War Industries Board drew on the expertise of economists to identify efficient monetary allocations and spending flows for meeting productive and distributive needs. Other social scientists, including psychologists and sociologists, gained employment in war-support campaigns, which were based on the idea that social scientists can specialize in persuading people, such as to believe that Germans were beastly creatures.

Psychologists already had been employed to develop advertising campaigns for consumer products, and in fact a textbook on the topic – entitled *Advertising and Its Mental Laws* (1916) – had been recently published.[12]

## To Advance the 'General Field'

When Ruml began his work at the Memorial, the transition in leadership was marked by a summary report on the Memorial's first four years. Ruml used the opportunity to introduce ideas about broadly supporting the social sciences. Perhaps the initial bridge from the Memorial's original focus to a new focus was Ruml's suggestion to focus on research capable of showing 'rather immediate relations to measures of human welfare'. The Memorial's interest in scientific research, he added, has 'as its foundation a belief that knowledge and under-standing of the natural forces that are manifested in the behaviour of people and of things will result concretely in the improvement of conditions of life'.[13]

Ruml continued to clarify his ideas. He prepared a memorandum that is somewhat well-known in the history of social science. In the memorandum he stated his vision for building the social sciences to be capable of truly attacking social and economic problems. Advancements in the social sciences would be used to eliminate a lag between knowledge about material nature and knowledge of the condition of society. A key to the success for a redirected Memorial would be to help create a greater balance between advancements in the physical sciences and advancements in the social sciences. By summer's end, Ruml had a plan.[14]

In October 1922, Ruml presented his 'General Policy Memorandum'. The memorandum came at an important point in the history of social science, as there was great debate at the time over what social science was, and what it could be. An outstanding question was how to provide greater support to social scien-tists. The centrepiece idea in Ruml's plan was a goal to achieve scientific analysis of social and economic problems, which would enable the development of a body of 'demonstrated principles'. Ruml spoke with great optimism of a world of impending breakthroughs in substantiated knowledge about humans and socie-ties. Yet he also communicated a message of lament: 'All who work toward the general end of social welfare are embarrassed by the lack of that knowledge that the social sciences provide'. The state of affairs resembled an engineer who would be forced to work without recent developments in physics or chemistry. Or per-haps it was more like a physician required to practise in the absence of medical science. Ruml admitted that 'The direction of work in the social fields is largely controlled by tradition, inspiration and expediency, a natural condition in view of our ignorance of individual and social forces'.[15]

Ruml took time to summarize the past and present conditions of the social sciences. But what he really cared about was setting a future course. For the year

1923, work needed to be done to allocate the Memorial's discretionary budget into a 'rich enough' range of opportunities 'to measure up fully to the resources available for its cultivation'. Ruml proposed developing scientific communities by employing the tactic of finding strategic entry points for carefully injected funds. Some focus needed to remain on traditional concerns at the Memorial:

> An examination of the operations of organizations in the field of social welfare shows as a primary need the development of the social sciences and the production of a body of substantiated and widely accepted generalizations as to human capacities and motives and as to the behaviour of human beings as individuals and groups.[16]

Most kinds of social research in the universities were not yet truly 'scientific'. University professors spent most of their time teaching, and society missed out on what these specialists could contribute as leaders in the discovery of knowledge. University research facilities were typically inadequate, and were too few in number. University-based social scientists remained overly speculative and deductive, and they typically performed their work 'on the basis of second-hand observations, documentary evidence and anecdotal material'. Such sources of knowledge helped little in trying to execute progressive 'social engineering'. Ruml consistently offered images of a notion of 'cultural lag', such as his stating that the need was for social scientists to match the realized results of new 'technological controls'. What was needed – he used the phrase – was 'social control'.[17]

The ideas of cultural lag and social control jointly made for a compelling point of view. While the second of these ideas had been under development for a quarter of a century, the first idea owed most recently to the book *Social Change with Respect to Culture and Original Nature* (1922), by Columbia University sociologist William Fielding Ogburn. Ogburn's thesis was that acute social problems owed to an imbalance between leading technological sectors on the one hand and reactionary cultural and political spheres on the other, with the result that new policies of social control were needed.[18]

Ruml employed these dual concepts in order to propose that a fundamental shift was needed throughout the social sciences. Any philanthropic organization that would offer money merely for palliative needs would no longer succeed; money needed to be allocated for the discovery of knowledge and the development of tools to be employed by a cadre of experts who would work to end social ills, and lift human welfare. The necessary increase in fundamental knowledge could be attained by putting social scientists into 'far more intimate contact ... with concrete social phenomena', and this in fact would be the core of the Memorial's new programme. The scientific attack on social and economic problems needed to begin at the colleges and universities, which possessed 'stability of organization' and a 'wide range of professional opinion', alongside 'scholarly and scientific standards of work'.[19]

Guiding principles and objectives were needed. Scientific research was to be done by permanent organizations, and never by the Memorial. Most supported institutions should feature both undergraduate and graduate programmes, which would enable research activities to be closely connected to teaching. Fellowship programmes were needed to attract quality faculty to universities, and new journals and presses were needed to assist in sharing scientific knowledge. Ruml got all of these concerns focused into some specific strategies, namely to strengthen existing research centres, begin multi-year fellowships programmes, establish a guiding committee of social scientists who would identify important problems and methods, and financially support some real-world experiments. Through all of this, those persons who do social science will need to have strengthened connections to those who apply social science. Ruml's concluding optimism was that owing to Rockefeller's recent gift to the endowment, financial resources were great enough 'to make it possible by planning over a period of years to attack really fundamental situations and to reach relatively remote ends'. Grant recipients should largely determine their own preferred use of their financial support – as there should be great value in placing much autonomous responsibility on those persons who actually conduct the social science.[20]

Ruml's policy statement received approval from the Memorial's trustees. Outside of the Memorial, Ruml's policy became known among leading social scientists. James Angell received a copy of the memorandum delivered to him as president of Yale University. He replied that the proposal seemed 'sufficiently flexible and at the same time sufficiently specific to try out what could be done in the general field'. John M. Glenn, director of the Russell Sage Foundation, also in time contacted Ruml to learn more about the policy.[21]

Ruml's other initial project was to surround himself with outstanding officers. He met with Foundation President George Vincent to exchange ideas, and he interacted with Arthur Woods and Raymond Fosdick, both Foundation trustees. In November 1922, Ruml appointed Woods as acting president of the Memorial, a position that Woods would hold until January 1929. Fosdick was made an advisor to the Memorial, while he remained a Foundation trustee. Fosdick believed that the social sciences were ready to quickly approach 'the growing edge of things'.[22]

Ruml recruited other assistants as well. He brought in Lawrence K. Frank, a Columbia-trained economist who sometimes taught at the New School for Social Research, and who also had interests in anthropological and psychiatric approaches to behaviour analysis. Frank had seen urban problems first-hand, especially while studying mortality in New York's Lower West Side. At the Memorial, Frank would specialize in child development and parent education.

Ruml assigned Leonard Outhwaite, with his wide-ranging sociological interests, to focus on the field of race relations. Ruml also soon recruited Sydnor Walker, Edmund E. Day and Guy Stanton Ford. Walker oversaw the Memorial's support of social welfare projects. Day, originally a professor of history at the University of Michigan, had interests in both history and economics, and would (in January 1929) be made head of the Rockefeller Foundation's Division of Social Sciences. Ford, a history professor at the University of Minnesota, seems to have been more of a generalist in his Memorial duties.[23]

Finally Ruml connected his guiding policy and his appointed personnel by establishing a manner of interaction at the Memorial. He developed a habit of introducing to the trustees and officers his policy resolutions, as drafted by himself. When it came time to consider any specific grant application for funding, Ruml's method was sometimes to present the original application to the trustees. But with any application not favoured, he sometimes saved troubles by summarizing only the application's content for the trustees. The trustees, it seems wholly clear, typically had a good sense of Ruml's preferred decision for any particular grant application. They were thus able to separate any decisions about financial support from any specific descriptions of research goals; it was Ruml who took this on as his concern.[24]

Ruml assigned a special project to Frank: to produce a second policy memorandum to assess the conditions of all the social sciences. By March 1923, Frank produced a lengthy report: 'The Status of Social Science'. He provided an overview of how five different social sciences had originated, and he suggested where they might be headed. He drew attention to various historical circumstances that led these sciences – economics, sociology, political science, psychology and anthropology – to be mostly non-empirical, entrenched in their 'speculative inertia' with methodologies 'largely inherited from moral and ethical disputes of the past'. Fifteen universities maintained doctoral programmes in the social sciences, but few dissertations made empirical investigations of any concrete sort; nearly all were 'works of scholarship, involving library studies and consultations of records'. Courses in scientific methods were nearly unavailable, and the general 'backwardness' of the social sciences was lamentable. Most distressing was 'the lack of adequate funds to support investigations and experiments'. Because so many universities lacked the resources to release faculty members from crushing teaching loads, 'The most promising method of giving assistance to these teachers would be to establish a research bureau or institute', that could include 'the needed clerical, statistical, and other help required for any worthwhile investigation'.[25]

Frank saw the field of economics as illustrative of how to support the social sciences. Any real scientific output had been quite sparse in economics; indeed most every economist recognized that 'there is an absence of real scientific work in their field'. Deficiencies in methodological training stemmed largely from the limited numbers of fellowships for graduate students in economics. This situation seemed representative of other social sciences as well. Each of the social sciences progresses only when 'concrete problems' are studied, and 'it is just in proportion that a science has addressed itself to specific problems that scientific progress has been made'.[26]

Frank agreed with Ruml on a number of points. They each saw faults in older styles of social science which aimed to classify cases and refine categorical definitions. Such research – stuck in 'typological thinking' – treated data just as does the naturalist, who 'compares and judges animal forms and activities, but stops with the superficial aspects'. Frank and Ruml each recognized the value in taking a long-term view to building the social sciences to include more quantitative rigour and empirical attitude. Frank again illustrated his argument with economics. What kind of social science do business persons now want, he asked?

> [B]usiness men find that the academic economic science tells them little about the concrete situation with which they are concerned. Economists are looking at the whole of economic life in its long term trend, seeking wide generalizations, while business men are concentrated upon scientific situations.

Businesses were doing scientific work. They were coming to understand economic forecasting. They had the resources to undertake research. As a result, 'the scientifically inclined men in the universities are being taken over by business organizations'. But a more empirical kind of economics could be built in the universities, in phases: first develop the scientific 'habit of mind'; then improve scientific methods; then discover knowledge. Research fellowships could help by supporting younger scholars while they gain training in scientific methods.[27]

Frank also warned social scientists to be careful of political forces on the social sciences. It was crucial to avoid allowing any supported organization to become 'classified as radical, liberal or conservative'. 'Social research in the absence of experimental work', he added, 'tends inevitably to become or to appear apologetic or polemic, to play the role of disputant and attorney, rather than that of scientific inquirer'. A neutral and objective stance, founded on experimental science, will require lighter teaching loads, teaching methods that are more in contact with active research programmes, more graduate training in scientific methods and an increase in research fellowships.[28]

As revealed in the words of both Ruml (October 1922) and Frank (March 1923), tensions still existed in the social sciences, especially between historical methods and empirical methods. Ruml and Frank were by no means the only ones to identify such a tension, as indeed a sort of combat was long-running between these two research styles. And if no side had yet prevailed, might additional money become a tipping force? Historical methods were relatively inexpensive to begin with, and really did not need more money. Newer approaches to empirical research were more costly, as they tended to be based on observation, measurement, experimental tests and statistical analysis. The shift to modern social science was a change that needed to take place, and financial resources were the biggest missing element.

## Social Science by the 1920s

Psychologists and economists began making the shift to modern scientific methods as early as about 1890, and within some thirty years, practitioners in all of the social sciences were aware of a potential to make a similar shift. Yet also by the 1920s, it seems that each of the social sciences had become divided within, with various 'camps' emerging in the different social sciences. At the Memorial, a goal was clearly stated: to promote scientific work with an overriding aim to discover causes of social and economic problems.

New leadership at the Memorial had to wait some six months, however, for various financial commitments to be worked out, before any full-scale programme could be initiated. Ruml was ready to make the move, when he could. He prepared by consulting with various leaders in the social sciences. With G. Elton Mayo he discussed problems in industrial research. Mayo's own work impressed Ruml, who as soon as he could, arranged a three-year grant to assist Mayo's work at the University of Pennsylvania. Another example of Ruml's inquiring dialogue during the initial period was with Charles Merriam, a University of Chicago political scientist. Merriam had already written about 'the new social science', and he shared with Ruml some ideas for developing a national-level organization to promote better research methods in the social sciences. Leaders at the Memorial were ready to discover how to award money to best promote the potential for social science to do great things for people.[29]

In 1923, Ruml began using millions of dollars to further his aims. In the first month of the year he received an inquiry that may have provoked some thinking about building a university-based 'research centre'. The inquiry came from the University of Pennsylvania, which was interested in projects that used applied psychology as a means for forging tighter interconnections between many social sciences.[30]

Psychology was a reasonably developed science, and by the 1920s, the 'new' psychology had been under development for some time. Psychologists tended to consider themselves 'professionals' (persons certified with 'expertise'), and they traced a proud tradition of experimental science from as early as some 1870s laboratory measurements of perception and sensation, performed especially by German practitioners of 'psychophysiology' (or, 'psychophysics'). The profession generally admired the research ideas of the American William James, especially in his *Principles of Psychology* (1890), which also emphasized the need for empirical research. James and his followers had ultimately taken their research ideas in wide-ranging directions, yet many of them were identified as empirical 'functionalists'. A basic idea for functional analysis in psychology was to study people's habits and other measurable behaviours as adaptive and even perhaps as heritable traits; functionalists understood the human mind to be adapted to its environment. In addition to the approaches of psychophysiology and functionalism, there were numerous other approaches to psychology by the 1920s, including psychoanalysis.[31]

There is another way to mark the rise of a scientific profession. In 1887 a small group of psychologists initiated the *American Journal of Psychology*. In 1892, following James's *Principles*, twenty-six charter members established the American Psychological Association, and two years after that, the organization helped to establish the *Psychological Journal*. While the first of these journals was not seen as particularly 'scientific' prior to about 1900, articles in the *Psychological Journal* were rich with data and analysis from pretty much the beginning.

A bit closer to the period of the Memorial, in 1913 John B. Watson published 'Psychology as the Behaviourist Views It'. In this manifesto paper, Watson advocated developing a psychological science based on externally observable behaviours. Yet his approach was somewhat determinist in its main assumption, which was that the way in which an organism interacts with its environment is the result of an aggregate of innate properties that awaits awakening by environmental stimuli.[32]

Watson's ideas were a bit slow to catch on. Perhaps the real prod came in 1919 when Watson published 'Psychology from the Standpoint of a Behaviourist', which triggered an intense five-year conversation between Watson and William McDougall, known as the 'behaviourist debate'. A culmination of this phase of disagreement came in 1923, resulting in joint publications in February 1924.[33]

Psychologists were thus excited and energized in 1923. Many approaches to psychology existed at the time, and potentially some better experimental methods could help sort some things out between the competing approaches. Psychologists were in a position to benefit from any financial assistance that they could obtain.[34]

## Applied Psychology

This was the context in which the University of Pennsylvania's proposal came to the Memorial, in January 1923. Faculty members at the school inquired whether they might receive a significant block grant. Such money would be left largely to a recipient to determine how to use. Penn's social scientists expressed interest in studying the relationships between work environments and psychological well-being. High levels of maladjusted habits seemed to have resulted from strong irrational forces at work in modern society. Penn's social scientists proposed studying industrial workers in real-world situations. They suggested that their school's department of industrial research was 'the only one in the country which has effectively brought into association a group of employers of a community for the study of personnel problems under university auspices'. Led by respected industrial economist Joseph Willits, Penn's department of industrial research forged contacts between business interests and scientific interests. Such contacts could be a promising way to better understand the 'irrationality principle' pervading everyday life.[35]

Shortly following Penn's initial inquiry, one of Penn's industrial psychologists, G. Elton Mayo, submitted a supplemental description. Mayo described his observation of an extreme psychological manifestation during the war. The phenomenon, which we today identify as extreme post-traumatic stress, was 'shell shock', and it was something that Mayo said he recognized appearing in a milder form in everyday life.

> Probably the work done by psychiatrists in 'shell-shock' hospitals with soldiers has, more than any other psychological achievement, drawn attention to the curability of many mental disorders. It has also drawn attention to the wide distribution of mental disorder, lack of 'balance' and unhappiness through the modern community.

Occurrences of a kind of low-grade 'shell-shock' could be found throughout modern society, and the growing presence of such traumatized people bred widespread social problems. Mayo believed he may have identified a core cause of social and economic problems. It seemed 'that prejudice, emotion and unreason are responsible for the origin and perpetuation of a great part of our social ills'. Unlike what was believed by earlier psychologists, 'irrationality of the type discussed by the crowd psychologists is not an inborn character of the human mind, but originates during the lifetime of the individual'. Mayo advocated an explanatory system that was firmly environmental in nature.[36]

At the time that the First World War broke out, Mayo was a professor of psychology and physiology at the University of Queensland, in Australia. Many Australian soldiers went to the war, especially in the winter of 1915, and they suffered horribly. Mayo became interested in the psychological reactions of soldiers, and he developed a view that physical experiences can very often provoke psychological disturbances. In 1923 Mayo got the opportunity to come to the University of Pennsylvania, which he did with the financial support of the Memorial.[37]

When the Memorial thus received Penn's letter of inquiry, Ruml responded by arranging meetings with both Mayo and Willits. He described for the Memorial's trustees his visit, in May 1923, as 'a profitable day in Philadelphia'. Fine ideas were shared about Penn's proposed research, and Ruml was 'favorably impressed not only by the quality of the work Mayo has done, but by the way he has interested manufactures in the possibilities'.[38]

Penn received its grant. Its research programme got underway, and it expanded over time. Mayo guided social scientists to undertake studies in Philadelphia's factories, especially in the textile works, while Willits guided another group of researchers, based at Penn's Wharton School of Commerce, who practised what the Memorial considered to be 'social technology'. Potential research areas for Willits's group, as he stated in May 1923, included medical insurance, labour turnover and studies of wages and earnings. Yet the central idea remained the belief that all research areas might connect around a central focus on the irrationality principle. As Willits explained, the connection between psychological research and problems studied by business professors began from Mayo's

> original idea to treat a factory as if it were a 'shell-shock' hospital and to examine every individual in it with the object of discovering: 1st, In what respect his attitude to life was abnormal or defective. 2nd, The effect of such abnormality or defect upon collaboration in work within the factory.

Willits wanted to discover what sorts of impacts harsh factory environments can inflict upon the qualities everyday life.[39]

With the Memorial's financial support, Penn's social scientists undertook a number of projects. Their central focus consistently remained to explain social ills in terms of psychological causes. Some successes were achieved, and by 1927, Willits's research team tied their projects together under a banner of 'Industrial Problems of Individual Adjustment'. Work on such problems required collaboration between physiologists, psychologists, sociologists and economists. Penn's researchers recognized that many problems in society require interdisciplinary teamwork, by specialists in numerous fields. Writing in 1927, Willits emphasized that perhaps the greatest benefit to be achieved from connecting all of Penn's industrial research projects together 'has been the gradual extension of scientific contacts that are available for effective cooperation'.[40]

A chief objective of Penn's research programme was to address institutional lag by helping people adjust to a changed world. But this was no ameliorative programme; it was a programme aimed at fundamental change. If the research choice was between changing a person's environment or changing a person to handle their environment, then Penn's focus was more on the latter. They selected to advance their fundamental research with a kind of methodological allowance that accepted the status quo of a changed world as it happened to be, at least for the time being.

The University of Pennsylvania was not alone in pursuing a research programme focused on learning about human nature at a psychological level. Another school that hoped to build a research programme based primarily on psychological research was Yale University. Yale shared their idea to help reorient people to a changed world, and similar to the situation at Penn, Yale's social scientists were led by another friend of Mayo, Robert M. Yerkes. Also similar to Penn's situation was the fact that Yale's faculty had both theoretical and applied interests.[41]

In May 1923, Yale's president James Angell contacted his old friend Ruml. Angell tested the prospect of obtaining financing for a new psychology institute at Yale. Ruml invited a proposal, and Angell set to work. 'There is unquestionably great need at the present moment', Angell declared, 'for the development of psychology – using the term in the broadest sense – to contribute light and guidance for the solution of many problems of our present social order'. The illumination that might result from research in psychology would come 'from a thoroughgoing study' of base-level motives, which were present from 'the earliest conditions out of which humanity has developed'. Angell argued for the value in studying 'the more primitive types of animal life in whose activities we may hope to discover some of the deep lying factors in human nature which occasion in us perplexity, both as individuals and as members of civilized society'.[42]

Yale's researchers intended to focus on discoveries at a biological level; yet their ultimate goal was to help redirect individual and collective behaviours. Angell believed it even 'conservative' to say that 'we are at the very threshold of the most important advances in our understanding of human activities and our ability, particularly through educational methods, to control human life for the betterment of all future generations'. One keen note of optimism that carried through the psychology profession was that modern societies were at a threshold of a new age, and that with the help of social scientists, each person's 'social bearings' will be better 'oriented' to a changed world.[43]

Yale's psychologists proposed projects in five areas: normal human behaviour; comparative psychology; mental testing; aberrant mental behaviour; and 'racial, and particularly primitive, human behaviour in its cultural and social aspects'. In this latter category they also included the potentially controversial area of 'sex research', which was of particular interest to Yerkes. Angell's application materials cited Yerkes as a leading specialist in animal behaviour, and as a great leadership presence at Yale. Yerkes's animal studies, which focused on experiments on cats and rats, had led him to conclude that 'savageness' (or 'killing instinct') was a 'heritable behaviour complex'. Yerkes thought of his experiments between about 1910 and 1920 as studies of the 'heredity of savageness and wildness'.[44]

Following some clarifying interaction and advice between Ruml and Angell, Yale submitted a revised proposal. They declared that the nation's rapid social and economic change had resulted in maladjustments requiring new forms of 'social control'. They now grouped their projects into three areas of study: 'the neurological and instinctive aspects of behaviour'; 'the social traits of man, both primitive and civilized'; and 'peculiarities of race, climatic habitat, and cultural and economic status'. Ultimately Yale's researchers aimed to make discoveries about the natural bases of human behaviour. Such research, wrote Angell, 'will especially stress aberrant forms of behaviour' in attempting 'to orient ... forms of abnormality in their individual and social bearings'.[45]

Yale's proposed fields of study differed from those described by Penn's social scientists. Penn's proposal focused on an environmental level of study, and a principle of social psychology; Yale's interests involved deeper bases of behaviour. While Penn's application seems to have been assisted by the high regard held for Mayo, at Yale it was the scientific ideas and methods of Yerkes that were highly regarded. Yale's research rationale fit with what the Memorial's trustees could approve, and Yale received a generous grant. By the late 1920s, the research programme at Yale resulted in the creation of a pair of fine institutes: an Institute of Psychology and an Institute of Human Relations.[46]

In addition to the research programmes at Penn and Yale, other 'concrete' directions for psychological research existed that could be of value. One group interested in some pertinent research was the National Research Council, which as early as 1922 shared its interest in studying psychological dimensions of human adjustment to the industrial workplace. NRC leadership recognized that multiple research groups could be useful in the field of occupational psychology, and that a coordinating body could greatly assist in this field. In the NRC's estimation, particularly useful would be an increased focus on developing tests of 'occupational fitness', and for such a project they advocated a 'purely psychological' approach to 'the study of techniques of setting tests of fitness for certain occupations found in civil service, business, and industry'. The Memorial provided some assistance to the NRC to 'stimulate original research in that field'.[47]

Another research organization that contacted the Memorial with an interest in studying psychological issues in the industrial workplace was the National Institute of Industrial Psychology, which did so in November 1923. The NIIP's application described the need for better measures of occupational fitness. The NIIP disclosed a willingness to undertake private investigations 'on behalf of Industrial and Commercial firms'. The group's statement of purpose reiterated this message by noting that 'Communications are invited from firms in regard to any problems in which they think the Institute may be able to render them assistance'. The Memorial decided to support this organization interested in working so directly with private interests, and within two months the NIIP received a Memorial grant to initiate a five-year study of how workplace conditions can be made better for workers. Their studies were done with an explicit view that both workers and owners can be assisted by any research work supported by the NIIP.[48]

The idea to pursue industrial research partly to benefit private interests was not new in 1923. One of the more prominent psychologists of the day, James McKeen Cattell, founded a 'Psychological Corporation' in 1921 as a sort of matching service to connect social scientists as consultants to industry. Cattell's work was one of the better known of a few such consulting organizations that came into existence at the time. Worth noting, as well, is the renowned example of 1920s consultancy, the Hawthorne study.[49]

The Hawthorne study stands as a marker in the rise of the 'new' behavioural science. Performed in 1924 at an AT&T–Western Electric factory on the west side of Chicago, a team of industrial engineers with sociological interests travelled from MIT and, supported by NRC funds, set up an experiment. For their control group they tried holding all working conditions constant, while systematically altering a series of workplace variables for their experimental groups. Changes were made in such attributes as work-station positions, table designs, chair heights and lighting levels. Yet whenever the researchers measured for productivity changes in the experimental groups, they discovered that both the experimental and control groups became more productive. What had happened – we now know – is that both groups discovered one basic fact about the experiments: the experimenters were there to measure for productivity improvements. This fact alone led both groups to want to improve their productivity. After some half a decade or so of puzzling over what had happened (and also including a subsequent series of experiments that tried other adjustments such as clustering employees into smaller work groups), it was in the early 1930s that one particular researcher was invited to the Hawthorne factory to get to the bottom of things. This person, who confirmed that the Hawthorne experiments revealed some unexpectedly complex psychological effects, was G. Elton Mayo.[50]

## Conclusion

In 1923 at the Laura Spelman Rockefeller Memorial, a remarkable experiment was underway. The experiment was to discover what could happen if a very substantial amount of money was put in the hands of a worldwide community of social scientists. The experiment was a one-time opportunity that Beardsley Ruml and the Memorial officers were called upon to implement with a rare balance of speed and sensibility, and they wanted to implement the experiment to the best of their abilities.

# 6 RESEARCH CENTRES

## Introduction

Between January 1923 and January 1929, the Laura Spelman Rockefeller Memorial supported the creation of five university-based 'research centres'. Each centre had a special focus. The London School of Economics focused especially on economic research. The University of Chicago focused on interdisciplinary urban research. The University of North Carolina focused on race relations. Columbia University focused especially on intersections between law, politics and other fields in the social sciences. Harvard University focused on industrial psychology, while also experimenting with a methodological shift from social ethics to empirical analysis.

## Origins of Social Science

By the 1920s, persons involved in academic social science made great strides toward becoming 'professionals' in their fields of expertise. Persons in the sciences of economics, sociology, political science and social psychology could all perhaps even come to believe that their science was the central social science.

The idea of a 'science' of humans living in society far predates the 1920s. Among the ancient Greeks in the western tradition, one can find keen insights in social, political, economic and even anthropological thought – but it was 'thought', not 'science'. In much more recent times it can be a challenge to commit to any exact order of the emergence of the 'modern' sciences of humans and societies. David Hume in 1741 wrote his essay, 'That Politicks may be reduc'd to a Science'. Giovanni Battista Vico, the political philosopher, published his *Scienza Nuova* even sixteen years before that. Later in the century, the American and French projects to articulate successful rules for self-governance were definitely grand experiments in political science, with the ideas of Montesquieu being a touchstone for both nations. Yet it was almost a century later that political science began to gain some momentum toward becoming a profession based on expertise. The American Social Science Association (ASSA), established in

1865, included various persons interested in politics and governmental reform, as well as some who were interested in learning about the ways of life of 'others', most often, Native Americans. A few scholarly journals emerged, including the *Johns Hopkins University Studies in Historical and Political Science* (est. 1883) and the *Political Science Quarterly* (est. 1886). The American Political Science Association got its start in 1903, and the association soon began the *American Political Science Review*. But for some number of years the articles published in the journal were not highly encouraging in terms of their scientific elements. In 1908 Arthur Bentley, a Johns Hopkins-trained behaviourist, could even notably declare: 'We have a dead political science'. However in 1921, University of Chicago political scientist Charles E. Merriam decided that the right research tools were beginning to exist to enable a 'new science of politics'. Merriam conceived of a political science that could be based on testable hypotheses, and he believed that rigorous methods should build especially upon the 'behaviourist' approach in psychology. Merriam was confident that in the face of some minor resistance (such as Charles A. Beard's 'anti-scientism'), political scientists could finally begin to discover what could be done to build an empirical political science.[1]

Sociology as a scientific field began in numerous places and times. The founding moment might depend on what sort of an argument we want for a 'founding' moment. Adolphe Quetelet, J. S. Mill, Karl Marx and Friedrich Engels, Emile Durkheim, Max Weber – all Europeans – were all nineteenth-century founders in the western tradition; as were others as well. One kind of a project that all of these writers produced were synthetic treatises designed to craft unifying arguments. The idea was that all other fields of the social sciences divide things up, and sociologists put things back together.[2]

Another measure of a modern status of sociology is when the field became a professional activity. The creation of the ASSA was, for many people, an effort to bring organized attention to major social and economic problems, including crime, pauperism, reservation conditions for Native Americans and education for African Americans. In Europe, a style of sociological analysis on the rise by the 1870s, and which may have culminated by the early 1890s, was based primarily on theoretical arguments pertaining to Europe's own social and economic conditions, including a view that such a vast amount of reform might be needed as to entail a full-blown 'Revolution'.[3]

By the 1890s, Durkheim interpreted sociology as emerging from some kind of 'heroic age' of encyclopedic thinkers and their quests for total explanatory systems. Durkheim had in mind that breed of system builders who, over the preceding 150 years, had imagined and refined an idea of a long trajectory of western societies following a movement from status-based to contractual relations – the idea that modern political and governmental order had emerged from ancient kinship ties. Yet all of these writings were conjectural histories at best. Durkheim criticized those who posited speculative arguments that were impossible to test. He advocated the pursuit of rigorous investigations to discover general facts about society – facts that were uniquely at the level of aggregate human communities, and which he called 'social facts'. There is a high level of agreement among historians of sociology that during the 1890s a genuinely scientific sociology began to emerge.[4]

The first academic sociologists in the United States came from religious backgrounds. Their motives in teaching and writing showed their Christian care for society. At Columbia College in New York, trustees in 1877 discussed establishing a department of charity and corrections. At Bryn Mawr College, in 1888, Franklin H. Giddings established a department of sociology; however, he was identified only as a lecturer. The first sociology professorship in the United States was assigned in 1892, when Social Gospel minister Albion Small received his appointment to the newly established University of Chicago. Small established the school's department of sociology in that year, and three years later he initiated the *American Journal of Sociology*. Columbia, in that same summer, hired Giddings to teach a course on 'Sociology' for their Faculty of Political Science, but Giddings's assigned 'chair' was abolished by the faculty the following spring. For a decade or more, relatively little was published in the *American Journal of Sociology* that can be called 'science', according to our modern sense of things.

But this began to change. In 1905 American sociologists met as a national-level organization, the American Sociological Society. The recent breakthrough in empirical methods that they discussed at length was W. E. B. Du Bois's case study, *The Philadelphia Negro* (1899), which employed the 'social survey' method and provided statistically sound conclusions capable of transcending singular case studies, thereby achieving the announcement of general principles capable of shifting sociology from explanations based on nature to explanations based on nurture – or, in other words, based on environmental and social causes. The method of social surveys was created over the preceding couple of decades, outside of the universities, and most notably in connection with the settlement house movement. Researchers associated with settlement houses – such as Hull House in Chicago – typically employed social surveys within their municipal, social and political agendas.[5]

Also at their national meetings, sociologists began an aggressive decade or so of self-conscious discussions aimed at establishing 'boundaries' between their subject matter and the subject matter of other social sciences, as well as biological science. One consequence of this effort was to further promote the creation of separate definitions for the different social sciences. But one problem remained through the 1900s and into the 1910s: while it was potentially a professional science, the religious sentiment remaining in sociology meant that an insufficient separation might exist between scientific objectivity and reform-oriented advocacy.[6]

Beginning with an initial spurt of conversation between about 1895 and 1905, sociologists regularly returned to engaging in defence work, as they aimed to retain for themselves an area of the social sciences with a unique mission, which was to analyse materials involving modern human groups and societies, and to find ways to holistically describe modern social processes of great complexity. By the 1920s, sociologists were settled on a couple of strategies to define their science: to recognize sociology as a project focused on organizing and synthesizing all available knowledge about all influences on human associations; and to respond to all of the other social sciences that might happen to encroach upon sociology's territory, i.e. sociology as a privileged point of view for studying certain social problems such as race relations, urban-group conflicts and matters of collective behaviour.

The optimism by the 1920s was that any rigid disciplinary divisiveness was about to end in the social sciences. A return to unity could be spearheaded by the sociologists. As Small phrased the idea in 1913:

> it is no longer possible for gentlemen who call themselves by some sectarian scientific name to be taken seriously by completely conscious scholars when they assume that the traditions of their scientific sect are authority enough for the selection of objects of attention which they please to make.[7]

By the 1920s the situation in economics was fairly similar to that in sociology. A period of professionalization began in economics as early as the 1880s, taking place primarily in the United States, as American economists nearly always journeyed to Europe to earn a doctorate in political economy (often in Germany). Formation of the American Economic Association came in 1885, and also in that decade, a few scholarly journals began to accept economics papers. But for any person who would purport to possess unique 'expertise' in economics, as represented at least by an advanced degree, a persistent concern was a potential appearance of some perceived political slant within their writings. This was a danger that could get a person fired. In fact, it eventually took the introduction of new mathematical and statistical methods during the 1930s and 1940s to provide enough safe distancing between a scientific stance for economists and an ideological stance for policy advocates. This move, to separate economics as a science from policy formation as values advocacy, could also benefit from increased financial resources.[8]

The fields of political science, sociology and economics were all well separated from each other by the 1920s. Also split and on its own path was psychology – which was once part of 'moral philosophy', became a 'social science', and then became 'behavioural science'. Practitioners in each of the social and behavioural sciences had an established body of specialized knowledge and methods. It seems overall there was an attitude of optimism that carried the day, and did so long enough that the money could arrive.

## The London School of Economics

In September 1923, the London School of Economics (LSE) began a long-running relationship with Rockefeller philanthropy. Ruml made a visit to London that month, and he arranged a meeting with William Beveridge, the director of the school. Faculty at the LSE were already engaged in a process of establishing their fields on empirical foundations, and the LSE's social scientists came across as persons highly involved in their professional dialogues. The LSE's administrators responded to Ruml's visit by introducing their understanding that the Memorial 'may be prepared to consider a proposal for assisting research in Economics and Social Science'; they wished to introduce two lines of potential projects. One area of projects would involve more 'immediate opportunities for investigation', and could include such problems as managing economic resources of undeveloped lands, studying causes of unemployment and analysing various sorts of population issues. The second area of projects was to 'make a systematic study of economic phenomena in their bearing on social welfare'. Within a few months, by January 1924, the Memorial awarded to the LSE a five-year, $1.4 million grant, supporting both proposed areas of research. This very substantial grant made the LSE into one of five research centres supported by the Memorial.[9]

Ruml much liked having the LSE on board. Founded in 1895, the LSE was becoming a preeminent British university for social science. Of great appeal to the Memorial was the fact that the LSE's faculty paid special attention to graduate-level education. Ruml struck up a friendship with Beveridge and they shared ideas about the need for research suitable for addressing 'concrete' problems. Ruml understood Beveridge as displaying a genuine interest in transforming the LSE from an institution based on part-time instructors and commuter students (and burdened by shortages in facilities and housing) into an elite research institution.[10]

The Memorial's decision to support the social sciences at the LSE included funds for research as well as general endowment, libraries and building improvements. In terms of supported research, most financial assistance went to broad programme development in international studies, as well as some funds to bring in visiting professors of political economy (such as Harvard's Allyn Young). LSE researchers had substantial freedom to make their own decisions about how to use the money, and it seems universally they decided to minimize teaching loads of senior faculty in order to encourage more research.[11]

After about a year and a half of Memorial support, LSE's social scientists shared some new ideas. In July 1925, they were interested in focusing greater attention on developing the foundations of the social sciences. LSE's researchers expressed an aim to connect the school's lines of research in 'economic relations' and 'politics and social relations'. Related to this, they wanted to study 'the borderlands' between social science and non-social science. Fitting well with what many social scientists were beginning to recognize, the idea was that a unity of the social sciences was becoming necessary primarily because most social and economic problems required cooperative attention from many fields. In addition, as the LSE's social scientists uniquely put it, there was a 'missing' piece to any complete structure of the social sciences. They described their synthetic vision, that to 'complete the circle of the social sciences' a field of studies was required that would deal 'with the natural bases of economics and politics, with the human material and with its physical environment, and forming a bridge between the natural and the social sciences'. This last area of study would be a big undertaking; that they recognized. Yet they saw the need to deal with 'the study of the natural bases of the social sciences as the most important development now to be made in the field of the social sciences'. To complete an integrated continuity of the social sciences, progress remained necessary in a range of other fields as well, including anthropology, social biology, economic psychology, geography, agriculture studies and public health. This was going to be challenging work to connect all of these sciences into a seamless web, and to begin making progress in this effort, a first objective was to make the social sciences methodologically more like the natural sciences, especially 'by bringing the natural and social sciences into contact and importing the methods of the former into the latter'.[12]

As the LSE's social scientists worked with their Memorial funds, they showed great interest in introducing new methods of analysis. One method, developed originally by anthropologists, was 'functional analysis'. This method was seen as a way to add greater generality to anthropology, making it into a robust science capable of enabling research into all aspects of societies, even modern societies. The goal was to learn how a society is adapted to meet its most necessary functions for perpetuating meaningful life. There was a sort of reductionism to the exercise. The idea was that some half dozen or so absolutely fundamental needs could be identified as societal universals. For any given society, an anthropologist can become absorbed within the culture and gain an intimate understanding of what the people believe and do. The thickly ensconced anthropologist can then unravel all of a ceremonial superstructure of interconnected norms, mores, rituals, codes of conduct and the like. While industrial societies might have more accumulated ceremonial procedures to enable them to be more functionally differentiated than primitive societies (in other words, a greater degree of specialization of labour), the same core functions must ultimately be met by any society. One chief innovator of the functional approach in anthropology was Bronislaw Malinowski, a social anthropologist at the LSE. Malinowski expressed to the Memorial his goal to broadly apply the new method. While he specialized in studying primitive societies in order to identify the material benefits that a group might receive from their systems of beliefs, Malinowski focused his interests not on learning about primitive societies, but on learning about 'the practical influence of social science upon policies'.[13]

In the early 1920s, anthropology was ready to explore the potential of functional analysis. This new method was a response to a wider debate in anthropology with respect to which research methods could best transform anthropology into a rigorous modern science. One tradition in anthropology that we now call the 'amateur' approach, involved 'spending time with the natives', who tended to be seen culturally and racially as the 'other'. The new research approach emphasized that culture and race are separate attributes of human social existence, and (as Ashley Montagu soon put it) race is not a factor in any anthropological equation. By the 1920s, Franz Boas and his followers had spent a quarter of a century supporting the argument that race attributes are not fixed, and that ideas and values of a community of people are often dependent on local circumstances. Contributions by Boas and his followers (sometimes called an 'American Historical School') helped to make anthropology into its own sort of a professional, 'expert' science. But having a basic objective to gain more intimate contact with a group of people, along with an assumption about the malleable nature of any attributes of 'race' – these were just the beginning points. Anthropology was finally becoming prepared to develop its own universal method of analysis. With functional analysis, anthropologists could systematically identify similarities and differences between wide-ranging cultures. They could do it with the confidence that each and every society must ultimately solve the same core problems of physical sustenance and emotional well-being.[14]

LSE's social scientists focused most of all on using the Memorial's funding to study economic problems. They produced a number of publications, some focused on theoretical concerns, and others on concrete problems. Overall they made good use of their freedom to explore wide-ranging research methods. They also aimed to fill in missing pieces in the unity of the social sciences. This latter interest potentially pushed them to learn what the older, historical methods could yet accomplish. Certainly important among LSE research projects from the time are such landmark accomplishments in economic history as R. H. Tawney and Eileen Power, *Tudor Economic Documents* (1924), A. L. Bowley and Margaret Hogg, *Has Poverty Diminished?* (1925), T. E. Gregory, *The First Year of the Gold Standard* (1926) and R. H. Tawney, *Religion and the Rise of Capitalism* (1926).[15]

An interesting study, by a sociologist supported by Memorial funds in his publication stage, is L. T. Hobhouse's *Social Development: Its Nature and Conditions* (1924). Hobhouse's project stands as something of a conceptual bridge. He attempted to connect together heredity and environment as two levels of causation in explaining modern problems. Hobhouse had deep compassion for the experience of impoverishment, which he saw as resulting in a loss of respectability of 'marginal' groups, or what he also called the 'submerged tenth'. His concern was to explore how much of the status of poverty owes to hereditary weakness, and how much this owes to social forces.[16]

Not only did the Memorial's support help the LSE's faculty to complete projects already underway, but it helped in recruiting leading scholars who could put new ideas and projects in motion. Notably we can identify the research appointment of Harvard economist Allyn Young (1928) and the faculty hiring of Oxford economist Lionel Robbins (1929). While Young stayed for one year, Robbins stayed for a career. Robbins's *Essay on the Nature and Significance of Economic Science*, published in 1932, stands as potentially the best-known LSE study supported by the 'fluid research funds' from the Memorial. The book is noteworthy for its attempt to bridge together concrete-historical and abstract methods in economics, which were thought, at least by some, to be incompatible. Another type of research favoured by the Memorial, and performed by LSE social scientists, was the social survey. The best-known was the 'New Survey of London Life and Labour', begun in 1927 by a team of LSE social scientists.[17]

These and other projects undertaken by LSE's social scientists were not the result of any direct agreement to identify particular problems for study. Rather these were projects that stemmed from choices made at the LSE. As Nobel laureate economist Friedrich Von Hayek later pointed out, the Memorial's support helped greatly at the LSE:

> It is scarcely too much to say that during most of the Beveridge era the growth of the School was dominated by the new developments, financed mainly from Rockefeller funds, which affected chiefly the library, the development of entirely new fields of teaching, and the provision for research.

The LSE's employment of Memorial funds produced a major research centre and, in time, one of the world's great research universities.[18]

## The University of Chicago

The University of Chicago, founded largely by John D. Rockefeller, opened its doors in the fall of 1892, with definite fanfare. The school's department of sociology and department of political economy opened in the same year. A main focus at Chicago was to sustain outstanding graduate programmes, and a couple of the school's premier graduate programmes were sociology and political economy.

During the university's first few years, their sociologists took some initiative in expressing a reform spirit. Chicago's sociologists were influenced by local successes of urban surveys, and by theories originating with some German scholars, such as Georg Simmel of Berlin. Such an essay as Simmel's 'The Metropolis and Mental Life' provided encouragement to focus on a whole constellation of problems as owing largely to phenomena of separation and alienation in everyday urban life.

A number of early faculty members at Chicago sought their training at German universities, and even those who did not still discussed German writings.[19]

But Chicago's social scientists wanted to bring together these influences – reform spirit, empirical methods and theoretical guidance – to produce studies that would be uniquely their own. The first leader of Chicago sociology was Albion Small, who in 1892 received his professorial appointment in sociology. Small had great interests in a reform orientation, and the Chicago appointment went to him based largely on his expertise in Baptist-motivated social work. From about the earliest moments of its institutional existence, Small brought to the university a willingness to perennially debate and reconsider what applied social science should do.[20]

Robert Park was another primary figure in early Chicago sociology. Park arrived at the school in 1914, having studied in Germany, directly with Simmel. Park also brought an interest in discussing the German Ferdinand Tonnies's notion of a broad historical shift, from traditional rural 'community' (*Gemeinschaft*) to complex urban 'society' (*Gesellschaft*). Tonnies's ideas were a kind of armchair theory developed from extensive reading. Small, originally a history PhD, was also drawn to such broad theories of history.[21]

Sociologists at the University of Chicago were never to be 'sociologists of the chair', for they advocated hands-on research, especially research that could get a social scientist fully into the city, in order to experience the city and to communicate with city people who themselves experienced the city. From this immersion method (certainly sharing something with methods in anthropology), there ensued a remarkable series of studies. The great study, which was some half a dozen years in the making, was published in 1918 by Chicago sociologist Florian Znaniecki and sociologist-journalist William I. Thomas: *The Polish Peasant in Europe and America*. An approach to sociology that would become known as the 'Chicago school' was being crafted, and this study was part of it. Znaniecki and Thomas drew upon dozens of interviews as well as all sorts of documentary materials (including family letters, social work files and church records) to develop 'life histories' of common people. From these life histories they could show a 'race psychology' (today we would call this an 'ethnic identity'), and they made the move to extrapolate this to a 'community portrait'. This was no sociology of abstract typologies, but was about real people and their daily activities described in detail. The essential property of Znaniecki and Thomas's approach to social science, as they themselves put it, 'is the direct dependence of its generalizations on new discoveries and new happenings'. The *Polish Peasant* is a lengthy study, from which sociologists could extract a general and neutral explanatory system: from 'social organization', to 'social disorganization', to 'social reorganization'.[22]

Another marker in establishing the reputation of Chicago's sociologists was Park's development of the concept of 'City as Social Laboratory'. Just as anthropologists worked to understand 'folk communities', sociologists should work to understand 'urban ecologies'. And in addition to achieving understanding, Chicago's sociologists had an added responsibility, which was to intervene and guide the development of cities. With this responsibility a contrast emerged at Chicago between 'social scientists' and 'social workers' – with the former having the task to discover how to guide change, and the latter setting out to do it.[23]

As Chicago's sociologists approached 1923, they were significantly influenced by the 'Americanization' project. Park's contributions to Americanization studies particularly brought notice to the university, including his analysis of groups and conflicts in his essay on 'The City' (1915). Park believed that a unity of the social sciences was necessary for studying all facets of any social or economic problem. Following this essay, Park teamed with Ernest Burgess to produce a breakthrough textbook, *Introduction to the Science of Sociology* (1921), which aimed to show that 'all social problems turn out to be problems of social control'.[24]

At about the same time, over in the school's department of political science, Charles E. Merriam wondered if an increased degree of social control might help solve various problems that he saw as associated with the public's level of participation (or lack of participation) in the political process. Merriam, as a proponent of the 'behaviourist approach' to political science, wanted to find paths toward greater empiricism in political science. The idea, shared by Park, Merriam and others, was to interconnect empirical data collection with actual experiments, so as to better identify successful mechanisms of social control.[25]

The outstanding work that brought together threads of both sociology and political science was one that involved a situation of great importance: race relations in the wake of Chicago's race riots of 1919. Charles S. Johnson, a sociology graduate student at Chicago, worked on a government appointment by the Chicago Commission of Race Relations to produce *The Negro in Chicago* (1922), a much discussed book at the time. The book was the result of research carried out for the governor of the state, and it included a number of methods emphasized at Chicago, including collection of personal documents, direct observation, intensive content analysis of press coverage and the gathering of official statistics by questionnaire. Johnson personally interviewed 274 families, living in all parts of the city. His interpretations led him to see a host of 'isolated' social problems as in fact an interconnected consequence of increased African-American migration toward northern cities following the First World War.[26]

The social sciences at Chicago were in a different state of development than those at the LSE. An injection of money – if it happened – could do different things at Chicago. Between August and November 1923, an exciting exchange of ideas transpired between social scientists at the school and leadership at the

Memorial. Park introduced ideas on behalf of the school's sociologists, while Merriam did so for the political scientists. In addition, Leon Marshall, a younger economist with interests in social science education, shared his ideas about the school's potential to promote great research in economics. It seems clear that it was the University of Chicago, more than any other school, which Ruml wanted for a research centre – and indeed the school received prompt word of the Memorial's major support, by year's end.

In March 1924, Chicago's local community research programme received its initial three-year Memorial endowment to establish a research centre. Ruml's indication, in 1924, was his approval of Chicago's focus on doing interdisciplinary social science through a 'local community research centre'; indeed he appreciated how it was 'concrete' to 'map' all regularities of interaction throughout an entire local community. Chicago's sociologists understood that all peoples and groups interact within a kind of 'social ecology', and such a systems-based understanding required the employment of research tools from multiple social sciences, including economics, sociology, political science, psychology and social work.[27]

Chicago's social scientists marched right into a rapidly changing urban world. Among their concerns were such problems as immigrant assimilation, immigrant housing, race and ethnic relations, criminality and inter-group conflicts. They emphasized a need to obtain 'scientific forms' of data, which meant an aim to obtain uniform categories of data to help make objective policy decisions.[28]

Many fine research studies resulted from the efforts of Chicago's social scientists through their local community research centre. Of great influence to Chicago's social scientists at the time that they received the Memorial's support was the 'nationality question' – as had been included in a study of immigrant assimilation titled *Old World Traits Transplanted* (1921), published by a research team led by William I. Thomas. The book focused especially on group relations between a majority population with an ancestral culture largely of Western European descent and more recent Eastern European 'races'; a conclusion was that while any event of group conflict could be anywhere on a spectrum between minor and severe, the ultimate outcome of group conflict will nearly always be assimilation of the smaller group into the larger one.[29]

Once the Memorial funds were fully in place, the rate of production of research projects simply exploded. Frederic Thrasher, with *The Gang* (1927), produced what is simultaneously a study of 'the gang' as a sociological phenomenon (i.e. a type of group) and of 'gangland' as a social issue (i.e. a type of problem). Thrasher studied 'gangs' and 'gangland' as social facts, and what emerged was another way to discover an 'urban ecology' – in this case, a discovery of zones next to zones, and zone within zones; Thrasher called the whole outcome an 'interstitial area'. The project was some seven years in the making, but it needed financial assistance toward the end; Thrasher nicely thanks the Memorial-supported Local Community Research Committee.[30]

Louis Wirth extended a thesis similar to that of *Old World Traits Transplanted* in his book *The Ghetto* (1928). By looking at the history of Chicago's Jewish population, Wirth showed an assimilation process in action. He also fitted it into a general pattern, with it being much like the process of emergence of the first 'ghetto' in history, in a section of Venice, where in a particular quarter of the city the first Jewish settlement was located, first by choice, but later by Jews being compelled to live there. Wirth extended the idea with respect to Chicago, and he saw similar transitions across the city, which was producing a great 'mosaic' of peoples segregated as racial and cultural groups. Wirth, in his language, was 'examining the natural history of an institution and the psychology of a people'. The institution was 'the ghetto'. Wirth said that he could not have completed the project without resources made available to him by the Memorial.[31]

Just a few years later, many accomplishments by Chicago's sociologists were in Wirth's thoughts when he summarized the 'ecology of the city' approach, which he saw as potentially both biological and cultural in nature. The city was no longer a place of so many isolated groups, he opined in 1938, but 'is a melting-pot of races, peoples, and cultures, and a most favorable breeding ground of new biological and cultural hybrids'. The city, he added, had become a place that 'rewards individual differences'.[32]

Another research area supported by Memorial funds at the University of Chicago was economics. There were already some important economists at the school, and one of them was Marshall, director of the National Council for the Social Sciences. This organization had a goal to make the social sciences as useful as possible for educational purposes. Marshall's approach to economics was different from a more mainstream attitude to support abstract theory, which thus made him a bit different from most of the school's economists. Marshall took a lead in working with the Memorial, as he proposed promoting increased communication between social scientists, so that together they could help reach the goal of making social science more useful. Perhaps it also mattered to Ruml that Merriam and Marshall were friends. Merriam was already doing wide-ranging and impressive research in political science and he was a known leader across the social sciences. Merriam and Marshall also shared ideas directly with each other.[33]

In early 1924, Marshall communicated with Ruml by providing pamphlets and reports, many authored by Marshall himself. One of Marshall's pamphlets was an 'Introduction to Social Studies'. The pamphlet explored many interrelations between the social sciences. Ruml showed an interest in Marshall's ideas, and he requested that Marshall prepare a new report to explore ideas about social science education 'for engineers' (by which Ruml meant social engineers).

Marshall provided this report in a matter of weeks, and in it he communicated a 'general recognition' that 'an outstanding deficiency in the preparation of engineers is in the realm of the social sciences and business administration'. Yet Marshall also expressed optimism that great progress was being made in putting knowledge into action across the social sciences, which will thereby 'enable interesting experiments to be made rather quickly and with quite as much probability of successful outcome as one could ask in experimental work'.[34]

Marshall also provided a third report, in November 1925. Again he evaluated possibilities for social science education for engineers, with a specific aim to bolster experimental applications of knowledge by 'indicat[ing] the importance of instruction in economics and the other social sciences in an engineering curriculum'. Engineers were recognized as persons 'concerned with the effective control of natural materials and forces – usually in terms of costs and returns, and always in terms of the social and economic institutions of our day'. What was needed in engineering education was an educational component focused on 'social technology'. Society's engineers needed to know the latest scientific understanding of the institutions of the day, for only with such knowledge could they best serve the public welfare.[35]

Also there was an interest within Chicago social science to develop and apply the anthropological method of functional analysis. Similar to the point of view at the LSE, the hope was to discover that functional analysis can be a general method suitable to studying modern societies. In addition to the main grant of Memorial funds, Chicago's department of anthropology received its own grant from the Memorial in 1925. This money enabled the three-year appointment of Edward Sapir, a follower of Franz Boas's emphasis on the importance of nurture over nature. Sapir was also a young leader in applying functional analysis. In 1926 Bronislaw Malinowski also joined Chicago's anthropology faculty, as he was brought over from London on a Memorial fellowship. Malinowski was excited to work toward clarifying 'the place assumed by science in American life, especially by social science'.[36]

One famous project that showed how to apply functional analysis to a modern society was called 'Middletown'. Undertaken by Chicago-trained sociologist Robert S. Lynd, assisted by his wife Helen Lynd, the Middletown study employed sociological as well as anthropological methods to thoroughly analyse an average American town, now known to have been Muncie, Indiana. In 1924, Lynd received Memorial funds to undertake just the kind of concrete research that Ruml wanted. Even though the Lynds were both sociologists, *Middletown*, when it was published in 1928, was a project in unified social science. Included in the project was even an aim to discover ways to help reduce a heightened level of 'irrationality' in an industrializing community.[37]

In April 1927, Max Mason, president of the University of Chicago, got personally involved in conversations with the Memorial. Perhaps having learned a
bit about what Ruml liked, Mason communicated his own ideas about how to
unify the social sciences. Mason believed that all of the sciences – natural, physical and social – were ultimately one body of science. It was time, he said, to move
from mere responses to 'pathological incidents in society', toward discovering
'the great fundamental processes in society'. Mason requested a combination of
grants in excess of $1.7 million. With his request he also included a lofty line
of sight: that while 'all science is one', it now seemed clear that the particular
branches of the sciences 'which can best serve man in mastering and shaping
his social environment to the end of effective living together are the social sciences'. Mason – following up on the reports provided by Marshall – proposed a
Memorial-assisted revamping of graduate education in the social sciences. He
expressed the need to end 'the present welter of miscellaneous formal factual
courses dealing usually in a routine way with problems of the day'. Such courses

> must yield to a functional arrangement in which a relatively small amount of formal
> instruction will open the student's mind to a preliminary understanding of the frame-
> work, the fundamental processes, the driving forces and the institutions of social
> living, and another amount of formal instruction to equip the student with essential
> methodological tools.

The essence of things was in Mason's closing point: to equip students with
'tools'.[38]

Marshall remained highly interested in revamping the structure of social science education at the graduate level. He produced another report, which agreed
with Mason, and which said that research and curriculum in the social sciences
must target the discovery of fundamental social forces and processes. Marshall proposed an approach to social science graduate education that focused
on 'knowledges' and 'skills'; specifically he advocated connecting the applied
emphasis on 'the engineering aspect' of social science to a corresponding 'fusion
program' in fundamental social science. He proposed that what was needed was
financial support to develop teaching materials for a tightly arranged, eight-
part sequence of courses that would take students through undergraduate and
then graduate education in 'Tool-Skills and Tool-Knowledges Foundational for
Advanced Work' in the social sciences.[39]

Marshall soon clarified that on the applications side of the proposed programme would be a focus on 'three schools of social technology' (law, social
service administration and commerce), all already operating at the university.
These three areas of social technology represented an educational arrangement
for 'the engineering aspect of the so-called social sciences'. Finally, when it came
to more tightly interconnecting all of the fields of the social sciences with the

social technologies, the key step would be to encourage perspectives of an applied character that could address concrete problems requiring 'A greater amount of research work of a true rather than a formal cooperative character'. What was needed, Marshall again emphasized, was encouragement of 'true cooperation and synthesis in social science work'.[40]

Finally worth noting are a few specific Memorial grants made to support the appointment of full-time research professorships. Three noteworthy appointees, all in 1927, were economists Simon Leland and Henry Schultz, and psychologist L. L. Thurstone. The Memorial also gave $1.1 million that same year to help build a new Social Sciences Research Building on the campus. Included among still other Memorial grants to Chicago were personal grants, such as $60,000 to Charles Merriam to study civic education, $30,000 to Leon Marshall to study business education and $100,000 to the University of Chicago Press to support publications in the social sciences. All told, by January 1929 the Memorial provided approximately $3.4 million to the University of Chicago, making the school its largest university recipient of Memorial funds.[41]

With its extraordinary support from the Memorial, the history of changing ideas and the emergence of interdisciplinary approaches at the University of Chicago can be seen as a fine microcosm of the Memorial's goals for an overall pattern of advancement in the social sciences.[42]

## University of North Carolina

During late 1923 and early 1924, Ruml was struck by some ideas of a friend of his, Howard W. Odum, a professor of social science at the University of North Carolina (UNC). Odum was a Columbia-trained social psychologist, but he had moved his research interests into race relations in the American South. He was editor of the newly establish *Journal of Social Forces*, and he was something of a known quantity to Ruml, who admired Odum for his expanding tally of scholarly accomplishments. Ruml particularly appreciated Odum's design of a comprehensive course covering all major issues in the social sciences. One subject of Odum's thinking was his theory of 'leadership evolution' in the South. In 1919's *Social and Mental Traits of the Negro*, Odum attempted to learn something about the balance between nurture and nature as two levels of forces contributing to what a person can become. In his book he also aimed to explain why the South seemed so acutely maladjusted, both economically and culturally. The South could be greatly helped by applying all of the social sciences, and so Odum decided to recommend basing one of the Memorial's research centres at his school.[43]

Ruml communicated with Odum about visiting the school. They discussed the Memorial's interest in building a research field in race relations, and Ruml made it clear that as part of this overall interest, one of the Memorial's specific research centres might do well to focus especially on African-American communities in the United States. Odum responded with shared enthusiasm that a research centre could bring a range of social sciences into a concerted focus on 'Negro studies'. Such a study could blossom at the University of North Carolina. However Ruml believed that more discussions were still needed.[44]

Ruml met with Odum in Chapel Hill, North Carolina, in May 1924. The two discussed the potential for creating a major research centre. They discussed the condition of race relations throughout the United States, and especially in the South. In some particulars they discussed an idea 'to make a general survey' of those southern institutions that were 'offering training for social work, to discover what this field of activity might offer for the Memorial'.[45]

Odum followed the meeting by writing down his concerns about lagging leadership evolution in the South. This idea might just join with race relations as a second unifying theme for social scientists at a research centre at UNC. Odum produced a memorandum to explain the shortage of leadership qualities produced by southern schools. He believed that the South had great potential for progressive improvement, and that to turn this potential into reality 'is a Southern promise'. As Odum interpreted the leadership deficiency, what he saw was 'the failure so far to make quick adjustments to social change and to the shortness of time for the evolution of new types' of leaders. The specific deficiency causing the lag in social institutions was 'that the South lacks experience and training for the newer leadership needs'. Odum sent his memorandum, along with a letter, to Ruml. He recommended particular developments that could assist the South, including establishing exchange fellowships and professorships, which could help transport leading scholars 'south to east, east to west, east to south, south to west, and so on'.[46]

The University of North Carolina certainly showed hints of being the kind of place that Ruml would want on board. Yet the school was still small and in a financially precarious position. Could Memorial funding be a powerful enough leverage mechanism to change all that? Ruml, in addition to being friends with Odum, began to correspond with UNC president Harry Woodburn Chase, a social scientist himself. Ruml shared his appreciation for the school's location, and said he was pleased to see that certain lines of research were already underway there. Ruml was clear about his purpose for making his May visit to Chapel Hill, which was to encourage an application for a major grant. He was following up with some encouraging kindness: 'I have never seen a university where the desire to serve the people of the state is as strong as in North Carolina'. Strong connections already existed at UNC between 'social science' and 'social technology', as well as between university departments in social technology and multiple state-level agencies. 'The Engineering Department advises the Highway

Commission, the School of Commerce is a member of the State Harbor and Shipping Board, the School of Public Welfare is technical advisor to the State Public Welfare Commission'. UNC's social scientists were highly competent, 'and all ready for cooperative work'. The school had all the basic prerequisites to satisfy the Memorial as the right institution for a research centre in the South: strong departments in the social sciences; an established focus on applications of science; a willingness to connect the two within the university; and an established pattern of interaction with policymakers outside of the university.[47]

In May 1925, Odum submitted the invited grant proposal. Briefly he described a range of projects, including some that specifically addressed the Memorial's interest in research that could extend beyond a state-level of interest. One interest was to publish African-American traditional songs, and another was to study black migration, both within the South and between the South and the North. Odum also had in mind a comparative study of economic concerns facing African-American communities in North Carolina and Mississippi, and he supported an idea (which he submitted jointly with UNC sociologist Guy B. Johnson) to study Southern community interactions from a point of view 'of two races living progressively together'. Odum's projects clearly focused on a recognized need for research in race relations.[48]

But as the Memorial saw things, Odum's projects were too general in description. Unlike what had happened so quickly for the University of Pennsylvania and Yale University with their proposals for financial support in psychology, and clearly differing from the relative ease with which the London School of Economics and the University of Chicago obtained substantial support for many projects in the social sciences, UNC's grant proposal was found not ready for approval. Memorial officer Leonard Outhwaite took some initiative in providing guidance. He informed Odum that a resubmitted proposal will need to state projects with greater clarity, and he emphasized the specific area of research of special interest: race relations in the South. Finally Outhwaite suggested that Odum would have to concede that he was having some difficulties getting his proposed projects into concrete terms. In a flurry of letters between them, Outhwaite and Odum worked to achieve the greater level of clarity. Finally, after a number of exchanges, Outhwaite came to the point that he emphasized a request of a friend:

> Now be a good fellow. Forget everything else for a while, get an old hat, a pipe, go for a walk and think over exactly what it is that you think you might do by way of Negro study during the current year at North Carolina. Set down the specific topics of Negro study that you feel you are best equipped to deal with adequately.

Outhwaite almost pleaded with Odum to 'set down something of the scope and the method that you think will be involved in each study', and to get onto paper how 'the whole plan will be consonant both with the purposes of your Institute and the University situation, and also with the known priorities of the Memorial'. Ruml was 'clamoring for just this type of statement from you'.[49]

Clearly the Memorial had made a decision to step forward and potentially guide Odum's efforts just a bit. Outhwaite's letter aimed to push Odum into action. But in what way? To what extent? In the case of this interaction between Outhwaite and Odum, the evidence might seem to reveal some direct engagement showing how the Memorial would grant money only upon some agreement over the planned projects at the outset. However, an alternative interpretation, which seems fair, is that Ruml and the Memorial simply wanted some level of concreteness to any description of planned projects.

Odum worked hard, and by September 1925 he developed a revised proposal. He described tangible projects in eight specific areas: race relations in the South; cultural studies of African-American folk traditions and 'Negro song'; African-American business enterprise; credit facilities for African-American communities; county convict camps; statistical studies of crime in North Carolina; a case analysis of black offenders; and black offenders given the death penalty. With the revised proposal the Memorial could support UNC's efforts to build the desired research centre.[50]

The Memorial awarded an initial $97,500 to UNC, primarily to establish an Institute for Research in Social Science. The Institute would be run by a small board of directors selected from the university's administrators and senior faculty, with Odum serving as director. Between 1924 and 1928, the Memorial further supported the institute to a tune of over $400,000. Of great appeal to Ruml throughout the relationship was Odum's applied interest in race equality, as well as his success at conceptually integrating the social sciences. Odum was also at work on a textbook to better unify the social sciences, which he produced in 1927.[51]

UNC's social scientists used the support to study many aspects of southern life, focusing especially on African-Americans and their living and working conditions, including factory relations between workers and management. They also studied a variety of economic problems in North Carolina. Some projects were already important to the Memorial, such as studies of fundamental causes of criminal behaviour, agricultural market problems and industrial working conditions. Others related to conditions specific to North Carolina, such as studies of traditional music and culture in African-American communities. The kinds of social and economic problems studied by UNC's social scientists ultimately involved nearly the totality of life in the region.[52]

Back in September 1924, Odum came up with an idea for something enjoyable to do. He contacted Ruml and recommended a road trip, and he suggested that the idea stemmed from his dream to start 'an all Southern renaissance'. The two exchanged another volley of correspondence, aimed at hashing out some additional projects that might help the South. The idea for the trip came together in these letters, and they agreed to visit some half dozen or more southern universities. The trip across the South actually happened. The following April, with Ruml and Odum joined by Memorial assistant Leonard Outhwaite and UNC president Harry W. Chase (who hoped 'to have plenty of time to loaf'), the group of four went for a long, somewhat meandering drive, ultimately visiting eight southern universities in rapid succession.[53]

As to research projects, many lines of research work got underway at UNC. The programme of overriding importance was 'Negro Studies'. At one point in February 1925, Outhwaite expressed what the Memorial saw as the heart of the matter: that 'so far as the American Negro is concerned, the problem of his economic status and economic opportunities is extremely important'. If opportunities could come first, then many good results should follow. Odum agreed that the economic situation was the fundamental intervention point for getting all sorts of improvements underway in the South. All persons were agreed that 'concrete information' on specific problems was what was now needed.[54]

Through the rest of the 1920s, UNC's Institute for Research in Social Science pursued important studies on African-American culture and broader race relations in the upper South. However, it was on the subject of studying race relations that social scientists could be in danger of passing into sensitive territory. UNC sociologist Guy B. Johnson wrote a memorandum in 1925 that introduced a kind of policy position. He believed what was needed to improve southern race relations was initially to prefer only a slow rate of change. One part of his argument was that reforms ought not to be enacted until all available conclusions are stated by social scientists. But his main argument for the recommended delay was due to the expected 'resistance' of white southerners. Any social scientist wishing to work on race relations is 'absolutely free' to study any subject matter that he or she pleases, but 'would have trouble down here if he tried to put into immediate action the ideas he had developed from his study of the race problem'.[55]

One measure of success for the Institute for Research in Social Science is that it received much public recognition in the region. According to one news article at the time, the institute 'has a single aim: to improve the State'. The institute aimed to 'collect and sift existing knowledge in the social field', so that 'no public official in the State ought ever be in doubt about where to apply for information regarding any question of public interest'. One cited research goal was to learn how much of an individual's tax bill goes to dealing with North Carolina's crime enforcement expenditures, including policing, jailing, reform and the like. Another identified goal was to inquire whether a majority of crimes really are committed by 'semi-idiots', and if so, whether it would then be possible to scientifically identify some least expensive ways to minimize crimes. Helping to smooth North Carolina's transition into the semi-industrial economy of the 'New South', the institute studied what sorts of roads the state required to get all of its products to market. This research was being done with a proper level of professional 'disinterest', in that a study of potential efficiencies in the shipping of state products 'is being made by a man who owns no town lots or marketable timber, who doesn't give a hoot whether a proposed railroad runs yan-side or this, but who has spent years studying transportation as an economic problem'. The Institute, it was added,

> does not inquire into the mysteries of chemistry or physics, for those are natural sciences, sciences of nature. It does not inquire into the origin of Greek verbs, for that is the science of language. But whatever touches society, that is, men in more or less organized groups, is within its fold.[56]

## Columbia University

In February 1925, Columbia University applied for a Memorial grant. Columbia's social scientists emphasized a rapidly changing world as the chief reason why their social science programmes needed strengthening. Columbia's approach resembled arguments made by other schools; however, Columbia's social scientists added at least two unique lines of reasoning: social scientists were in a critical phase of work in attempting to overcome cultural lag, and this critical phase involved the need for more quantitative research methods.[57]

Columbia's social scientists made their case for financial support. The fact that 'research in the social sciences has turned largely from qualitative to quantitative methods' was a major reason why cooperation was needed across the social sciences. There were at least two special needs: one was to play catch-up to a changed technological world; the other was to become more interconnected with each other in order to attain the fullest benefits from quantification. A selling point for their argument that they were uniquely suited to make quantification a focal point was a much-acclaimed work at the time, *Negro Migration* (1920), authored by Columbia University sociologist T. J. Woofter. The book was on the subject of the African-American 'Great Migration', and it was a work which represented the first major application of multiple regression techniques in social science.[58]

Columbia's social scientists also explained to the Memorial that they aimed 'to consider ways and means whereby their common interests in research in the Social Sciences might be encouraged and supported through mutual cooperation'. Financial support would assist their effort to better organize communications between all departments in the social sciences, 'which have a common interest in encouraging research in the social sciences generally'. Communications also needed to improve between social scientists and persons practising social technology.[59]

Columbia's grant proposal was fairly specific by identifying thirteen potential projects, ranging from studies in animal behaviour, to anthropology, to international economics. Some projects fit nicely with the established interests of the Memorial, whereas others fit nicely with Columbia's interest in the quantitative nature of the social sciences. One particular area of projects would be to study managerial approaches in business; this was something that Columbia described as being an aim, in part, to be 'a systematic and critical study of the laws – both judicial and legislative – governing the organization, control, and financing of American business corporations'. Columbia's social scientists noted their willingness 'to criticize existing law from the point of view of its effectiveness in service to the public welfare, and even to suggest what changes in the law are desirable'. It would be 'essential to study, more systematically than has ever been done before', the nature of 'corporate conduct which is conditioned by this law'. In effect, Columbia's social scientists wanted to evaluate policy. 'Economics, like all the other social sciences, tends to lag', and specifically it lags behind changes in the real world 'which form its subject matter'.[60]

Columbia received a substantial Memorial grant in May 1925, with which they established a research centre. Columbia's projects were fairly wide-ranging, although there were some interconnecting themes. Columbia's research programme grew quickly, especially with international projects in focus. Their social scientists also had an outstanding reputation for public service, and this interest was maintained through their newfound financial stability, which among other things allowed for the hiring of more replacement faculty. The school was also just coming out of a period of some turmoil. Back in 1917, at a time of uncertainty about US involvement in the First World War, a handful of Columbia professors were dismissed for protesting against new laws denying fundamental freedoms of expression. One of those dismissed was James McKeen Cattell, an important professor of psychology. A week later, historian Charles Beard resigned in protest over a general climate in which the trustees of the school will 'drive out or humiliate or terrorize every man who held progressive, liberal, or unconventional views on political matters'. In the half a dozen years that followed, John Bates Clark, Bassett Moore and Munroe Smith (editor of the *Political Science Quarterly*) all retired in some frustration.[61]

But during the time of the Memorial's support, new hiring increased, and many fine works were supported for publication. From the faculty in the department of public law and government came Lindsay Rogers's *The American Senate* (1926), Munroe Smith's post-retirement volumes *A General View of European Legal History* (1927) and *The Development of European Law* (1928), and Raymond Moley's *Politics and Criminal Prosecution* (1929) and *Our Criminal Courts* (1930). From the faculty in the department of sociology came Edmund Brunner's *Rural Korea* (1928) and *Immigrant Farmers and their Children* (1929),

Frank Ross's *The Near East and American Philanthropy* (1929), and Robert Morrison MacIver's *Society, Its Structure and Changes* (1932). Memorial funds were also used in 1931 to establish the Parker Institute of International Affairs, an institute that fit well with the Memorial's goals. The institute was designed, in the words of Columbia's Dean of the Law School, Howard Lee McBain, to 'enrich and to supplement, not to duplicate nor to absorb that which long has been and still is under way'. Initiated by the institute, and pushed forward with the support of a 1934 Rockefeller Foundation grant, was a series of volumes on 'the principle of neutrality' as a doctrine of international relations.[62]

By 1926, the school proposed a stand-alone project as well. This was aimed at studying interactions between economic, cultural and political situations in France. Post-war conditions in France were seen as representing 'a most significant laboratory of the social sciences', a situation in which capitalism, communism, socialism, nationalism and even Italian fascism were all somehow battling it out for primacy in organizing a nation's political and governmental forces. The Memorial approved this particular grant. All told, by 1929 the total number of projects that Columbia's social scientists operated with the Memorial's financial support expanded to thirty-one, and by the end of the decade, projects also included research on causes and consequences of African-American migration and the economics of industrialization in the Far East.[63]

## Harvard University

In February 1926, at the encouragement of eminent Harvard University physiologist Lawrence Joseph Henderson, Harvard's School of Business Administration recruited G. Elton Mayo from the University of Pennsylvania. Harvard's business faculty wanted to study psychological adjustment in an industrial economy. With Mayo in residence at Harvard, Ruml and the Memorial trustees soon decided to designate Harvard as one of five Memorial-supported research centres in the social sciences.[64]

By the 1920s, the scientific status of social research was advancing nicely in a number of fields at Harvard. Good work in anthropology had been underway at Harvard's Peabody Museum for over a half century, and a renowned department of political economy was also established at the school during the 1870s. By the 1890s, the school also featured an outstanding department of government. Yet by the early 1920s, Harvard still had no department of sociology.[65]

The explanation for why Harvard waited so long to establish sociology is that the field was seen as lacking 'rigor' enough to fit within an established disciplinary organization at the school. But this was something of a traditional organizational structure, and it could change, particularly if and when significant outside money arrived.[66]

It wasn't that simple of course. Harvard's administrators applied some serious thought to it all. They recognized that a guiding framework for social inquiry already existed at Harvard. A long-running department of social ethics tended to cast a bit of a shadow over all other areas of social inquiry at the school. Long-time University President Charles William Eliot oversaw the creation of the department back in 1869, and for forty years until his retirement in 1909, the university strongly favoured a blend of philosophical and reformist approaches to social inquiry. The guiding framework that came from such an emphasis was a belief that, largely through inductive reasoning, there will emerge an identification of a single principle of social order. The new president, A. Lawrence Lowell, who was originally a professor of government, maintained this emphasis as well.[67]

In February 1926, Harvard submitted to the Memorial an invited proposal that evidently had been requested for some time. A centrepiece research focus, as Harvard described it, would involve Mayo's style of industrial psychology as part of an experimental programme to study mental health problems in the workplace. Harvard believed that great benefits should result from applying Mayo's ideas and methods. Thus the proposed programme would focus on connections between physiology, psychology and the physical nature of the workplace. '[T]he cultural benefits of Dr. Mayo's work to industry and business', declared Harvard's James Curtis, 'are of tremendous importance'. At the Memorial, Leonard Outhwaite received Harvard's proposal, as submitted by Curtis. Outhwaite informed Ruml that Mayo's ideas made sense as a way to deal 'with maladjusted individuals in industrial life and with the conditions in industry which tend to generate and foster maladjustment'. It seems probable that when the Memorial assessed Harvard's application, the school's reputation along with Mayo's presence were the only elements really necessary to obtain approval.[68]

In early 1927, a substantial Memorial grant went to Harvard. One of Harvard's prime responsibilities, according to a division of labour in the social sciences that was being created by the Memorial, was to study problems of mental and physical fatigue in the workplace. They were also to bring together and begin to interconnect a number of studies in this research field as was being done elsewhere. At Harvard, studies of such problems would be part of a research programme described as 'individual industrial efficiency'. But beyond this, Harvard was to receive enough support to become one of the Memorial's five major research centres.[69]

Harvard expressed a goal to better clarify the content and boundaries of psychological research. Such an objective was of real interest to psychologists at the time. The American Psychological Association was actively reevaluating its own division of subfields, and in 1926 they settled on distinctions between sixteen different 'fields' or 'schools' of psychology.[70]

With the Memorial's support, what grew most quickly at Harvard were the school's Psychological Clinic (est. 1926) and Fatigue Laboratory (est. 1927), the latter of which was connected with Harvard's School of Business Administration. One emphasized goal at Harvard was to better separate psychology from moral philosophy. In fact, as impacted by the infusion of targeted funds, the university's legendary department of social ethics came to an end in 1927.[71]

By January 1929, when the Memorial's programme was absorbed into the Rockefeller Foundation, Harvard's research projects in the social sciences included some half a dozen or so identifiable fields of study. Worth specific identification is their focus on economic studies of industrial hazards, while another important addition to their specialties was an emphasis on international relations.

When Harvard's new research programme in the social sciences is evaluated as a piece, all of their research efforts ultimately had two central goals. From the Memorial's perspective, one goal was to explore how far Mayo's ideas could reach. From Harvard's perspective, a grand goal was to transform fields of research that were still in a philosophical tradition into fields of research in an empirical tradition.[72]

## Conclusion

Between January 1923 and January 1929, the Laura Spelman Rockefeller Memorial helped to establish five university-based research centres in the social sciences. Each centre was relatively unique and non-overlapping with the others, and this was by design. Beyond the approach of establishing research centres, generous Memorial support also – over the same period of time – broadly targeted the development of some dozen or so research fields in the social sciences. One research field, as already introduced, was industrial psychology. The basic idea observed in that case was to coordinate a number of smaller-scale projects supported at many institutions.

# 7 RESEARCH FIELDS

## Introduction

Between 1922 and 1929, at the same time that the Memorial worked to build five research centres in the social sciences, it also focused on building about a dozen research fields in the social sciences. The Memorial did this by supporting many smaller-scale projects at numerous institutions. It is up to today's scholars to fully identify the specific research fields emphasized by the Memorial, at least in terms of their exact boundaries and definitions; it seems there was never any singular and definite statement by the Memorial to identify all of these fields. This chapter studies nine research fields: race relations in the United States; problems in the American South; problems in the American West; problems in non-capitalist regions; land usage and population change; group biological similarities and differences; child welfare and parent education; international relations; and coordinated data collection.

## Race Relations

The Memorial's main research centre for studying race relations was at the University of North Carolina. But given the profound impact of America's Great Migration that began in the 1910s, projects at both the University of Chicago and Columbia University were also involved in this research field. At the University of Chicago, social scientists studied matters of race relations within their local community research programme, where their chief focus was the process of assimilation. At Columbia University, social scientists focused on African-American communities embedded within and interacting with the social forces of a major city. But certainly everything that was needed from such a research field could not be accomplished at just a few institutions alone. The question to be asked was what kinds of research projects might best advance the scientific status of the field of race relations.[1]

During April and May 1925, the Memorial added some support for research on race relations in another northern city, Providence, Rhode Island. Problems of race relations were considered appropriate for study by social scientists at Brown University, who saw the city of Providence as uniquely set up as a natural experiment. The person best suited to direct the project was sociologist Bessie Bloom Wessel, who was new to the school's faculty. Ruml, who was unfamiliar with Wessel's accomplishments, requested additional information from outside people, until he was satisfied with the decency of Wessel's 'personality', as well as the 'scientific' nature of her work. Contact was initiated with James Quayle Dealey, chair of Brown University's department of social and political science. Dealey provided, to Guy Stanton Ford at the Memorial, a report from a number of Brown's social scientists who conveyed unanimous confidence in Wessel. Dealey remarked that Brown's social scientists asked that funds 'for a period of three years be granted so as to give a fair opportunity to make a thorough study of racial situations in the city of Providence'. Their proposal, prepared by Dealey's department, was supported by other departments as well, with all 'agree[ing] to give hearty cooperation in bringing the study to a successful conclusion'. The city of Providence represented something special, a city which 'with its industrial population so largely foreign in birth and descent, furnishes a splendid field for a racial study involving a constructive program'. What they had in mind as a 'racial study' included blacks, whites and all immigrant groups as well.[2]

Brown University received its grant. After a few years of success with their 'Study of Ethnic Factors in Community Life', Wessel applied to the Memorial for additional funding. But this time the funding was not to go to Brown University, since Wessel had decided to return to her old school, Connecticut College, then still a women's college. In connection with what Wessel figured made sense for a research emphasis at Connecticut College, the project she now proposed was to expand the original study, already in action in Providence, and which had developed into a study involving not only race relations, but also various other migration issues. Research work in urban Providence could serve as a training ground for younger social scientists and social workers, who could take their knowledge and apply it to similar applications of these 'laboratory techniques' in other cities. Hence a project that had begun by including a 'single study testing out techniques for the examination of population changes' of specific racial and ethnic groups was ready 'to supply a working base for any students who might be interested in experimental work in this field'. Wessel received her grant renewal in 1928.[3]

Another study in US race relations was in the northern city of Cleveland. In November 1925, faculty members at Western Reserve University applied for a grant to support their work to bring together social science and social work. They proposed to study a host of problems associated with a suddenly maladjusted, industrial–urban world. They were seeing first-hand much hardship in their city. 'Modern urban life has created a radically different society', they observed. 'There are many persons who cannot adjust themselves effectively to this new society;

their need for assistance has made social work an imperative necessity'. To help support more progressive social work, focused efforts were needed at two levels. One level of attention needed to include family welfare, child welfare, group services, health administration and public health nursing. Second, with race relations being especially severe in Cleveland, better work in the sciences of sociology and economics was also necessary. Western Reserve received a grant.[4]

In February 1926, researchers at Fisk University, a traditionally African-American institution in Nashville, applied for a five-year grant to study the economic progress of African Americans. The premier objective expressed in Fisk's application was to uncover 'well-attested' and 'true facts' about social and economic conditions of African-American communities in the South. Fisk hoped to restructure their department of social science, and they requested additional support to help develop black leadership programmes at the school. Fisk's social scientists may have been aware that this latter idea fitted well with the ideas of Howard Odum, which were already acknowledged by Ruml.[5]

Fisk's department of social sciences, in 1927, received a Memorial grant of $125,000 to reorganize and strengthen its department. Within just months the Memorial could evaluate some successes by Fisk's social scientists, and they saw that 'considerable progress' was made and being made 'in the development of scientific studies dealing with negro economic and social life'.[6]

The Memorial's support of Fisk provided an outstanding opportunity, and an extraordinary young social scientist saw this. Charles S. Johnson was one of the best graduate students that Robert E. Park ever had at the University of Chicago. Johnson, who was African-American, accepted a job at Fisk, and upon his arrival he prepared a focused memorandum in September 1928. Johnson recommended that Fisk would be wise to select one area of research on which to focus. He concurred with others that 'the most logical field is that of the Negro and Race Relations in the United States', and he added that it was enough to focus on the city of Nashville: an 'ideal laboratory as an educational centre'. The city had a large African-American population, and it was 'within reach of interesting rural communities'. Johnson suggested some specific projects, and with the school's administration on his side, he went forward and recruited outstanding graduate students. Johnson, with these students, soon built a great department. In 1930, with the help of Memorial funds, Johnson published *The Negro in American Civilization*.[7]

A primary geographical emphasis for studying race relations needed to be made throughout the American South, and potentially the projects at UNC and Fisk did not yet support all the research that was needed. Southern attitudes toward race relations were, according to increasing numbers of social intelligentsia, in a state of acute maladjustment. Leadership at the Memorial decided that more attention needed to focus on Southern race relations. But the question was, how?

Higher level discussions were needed. In various grant applications as well as internal memoranda, problems of race relations were seen as stemming largely from economic circumstances. If the problem was differential rates of crime between whites and blacks, then the root cause should be found to be largely economic. If the issue was contributions to overall economic production, then black workers could be interpreted as representing an underemployed asset. The Memorial's focus for research in race relations should be to identify problems for which comparable classes of facts can be obtained for both black and white groups.

In January 1925, at a time when the Memorial was still much involved in discussing how to establish a research programme in 'concrete Negro problems' at the University of North Carolina, Ruml obtained a report from James W. C. Dougall, a leading missionary advocate for education in Africa, and an outside advisor to the Memorial. Dougall, who was informed about the contemporary movement called Pan-Africanism, focused on the conditions of African-American education in the South. But his focus was ultimately not so much on educational methods 'in practice', but 'on the social reactions of negro education' – that is, 'the study of results as they are to be seen in the life of the negro communities and the relationship existing between white and coloured people in the South'. The pernicious problem, the report concluded, was not any intrinsic inequalities between race groups, but the beliefs harboured by white southerners about such supposed inequalities. Fortunately some southern white leadership was emerging with a focus on advancing an equalitarian mindset. 'The proof of the negro's progress lies not only in what he has accomplished when given the chance but by the growing sentiment of faith in his possibilities which can be clearly seen in all sections of the South'. The fundamental factor, the report pragmatically concluded, was that white persons in the South have, if nothing else, begun to recognize black persons as people with 'value as an economic asset in the community'. What the South needed was to create more job opportunities. 'It has been seen that the South must offer greater inducements if the Negro is to refuse the call of the North with its greater wages, more abundant school facilities, and the removal of disadvantages, fears, and persecutions'.[8]

Another report on race relations, produced in April 1926 by the Memorial's Leonard Outhwaite, was substantial as well. Outhwaite offered some thirty-five pages of analysis that aimed to 'set out some general facts regarding the position of the Negro in American social life'. He addressed possible research methods by writing that 'an increasing acquaintance with the field leads me to believe that the general approach and methods advocated are the most likely to yield scientific and social results'. Any uncritical focus was unwelcome, as there would be no easy solution for America's race problem 'as a whole', or 'as a thing in itself'. Any reasonable and responsible social scientist should attempt to make 'systematic' analysis along 'broad functional lines of the various physical and social facts on which

Negro life is based'. What was needed was to study all aspects of race relations as a whole, and the best way to do this was through comparative study. Studies of any particular facet of African-American life 'should, wherever possible, be joined to similar studies or activities being carried on in the whole group' of Americans. At a time when so many social scientists focused on ideas about the 'unity' of the social sciences, Outhwaite emphasized that not every scientific method might be appropriate anymore. Such measurement approaches as psychometry and anthropometry were anathema. In contrast, a 'major field of genuine social as well as scientific importance' was psychopathology, which was quite needed, especially given that facilities 'for insane Negroes' were severely lacking.[9]

Outhwaite recommended undertaking more studies of 'negro crime and the negro criminal', and he advocated increased attention to research on 'negro business and negro credit', 'negro education' and 'negro legal justice'. In all of these cases, what stood out was a need to investigate environmental rather than innate factors. 'New economic and social pressures are developing and migration continues as a symptomatic phenomenon', he observed. 'In particular the mores and social customs which served an older generation as methods of control and of adjustment are breaking up or are no longer adequate'. Greater opportunities elsewhere, coupled with broken community ties at home, could be seen as contributing to the increased rate of black migration. More community-level studies were needed to better understand the complex nature of this phenomenon, and all of the social sciences were needed to begin 'approaching the whole field along a variety of functional lines' – notably, living conditions (e.g. building, housing, sanitation); economic conditions (e.g. employment, business, credit); health conditions (physical and mental); schools, legal and penal problems; mental well-being and social and political relationships. When all of these interconnected lines of analysis are understood to be parts of concrete, real-world subject matter, 'the problems of Negro life' will be seen to be 'largely parallels of the problems of White life but appearing in a different context'.[10]

All persons interested in scientific studies of race relations must be realists. Perhaps recalling what UNC sociologist Guy B. Johnson had already expressed as a perceived need for any changes in southern race relations to be slowly executed, Outhwaite held that the pursuit of a scientific approach to race relations

> should not obscure the fact that we are faced ... with the belief, and the behaviours growing out of the belief, that these physical differences are attended by differences in capacity and adjustment which demand, for one group, necessary specialized treatment.

What mattered, in effect, was not the reality of any equalities or inequalities, but simply that too many people still believed in race inequalities – 'that as a social phenomenon, race counts because we think it counts'.[11]

There was also a third report on race relations, this one compiled by the Memorial itself. The 1927 report, titled 'Race Relations and Negro Work', aimed to clarify reasons for undertaking an 'intensification of effort' to promote a 'reasonable' rate of change. The Memorial introduced its view: 'That development in this field should take place slowly is both natural and desirable'. The report noted a widespread belief in the need for slow adjustments in race relations, and some reasons were offered for somewhat agreeing with such a view:

> That progress should be slow arises in part from the very nature of the field: from the fact that many of the important features of negro life and interracial relations have in the past been the subject of imperfect knowledge and acrimonious debate rather than of scientific inquiry.

The idea, in essence, was that the South was simply not ready for any scientific plan to direct any rapid transformation in race relations. Yet there was also a counterpoint, which was that one particular contribution to slow progress in race relations was

> the fact that aside from the sensational features of racial and social conflict there has been a certain public apathy which is frequently reflected in the work of organizations whose activities might properly cover negro as well as white welfare.

The stated problem, to be clear, was that many welfare organizations equally address circumstances in white and black communities.[12]

Leading persons at the Memorial held great confidence in the potential for achievements of the highest order, by all persons. The general belief was that southern race relations unfolded as an historical accident, and that a paced approach to remedying the situation was what was needed. This was not because of some belief that any individual persons were not capable of making great strides of self-improvement, but because of an idea that the greatest prospect for long-term success in lifting everyone out of their impoverishment was to provide opportunities for the entire African-American community to be lifted and to lift itself as one.

With respect to studies of race relations, the report concluded that

> the amount of work undertaken has to a certain extent been determined by deliberate Memorial policy ... The Memorial has felt that an orderly development along a variety of lines, negro education, the development of public welfare agencies and of channels for inter-racial cooperation was greatly to be preferred to a sudden or spectacular development in any of these fields.

A many-pronged attack on the problem was necessary, and should be performed based 'upon the results of scientific studies and deliberate inquiry'.[13]

Special meetings were now considered useful to arrange. One conference was in December 1927, on 'Problems of Contemporary Negro Life and of the Field of Interracial Relations'. Planned by the Memorial and held at Yale University, this was actually a 'confidential' gathering of some specific invitees, including 'heads of negro educational institutions, leaders of negro national organizations, and white administrators of organizations working in the interracial field'. James R. Angell, president of Yale, attended, as did Leonard Outhwaite, on behalf of the Memorial. It seems that the main result that we know of from the conference was a plan for another conference.[14]

Leaders at the Memorial organized the next conference for December 1928, on the topic of 'Race Problems in the United States in the Light of Social Research'. The purpose of the conference was to survey existing research, and to plan a future research programme. The Memorial, working with other groups including the Russell Sage Foundation, helped pull off the conference, which took place in Washington, DC. Participants produced reports on topics relating to health, education, industry and agriculture, housing and education, crime, citizenship and race relations. Conference reports were brief statements generally declaring that more research was needed.[15]

In March 1929 (two months after the Rockefeller Foundation absorbed the Memorial's programme), an open conference was convened to discuss black welfare programmes. A question as a focal point for the conference, which historian Vanessa Northington Gamble has identified, was this: did enough data exist 'to determine whether blacks were worth educating'? Ruml attended the conference, and thinking scientifically and using results from recent scientific arguments, he reasoned 'that although the average intelligence of blacks was lower, variability would compensate and thus make the support of black education a worthwhile endeavor for the Rockefeller philanthropies'.[16]

## Problems in the American South

The American South was of great interest to the Memorial. In addition to research on race relations, some sort of a broader research field also seemed possible. In April 1925, Ruml, Outhwaite, Odum and Chase made their great car trip across the South. Many of the schools that they planned to visit contacted the Memorial with expressions of interest. Some of these schools began their letters with ideas about connecting with projects already planned at UNC.

In January 1925, while the Memorial and UNC were still negotiating the possibility of a major grant, and while the car trip was some still six weeks away, Vanderbilt University contacted the Memorial. Vanderbilt's social scientists wondered if they might help with any projects to be undertaken at UNC. They explained that their school could particularly be strengthened by better connecting their own social science departments. Vanderbilt's Chancellor, J. H. Kirkland, wrote to the Memorial to arrange a meeting with Ruml. The letter described

Vanderbilt's departmental organization, which featured thirteen social scientists divided between five departments. The letter briefly described twenty-four projects that they had in mind. Mostly the projects focused on problems pertinent to the state, which ranged from 'the economic position' of African Americans in Tennessee, to 'the county court in Tennessee', to 'the social origins of the aggressive personality'. This last point was important, as it indicated their intent to study nurture over nature. Vanderbilt hoped for support to add three or four new professors in the social sciences, who would fill gaps in their unifying structure of the social sciences. Kirkland nicely employed the sort of language that the Memorial tended to respond to, as he noted in particular the school's respected programmes in 'social technology'.[17]

Ruml responded by asking Kirkland to apply more thought to any truly unique contributions that Vanderbilt could offer. An interaction process continued for nearly a year, and in November 1925 Ruml interviewed Kirkland. Ruml aimed to help the process by emphasizing that the Memorial did not want 'to simply support the traditional type of teaching in social science'. Each of Vanderbilt's social scientists needed to show 'an interest in any new experiments' that might be undertaken, and the hope was that Vanderbilt would prove well prepared to explore experiments in teaching social science. Yet more clarifications were necessary in Vanderbilt's proposal.[18]

Ruml contacted Vanderbilt's Dean of Social Sciences, Walter L. Fleming, in January 1926. Ruml decided to help guide Vanderbilt's efforts to articulate innovative experimental approaches in pedagogy. Ruml's interactions with Fleming were direct: 'The Memorial now has under consideration the question of strengthening undergraduate as well as graduate work in the social sciences'. All possibilities for improving undergraduate education needed to be kept in mind as Vanderbilt refined their proposal; however, Ruml also pointed out that 'no final decision has been reached as to whether we should enter this field'. Ruml asked Fleming to continue providing information regarding Vanderbilt's plans for developing social science education, 'both from the standpoint of research and undergraduate instruction'.[19]

Vanderbilt's revised application, dated April 1926, asked for five years' support. Its main goal was to better 'correlate' the social sciences, in both undergraduate and graduate curricula. The revised application described thirty-four projects with enough substance that the Memorial could hone in on what it wanted. Ruml responded with a request for still more information about two issues in particular. When it came to undergraduates, he wanted to know about 'problems and methods in the study and teaching of the social sciences'. When it came to teaching graduate students, he expressed his interest in seeing Vanderbilt 'guide the student in working across the field regardless of departmental lines'. Vanderbilt concurred that these were goals that it wanted, and it received a grant. What we see in the case of Vanderbilt University's efforts to obtain a grant is a situation in which Ruml and the Memorial encouraged the applicant in such a way that they could sharpen some ideas for how certain projects could uniquely contribute to the Memorial's broad programme.[20]

The University of Virginia also wanted to join with UNC. In March 1925, E. A. Alderman, president of the school, contacted Ruml to invite him to a meeting during the planned southern road trip. Alderman recommended a personal chat so that he could showcase the school's work in the social sciences, which were his 'chief concern for some years'. About the same time, Alderman also contacted Wickliffe Rose of the Foundation's International Education Board. He shared with Rose how impressed he was by Ruml's work underway at the Memorial. In these letters to Ruml and Rose, Alderman added his idea that UNC's planned research centre might be nicely extended to include the University of Virginia. Social scientists at Virginia were working on a grant application that would reinforce the opinion that southern institutions were lagging and maladjusted. The South was a region in need of some good social science.[21]

Ruml visited Charlottesville in April 1925, and he was encouraged by what he found there. Yet following the visit it took eight more months before Ruml made a second visit to the school, in part because he took a lengthy vacation to Europe. In January 1926, UNC's Howard Odum contacted Ruml to add his word on Virginia's behalf: 'We do not know of any step in the South which would help the whole situation now more than a definite progressive movement at the University of Virginia in the social sciences'. Alderman also wrote, contributing more of his thoughts:

> The greatest need of the State of Virginia at the present time is for scientifically determined information regarding the vital problems in the life of its people and their institutions through which this life seeks to find its highest expression.

Alderman hoped that a major grant could help remedy 'many defects in the path of southern development'. The University of Virginia was now well into planning stages for improving their social science programmes, with a goal to organize six departments into a single Institute for Research in the Social Sciences – which, said the application, would be 'modeled somewhat after Columbia and Carolina'.[22]

Ruml again went to Charlottesville, this time in March 1926, to meet with President Alderman. A few social scientists joined in the meeting, including agricultural economist Wilson Gee. Ruml asked Alderman to contact more of the school's social scientists and gather descriptions of the kinds of problems that they could study. Alderman did this and reported back that he could now provide 'a more concrete idea' of what the school's social scientists 'wish, with your help, to get under way at this institution'. Alderman submitted a 'Suggested

Program' identifying nine specific problems. The overall stated goal was to study 'very concrete situations' in Virginia. All they needed was money. '[T]he curse of intellectual undertakings in the south and southern institutions', Alderman opined, 'has been in attempting to do big things with small means, to make bricks without straws'.[23]

In June 1926, the University of Virginia received a five-year Memorial grant. The Memorial followed the award by contacting Professor Gee, who Alderman appointed as director of the institute. The Memorial encouraged Gee to emphasize to the school's social scientists that they should have no aim to merely imitate research at UNC. Virginia's research programme, Gee concurred, was to be uniquely suited to 'very concrete situations' in the state. One noteworthy product of the grant money was a 1929 volume, edited by Gee, entitled *Research in the Social Sciences: Its Fundamental Methods and Objectives*.[24]

## Problems in the American West

There was another major university that wished to join an enlarged southern research centre. This institution, however, is actually located in the American south-west. In January 1926, University of Texas president W. M. W. Splawn contacted the Memorial. Splawn asked whether his school's social scientists could begin any work in conjunction with projects underway at UNC. Perhaps having learned from the Memorial's responses to Vanderbilt and Virginia when they asked to join with UNC, Splawn included a bit of an advertisement for the regional uniqueness of problems in Texas. Ruml responded that no extension of any projects was planned, and what UNC's social scientists were doing was 'on a purely experimental basis' in that region. Splawn needed to think about research opportunities uniquely 'concerning the Texas situation'. Ruml was willing to help Splawn get some of his thoughts in order. Texas reworked its grant application, to which was added the awareness of Ruml's desire that Texas contribute toward better 'coordinating the work in the social sciences'.[25]

Splawn took charge of the application's revision. He identified the school's separate departments of anthropology, economics, sociology, government, history and psychology, and he emphasized a goal to use any received support 'To promote closer and more stimulating relationships between the faculties of the several departments of the social sciences'. Separation of the departments had been 'in large part artificial', and was definitely 'disadvantageous' to any continued advancement of useful social science. The ideal situation would be that researchers in all these departments 'should work in cooperation with one another on a common problem or problems', and would come to 'realize more clearly the importance of each of the social sciences as an approach to the study of man and his environment'. Texas's grant application focused especially on the diversity of peoples and conditions in the vast Texas region, which 'truly constitutes an empire'. Texas's social scientists recommended 'studies relating to the conditions and the problems of the Southwest, such as the study of the Mexican population in this section of the country'. Overall they now recognized that they could best merit a grant if they studied social and economic problems unique to their region, and did so by using all of the social sciences.[26]

Texas received a Memorial grant. President Splawn then resigned his university presidency, and assumed directorship over research projects under the grant. That aside, the strategy that helped to produce success for the University of Texas's application was the case that they made for their regional uniqueness in terms of social and economic problems. They did not receive a major research centre, but they certainly received generous support.[27]

The University of Texas was not the first western school to make a case for its regional uniqueness. At least two other schools developed strong arguments along similar lines, perhaps to play into the Memorial's strategy to maximize coverage of research fields. These schools were Denver University and Stanford University.

In April 1925, Denver University – a premier research university in the Rocky Mountain region – presented its case that the Memorial should direct attention to certain social and economic problems in the West. Denver's social scientists claimed that social problems and welfare issues were unique enough in the Rocky Mountain region to merit detailed study. They said that any attempted 'organization of the economic facts pertaining to the great area west of the Mississippi and Missouri Rivers presented one of the important social problems of today. The future of this area', they added, 'depends upon the enlistment of outside capital'. One great need was for resources to support 'some agency of a scientific nature that can take the problem of organizing the economic information of the Rocky Mountain and Prairie States and work it out'. Denver's letter of inquiry was well received at the Memorial.[28]

Upon receiving Ruml's encouragement, Denver University set about developing a specific plan to undertake projects 'directed toward the collection of fundamental statistical data dealing with the physical, economic, industrial, business, social, political and legal aspects of this region'. Denver's social scientists had in mind a unified research programme that would employ all of the social sciences at once. Included in their studies would be regional consumption patterns, growth and character of regional population and various other practical needs in the West.[29]

Denver's proposal arrived at the Memorial where Arthur Woods expressed his belief in it. Denver's social scientists had not expressed any interests in developing mere theory; they were interested in helping a region. Yet Woods worried that a grant to Denver might encourage a precedent resulting in an 'avalanche of appeals' based solely on some argument about geographical uniqueness. Such a danger could be avoided by including some specific research on the training of mining engineers. Ruml accepted Woods's recommendation, yet he also sought some outside feedback. After a final round of interactions within the Memorial, in November 1925 Denver received a three-year grant.[30]

Stanford University also claimed regional uniqueness. In May 1926, Stanford's School of Social Sciences suggested that the state of California was a distinct enough social and economic unit to merit specific study. They hoped to initiate research in such fields as local water conservation, public finance in the region and cooperative marketing practices in the West. They also wanted to expand a programme of inter-racial studies in California, and they wished to strengthen their programme of Russian studies, especially Russia's Pacific coastal presence.[31]

After some interactions with the Memorial, through which Stanford's social scientists slightly elevated their emphasis on the regional nature of their projects, in March 1927 Stanford received a five-year grant.[32]

Taken together, the University of Texas, Denver University and Stanford University were capable of being seen as representing a research field, one defined and supported on a geographical basis as a field focused on problems in the American West.

## Problems in Non-Capitalist Regions

Leadership at the Memorial also believed that an important research field could involve studies of various problems overseas. To tie it all together, perhaps one major goal was to learn what might work within regions of the world where national systems were not purely democratic and capitalist. A second goal was to find ways to help people in such regions, including preparing them for eventual participation in Western-style democracy and capitalism (if and when they were allowed such participation). The Memorial decided to apply funds toward such research with respect to the Far East, the Middle East, Russia, Africa and even Europe.

By the 1920s, one focus at the Rockefeller Foundation was to support education in China. Rockefeller, Sr, motivated by his religious convictions, had worked with Frederick Gates to help establish a new university in China. The university, to be modelled in some ways on the University of Chicago, was to develop home-grown leadership that could help 'civilize' the nation. The main idea, according to a report at the time, was that scientific rationality 'was the solution to the riddle of China's modernization'.[33]

One important goal for the Foundation during the 1910s was to introduce modern scientific medicine to China. This it began doing in 1914 by establishing the China Medical Board. In 1919, aided by the Board's funding, a new medical school began operations as the Peking Union Medical College (PUMC).

The PUMC's ultimate mission, as Rockefeller, Jr phrased it, was to contribute to China's 'mental development and spiritual culture'. One of the six departments in the PUMC was a Social Service Department, and the presence of such a department, says historian Thomas Rosenbaum, 'gives further evidence that the PUMC administration sought to establish a completely up-to-date medical school and hospital where the practice of medicine was informed by a concern for the emotional needs of the patients and staff'. This objective, in other words, could draw the social sciences into the picture.[34]

During Ruml's period of leadership at the Memorial, the Memorial's officers identified some of their own opportunities in China. They believed that a supported project might do especially well if it aimed to teach the people about economic, cultural and political matters of the West. A specific proposal came to the Memorial in 1928, from social scientists at Yenching University, a missionary college in Peking. The proposal described an idea for studying a natural experiment; the idea was that entire regions of the world can lag behind the world's industrially advanced regions. Yenching University, established in 1916, had begun a programme of economics education by 1917, as introduced there by British-trained economist, John Bernard Taylor. Economic analysis, as Taylor taught it, was similar to a contemporary movement in America known as 'institutional economics', which aimed to make economics relevant to real-world institutions.[35]

The Memorial's leading mind in economics was Lawrence Frank, who understood the kind of economics taught by Taylor. Taylor's activities at Yenching were soon joined by three more economists, one from Europe and two from China; and by 1928, as historian Paul Trescott observes, the group of economists at Yenching had an overriding objective 'to develop innovative institutional forms to enhance China's economic performance'.[36]

The Memorial's interest in China became an interest in assessing the consequences of China's own historical circumstances. This came about when, in March 1928, Yenching University's social scientists submitted their grant proposal with a stated belief that the rate of social and economic development in China had been delayed. If China's social and economic institutions had a chance to catch up to where they should be, then not only could China be assisted, but all other nations would benefit as well. Yenching's social scientists introduced their arguments that 'China will in the future become a very important part of the family of nations', and that 'earnest effort is being made to improve human conditions in the country and to evolve, through education, a system that will elevate the Chinese and command the respect of Western nations'. Yenching's social scientists emphasized the need to discover 'the facts and conditions' that caused such 'a slow evolution' of a region of the world to begin with. They used language that Ruml liked, as they requested financial assistance 'to knit closely together all departments of study, instruction, and research constituting the social sciences'. Social scientists could thus 'unite' in investigating, 'with unbiased clarity of observation', the true facts about China's evolution. Yenching's social scientists would not judge, but would 'discover where the economic factor is dominant and where the social factor is [dominant]', in accounting for how China had fallen so far behind the rest of the world.[37]

In the last year of the Memorial, they became a major supporter of Yenching University. The school's social science departments received a substantial grant of $140,000 for seven years. Development of the social sciences in China was thus able to begin from a foundation that enabled many of China's social scientists to study economics overseas and return to Chinese universities. By the early 1930s, with financial support from both the Memorial and the Foundation, the development of economics programmes were greatly underway at Yenching University, as well as at Nankai Institute of Economics (in Tientsin) and the Agricultural Economics Department of the College of Agriculture and Forestry in Nanking University. All three efforts are considered success stories.[38]

Another source of support for the social sciences in China came from Rockefeller, Jr. For in addition to the work that was supported by the Memorial and the Foundation, Rockefeller, Jr decided, in 1925, to support the Institute of Pacific Relations (IPR). In December 1930, British economist and historian R. H. Tawney visited the Nankai Institute in connection with his IPR-sponsored study of China's economy. Based on his research during the visit, Tawney published *Land and Labour in China* (1932). Another important book, *Chinese Farm Economy* (1930) by J. L. Buck, also had the support of IPR funds, which enabled the processing of much survey data for the book. Thus when it came to Rockefeller support of the social sciences in China, the fertilization of ideas went both into and out of China.[39]

China was by no means the only foreign nation capable of attracting the attention of Rockefeller philanthropy. The Memorial had an interest in supporting education programmes for Russians. In addition to the support for research on Russia, in early 1923 the Memorial helped to establish a programme to support Russian students who were dislocated to other nations. According to one of Ruml's outside advisors, displaced Russian students needed to be ready for when 'the time comes and Russia does straighten out'. The belief, then still widespread through the West, was that Russia would soon rejoin the free world. Ruml evaluated the idea to support student émigrés, but he first needed to obtain proof that a group called the 'Russian Student Fund' was legitimate. The organization needed to be incorporated under US law, as such a status would be important given that communist Russia had formed a recent habit of unilaterally cancelling international debts. Ruml obtained trustee approval for a grant to support Russian students who were interested in pursuing their education outside of Russia.[40]

Still another approach to employing Memorial funds in a non-capitalist region could be to support research that might aim to discover what happens when a non-capitalist economy operates on its own terms. Because non-capitalist economies already existed, they might as well be studied.

In March 1925, the Memorial became interested in Russia along just such a line. This interest developed when it began to seem likely that post-revolutionary Russia might sustain their planned economy for some time to come. Therefore it was time to consider Russia's economy as an 'experiment'. A Stanford University research group proposed gathering data on Russia's economy, and they phrased their purpose with care:

> In making a study of the revolution the purpose should be to ascertain what the leaders of the movement hoped to bring about, how far they succeeded and failed, and the actions and reactions of their experiments on society. It should not be the object of the study to prove anything in particular, but merely to gather such social, economic, and psychological data as can be had at the present time.

The Russian Revolution, Stanford's F. A. Golder added, 'should be studied as a social experiment in the making'.[41]

Memorial officials were willing to go along with the reasoning that since it happened that there was this unprecedented experiment of partitioning an industrializing nation 'into economic units according to resources and industries' (these being Golder's words), scientists might as well study whether any such division into economic sectors could rest on fundamental truths about the organization of an industrializing economy. Because financial support for such studies was highly unlikely to come from any university endowments, the Memorial agreed to fill the gap, doing so with a two-year grant to Stanford.[42]

Another example of ideas about capitalism being introduced to people living in non-capitalist regions arose in connection with a school in Beirut, Lebanon. An objective for the Memorial was to promote better research and teaching in all the social sciences, which could include 'commercial studies'; and the American University of Beirut was an appropriate place to emphasize such teaching. In 1925 the Memorial trustees approved six years of support for two new professors at the school. Each was to be a person 'native' to the region, and each was to help prepare students to participate in world business.[43]

As to the Memorial's support of the social sciences in Africa, this story is more subtle than most. Potentially the story began in 1925, when two speakers came to New York City to discuss conditions in Africa. They made their presentations before two different meetings of the Interboard Luncheons, which were held for leaders representing all of the Rockefeller philanthropies. Thomas Jesse Jones, a progressive educational reformer and the education director of the Phelps-Stokes Fund, presented a discussion on 25 May 1925. His topic was education and health in Africa. Later that same year, on 26 October 1925, Dr J. H. Oldham of the International Missionary Council discussed the needs of Africa, and how philanthropy might help. Oldham discussed plans for an International Institute for African Language and Culture. In October of the following year, the Memorial voted to support the institute, based in London, at a rate of $5,000 a year for five years.[44]

Also during 1925–6, representatives of the Memorial discussed in some detail an idea to support scientific studies in Africa on a general theme of 'race psychology'. They met with Clark Wissler, an American anthropologist with a PhD in psychology, who recommended doing simultaneous studies, one in Africa and one in black populations in the West Indies. These could be comparative projects designed to find out more about the psyches of people who were working to overcome a lack of freedom during a life within a repressive regime. Memorial advisors also visited with a former missionary in Africa, Ellsworth Farris, who recommended doing a similar study in the Congo, where a highly brutal Belgian colonialism had ended some decades earlier.[45]

In November 1927, Leonard Outhwaite of the Memorial met with Edgar Brookes, the South African representative in the League of Nations, and a leader with the South African Institute for Race Relations. The two discussed various possibilities for better developing the social sciences in South Africa, although in this case no specific funding decision was made by the Memorial.[46]

The idea to interpret a situation in a non-capitalist region as an experiment came up quite explicitly in the case of Sweden's 'mixed' economy. Communications began during 1924 and 1925, when Swedish economists contacted the Memorial to say that their nation truly represented a 'laboratory for social research'. An experiment in a new kind of 'welfare state' was in action, prompted by the demand of the Swedish people. Faculty at the University of Stockholm wanted to learn all they could from Sweden's experiments. A cadre of social scientists and social workers were already prepared at the school, and they asked for a five-year grant. One particular stated objective, which was agreeable to the Memorial, was to use a grant award to promote tighter connection between the social sciences and social technologies at the school.[47]

An interesting matter is how the University of Stockholm's grant proposal made its way to the Memorial. In September 1924, Swedish economist Gösta Bagge came to New York City. Bagge arrived at Ruml's office with a letter of introduction in hand. The letter, from Russell Sage Foundation Director John M. Glenn, helped Bagge through the door, whereupon he worked to persuade Ruml that a lack of funds prevented fulfillment of the school's goal 'to initiate and carry on scientific research in the social and municipal field'. Bagge added that 'There is in fact no institution in Scandinavia today where scientific social research is being carried out on a systematic plan', and such a lack of research was 'unfortunate not only from a Scandinavian point of view, but also it seems from an international viewpoint'. The community of nations could benefit if Sweden's social scientists received support to 'analyze properly from a scientific point of view' the consequences of the various sorts of institutional innovations being tried in Sweden – including an eight-hour working day, regulation of wages and the creation of a Swedish Trade Union.[48]

Ruml had never before met Bagge, and he did not just hand over the money. Ruml responded to Bagge's inquiry by seeking outside advice. He contacted two economists, Gustav Cassel in Sweden and William Beveridge in London. Cassel was likely to provide the most valued feedback, and in fact did so, through Beveridge. Cassel, a friend of Bagge, decided to express some doubt as to whether the University of Stockholm could 'concentrate itself upon forming the habit of scientific thinking'. He was willing to believe that the school potentially could serve 'to fill up the former lack of economic education of those who take care, in the democratic society of ours, of local government and of social work generally'.

Following Ruml's push for more details, Bagge responded in June 1925. In what became the successful grant application, awarded in November 1925 for $75,000, Bagge emphasized that, 'from a scientific point of view', Sweden is 'in many respects an almost ideal "laboratory" for social research'. Many variables could be held relatively constant:

> Sweden is a small, well administered country with a homogeneous population, which makes it so much easier to get the necessary statistical and other material to isolate social phenomena, to make observations without all the bewildering tendencies in different directions, which characterizes the large countries and their mixed populations.[49]

The Memorial's interest in studying Sweden's national economic controls connected to ideas about imbalances between social science and social technology. There was an opinion at the time that while social science in Europe lagged behind even the tardy arrival of modern social science in the United States, applied social knowledge (i.e. social technology) in Europe appeared to run ahead of that in the United States. Finally, there is a possibility that the idea to support research on non-capitalist regions may have been part of a broader interest in studying some competitive process between alternative economies; for if such a competitive process was happening, then it was a process with an undecided outcome.

When all of these supported programmes outside of the United States are considered together, it seems clear that there was a research field at the centre of it all; these were projects encouraged for the purpose of studying alternative economic forms. In addition to the idea that places in China, Russia, the Middle East and Africa all might have experienced some degree of institutional lag or repression, and in addition to the idea that such a place as Sweden might also be attempting some degree of institutional correction, yet another intriguing possibility could be that an entire sector of an economy could lag behind other sectors.

## Land Usage and Population Change

Scientific studies in land usage and population change represented a major research field supported by the Memorial. In fact some of the earliest areas of Rockefeller philanthropic activity were efforts to help modernize farming practices in the American South during the early 1900s. By the 1920s, when both the American and European agricultural economies faced trouble, one of a number of possible interpretations could be that industrialized nations experienced regional population imbalances. A result could be regions of over-population, under-population or some other skewing away from what seemed normal. One goal was to discover fundamental causes of migration patterns that link different regions and their populations and land uses. Such an area of research could relate as well to research in race relations, especially following the heightened phase of America's Great Migration. Social conditions were severe for southern African Americans in the 1920s, and many black families – and even entire communities – moved northward for better living and working conditions. The issue of bringing white families and black families into peaceful and productive coexistence was seen by many social scientists to be an urgent matter. Another issue, having more to do with population flow from rural to urban life, was found to relate to problems of regionally maladjusted land usage.[50]

In December 1922, a broad research proposal arrived at the Memorial, at perhaps the earliest possible moment that it could have arrived. It came from Richard T. Ely, an established land economist and director of the Institute for Research in Land Economics and Public Utilities at the University of Wisconsin. Ely recommended a land-use study that would be 'vital to the national welfare and survival', and he applied for support for multiple years to operate the programme.[51]

Ely asked for a tremendous amount of money: $100,000 annually for at least three years. The proposal was also fairly broad and general. Yet it arrived at the Memorial well supported by recommendation letters. One supporter, Albert Shaw, was editor of the *American Review of Reviews*. Shaw was convinced 'not only of the scientific value but of the intensely practical character of the work in land economics' as proposed by Ely. The project, Shaw added, would involve wide-ranging problems 'relating to the public domain and the natural resources' of the nation. With respect to areas of knowledge still in need of development, 'the methods of Dr. Ely's institute seem to me particularly adapted to the supplying of trustworthy information'.[52]

A personal meeting was arranged between Ruml and Ely. They met in Washington, DC, and the meeting evidently went well enough. Ely followed up by acknowledging his high regard for Ruml's 'interest in the scientific aspects of our work'. Ely also noted his belief 'that economists have not attained as high of scientific standards as have other scientists'. But new statistical data was helping to improve the situation, and a next need was for greater coordination between all social scientists. The problem of land-use analysis 'has become too great for isolated workers', and the promotion of closer contact between all social scientists 'is the reason for our Institute'. Ely used a familiar analogy that compared economic research to medical research, seeing it as a 'fact that the best scientific work in economics as well as medicine is the result of efforts by scientific men, following scientific methods, to solve actual problems'.

Ely identified three problem areas that could benefit from the Memorial's support: 'prevention of human misery involved in unwise land settlements'; 'problems of starvation in India and China'; and 'the problem of world peace to which we could make a contribution if we work out plans for the distribution of the food and raw materials among the nations of the earth'. Clearly Ely proposed studying social and economic problems that existed far beyond his own geographical region.[53]

Ely and Ruml got into deeper discussion. Ruml asked for more specifics, and Ely tried to oblige. Ely recommended studying consequences of large land holdings on the US economy, as well as exploring problems associated with utilizing low-grade land and problems connected to extreme fluctuations in land values. He emphasized the solid reputation of his institute, and he noted his concern to 'take up practical problems of human welfare and attempt to solve them by scientific methods'. But in the end, Ely's proposal was denied. Were his proposed projects too general? Were his views too controversial? Did he ask for too much money? Perhaps the situation reflected a bit of each of these. One potential problem, surely at least considered by the Memorial, was Ely's failure to specifically state his projects. Yet there were other proposed projects that were supported by the Memorial that were stated with roughly the same level of generality. The Memorial may have been wary of the likelihood that policy implications could come from Ely's studies. But this too was no different from other supported projects. Could it have been that whatever policy advocacy might come from Ely's scientific findings would be a bit on the radical side? Ely did have a reputation as something of a radical, and Ruml was new at the Memorial – meaning that he may not have wanted to risk losing any 'good will' invested in him in his new position. Or maybe $300,000 allocated to one of the very first proposed projects during the Ruml years was simply too much. What we do at least know is that it was upon Ruml's advice that Ely withdrew his proposal just prior to its expected denial by the Memorial's trustees; Ruml told him that it was 'doubtful' the trustees would award the grant.[54]

Another proposed project, also denied funding by the Memorial, came from Stanford University's Food Research Institute. Stanford's project was seen as too impractical. The project, initially submitted in May 1922 by Institute Director

Carl Alsberg, asked for $80,000 to develop better annual harvest predictions by 'dealing with the technique and methods of crop estimating'. Accurate crop estimation, Alsberg pointed out, 'lies at the base of all rational agricultural production and marketing'. To the best of Alsberg's knowledge, there existed 'no complete and thorough study of all the methods in use in the past and present for crop estimating and no critical study of their respective values'. The proposed project would be economic analysis, based on statistically analysed data. An interesting added idea was that accurate crop estimation 'involves psychological factors', which 'loom particularly large' in any estimation errors. Or was that maybe a stretch? Ruml hesitated to support the project. Possibly the project seemed a bit far-reaching in how it aimed to connect the work to estimate seasonal crop levels to an analysis of psychological factors. Perhaps the proposal arrived at the Memorial too soon, in fact prior to when Ruml officially instituted the change of Memorial policy.[55]

Even though Stanford's Food Research Institute was highly regarded, the proposal was denied. This decision was probably based not on any ideological or political grounds, but most likely owed to Alsberg's general and lofty description of the project, and perhaps to the timing of its arrival. One attribute that the proposals from Ely's institute and Alberg's institute had in common may have been the grand scale of what they put forward. Another shared attribute is that the two project proposals arrived at the Memorial very early in the Ruml years.

In June 1922, Ruml decided to support some research in the closely related field of population and migration. The project was overseen by the National Research Council (NRC), and a described goal was to support improved communications between social scientists and their variety of research methods. The Memorial decided to fund some research supported by the NRC's Committee on Scientific Problems of Human Migration. While the Memorial might have hesitated to commit any large sum of money to supporting one particular research method in a new field of research, it would have made sense to support the NRC's proposal. The Memorial was interested in providing support through the NRC at least in areas relevant to the Memorial's interests. The nature of the specific project was to establish uniform measurement categories and methodological standards for data collection. The Memorial's support for the NRC's projects in population and migration studies began when Ruml inquired if there were any research ideas at the NRC that might relate to the social sciences. NRC secretary Vernon Kellogg responded that Memorial funds could be appropriately directed to the 'promotion of scientific projects sponsored by the Council', and that it would be best for these funds to be placed into a general endowment, 'rather than to give the money for the support of a specific list of projects made up in advance'.[56]

NRC chairman George Ellery Hale also believed that any grant from the Memorial should be distributed to the NRC as a general endowment. The NRC was already supported by the Foundation for research in the physical sciences, and Hale recommended developing a new project which would aim to study how society actually used the products of physical science, or as he put it, to 'briefly survey the wide field of science and discern its true place in any intelligent scheme of national development'. This was a grand idea. Hale recommended even trying to identify the best societal applications for every specific scientific discovery. This proposed project did not receive a Memorial grant.[57]

Another study in land usage and population analysis came forward in 1924, in a proposal from the New School for Social Research in New York City. An idea was to make better scientific studies in agricultural economics. The New School was an institution with which the Memorial had some familiarity. A couple of Ruml's friends, Lawrence Frank and Wesley Mitchell, sometimes taught there. The New School's economists proposed to study human migration from a kind of 'selection' point of view. They displayed solid understanding of connections between increased human migration and increased agricultural problems, and their grant proposal opened by declaring: 'The agricultural problem in the United States stands in dire need of reformation at this time'.[58]

The New School proposed a project primarily economic in nature. A recent recession had left agricultural prices out of balance with other prices in the American economy. Farmers faced a crisis, which was compounded by inadequate loan credit. But the 'deeper cause' that underlay both the farm crisis and credit crisis, and which was perhaps familiar only to the 'hard-boiled economist', was 'that the problem is one of decreasing costs by improving the technical methods of agriculture'. That is to say, economic institutions were not easily catching up with advances in technology. Part of the problem dated from the 1890s, when highly marginal western prairies were brought under cultivation. That was the last wave of substantial acreage available for industrialized tillage. 'Sooner or later the food supply of our nation must begin to lag behind the growth of population', declared the New School's social scientists. The proposed project would aim to better connect technological know-how with scientific understanding of population growth and migration patterns.[59]

Because the New School was located within the confines of New York City, the school's social scientists believed they should be clear as to why they wanted to undertake this project associated largely with rural America. Their explanation was that recent migration trends often had the city as the destination, and 'the city-ward move of population which has been going on in this country for half a century is undesirable'. This undesirability came partly from the seeming fact that 'the city is a poorer place in which to grow up than in the country'. Yet there was also a factor that led the New School's social scientists to conclude that they needed to study changes in the qualities of people who were left behind.

> As the process of migration from the farm to the city continues, a selection of persons who go as against those who stay is continually taking place. Is the city draining from the rural districts the most intelligent and energetic part of the population?

The New School's social scientists wanted to research all major factors involved in rural-to-urban migration, and they believed that 'the most difficult part of the problem is the formulation of an adequate culture for the rural community'. The key ideas were to identify policy tools that might keep more people living in rural communities, and in some cases to see that people moving to cities are better prepared for the difficulties of urban life. Leadership at the Memorial advised the New School's social scientists to improve their proposal.[60]

In a refined proposal, the New School's social scientists emphasized their confidence that multiple projects were ready to go. A number of projects aimed to use applied social science to strengthen the economic and cultural foundations of rural communities. Added projects now included studies of federal taxation and finance, research on the 'Agrarian problem', analysis of organized labour in the public service, studies of religious life of a typical American community, general work on race problems, social studies of races and cultures, research on crime and delinquency and measures of personality development. Even though all of these listed problems were still a bit generally described, and were wide-ranging, a five-year grant was awarded.[61]

Within the Memorial's supported research field in land usage and population change, Ruml decided, by January 1925, that it was time to develop a stronger focus on agricultural economics. That month he requested a report from Edwin G. Nourse, head of the agricultural section at the Memorial-supported Institute of Economics. Nourse, who had done his graduate work with Leon Marshall at the University of Chicago, and who had taught at Iowa State, had his own research expertise in farmers' cooperatives. He was well prepared to assess these programmes, and Ruml saw him as an advisor whose views carried weight.[62]

Ruml asked for details about the quality of scientific work in agricultural economics in the nation's leading universities; he shared his idea that issues associated with rural land use must be better connected to the web of social sciences. Nourse came through with detailed information about all of the nation's major programmes in agricultural economics. His opinions ranged from low points of 'no good men' (at Penn State) and 'no one ... who is regarding American farm policy from a national point of view' (at Cornell), to high praise, especially for three departments, namely the University of Wisconsin, the University of Minnesota and Iowa State College.[63]

Following his discussions with Nourse, Ruml decided to explore agricultural economics as a kind of special field in need of development. Ruml produced a report, in November 1926, which recognized agricultural economics as now standing equal in importance to research in race relations. While the level of demand for better social science was seen as increasing in a number of fields, such demand pressures were especially strong in agricultural economics.[64]

During the last few years of the Memorial, Ruml got a number of major studies supported in the field of land usage and population change. Problems associated with human migration were central to a 1927 proposal that came from the National Bureau of Economic Research. The National Bureau aimed to study patterns of international migration, and no real reason could exist for any objection to awarding the grant, especially given the fine reputation of the National Bureau.[65]

The following year, in June 1928, Ruml decided to support a particular study in agricultural economics that was much of his own design. The project was an analytical exercise designed to study 'agrarian reform'. It was overseen by J. D. Black of Harvard University, and it focused on exploring an agricultural relief plan by designing an experiment in alternative approaches to responding to tariffs that might be imposed on agricultural products. Black's team studied the effects of various hypothetical tariffs. A central part of the project was to provide farmers with certificates that gave them 'transferable rights' to harvested crops, which ensured that even if their crop (which was wheat) sold below a tariff-level price, that farmers would receive the difference. The project became a quantitative study based essentially on running a sort of simulation of alternative scenarios for multiple harvest seasons (from 1928 to 1930). The year after beginning Ruml's 'Surplus Study', Black took the results of the study to Congress in testimony that he provided to Senate and House Committees on Agriculture.[66]

Ruml's study focused on factors that might help tie together agricultural economics, international trade and agrarian reform. Ruml in fact also helped to build an earlier study, a long-term project that began in 1924, and which was based on ideas developed by agricultural economists Richard Ely and H. C. Taylor. The experiment was put into action on the high plains near Helena, Montana, and was known as the 'Fairway Farms' study. On parcels of land purchased by both the Memorial and the Foundation, the study (in words of a contemporary news reporter) was to test 'the theory that farming in the northwest, when undertaken on a proper economic foundation and carried on in a scientific manner, will pay'. In addition to testing the ability of America's northern high plains to sustain farming, a second objective was to learn about human behaviour within the context of landlord–tenant relations; the objective was to identify the kinds of relations that could best promote farm ownership by the largest number of farmers. As implemented initially on just nine purchased farms, work got underway to build an entire farm community.[67]

The Memorial also supported a project in land usage and population change that began in June 1928, when social scientists at the University of Vermont received a Memorial grant. The research team was already involved in an ongoing study, and it featured some intriguing ideas. A project known as the Vermont Commission on Country Life was guided by Henry F. Perkins, a professor of zoology at the University of Vermont. The state of Vermont had a situation in which 176 of the state's 251 rural communities had lost population since 1850, and so Perkins initiated a population survey in 1925 which aimed to determine the status of what he described as the 'good old Vermont stock'. In connection with the population survey, Perkins established the Eugenics Survey of Vermont. With a goal to better understand the 'state of degeneracy', he proposed studying sixty-two 'low grade' families.[68]

The idea to try and establish the level of degeneracy of a rural population was actually a familiar one. Perkins cast his study within a framework of analysis similar to what existed in such projects as Richard Dugdale's study of the 'Jukes family' (1877) and Henry Goddard's study of the 'Kallikak family' (1911). Each of those studies tended to argue – sometimes vigorously – that immorality, imbecility, pauperism, prostitution, alcoholism and other weakened human attributes were largely controlled by genetic inheritance.[69]

But something happened in 1927. And it changed Perkins's view. The event was the devastating 'Great Flood', which 'opened the minds of people' to an alternative cause of poverty: the environment. Perkins began to rework his thinking into an environmental viewpoint, and he wondered if a high frequency of moral 'deterioration can only take place in poor isolated communities'. He set to work creating his broader project for the Vermont Commission, and it was this project for which he sought the Memorial's support.[70]

Perkins introduced to the Memorial a goal to evaluate the social and economic causes of rural-to-urban migration. Social scientists at the University of Vermont had the idea to make their study from a 'selectionist' point of view, which they saw as an underappreciated method for understanding the causes and consequences of declining rural populations. In March 1928, Perkins contacted Edmund E. Day at the Memorial. Perkins suggested adding to the eugenics survey a significantly more comprehensive survey of social and economic factors in rural Vermont. His main concern was that 'the declining population of the rural areas of the state ... seems to be no local problem, but one of widespread significance throughout the country'. Reasons for the decline were not yet known, and in research already underway, 'there are almost as many answers to the question as there are individuals who have investigated the matter'. The Memorial asked for more details.[71]

In June, Vermont's social scientists submitted a revised proposal, refined with more details. The study would now focus on ten dimensions of social and economic analysis in order to explain rural population decline. The study also had a clear applied goal, which was to discover how to better meet the needs of Vermont's rural communities. The proposal sold the idea that the study would have national implications.[72]

The Memorial awarded the funds. Perkins hired H. C. Taylor as project director. Taylor, an agricultural economist, was chairman of the Social Science Research Council's Committee on Economic Research on Agriculture. Together these two settled on an organizational structure for the major project, which would be comprised of seventeen committees. Perkins and Taylor were agreed with Ruml that there must be a careful degree of scrutiny concerning the kinds of research to be included. Taylor wrote to the Memorial to express his admiration for the way 'the human factor and the life of the people is receiving unusual emphasis' in the Vermont study. The study was different from other studies by rural commissions in Maine and New York, he said, because while other studies tended to take land utilization as a 'starting point', the Vermont study aimed to begin with the condition of people. The project, as Taylor put it, involved 'the sifting of facts' for study until 'their significance is clearly seen in their true relation to everyday life of a forward looking people'. The project was 'the first to use the methods of scientific planning ... as a means of insuring progress'.[73]

The projects pursued at the University of Vermont again marked a recognizable shift in thought about human nature. These projects began in the early 1920s, with ideas based on eugenics. By the end of the decade, however, the ideas were very much along the line of environmental determinants.

In Europe there were also problems of land use and population change. One project that the Memorial supported was based at the International Institute of Agriculture in Rome. The goal of the project, as expressed in 1925 by its researchers, was to distinguish between rural problems specific to Europe and rural problems likely shared with other nations. As they phrased it: were the problems encountered on Europe's path to 'rural life improvement' rooted in the same basic causes as in other countries? The institute's researchers wanted to do better science as well as establish better ways to translate their current science into instruction, including instruction for policymakers. They received a three-year award.[74]

Another project in Europe, based at the University of Copenhagen and supported by the Memorial, was one that focused on building 'cooperative' social science. The specific goal was to increase the level of cooperation between different kinds of social scientists who study agricultural and rural problems. Denmark, a major agricultural nation, had faculty at the University of Copenhagen's Institute of Economics and History who explained to the Memorial their aim to study agricultural and rural problems within a context of 'mak[ing] an organized study of political and social-economic history of the past few decades'. Economics professor Aage Friis, in contact with the Memorial in September 1926, introduced some specific rationale while applying for the grant. He identified a cooperative attitude, nicely suited to the Memorial's interests; and in particular he offered the school's view that 'the subjects and the materials forming the history of the past generation are so comprehensive in extent that one investigator would be unable to work through all this material by his own unaided efforts'. Friis's wording also touched upon a kind of comparison that was familiar to the Memorial: 'In the natural sciences the work of research is now carried on in great institutions'; however 'in the historical and economic sciences, each investigator as yet works on his own particular subject ... without considering the possibility of cooperating with others'. The isolated researcher no longer succeeds in the social sciences. In 1927, Copenhagen received its grant.[75]

Thinking about problems of land usage and population change could get people thinking about processes of human biological change – indeed, we have seen some linguistic evidence that show this.

## Group Biological Similarities and Differences

An idea that appeared multiple times in connection with research on land usage and population change was a notion that potentially too many people live in some areas while too few live in other areas. A related idea was that changes in rural and urban population numbers can involve changes in the qualities of people. Research into factors affecting population numbers – and population qualities – was a widespread interest during the 1920s.[76]

Before the years of the Memorial, Rockefeller, Jr established the Bureau of Social Hygiene in 1913. The Bureau was still active in the 1920s, and through the Bureau Rockefeller, Jr donated money to the eugenics movement, which included the American Eugenics Society (AES). At least two archived items help us to investigate the matter. In 1925, Rockefeller, Jr received a letter from the AES, and he responded in two ways. One response was to put his pen to work, as he appears to have put a margin note on the received letter to concur with the society's views at some level: '[T]he people make the slums; moral people are born, not made; the criminal is a defective human, also born, not made; the intelligent will be successful anyway'. Yet his other response was to state a view through an internal memorandum, in which he offered that 'The matter of which the letter speaks is, I believe, a profoundly important one to the future of this country'. But although he would want to be helpful in this field, Rockefeller, Jr wanted it stated that he 'could not take any personal part'.[77]

Rockefeller, Jr also donated money (as much as $15,000 per year) to the American Birth Control League (ABCL), recently founded by Margaret Sanger. Of interest was the ABCL's work to get birth control information and technologies to lower economic classes. Rockefeller, Jr believed that financial assistance for birth control was preferable to imposing any severe eugenics programme. He discussed ideas with his staff; there is a Foundation memorandum from one staffer that introduces a reason for his stance: that 'birth control' and 'family planning' are preferred by persons with reasoned opinions, in comparison to others 'who hold debatable opinions, the most capable group being the Eugenists'.[78]

The Foundation received at least a few applications for support that may be pertinent here. During 1920 and 1921, anthropologist and eugenicist Harry Laughlin applied to the Foundation multiple times for funds to help publish *Eugenical Sterilization in the United States*, but repeatedly he was turned down. In 1923, Elliot Smith, an anthropologist and race theorist at University College London, communicated with the Foundation, which decided to provide him some support for drafting a plan for the development of Australian anthropology. The Foundation ultimately funded Smith with $100,000, and his plan (with contributions by New York attorney Madison Grant, the eugenicist author of 1916's *The Passing of the Great Race*) is considered an important achievement.[79]

Beginning in November 1924, the Foundation awarded $100,000 over four years for a series of studies in Australia. Director of the project was A. R. Radcliff-Brown, a Cambridge-trained anthropologist who focused on developing a version of functional analysis. Radcliffe-Brown used the method to explain how an aggregation of behavioural norms, rules and guidelines can emerge in a society and become 'social structure'. He worked also to establish *Oceania*, a scholarly journal to focus on a vast region of peoples and cultures from Australia throughout the Pacific. Foundation support of Radcliffe-Brown and his research on aboriginal Australians and Pacific Islanders continued into the 1930s, when the programme became a 'special field of interest' within the Rockefeller Foundation's Division of Social Sciences.[80]

Other directions of thought were taken when it came to ideas about the intersection between human genetics and problems in society. During 1925, Rockefeller Foundation secretary Edwin Embree, in communication with Foundation President George Vincent and Memorial Director Ruml, briefly set up a 'Human Biology Program'. Scientific projects supported by the programme could involve a range of fields, including anthropology. One particular project supported by the Foundation was the research work of Raymond Pearl, a Johns Hopkins biologist, editor of *Human Biology* and author of *The Biology of Superiority* (1927).[81]

But Embree really only briefly explored the possibility of supporting a quest for greater knowledge of eugenics. As he once expressed a thought about the education of children, he opined that it was even 'harder to give a good inheritance than good surgery'. Yet as Abraham Flexner cautioned him, the Rockefeller

Foundation 'should not itself undertake studies, particularly in such controversial topics as population and eugenics. The fact that it is not proposing to enter directly into such fields should be made clear from the outset'.[82]

With respect to this whole temporary experiment by the Foundation, one positive way to interpret the effort may be to see it as an idea to discover if social evolution could be helped along. We can consider the view of Frederick Gates, who contemplated social evolution briefly in a 1926 Foundation memorandum. In his own way Gates connected an idea of 'scientific philanthropy' with an idea of competition, which he did by asserting that grants should be awarded to 'reach the sources of the evil they seek to correct'. The idea, as we have seen in previous chapters, was to locate fundamental points of intervention, where allocated money could best promote long-term benefits. More than ever it seemed to Gates that funds not carefully targeted would be only 'temporary opiates' working against the 'stern logic of evolution'.[83]

A few applications for the Memorial's support should also be noted. First, it is said that the first major effort to study racial questions after the First World War was the NRC's formation, in 1922, of its Committee on Scientific Problems of Human Migrations, established within their Division of Anthropology and Psychology. The committee, chaired by Robert Yerkes, received support from the Memorial and focused on concerns about immigration, including persons from Eastern Europe and Asia. The committee sponsored some conferences, which were well attended.[84]

An interesting topic of discussion at the time was human social evolution. Ruml personally recorded a bit of a personal stance on a large controversy, which was whether evolution should be taught in the public classroom. In May 1925, the nation followed the Scopes Trial, in Dayton, Tennessee. At about that time, Ruml was working with social scientists in the adjacent state to the east, as he helped to guide the University of North Carolina's establishment of their research centre. Ruml was interested in the cultural climate surrounding the teaching of evolution, and he learned that UNC's President Harry W. Chase had, in February of that year, delivered some testimony before a North Carolina legislative committee. Chase spoke in defence of teaching evolution in public schools, and Ruml wanted to know more about this. The person at UNC who shared with Ruml the recorded response was Howard Odum, who observed how at least one newspaper admired Chase's testimony as perhaps 'the most notable example of courage and faith in a high ideal which North Carolina has witnessed in recent years'.[85]

Ruml showed interest in other questions about human social evolution. In one collection of saved letters he shared his sense of the importance of a proposed anthropology project at UNC. The project was something he admired for its methodology, which aimed 'to assist in the study of Australian aborigines'. Sharing a thought with Arthur Woods at the Memorial, Ruml stated his hope 'that a very definite step had been taken toward the opening up of the general field of anthropology, ethnology and biology as it bears on human evolution'.[86]

One noteworthy case of support for research in human biology was a Memorial-supported project at the London School of Economics. Support at the LSE came with the school's receipt of fluid funds between 1923 and 1929. One particular area of research emerged at the LSE about which the Memorial had concerns. In their original proposal to the Memorial, one of the LSE's many expressed interests was to focus on 'the physical or natural bases of the social sciences, including Anthropology, Social Biology and Psychology'. LSE administrators targeted some of the money toward creating a Chair of Social Biology.[87]

By July 1925 the idea began to percolate for establishing an entire department of social biology. A first move was to identify some combination of interdisciplinary expertise that would make a good social biologist. One idea, by 1927, was to find someone trained in both economics and biology. Conversation continued for a couple more years, and in October 1929 a job opening was advertised. Various names were discussed, a couple of names went on the short list, and the choice was a professor of zoology at Cape Town. Lancelot Hogben, a Cambridge graduate and a well-trained statistician, began his work with an inaugural lecture in October 1930, on the 'Foundations of Social Biology'.[88]

Hogben came to the LSE as a self-identified refugee from South Africa, which was at the brink of imposing apartheid. Hogben aimed to use his LSE chair to fight global racism. But the timing was not right. A tide was turning against anything that could hint of being eugenics, even though Hogben was much on the side of environmental arguments designed to oppose eugenics. Also not helping things was that Hogben's research focused on subject matter that the rest of the LSE faculty could not much relate to, such as rabbits, rats, toads and guinea pigs. He published a paper on 'chromatic function in the lower vertebrates'. Hogben left the LSE in 1938.[89]

The tide was turning against eugenics in large part because of events outside of any control by Rockefeller philanthropy. During the 1920s and into the 1930s, scientific contacts were close between many German and American scientists, and especially close between eugenicists. In areas related to the social sciences, among notable recipients of Foundation funds were the Kaiser Wilhelm Institute for Psychiatry and the Kaiser Wilhelm Institute for Anthropology, Eugenics and Human Heredity. These relationships have been assessed by historians. Edwin Black has developed interpretations, as has Angela Franks. Franks, for one, recently concludes that without Rockefeller support at these institutes, 'the scientific development and acceptance of Nazi eugenics would have been greatly impeded'. Historians recognize the difficult situation that comes from the fact that financial support of German eugenics research continued, for at least a few years into the Nazi regime. Often cited is the Foundation's support of German physician and demographer Hans Harmsen; for at the time that he received this support, Harmsen was well into the process of becoming an influential supporter of Nazi policies, including advocating for the sterilization law of 1933.[90]

Trying to figure out the nature of German scientific thought in the late 1920s and early 1930s is challenging, and if the topic challenges historians, then it would have challenged people living at the time. Investments in early-1930s Germany were made by many Americans, both on the business and philanthropic sides, and there was no definite indicator for when precisely it was time to cut ties.

When taken altogether, supported research projects in human biology were, in many ways, about discovering interactions between the processes of individual development and societal development. There was also another supported research field in which researchers were interested in such interactions.

## Child Welfare and Parent Education

The original purpose of the Memorial was to support the welfare of mothers and children. Thus, prior to 1922, quite a number of programmes had already received Memorial support to help promote 'the well-being of children in home, legal and institutional settings'. Supported programmes oriented toward the social-work side included the Boy Scouts of America, the Girl Scouts of America, the Playground and Recreation Association of America, the YWCA and the YMCA. Supported organizations of social scientists included the American Home Economics Association, the Child Study Association and the National Council of Parent Education.[91]

During 1922 and 1923, Lawrence Frank took the lead in planning improvements to the programme for supporting child welfare and parent education. Frank already held the respect of many for his ideas about family education, and it made sense for him to head the Memorial's work in this field.[92]

Ruml and Frank were in agreement that perhaps one kind of scientific approach to the field could involve laboratory schools, which could begin at the nursery-school level. At select universities, especially in the United States and Canada, social scientists could make use of a 'world-as-laboratory' conception of social science. By 1922 a few schools were already working in this field. Among the most established programmes were those at the University of Toronto, Cornell University, the University of Minnesota and Iowa State College. All were places where 'lab schools' were well positioned to gain support.[93]

One change at the Memorial during 1922 and 1923 was to direct a more scientific approach to the same purpose for which the Memorial was established. Social scientists and social workers were to join forces in studying the rearing, socialization and general well-being of children. In addition to studying child development and parent education, researchers also looked at the adoption and care of orphans, child health and hygiene, day care, family welfare and services, juvenile delinquency, recreation and social clubs and even youth unemployment. Some twenty-five or so colleges and universities received Memorial support for research in child studies and parent education.[94]

As the Ruml years got underway, the trustees could be pleased with the continued attention to the Memorial's original field of interest. The only question when it came to this field would have been: how far from the Memorial's original focus should such a broad scope extend?[95]

Lawrence Frank assumed the responsibility to promote scientific research in child welfare and parent education. He strongly agreed with the Memorial's redirected emphasis that to address symptoms of social and economic problems was not good enough, and he developed a series of reports during 1924 and 1925 to establish the need to focus on underlying causes of society's problems. Frank decided that a major issue with the existing child welfare programmes was the continuation of faulty parental behaviour; parents simply needed better training to raise healthy children. Society needed to help parents attain the knowledge to raise children who are healthy, and money was needed to support organizations that focus on developing educational materials on childcare. As Frank expressed it in 1925, the ultimate goal was that the 'home as a child welfare agency will tend increasingly to reduce the need for specialized remedial services'.[96]

Frank recognized the value in preexisting, federally-funded extension service programmes, which were created through the 1910s and the 1920s, and were quite established in many states. Extension service was designed to put research experts into direct contact with the public. Such contact helped farmers learn the latest information and techniques in agricultural science. Extension service contacts were also prized for their role in assisting the spread of better home management practices. Frank contemplated using extension service to help establish parent education programmes. He also stated a key question in 1926: 'How can college Home Economics Departments best make their contribution to pre-parental education'?[97]

One of the more dedicated traditions of using extension service programmes was at Iowa State College. In 1925, Frank worked with Anna E. Richardson, the school's home economics dean, and also president of the American Home Economics Association. With the Memorial's support, Richardson established instruction programmes in parent education as part of the school's extension service. Strongly influencing the Memorial's decision to provide the funds was the presence of unique child 'laboratories' at Iowa State. Richardson wanted to use these lab facilities to study child rearing and socialization, and she worked to enable Frank to recommend a three-year grant, which was approved.[98]

One project began at Iowa State in 1925, and it involved the creation of a new kind of home, right on campus. Undergraduate students could live in this home, where they could help raise an infant boy. The project was a success, and continuing for some quarter century after that, baby wards of the state lived in a few houses on the Iowa State campus, where women students in home economics learned the principles of child rearing as well as home management. By about 1930, some attention also went to equipping Iowa State's 'home management house' with the newest sorts of household equipment and appliances; all of these introduced 'variables' constituted experimental adjustments in the tradition of 'scientific management'. As Richardson phrased it, young women should develop some understanding of 'household scientific management', which included the blending of technology applications and childrearing practices. The success of the programme was measured in part by the dissemination of knowledge around the state, and this success resulted in significant grant extensions into the 1930s.[99]

Another focus on developing scientific understanding of child development was pursued in Iowa, near the opposite end of the state. The emphasis in this case was on research to better understand child intellectual development. Whereas research efforts at Iowa State employed the benefits of extension service and focused especially on rearing physically and emotionally healthy children, at the University of Iowa the research work focused more on designing scientific methods for measuring intellectual attributes of children. The central interest was the developmental stability of a young person's 'IQ'. With financial assistance from the Memorial, researchers in Iowa City developed one of the leading 'child welfare centres' in the nation. Benefitting from the resources of the university's strong department of psychology, scientists at the Iowa Child Welfare Research Station established a nursery-to-preschool system designed to bring together groups of normal children (aged two years to five years) for observation under controlled conditions. Researchers focused on children showing 'normal development', as a main goal was to learn how to provide favourable environments for normal mental development.[100]

At Cornell University, the land-grant school in New York State, the Memorial in 1925 supported the establishment of a new department of family life, grounded in psychology. 'The grant', says historian Nancy Berlage, 'also helped to initiate resident work and courses in child training and to develop a nursery school'. It was now possible to do modern work in child training and parent education, as the school's home economists 'tied child study to the social sciences – intellectually through psychology, and methodologically through both research and reform models'.[101]

Another possibility for increased scientific attention to women and children was to develop better-trained social workers. This was a focus at Tulane University, in New Orleans. In 1928, Tulane contacted the Memorial with an idea to better interconnect all of their social science programmes. Once these pro-grammes worked more cooperatively together, they could better contribute to the school's flagship programme, its School of Social Work. Tulane focused on a belief 'that we should consider first the establishment of a comprehensive plan of child research and parental guidance in the University, which would furnish the proper background and facilities for all studies of the child and parent'. Tulane received its grant.[102]

A social work programme at Smith College in Amherst, Massachusetts, expressed an interest to better mesh together 'social science' and 'social technol-ogy', by which was meant the discovery of knowledge and the application of knowledge. In 1924 Smith College applied for and received a three-year grant to help produce better-trained social workers. One rationale for their request was that social workers needed better knowledge about factors and conditions unique to Boston and other north-eastern cities.[103]

Washington University's social work programme, the Memorial determined, could be used to prepare social workers as problem solvers. The Memorial pro-vided a grant in 1927, partly in response to Washington University's request for support to reorganize all of their social science departments at the school. An idea also came through in the grant application that social workers at Washing-ton University were to benefit from a training programme designed to employ discoveries of knowledge toward better supporting applications of knowledge.[104]

In March 1927, social scientists at the University of Liverpool contacted the Memorial with an idea to use their city as a laboratory. They wanted to bet-ter understand interactions between economic opportunity, family quality and urban problems. Liverpool's social scientists and social workers had an under-standing that leadership at the Memorial 'is interested in new schemes of social research and experiment'. Liverpool's investigators were 'taking the liberty of bringing to the notice of the Memorial certain projects which are in contempla-tion in Liverpool'. They had in mind a range of 'experiments in child guidance, health education, employment and after-care of boys, social centres, and adult education among casual labourers', and they believed they might even discover new approaches to 'research into problems associated with the experimental work' on the alleviation of poverty. They proposed establishing a 'settlement research' centre where they would do research on child development and general social welfare. They hoped also to examine 'physical geography', as well as 'the economic, political, and social factors of present Liverpool organization'. Their grand goal, as one leader at the Memorial interpreted all of this, was nothing less than 'to discover the causes of poverty and its effects upon the population'.[105]

Ruml responded positively to the University of Liverpool's proposal. He contemplated an idea to connect the proposed study to an ongoing LSE study known as the 'New Survey of London Life and Labour'. The name of that study was a clever reminder of one of the great social surveys of a previous generation, some quarter of a century earlier when Charles Booth published the extraordinary 'Survey of Life and Labour of the People in London 1886–1903', which resulted in the seventeen-volume *The Life and Labour of the People of London*. Booth's idea, so grand and direct, was to systematically confront the 'Poverty Question'. Liverpool's social scientists received their Memorial support, and in time their projects produced useful results.[106]

One theme shared by many projects in child welfare and parent education was an expressed confidence that mothers, infants, younger children, immigrants and all other persons trying to learn new strategies for living in society, could indeed be helped by adapting to a changing world, i.e. that people are not stuck with any specific habits and behaviours, but can learn new habits and behaviours. In connection with this environmental emphasis, a shift took place in the public's general perception of the 'intelligence–morality' relationship. Something interesting about mental tests (IQ tests, military selection tests and even a proposed US national intelligence test for all 'races') is that such tests tended to crystallize certain beliefs associated with scientific 'expertise'. A reason why social scientists were expected to administer these tests to individuals and groups was a commonly held belief that a person's level of intelligence was fixed, and that one's level of intelligence strongly determined one's life-long qualities of character. But by the 1920s, such an idea was beginning to give way. Strongly affecting this shift was the discovery with American soldiers during the First World War, that a person's performance on an intelligence test can be greatly determined by one's level of education.[107]

Something also happened overall with the increased emphasis on scientific studies of parenting: a tightening of the connection between fundamental and applied social science. Much discussed at the Memorial was the idea that applied social science was, in effect, 'social technology'. A clear statement of this appears in a 1924 memorandum, where Memorial trustees focused on distinguishing between 'social science' and 'social technology'. One question was where the boundaries might exist between the two. 'The Memorial's interest in "social science"', the trustees said, 'leads naturally to a consideration of schools of "social technology"', – to use a term to suggest the analogy between medical science and the professional medical schools'. Examples of schools of social technology were law schools, business schools, schools of social work and schools of public welfare. The essential idea was that attainment of knowledge is never fully separable from employment of knowledge; or in other words, that discovered knowledge cannot ultimately exist separate from its applications.[108]

When the Memorial ended in January 1929, this work to understand relationships between social science and social technology was an important line of critical thinking to be merged into the Foundation's Division of Social Sciences. However the specific research field in child welfare and parent education was not merged into the new division. With the closure of the Memorial, much Rockefeller support for child studies was continued by the General Education Board. The National Research Council also had a Committee on Child Development, and the Commonwealth Fund was an important supporter of child welfare needs as well.

## International Relations

Another research field of great interest to the Memorial was international relations. The importance of research in international relations was greatly recognized by the 1920s, owing especially to the efforts being made by all nations to help establish a successful League of Nations. Some historians have tended to suggest that the beginnings of the modern field of international relations came with the founding, at the University of Chicago in 1931, of the first cross-departmental, degree-granting academic body: the committee on international relations. Chicago professor Quincy Wright might well be argued to be the principal architect of an interdisciplinary social science of international relations. Or, perhaps one could make the case for Columbia University's establishment of the Parker Institute of International Affairs, in 1931, as a foundational moment for a social science of international relations. Both the University of Chicago and Columbia University were of course supported by the Memorial to establish research centres in the social sciences. At Harvard University, another Memorial-supported research centre, various projects in international relations were undertaken. The LSE used the Memorial's support to establish a department of international studies, with three chairs in the field.[109]

Potentially the scientific field of international relations got its start within Rockefeller philanthropy's ways of assisting the prospects of a new research field. When Ruml came to the Memorial, Raymond Fosdick advised him that a peaceful international order should be a major objective – that a focus needed to be to study and promote cooperation. The Memorial would, in its years under Ruml's leadership, support a handful of institutions that aimed to 'scientifically' investigate the causes of international misunderstanding and conflict. The Memorial held hope that accomplishments in this research field would be highly applicable research findings, useful to the League of Nations. At a time when the field of international relations was just getting started as a discipline, one commonly held idea was that a scientific approach to international relations and support for the League of Nations were nearly inseparable. Scientists and philanthropists held optimism in the human ability to solve problems at all levels, including the international level.[110]

In January 1926, Ruml exchanged ideas with Abraham Flexner on the subject of social scientists studying international problems. Just one year earlier they had exchanged subtle ideas concerning what the term 'social science' even meant, and in their renewed exchange, Flexner was overall optimistic about the progress of social science. When it came to international problems in particular, Flexner believed it might be possible for a small team of science advisors to identify, even somewhat specifically, every important problem that there was. All identified problems could then be attacked relatively in concert. The Memorial, Flexner suggested,

> must try to ascertain in every possible way what the specific problems are which could be studied, and a knowledge of which, if authoritatively disseminated, would give statesmen and officials who want to do right the light they do not now possess, or might influence public opinion.[111]

Ruml replied by emphasizing 'that in our approach to the social sciences we should conceive the matter on the broad basis of a fundamental search for truth, without too much reference to the immediate possibilities of application'. The Memorial, for the time being, would still favour a primary emphasis on fundamental social science – and one subject requiring more careful study was the League of Nations. Ruml saw the League as an experiment which 'presents certain new educational and scientific opportunities and responsibilities'. The Memorial needed to provide greater support for research on 'problems of an international character in the field of the social sciences', which would involve methods that 'may be political, economic, sociological, ethnological'.[112]

Not long after Ruml's exchange with Flexner, a Memorial memorandum in 1926 stated some specific objectives, especially in Europe, where security and stability were greatly needed. Especially worth attending to was the 'prevention of war'. Thus recognized was the need for projects to increase our scientific understanding of international relations. Desirable as well would be to support a few research projects.[113]

During 1925 and 1926, the University of Geneva shared with the Memorial their interest in cooperative social science. Social scientists at the school hoped to share with Ruml a description of their envisioned programme to establish research focusing on European international relations. Initial contact took place in March 1925, when the Memorial's European advisor, Huntington Gilchrist, contacted Ruml on behalf of the University of Geneva. Ruml and Gilchrist had already shared thoughts regarding some potential lines of research that Geneva's social scientists might emphasize, and Gilchrist took the stance of reiterating Geneva's interest in 'establishing a special school or institute, for work in political science and in international problems'. Pertinent for Gilchrist to add was that the institute was nearly ready to begin an active programme of research. Upon further encouragement from Ruml, in September 1925 the University of Geneva submitted a formal proposal, which emphasized the rigour of what they planned as 'a permanent centre of scientific studies with special reference to problems coming up for discussion in various sections of the League of Nations'. Nine months later, the University of Geneva received its five-year grant, and with it they established the Geneva Postgraduate Institute for International Studies.[114]

Undoubtedly important in the years following the First World War was the need to better understand European political situations from a German perspective. In late 1925, the Memorial interacted with the Hamburg Institute of International Affairs. The Memorial decided to award a grant for 'work of scientific research' on seven projects, all dealing with European political affairs. The projects ranged from studies of specific conditions in Germany, through a study of the constitutional position of Germany under the League of Nations, to studies of techniques of treaty making. The grant award came, in the words of the institute's director, 'at a time when such help is of the highest moral and material value ... for the rebuilding and stabilizing of Europe'. Political stability was seen as a crucial prerequisite for anything else happening that might be good for Europe. Support of the institute, as well as a separately planned Institute for External Politics, was maintained until 1930.[115]

One of the first programmes in the United States that aimed to use Memorial funds to support research in international relations was a project at Radcliffe College, the women's school located effectively next door to Harvard. Radcliffe had a small group of social scientists who perceived the need to help government leaders make sound policy, 'on an understanding of facts'. But even though persons at the Memorial agreed with such an idea, it took some effort to get Radcliffe's social scientists their grant.

In November 1923, the Radcliffe faculty submitted their proposal. They described a programme aimed at improving their research and teaching in international relations. Radcliffe's important goal, which should 'require no emphasis', was to help 'spread authentic information regarding international affairs and relationships'. But leadership at the Memorial had some doubts, not about the need for such research, but about who would do the research. The Memorial guided Radcliffe's social scientists to develop a more detailed proposal, which they did. The revised application expressed an objective to establish a Bureau of International Research, which would be founded on a belief that 'sound policy in international affairs can be based only on an understanding of facts, and that such facts may be discovered and made known'. Radcliffe's social scientists proposed a research programme designed to focus on discovering all pertinent facts, but the Memorial responded somewhat negatively once again. This time the Memorial put a pause into the whole process until they could gather advice from other persons, especially persons at Harvard. The question was whether Harvard's social scientists believed Radcliffe's social scientists were up to the task. Harvard's chair of its department of economics, Allyn Young, looked at Radcliffe's proposal to see if it was specific enough, and he hesitated. Young was challenged to see how an approach to an economic analysis of cooperation could work. He said that, in general, 'I find it difficult to formulate a definite proposal for the conduct of research in the field of international economic problems'. Harvard's head librarian assessed Radcliffe's library resources, and determined they were adequate. Harvard's law school consulted with the Memorial as well, as did Harvard's president. Harvard's office of the president stated its support for a grant to Radcliffe, and even cited no fewer than thirteen Radcliffe professors whose research related to the fields of international relations and affairs. Radcliffe received its grant in November 1924.[116]

By 1929, at the time of creation of the Foundation's Division of Social Sciences, a heightened level of debate was ready to take place about how best to continue building and supporting a research field in international relations. One idea was to support exchanges of ideas between prominent intellectuals in different nations. Another possibility was to look at the Institute of Pacific Relations (IPR), with an eye toward developing a global version of such an organization. John D. Rockefeller, Jr personally supported the IPR, and the Memorial did as well, beginning in 1926.[117]

Owing to the Memorial's work to support research in international relations, by the end of the 1920s this research field was in a position to support individual scientific studies, research institutes and think tanks in such ways that all of the actors could become coordinated in a new international political order, which they sought to make rational or 'rationalized'.[118]

## Coordinated Data Collection

Another kind of research field could also be developed around a focus on promoting better communications between social scientists. In fact the idea of a research field focused primarily on coordinating the social sciences proved interesting. Such a field could even help guide the Memorial's efforts to identify additional funding needs with respect to any gaps that might exist between fields or groupings of social scientists. One idea was that certain research needs tended to fall through the cracks due to their remaining too underappreciated or impractical for any particular institution to directly support them.

One example of such a funds gap was in connection with data collected at the municipal level. In this case, the need was for funds to support efforts to standardize the categories of data collection at local research bureaus. In 1926 the Memorial awarded money to the National Municipal League for the purpose of achieving better coordination between research by 'local bureaus of municipal research and other civic agencies'. By supporting such coordination, the Memorial hoped to 'make the most' of all discovered facts.[119]

Another need was to better coordinate research work at the state level, where public welfare statistics needed to be standardized across states. Serving this purpose was a grant to the American Statistical Association (ASA). The ASA's plan in 1928 was to draft a 'model law ... for the development of uniform statistical procedures in all states'. The goal was to develop comparable and meaningful welfare statistics.[120]

Especially noteworthy as a need for consistent statistical categories was a national project to establish a 'Uniform Crime Reporting System'. In 1926, the Memorial trustees received a memorandum from the Social Science Research Council outlining various improvements necessary in crime reporting; the memo advocated in favour of a single 'crime accounting system'. With the assistance of Memorial funds as well as some support from the Bureau of Social Hygiene, a crime reporting system was soon under development. Today's historians identify the beginnings of modern criminology as having been propelled mightily by the effort that took place between 1927 and 1929, when the Memorial supported the International Association of the Chiefs of Police to develop the modern crime report. The standardized crime report marks an important moment in the history of crime fighting, and the production of such a crime report typified what could be accomplished by bringing together the efforts of the Memorial with other funding organizations, the services of social workers and the commitment of social scientists.[121]

Another example of coordinative work emerged in connection with the resources for publishing materials in the social sciences. The realization was that increased publication of research results would help improve communications between social scientists. During 1923 and 1924, the Memorial supported social science publications especially at its research centres at the University of Chicago and the University of North Carolina. The basic idea, well stated by the Memorial's Arthur Woods, was that leaders in the social sciences had expressed that 'worthy books are not being published because they are commercially unprofitable'. Woods agreed that it was worth asking 'whether or not, perhaps, worthy books are not being written because the men who would naturally write them appreciate the difficulty, if not the impossibility, of having them published – and therefore is not scholarship being retarded?' Each of these university presses has over the years gained an outstanding reputation for the quality of their offerings in the social sciences.[122]

Finally there was a strategy that came along during 1927, when an idea was hatched to develop a multi-volume encyclopedia to include every major field and subfield in the social sciences. Such a project, to be overseen by Columbia University economist E. R. A. Seligman, related closely to the ideal of integrating a unified structure of the social sciences. The project became the *Encyclopedia of the Social Sciences*, and it was a massive undertaking. Editors and contributors were called upon to do nothing less than draw together 'the interrelations of all these sciences' in an 'attempt to take stock of our present knowledge'. As was expressed in 1927, in the proposal for the project, the encyclopedia was to be made widely available 'so that the fundamental ideas' discovered by social scientists 'would gradually percolate down to the wider public'.[123]

Once the project was funded by the Memorial (to a tune of nearly half a million dollars at the outset), in 1927 Alvin Johnson, a social scientist at the New School for Social Research, was appointed to serve as associate editor of the encyclopedia. Johnson worked well with Seligman, who remained the project's editor. Johnson held conversations with Alexander Goldenweiser, who had just finished co-editing a renowned volume in which thirty-three contributors attempted to draw interrelationships between fully a dozen social sciences: including anthropology, economics, history, law, political science, psychology, sociology, statistics, education, philosophy, ethics and religion. That book, said Goldenweiser and William F. Ogburn, was motivated by a growing realization 'that many problems lie in several different fields and that their solution demands methods from the various social sciences'. Goldenweiser has been credited with the original idea for an encyclopedia of the social sciences.[124]

The envisioned encyclopedia would come in at an enormous eight million words, and this was going to take a great many contributors. Johnson travelled between Europe and the United States and coordinated the project superbly. The encyclopedia came together in fifteen volumes between 1930 and 1935. The instrumental part of the daunting exercise to establish connections between all fields in the social sciences was in the very act of arranging the content for the encyclopedia; for it was during a series of planning sessions that the editors and contributors identified how best to arrange all of the major outlines of social knowledge.[125]

The Memorial's efforts to help fill funding gaps in the collection of data and the communication of results was the development of a research field in the social sciences; yet this was a field that applied itself not to any specific social or economic problems, but rather to all fields in the social sciences that were in need of assistance in meeting their roles in the grand project to forge interrelations between the social sciences.

## Conclusion

A handful of historians have studied the Memorial's efforts to support the broad advancement of social science. Persons connected with Rockefeller philanthropy also on occasion reflected on these efforts in their in-house reports. Yet in all of these reflections on the Memorial's efforts between 1922 and 1929, there is always some ambiguity as to what precisely the supported research fields were. This chapter has been an attempt to sort this out.

# 8 RESEARCH ORGANIZATIONS AND RESEARCH BOUNDARIES

## Introduction

Just as the Memorial was developing programmes to provide financial support to major research centres and also many smaller projects woven together into research fields, the Memorial implemented strategies to help develop a few major research organizations. One project was to develop an organization to oversee a research focus on business cycles. The Memorial also helped build the intermediary organization: the Social Science Research Council. We can also return to an interest in the Memorial's support of research fields by considering some support of research in humane studies, and support of research at intersections between legal research and the social sciences. These last two research fields helped to define boundaries at the edges of the social sciences.

## A Fellowships Programme

One way to assist the coordination between social sciences was to award research fellowships. Leadership at the Memorial developed methods for establishing fellowships programmes, covering a range of needs, both domestic and international. A fellowships programme is itself a kind of research organization.

One approach was to establish a programme to provide international fellowships. Such fellowships can serve multiple purposes, including enabling the movement of ideas, which in the early 1920s tended to still stay a bit provincial. In 1923, the Memorial created a fellowships programme to provide 'direct fellowships' to social scientists outside of the United States. The aim was to help researchers better develop their methods and approaches. The Memorial began in 1924 to award these fellowships in earnest. Within the following year, Ruml decided to establish a domestic fellowships programme, which was especially for younger scholars. As he explored ways to make the domestic fellowships programme work, perhaps in tandem with the international fellowships programme, Ruml identified two basic needs: to use a system of advisors in other nations to help operate the international fellowships programme; and to establish an over-sight organization to help distribute fellowships in the domestic programme.[1]

The international fellowships programme, established and operated by the Memorial, was initially primarily for European social scientists. An initial round of awards went to established names, including the likes of French economic historian Charles Rist and British anthropologist Bronislaw Malinowski. Australian industrial psychologist G. Elton Mayo received a grant as well. While recipients of the Memorial's international fellowships could travel to many locations around the globe for their continued research and education, a prime goal for many of them was to work in the United States.[2]

The Memorial's international fellowships programme required that each fellowship candidate be nominated by a Memorial-appointed representative, based in Europe. By 1924, five representatives were in place, located in Austria, Czechoslovakia, France, Germany and Great Britain. These representatives forwarded names and details about nominees to the Memorial, where officers and other advisors evaluated the nominees. One example of an outside advisor was Edwin G. Nourse, of the agricultural division of the Institute of Economics. By 1928 a smooth bit of 'machinery' seems to have been put in place, with each of the five European representatives conducting dozens of interviews, producing multiple hundreds of applicants in total; at least 165 European social scientists and scholars received fellowships, nearly always to facilitate travel to other nations, most often to the United States. A small number of social scientists from the United States and elsewhere received support through the international fellowships programme, with American social scientists nearly always visiting Europe.[3]

One favoured group of applicants for the Memorial's international fellowships programme was the group involved in economics. By the beginning of 1930, when the last traces of Memorial-based decision-making came to an end, nearly half of all fellowships awarded by the Memorial to persons outside the United States went to persons listing some field of economics as either a primary research or teaching interest. Given that these fellowships candidates were recruited by the Memorial's representatives, it seems clear that persons with skills and interests in economics were actively sought. Such a reality fits with the fact that economic research was a growing interest for the Memorial throughout the 1920s.[4]

The Memorial's international fellowships programme received high praise. Commenting, for example, was Julius Rosenwald, the Chicago industrialist and philanthropist. Rosenwald recognized the value of an exchange programme for scholars and scientists, especially the benefits of diminishing the isolation of many alternative theories and points of view. The exchange programme served well to enable the sharing and coordinating of developments in the social sciences. Ruml and Rosenwald shared ideas numerous times, and they saw such a fellowships programme as an essential aid to the worldwide development of the social sciences.[5]

For a domestic fellowships programme, the Memorial leadership decided it was best to distribute grants through a central organization that would be separate from the Memorial; a level of control and oversight was needed that would go beyond anything the Memorial would want to do. To operate it right would require a level of trust comparable to what the Memorial required when allocating large grants to research centres. Ruml understood the task, which was to direct funds in ways that are legitimate 'under the Memorial's policies' to projects of 'almost a bewildering fertility'. He expressed his expectation that supported projects, 'in spite of far-reaching implications, are concrete and practical; and they associate themselves together with reasonable coherency'.[6]

The Memorial also started a fellowships programme to make small direct grants to US scholars and scientists. These grants were for limited travel needs, which could be useful for spreading and coordinating knowledge. One group of persons receiving such grants was recent doctoral graduates, who would spend a year or two visiting different research institutions. Recipients of travel grants could share what they learned at their home institution, while also considering other points of view offered at host institutions. It was of little if any concern what these different points of view were, for what mattered was only that a greater number of younger social scientists could learn a greater variety of theories and methods. This was the kind of programme that the Memorial could get involved in, and they did. As travelling grants were awarded, a significant number of travel grants happened to go to persons trained in economics, most often in labour economics.[7]

Responding to these new fellowships programmes was Robert S. Brookings, the economist and philanthropist. Brookings had an idea to establish a new graduate school to serve as a home base for many fellowship recipients, both as students and as teachers. The graduate school, located in Washington, DC, began as a satellite campus of Washington University in St Louis – and initially it was the Washington University Graduate School of Economics and Government. Memorial leadership saw the graduate school as playing an important role in helping to coordinate research in the social sciences. The school was a place where doctoral students, post-doctoral students and faculty members could gather to emphasize their pursuit of social science. The Memorial awarded nearly $800,000 to get the school started by the end of 1924. Over its first five years, the school received $2.8 million in total support from the Memorial.

Brookings soon recommended joining together the Institute for Government Research and the Institute of Economics with the new graduate school. The merger of the three organizations happened in 1927, when they formed the Robert Brookings Graduate School – today's Brookings Institution.[8]

## The National Bureau and the Economic Foundation

In the winter of 1920, as already noted, Columbia University's Wesley C. Mitchell led the creation of the National Bureau of Economic Research, initially established independent of any philanthropic support. The National Bureau began its work during a time of economic turbulence involving inflation as well as recession. The group's first major project was to measure national income in the United States. National Bureau economists completed the project, which included some breakthrough methods for analysing income distribution. The nation's policymakers viewed the National Bureau's findings as important, particularly because their methods established what previously had been only theorized: that the top 1 per cent of the nation's property owners received a very great percentage of the nation's total income, around 15 per cent.[9]

From the point of view of the Memorial, an important question was clear with respect to the National Bureau: how active should the Memorial be in helping to guide the activities of a research organization? Ruml and the Memorial trustees considered this question and answered, effectively, 'Yes' – it can be acceptable to play some kind of a role in the process. One of Ruml's early decisions at the Memorial was to support a new independent organization that could work in coordination with the National Bureau. The project gained conceptualization as a strategy to obtain greater financial support for the National Bureau, without becoming involved in any selection of particular research projects at the National Bureau. In January 1923, the Memorial established an 'Economic Foundation' (EF), which was carefully affiliated with the National Bureau. Legal establishment of the EF came with an express purpose 'to encourage and support such public educational, charitable or benevolent uses and purposes as will in the judgment of the trustees and without resort to propaganda most effectively further the economic, social and industrial welfare of humanity'. The EF was to be little involved in any science or policy deliberation, but was primarily to 'assist in the making of exact and impartial investigations in the fields of economic, social and industrial science for the advancement of human knowledge'.[10]

Leaders at the Memorial and at the National Bureau worked well together to obtain financial support for the EF. Mitchell had an outstanding reputation and was willing to oversee the operation of the EF based on a relationship of trust. With substantial Memorial funds now coming through the EF to the National Bureau, the first major objective, in Mitchell's estimation, was to study 'Unemployment and the Business Cycle'. An important factor in all of this was Mitchell's assurance that the EF would be kept sufficiently separate from any research decisions made at the National Bureau. Business cycles were urgent and concrete problems in society, and this made the Memorial's support appropriate.

In October 1922, M. C. Rorty, now the assistant director at the National Bureau, composed a formal statement of rationale for the EF; thus it was on record that Memorial funds go first to an 'independent' entity, and that all money that goes onward to the National Bureau 'involves the support of scientific work of very general significance'; and it is work that will 'lie clearly in the field which foundations can properly cultivate'. What was accomplished in framing the stated purpose for the EF, said Rorty, was to 'very cleverly overcome all the difficulties that exist in creating an endowment specifically for the National Bureau of Economic Research'. With this situation perhaps as precedent, the door was now open for the Memorial to support other research organizations of a similar kind.[11]

It was also in this context that in July 1924 Ruml constructed a statement of guiding principles for the Memorial. He provided twelve principles, arranged in two categories. Six principles served as criteria for identifying organizations 'inadvisable' to support with a grant, while six others helped to identify the kinds of research projects potentially desirable to support. Ruml's principles could be useful in the situation of trying to help develop new research centres, research fields or research organizations. The trustees approved Ruml's twelve principles.[12]

## The Social Science Research Council

In May 1921, Charles E. Merriam, a professor of political science at the University of Chicago, expressed an interest in building a new organization for social scientists. Merriam emphasized the need for a kind of umbrella group to assist in coordinating activities of all social scientists. 'Science is a great cooperative enterprise in which many intelligences must labour together', he wrote. 'There must always be wide scope for the spontaneous and unregimented activity of the individual, but the success of the expedition is conditioned upon some general plan of organization'. Merriam's view was somewhat akin to Ruml's view, as expressed in October 1922.[13]

Believing in the 'communal nature' of social science, Merriam was a rigorous investigator and a compelling writer. He was devoted to his belief that modern social science must be driven by data and hypotheses. In 1922, in a committee report for the American Political Science Association (APSA), Merriam first proposed establishing a Social Science Research Council (SSRC). What every social scientist needed to begin achieving greater success was to forge closer patterns of interaction between all social scientists in all fields. Merriam contacted Ruml, and the two agreed that such an organization was needed.[14]

Merriam was the right person to spearhead the creation of such an organizational advancement in the social sciences. In two papers in 1925, he further worked out his thoughts. It was time for social scientists to leave behind the 'softer', descriptive styles of inquiry. Too often what political scientists still did was 'to meditate and then elaborate in literary form an idea, without verification or with very inadequate verification'. While a slight role was still permissible for a 'guess or hunch' in guiding the direction of 'measurement and the analysis' of a particular problem, the world had changed so fundamentally that an increased complexity of social and economic problems necessitated greater research coordination.[15]

In another paper (his 1925 address as president of the American Political Science Association), Merriam asked the question: what sort of an organizational design should perform the necessary integration? He emphasized that while different fields of social science might look at the same problem from different viewpoints, ultimately there is a communal nature of any practical work in the social sciences. 'The problem of social behaviour is essentially one problem', he said, 'and while the angles of approach may and should be different, the scientific result will be imperfect unless these points of view are at times brought together in some effective way, so that the full benefit of the multiple analysis may be realized'. Much of Merriam's presidential address revolved around an idea that a unity of the social sciences need not require any common agreement between social scientists; only that they must develop channels of communication to foster their exchange of views.[16]

Creation of the SSRC was already underway by 1925. Planning meetings began in May 1923, pushed forward by Merriam and the political scientists. In July of that year, Ruml met with Merriam who reported on a decision reached by leading persons in the social sciences, that it would be desirable 'to form a council similar to the National Research Council that should operate in the fields of Economics, Sociology and Political Science'. Ruml agreed:

> There is no question in my mind but that there must be brought into existence sooner or later an organization that will function in the field of the social sciences in the same way as the National Research Council functions in the field of the physical and biological sciences.[17]

Rockefeller philanthropy already had great success supporting scientists through the NRC; this bolstered confidence. Appealing in particular was that the SSRC could, like the NRC, include a committee-based model to operate fellowships programmes for individual researchers.

Legal incorporation of the SSRC took a bit of time, but it came on 27 December 1924, with the political scientists joined initially by the American Economic Association and the American Sociological Society. With the legal incorporation accomplished, funding could follow, especially from the Memorial. In early 1925, a five-year appropriation of $425,000 was made for fellowships awards, including an expressed focus on post-doctoral support. Leadership at the SSRC advocated a cooperative focus on 'social problems' and a main objective was to expand and improve 'real-world' research opportunities. By the spring of 1925, seven disciplinary associations were on board with the SSRC, representing the fields of sociology, anthropology, political science, economics, history, psychology and statistics.[18]

With their receipt of generous Memorial support, which would grow to $2.7 million by the end of 1928, the SSRC's leadership knew to respect the views at the Memorial, where the belief was held that the SSRC should strictly complement and never rival other research organizations.[19]

At the time of establishment of the SSRC, two leading sciences were psychology and economics. Each of these sciences may have been more data-seeking than the other social sciences. In terms of their applied dimensions, psychology and economics could each contribute to helping correct maladjustments in relationships between people, groups, institutions and technologies. Psychologists can show people how to adjust to changed conditions, while economists can discover how to adjust the changed conditions. Psychologists and economists recognized that other sciences such as sociology, political science, anthropology and history were all necessary for this work. Many social scientists tended to believe that true science should focus on demonstrable conclusions, and that an empirical attitude would propel the social sciences forward.[20]

The SSRC got underway especially on a foundation of research in social psychology. To Merriam, 'measurable behaviours' and 'social forces' should be the centrepiece elements in a 'new synthesis of knowledge'. The SSRC encouraged a plurality of research methods, which would help to coordinate multiple 'angles' from which to study any particular social or economic problem. One friend of Merriam was Mitchell, who was also instrumental in building the SSRC. Mitchell encouraged respect for the SSRC within the economics community, and the SSRC in turn supplied generous financial support to economists.[21]

## The Hanover Conferences

Between 1925 and 1930, a series of almost legendary summer meetings took place annually, at Hanover, New Hampshire. At these meetings, a great amount of strategic and conceptual groundwork was created for the SSRC, including a statement of goals. Lasting about two weeks during each August and September, these meetings became an entry point for ongoing influence by the Memorial. One form of influence was the Memorial's financial underwriting of the conferences.[22]

The first of the conferences was initially called the 'Dartmouth Convivium'. Memorial leadership took the initiative to arrange the conference. Arrangements proceeded with a division between psychology on one side, and all other social sciences constituting another group entirely. Ruml began the work to organize the psychology section by sending letters to leading scientists in the field. Numerous responses helped produce a list of forty-two names. The Memorial's Executive Committee approved plans for a psychology conference, and another round of letters focused on two points of concern: psychologists worked too much in isolation, and particularly inadequate were research facilities for studying infancy and childhood development. Ultimately at least thirty-five psychologists were able to attend that summer's conference.[23]

The second section of the conference actually came about as an afterthought when some half a dozen social scientists from other fields were initially invited to the psychology conference. In that initial small group was Charles Merriam, and it was he who suggested some additional names for inclusion, including sociologist Robert Lynd and economist Clarence Ayres. Following this move, other invitees began to recommend more names. Through a back-and-forth dialogue, a final plan was hatched, and it was for a two-section conference, which became the Hanover Conference. Social scientists invited to the 1925 conference believed the meeting was an important gathering. Mitchell offered an impression of 'how large a service it seems to me that the Laura Spelman Rockefeller Memorial is rendering to the social sciences' by arranging such a gathering. Other invitees expressed similar words of appreciation.[24]

Participants in the conference produced a number of reports. The psychology section produced two: a 66-page compilation of comments, and a hefty 780-page final report. Clear above all else is that the psychologists spent a great deal of time discussing the purposes of psychological research, and that they extensively discussed relationships between their science and other social sciences. Participants in the general conference produced reports as well, and there was a central purpose that emerged from this half of the conference, which was to compile a list of important problems in need of study. One report from the general half of the conference was a 127-page statement, produced by a newly established 'Committee on Problems and Policy'. The statement included a 'Source List of Research Problems' which identified 268 different problems in need of scientific study. Identified problems were wide-ranging, from a study of child labour in the South, to an analysis of relationships between shopping centres and economic progress, to a 'study of thwarted ambitions'. A second report from the general conference was a 192-page record of all presentations at the conference, and it included its own 7-page list of recommendations for future fields of activity. The general conference provided an overall recommendation for the SSRC, which was to increase its focus on promoting interactions between the social sciences. Specific recommendations were to compile a list of research agencies gathering information on university endowments, to learn about the financial status of other agencies supporting social science and to recommend that SSRC members prepare for the next summer's conference. The SSRC's members were to focus especially on the 'gathering of data on specific interests and projects of those of its members engaged in research', and they were to see 'that this data be at the disposal of the Council'.[25]

Months of group meetings followed the first Hanover Conference. Preparations got along well for a second conference the next summer. The Memorial indicated its interest in again supporting the conference, and indeed would end up supporting all of these summer conferences through to 1930. Taken together, the half a dozen Hanover Conferences proved to be a highly exciting environment for all participants. Often the meetings included discussions about interconnections between the social sciences, as well as some attention to exploring changing boundaries around the social sciences. In 1926, for example, the renowned historian Charles Beard emphasized a need for increased research on 'economic motives in politics'. 'Some people', he declared,

> think that the economic motive has been overworked in the study of history and sociology and current politics, but I am inclined to think that it not only is not overworked but has never been systematically and thoroughly and intelligently applied as it might be.

As just one of many examples of thinking about integration in the social sciences, Beard's approach was to strengthen the economics component throughout the social sciences.[26]

In 1927, a leading speaker at the Hanover Conference was Ruml himself. Ruml discussed the workings of the Memorial. He shared the fact that his assistants all had significant flexibility of decision-making within their areas of specialization, with one result being that the Memorial's home office was a place rich in conversation. Ruml indicated that the Memorial's leadership increasingly recognized the fundamental importance of economic research to any successful programme of social reform.[27]

At the next Hanover Conference, in 1928, attending economists received their own subsection of the conference. They discussed various sorts of economic problems, as well as explored ideas about the overall organization of the social sciences. They considered numerous contact points between economics and other social sciences, and they produced a 418-page report, focused largely on what economists can contribute to problem-solving. The report included discussion provided by Frank Taussig, Jacob Viner, Frank Knight, Wesley Mitchell, William Beveridge and E. R. A. Seligman, among others. Also important was a new goal stated by the economists to identify every single economic problem requiring attention. Participants explored ways in which economic science might be affected by increased government activity in the economy. They explored new interrelations between economics and management studies, and they explored many other promising lines of future research as well. 'In general, our idea is that the discussions ought to indicate where we are in economic science, briefly whence we came, where we seem to be going, and possibly the direction in which we ought to be headed'.[28]

Through the six Hanover Conferences between 1925 and 1930, SSRC participants designed a committee structure for their organization. Led by frequent attendees such as Merriam and Mitchell, and with the likes of James Angell (Yale University), Frederick Woodbridge (Columbia University), Howard Odum (University of North Carolina) and Guy Stanton Ford (University of Minnesota) often chiming in, the SSRC developed a statement of general objectives for a committee: 'The objectives are a coherent conception of the area in terms of its central or major problems, the subordination of its minor problems, and a decision as to the most promising point or points of attack'. Social scientists must remain always receptive to the 'continuous reworking of any plan of a field', and the stated aim for any committee was 'to attain the best picture it can through the agency of the most competent group judgment it can secure'.[29]

A number of SSRC committees were established to oversee identified problem areas. The first two committees (created shortly before the first Hanover meeting) focused on human migration and on the mechanization of industry; these committees lasted only until 1927. Committees were established at the first Hanover meeting to focus on eighteenth amendment studies, crime research and agricultural problems. In 1926 committees were established to focus on industrial relations and on international relations.[30]

The Hanover Conferences were great events for building a sense of togetherness. People became chums at these conferences; there were even whole families who attended. Participants found plenty of opportunity to blend intensive work schedules with much socializing. There was fine food and drink, golf and shuffleboard were available, as well as simple hillside strolls. These conferences seem to have been great pleasure. One pleasing illustration comes in a letter from anthropologist Robert Redfield to his wife, at the time of the 1930 conference. Redfield reported on how plush the situation was. 'The Social Science Research Council pays their fares, and boards them, and feeds them and washes their clothes, and gives them carts to go to the golf club, and then expects them to produce "significant results"', Redfield wrote. He added:

> The place is overrun with pedants and potentates. The potentates are the executive secretaries of the big foundations – collectively they represent huge (staggering) amounts of money that has been set aside for research. The pedants have invited the potentates so that the potentates may see how the pedants do their most effective thinking, and how they arrange to spend that money.[31]

Although the Hanover Conferences came to an end in 1930, annual summer meetings for SSRC leadership continued for many years thereafter.[32]

## Boundaries Reassessed

In addition to the SSRC's committee reports and numerous publications, especially by sociologists seeking unified social science, another approach to identifying new projects was tried at the Memorial in 1926. The Memorial requested its own report, to be prepared by Arthur Woods. In seventy-two pages, the report surveyed early successes by three research organizations: the SSRC, the Institute of Economics and the Brookings Graduate School. These three organizations pursued their supported fields of social science with a relative lack of duplication. One assessment, offered regarding Brookings, was that faculty at the school were careful to differentiate between social science and social technology, including regular discussions about how to separate social science from the practices of political action. They had a goal to defend their organization against any accusation that it was becoming a politically-aligned agency.[33]

As to the Institute of Economics, Woods cited a question that was sometimes asked about the organization: had it become merely a 'propaganda institute'? The report noted the four areas that were dealt with by the institute (namely, international commercial policies, post-war international reconstruction, agricultural economics, and industry and labour), and he opined: 'There seems to be some question as to the actual purpose of the institute – whether for unbiased research, or for propaganda to influence public opinion and legislation'. Also worth noticing in the report were Ruml's own words regarding the institute: that with respect to propaganda purposes, the institute 'has never, as a matter of fact, performed' that way. '[W]ith the selection of its Director, Dr. Moulton, formerly Professor of Economics in the University of Chicago, the Institute became essentially one of research and not of propaganda'. However, the report also cited Abraham Flexner's contrasting view, that when the path was charted for the Institute of Economics, 'research and propaganda [we]re inextricably mingled in the conception which was presented'. The matter evidently remained unresolved.[34]

In addition to Woods's 1926 report, there were occasions when the Memorial identified itself as in a position to help define what social scientists do. One example of Memorial support for research that potentially could pertain to public policy came in 1928, when the SSRC recommended supporting a field of studies in sex and family. One goal was to help scientists discover fundamental causes of social problems, and the idea was that by encouraging studies of couples and families, progress could be made in this regard. Scientists who advocated for such research, for example sociologist William F. Ogburn, emphasized that the SSRC was supporting research not on human physical intimacy, but on problems of sex and family 'from the social angle'. The research would aim to be a 'systematic investigation of those social problems which pertain to the relationship of the sexes, such as marriage, sex education, and the family'. A 'Committee on Sex and Family Relationships' was established at the SSRC that same year.[35]

Already supporting scientific research on problems of sex was the National Research Council, which in 1922 (in cooperation with the Bureau of Social Hygiene) established a Committee for Research in Problems of Sex. Thus when the SSRC established its Committee on Sex and Family Relationships, research projects were selected in coordination with what the NRC was already doing. The SSRC focused first on producing a report on 'the possibilities of research in the family and in the field of sex', and in November 1928, the SSRC's 'sex committee' worked with invited NRC members to identify potential lines of research for social scientists, which included family conflicts as well as problems associated with home management, home consumption and family housing.[36]

By interacting with each other, the 'sex committees' of the NRC and SSRC were able to identify what subjects of study were most appropriate for each of their committees. Notably the NRC supported the primate studies of Robert Yerkes at Yale. Beginning in 1926, the Foundation provided some support for sex research at the University of California, Berkeley as well.[37]

In 1929, US President Herbert Hoover became interested in the SSRC. He asked for a new committee to study 'social problems of national importance'. The SSRC established the 'President's Research Committee on Social Trends', just prior to the October 1929 stock market crash. The committee's task was to put together 'a complete, impartial examination of the facts', so as to better see 'where social stresses are occurring and where major efforts should be undertaken to deal with them constructively'. Led by Merriam, Mitchell and Ogburn, the committee began its work to make sense of many facts in wide-ranging fields, and they kept any policy recommendations to a minimum.

The SSRC's 'president's committee' continued its work on a multi-year plan of data collection and analysis, and in 1933 they published a two-volume report, *Recent Social Trends in the United States*, completed right at the end of Hoover's presidency. The report introduced detailed analysis of various topics, including such fields as population, race and ethnic groups, women and family, consumption and leisure, labour, crime, health, education, public welfare, economic organization, public administration and government. One of the most popular research methods in the social sciences during the first quarter of the twentieth century, the social survey of a single community, was not in *Recent Social Trends*.[38]

President Franklin Delano Roosevelt warmly received the Memorial-supported, SSRC report on *Recent Social Trends*. Roosevelt was friendly with the SSRC, and as early as 1928 he served on an SSRC Advisory Committee on Business Research. A version of that committee remained as the National Resources Planning Board, refashioned by Roosevelt in 1933.[39]

Another basis for government leaders to think highly of the SSRC's social scientists would have been the organization's statements of objectives. One document from 1928 was labelled a 'Definition of Council Objectives', and it stated the seven tasks: to develop research personnel, improve research organization, improve research methods, preserve research materials, disseminate research materials, facilitate research projects and boost 'the public appreciation of the significance of the social sciences'.[40]

Another SSRC policy statement, from about the same time, introduced five 'interlocking principles' to serve as operating guidelines. Chief among the guidelines was that all of the social sciences are a collective enterprise requiring 'interdisciplinary' interaction. The SSRC's committee structure, aimed at regularly reevaluating research objectives, was an important foundation for promoting the 'interdisciplinary' point of view. Indeed, the very term 'interdisciplinary' is found to have begun at the SSRC. The term, according to historian David Sills, 'seems to have begun life in the corridors and meeting rooms of the Social Science Research Council as a kind of bureaucratic shorthand for what the Council saw as its chief function, the promotion of research that involved two or more of its seven constituent societies'.[41]

## Humane Studies as a Boundary

A somewhat popular topic of discussion during the 1920s had to do with identifying the furthest reach for subject matter that could be included in the social sciences. One such research field was human social biology, which both the Memorial and the Foundation recognized as a bit on the controversial side. Another field located somewhere near a boundary of the social sciences was 'Humane Studies'.

As early as June 1923, Ruml contacted French economic historian Charles Rist to ask for a report on the social sciences in Europe. Rist produced a memorandum which emphasized the need, especially in his home country, to better cluster together economics, political science and sociology. Such a proposed conjoining of these three social sciences would have 'as its aim to direct and encourage scientific work in this field'. The group could be arranged as an 'organized teaching system', comparable to what already existed in France for history, psychology and anthropology – each of which was a field 'already provided with laboratories and libraries, scientific meetings and regular publications'. Rist even suggested that Europe's relatively more interwoven condition of the social sciences might be a bringing together of somewhat different breeds of social science than in the United States. One potential difference was that the social sciences in Europe could include more facets of research in the humanities. In his response to Rist, Ruml recognized Rist as an important figure in 'the development of economic science in France', and he was clear about his valuing of Rist's input. Ruml shared his understanding that Rist's survey involved an informal bringing together of the views of a number of persons

who have an interest in the scientific aspects of this subject, for the purpose of examining what is desirable in the development of this field and for the carrying on of
various investigations which will be determined upon from time to time.[42]

Ruml also gained advice from Abraham Flexner. In 1925 the two exchanged
thoughts to contemplate the nature of 'good' social science. Ruml used the
opportunity to explore the extent to which the quality of any particular work in
social science might be best defined on a case-by-case basis – essentially a situation that 'you know it when you see it'. Because the social sciences seemed on
the path to integration, researchers should also attempt no prior declaration of
whether any specific problem should primarily belong to any particular field in
the social sciences. The better way to identify all appropriate fields of social science is through an open process that allows scientists in all fields to discover
what they can contribute to studying any particular problem. Any definition of
a particular social science's boundaries 'in the abstract' would be challenging,
while 'in concrete cases the limitation is easier'. Ruml explained to Flexner: 'The
field which the Memorial is exploring under the term social science is intelligi-
ble only in terms of our purposes. We are interested in the problems that arise
in connection with the tendency of human beings to associate'. The Memorial
needed to rely on grant applicants to identify the kinds of problems that tend to
arise in society; for in many cases the question of whether a particular problem
can be addressed by any particular social science, 'hinges primarily on the interest and approach of the individual investigator or group of investigators'. The
nature of social science will likely remain 'extremely broad' in the future, partly
because of the Memorial's strategy to provide grants to all outstanding applicants who can convince the Memorial that their described problem and research
approach deserve support.[43]

Ruml sometimes sought input from outside advisers. One advisor from
whom he received ideas about the nature of social science was John Candler
Cobb, who in September 1925 submitted to Ruml a memorandum titled, simply, 'The Social Sciences'. Cobb, a Boston operator of a private railroad, was a
self-formed scholar who was recognized in the mid to late 1920s for his articles on how to transform the social sciences into quantitative sciences. In his
memo, Cobb emphasized the 'appreciation' many persons are coming to have
of the social sciences for 'their existence as important factors in the ordering
of our lives'. Yet Cobb saw that 'The principle obstacle to their development is
the entire lack of agreement as to what they are and the existing confusion and
indefiniteness as to their province'.[44]

A question asked in 1925 was whether boundaries should be established for
the social sciences in Europe. To some persons it seemed that boundaries between
the social sciences and non-social sciences differed in Europe, at least when

compared to the United States. Leaders at the Memorial wondered whether any continuing state of 'disorganization and depression in the social sciences in Europe' might have impacts upon future peace in Europe. Ruml assigned to the American Historical Association a task to provide historical perspective on the social sciences in Europe, while to the American Council of Learned Societies he assigned a project to compare the states of 'humanistic studies and the social sciences' in Europe and the United States. The work undertaken by the ACLS produced substantial feedback, resulting as it did in a lengthy report by Frederick Austin Ogg, published as *Research in the Humanistic and Social Sciences* (1928).[45]

The idea to support scientific research in the humanities turned out to be a popular one. Arthur Woods, writing in 1925, advocated seeking 'the best methods of procedure with reference to securing men for looking up facts' about what is being done in humane studies:

> The plan that had gradually formed itself is for a survey of the field in Europe, to find out in general, what is the state of the Humane Studies, and in particular, who are the very great men in these subjects, under what conditions are they working, what, if anything, need be done to help them produce their best work, whether of aid of some kind at home, or the possibility of international intercourse.

In another memorandum on 'Study of the Humanities', written for the Memorial at about the same time, an expressed recognition was 'that the Humanities have had the tradition of putting a premium on originality, which has exercised a very marked influence on the development of culture'. One added thought was that 'the role of the arts in encouraging originality and the breaking of tradition will be seen to be considerable'.[46]

One group of European scholars who were interested in surveying the condition of the social sciences was at Cambridge University. In 1925, Cambridge submitted to the Memorial a grant application which emphasized the value of 'humane studies'. Of interest to Cambridge was a possibility that concrete modern-day problems might be researched in this field. What the Cambridge faculty put on paper played to their strengths by asking for support for one or two professors who would explore new approaches to research in the humanities. For example, Geoffrey Winthrop Young, the lead investigator on one proposed project, wanted to use concrete historical examples to learn what makes great leaders. Knowledge of such attributes could help future leaders accomplish greater good for society. Young also proposed to include a general survey of the condition of humanities research in Europe. Memorial trustees approved the proposal and granted the funds.[47]

Young began his survey in September 1925, and a year later he submitted to the Memorial a 143-page report aimed largely at evaluating whether additional funding might help promote a more 'rigorous' and 'objective' quality of research in the humanities. Young remained interested in developing more uniform methods for gathering useful information from humanities research. He described a 'scope of inquiry' that could identify ways 'of discovering the type of individual interested by nature to exercise an influence upon his own or succeeding generations'. The chief goal was that 'of developing – in the case of the still immature – these natural characteristics, so that they should be used beneficially and in the interests of a better humanity'. Young then set to work compiling a history of leadership, which he constructed from archival sources and interviews. He was clear about his aim to knock down a boundary wall:

> A little thought, and a good deal of conversation, soon made it clear that the distinction between 'Humanities' and 'Science', in so far as the terms are popularly used in education or to define departments of learning, could not effectively be maintained. For hardly any single subject could a line of demarcation between the two be definitely traced.

Case by case attention was required, since any scheme to classify materials 'into "scientific" or "humane" must be of individuals, not by subjects'.[48]

While Young was preparing his second report, this one on his actual findings about the history of leadership qualities, Cambridge further committed itself to a decision to support humane studies as a potential field in the social sciences. In April 1926, faculty at the school submitted a proposal that they hoped would fit with 'the project of extending the activities of the Laura Spelman Rockefeller Memorial Fund into the field of the humanities'. Cambridge's Robert Eisler, a fine humanist specializing in Greek and Christian symbolism, saw the value in extending research efforts into the humanities as being something more than a mere 'great man' theory of history. The kinds of humanities research that were proposed by Cambridge could indeed be seen as social science, Eisler explained, since one goal was to rigorously identify and describe how and why people do things. A second goal was to help rebuild European culture. And finally, studies of art and literature could assist in learning about the condition of the United States; for 'nothing could be more helpful for a student or professor of social sciences than the opportunity to see and study the rich, complicated social and industrial life of America', and to do so through the study of art, music and literature. As 'most of the material for study and research work in the field of the humanities is concentrated in European libraries, museums, and excavation fields', said Eisler,

> European scholars have developed peculiar methods of dealing with such subjects and have put in motion a very efficient machinery of collective research in order to make those documents and monuments of its common past available to whole civilized worlds.

Eisler emphasized the importance, therefore, of scholars travelling between the United States and Europe.[49]

Ruml deliberated over whether to support humanities research at Cambridge. One round of discussion had taken place beginning in May 1925, and the tentative idea was for potentially two funded faculty positions in the social sciences. One year later, the Memorial offered, and Cambridge accepted, a funded professorship in political science. But when the Memorial offered to arrange for the funded professorship in sociology, Cambridge declined it.[50]

Historians have worked to interpret these interactions between Cambridge and the Memorial. It is fair to interpret the Memorial's financial support of Cambridge as part of a broader experimental move to support some humanities research. But if looked at as a stand-alone matter, then it can seem possible that the Memorial intended to use the confirmed grant for the political science professorship to encourage some specific directions of research. Another possibility is that the supported chair in sociology was not yet arranged because Cambridge's own administrators were not sure of the kind of sociological research that would meet the Memorial's scientific standards. This latter explanation would fit with Ruml's nature, in that he would have kept a door open to persuade Cambridge to accept financial assistance at such a time that a sufficiently scientific approach is described. In other words, Ruml might simply have withheld support for the sociology chair until Cambridge stated a research plan with which the Memorial could agree. These at least seem to be some additional possibilities.[51]

We can also step back in time and notice that interactions between Cambridge and the Memorial began within the context of Ruml's general views toward Europe. He already had an impression about the nature of the social sciences in Europe. He also had a preference for relying on trusted acquaintances to evaluate potential grant recipients in Europe. One such report came to Ruml in February 1924, from European advisor J. J. Coss, a Columbia University philosophy professor who specialized in pragmatism and the idea of social control. Coss identified the school's contentment as an 'isolated' institution 'not at all anxious to grow', and he specifically recommended that the Memorial 'not do anything at Cambridge'.[52]

Some pertinent language also appears in an August 1926 letter by Ruml. He shared some thoughts with E. M. Hopkins, a professor of English at the University of Kansas, and a long-time director of a project (supported by the United States Bureau of Education) to study the cost and labour needs of English education in the United States. Regarding Cambridge in particular, Ruml described how he maintained a hope that the Memorial was making progress in 'getting an edge into one of the most conservative of universities'. The real matter of concern was only that Cambridge's own statement of intent in the field of sociology was not framed in concrete enough terms. In fact the Cambridge faculty even openly said that 'the outline of what was proposed in Sociology did not seem sufficiently detailed to justify recommending that Chair at this time'. Ruml, in response, stated his hope to encourage Cambridge 'to re-examine their position in Social Science a bit'. His own explicit goal was that 'of meeting the Cambridge people on their own ground and not trying to inject too many of our own notions into a foreign soil'.[53]

Still one more voice that chimed in with a thought was Lawrence Frank, who agreed that the overall Memorial strategy would be made stronger by adding to their support of research fields across the social sciences, a supported field in 'that branch of philosophy which deals with the history of ideas'.[54]

## Legal Studies as a Boundary

Another boundary question at the Memorial concerned whether to support research in legal studies. Would such a field fit into a programme to fundamentally build the social sciences? An idea was that research activities within law schools (even though previously identified as schools of 'social technology') might soon be placed more on the side of social science. Somewhat resembling the pliable abutment between 'social science' and 'humane studies' for which the Memorial largely focused on Cambridge University as a kind of test case, a similar question was whether legal studies could be made more scientific.

In early 1927 a Memorial statement was made on the idea of 'social technology'. Expansion in the Memorial's support of 'social technology' had been well accomplished over the preceding four years, the statement said, and it was time to wonder if it might be best to hold off on any further efforts to promote social technology, with the reason being that 'the social sciences have as yet contributed few tested facts upon which a social technology may be constructed'.[55]

Memorial leadership was able to explore the possibility of such a research field by focusing especially on grant proposals from Columbia University and Yale University.

Columbia University's law school contacted the Memorial in January 1927. Columbia's law faculty introduced an idea that legal analysis might be ready for tighter connection to the rest of the social sciences. A minor movement to connect law and economics was already underway. Columbia recommended that a next step was to supplement constitutional law with a body of 'real facts' coming from research in the social sciences. In particular Columbia cited the work of Leon Marshall, the University of Chicago economist, who was now a visiting professor at Columbia's law school. Marshall was exploring methods for studying the law along economic lines. One idea was to pool together all branches of the law applicable to business and industry, so as to 'assemble the rules which apply to the different processes and stages in the economic activities'. Funds were needed for another area of research, which aimed to establish links between criminal law and a body of facts in sociology.[56]

Columbia's law school dean, Huger W. Jervey, sent a letter to the Memorial explaining the main issue motivating the funding request: 'the development of thought in the law' had reached 'the point where we see clearly the necessity of having definite studies made towards programming the establishment of two lines of work in those fields where law and economics and sociology overlap'. Columbia's overriding hope was that 'the fence' between abstract law and applied law 'can be broken down', so that the law can be studied 'against a realistic background of contemporary social and economic thought and fact'. Jervey emphasized that the proposed lines of research promised to help guide efforts that 'must be made by the lawyers and the economists working together ... to tackle the fundamental problems scientifically'. The grant was awarded in May 1927.[57]

Yale University's law school, also in early 1927, introduced to the Memorial their argument that the time was right to place legal research more in contact with empirical knowledge based on 'the facts of life'. As encouraged by Yale's president, James Angell, Yale's law faculty recognized that the Memorial had an interest in promoting the methods of modern social science in every possible field. Yale's law faculty drew up a prospectus that explained how the administration of the law is a 'chaotic and maladjusted field, chiefly because of inadequate knowledge of the rules of procedure, their operation and their relation to the social sciences, psychology, criminology and penology ... This lack of knowledge', they added, 'can be removed only by a definite and concrete programme of research, directed to the collection of facts'. Such a programme – 'definitely an experiment' – was believed necessary, as the entire field of administration of the law 'must be subjected to rigorous investigation'. Workers active in administering the law, as well as active in the field of legislation, needed 'accurate information soundly analyzed'.[58]

Yale's application was a bit more abstract and general than the one submitted by Columbia's law school. Yale's application was denied. In the words of Lawrence Frank, writing to Yale's law school dean Robert M. Hutchins in March 1927, the Memorial hesitated because it felt 'hedged in by matters of policy and precedent which make it difficult to move unless conditions and prerequisites are present'. Precedent had been set, in other words, such that Yale's application would need to be made more precise with respect to what they proposed to do. Following the decision on Yale's initial application, the better part of a year went by with only minor discussions taking place between all parties.[59]

In December 1927, Yale's president Angell contacted Ruml, believing the time was right to get the ball rolling again. Angell aimed to convince his friend that Yale's law faculty had been wisely establishing the kind of projects that the Memorial could support. Yale's law faculty had shown the initiative to 'carry forward much further' their plans 'by new appointments and change of procedure, whereby the various social sciences have been brought into much more intimate contact with our legal teaching and study'. Worth citing were recent successes forging connections between criminal law, evidentiary procedure and psychology. Stronger links were also being made between public utility economics, labour research, tax studies and corporate finance. Finally, new connections were being tried between law and sociology. Angell reported that the Yale law faculty had contacted the University of North Carolina, and had learned how a few smaller projects in legal research were also underway at UNC. Yale had UNC's blessing to proceed with recommending that a matched pair of studies of legal administration could be established, one in a northern region, and the other in the South.[60]

At about the same time that Angell corresponded with Ruml, Hutchins wrote to Edmund E. Day at the Memorial. Hutchins reported that Yale's law school had a five-year programme underway to connect law and social science, and that the programme already 'has gone further than any other in the attempt to place the law among the social sciences'. Hutchins reported that Yale had recruited Walton Hamilton, already a Memorial-supported economist at the Brookings Graduate School, to teach law and economics at Yale. Hutchins concluded the letter by describing future plans with language quite befitting Ruml's preference for concreteness: 'The general drift of the School is toward the social sciences and toward the facts of life rather than the library alone as the material for research. These two aims are in fact one'.[61]

Ruml responded to Angell in December 1927. He reported on the high likelihood that the Memorial would soon approve financial support for the 'experimental project' at Yale's law school. Day responded, near the same time, to Hutchins. He reported on the impending final assessment of Yale's proposal by the Memorial's trustees – and that confidence was in place for a grant that 'would carry the Memorial into a field in which it has as yet developed no definite program'. A five-year grant was soon awarded, in January 1928.[62]

The project to financially support research connecting law and social science proved to be successful. Today's intersections between law and social science are rich and many. It seems likely that the development of closer contact between law and social science benefited greatly from the Memorial's support.

## Conclusion

This chapter focused on the support of research organizations and two areas of inquiries into potential research boundaries for the social sciences. We now have a systematic understanding of what Beardsley Ruml and the Laura Spelman Rockefeller Memorial accomplished between 1922 and 1929. The accomplishment was to help construct the foundations for modern social science. When the work was completed by January 1929, it was time for the Rockefeller Foundation to recognize that the social sciences were ready to become a division in the Foundation on par with divisions dedicated to the natural sciences and the medical sciences.

# 9 PREPARING FOR THE MERGER WITH THE ROCKEFELLER FOUNDATION

## Introduction

In January 1929, full operations began at the Rockefeller Foundation's Division of Social Sciences. By assuming oversight of many programmes developed by the Laura Spelman Rockefeller Memorial, the reorganized Foundation now had four divisions – the others being the medical sciences, the natural sciences and the humanities. The process of merging the Memorial's programme into the Foundation was a couple of years in the making. It included rounds of discussion between leaders in Rockefeller philanthropy and leaders in the social sciences. Memorial officers especially prepared for the transition by initiating a self-evaluation study.

## Self-Review

By November 1927, Beardsley Ruml had a clear list of guiding principles articulated for the philanthropic support of social science; the Memorial's trustees formally adopted Ruml's principles that month. He had worked on the principles for five years, and in the end there were eleven of them. They were to increase the stock of knowledge and appreciation of scientific methods; to promote diffusion of knowledge; to pursue studies of broad subject matter; to include both pure and applied projects; to have a programme that was international in extent; to disallow the Memorial from any direct influence on research findings; to find workable ways to support studies of controversial subjects; to support a variety of institutional types; to recognize that practical applications are necessary for testing scientific progress; to provide individual fellowships; and that 'the general aim of the program is better understanding of modern society'.[1]

When the Memorial trustees adopted Ruml's guiding principles, a phase in an experimental relationship between philanthropy and modern social science was nearing its end. Ruml's programme had done well, and a plan was coming together for the Rockefeller Foundation to absorb the Memorial's programme.

The Memorial's leaders spent the year before the merger taking stock of their goals and accomplishments.

In November 1927, in that same month of the approval of Ruml's guiding principles, the Memorial's leadership established a 'Committee on Review'. The purpose of the committee was to evaluate every field of social science supported by the Memorial. The Memorial sent out a request for comments, and they received many replies. Taken altogether, the feedback suggested a range of questions for the Memorial to consider. Had the Memorial spread its financial support widely enough? Had they dispersed money into some fields too widely? Had too many applicants merely taken advantage of the Memorial's generosity? Or, had the Memorial found some sort of a successful ratio between money distributed and successes achieved?[2]

The Memorial received a lot of feedback, and more than any other field of social science that drew attention, it was economics. Henry S. Pritchett, Director of the Carnegie Foundation, critically inquired whether the application of methods of physical science to social phenomena might be misguided to begin with. Is it possible that 'we are seeking to apply the methods of physical science to phenomena that are not amenable to such treatment'? Pritchett also believed that the fundamental social science might have become economics, 'which affects profoundly the conditions that make for true happiness or unhappiness of society'. Economics was on 'a somewhat different basis' than other social sciences, and while economic research can be made scientific, the persisting difficulty in attaining such a status

> does not arise from the fact that the methods of exact science cannot be applied, but from the fact that the phenomena to be observed are often times so complicated that it is not always possible to disentangle separate factors.

Yet economics, when applied responsibly to real conditions, 'can be completely scientific when the facts are ascertainable'.[3]

Wesley C. Mitchell, the Columbia University economist, responded with many ideas. He contemplated relationships between the discovery of knowledge and application of knowledge, and he emphasized that real-world problems will require attention from all the social sciences if there is to be any real hope of attaining complete understanding of all causes and consequences; problems studied by social scientists 'are not purely economic, purely psychological, purely political, or the like, but problems which have economic, psychological, political, sociological and other aspects'. Social scientists now understand the social sciences as 'a family' of sciences 'having common interests'. Yet still under debate was which problems will require the most immediate attack. 'What seems to be needed', Mitchell offered, 'is a reformulation of the problems which engage the attention of psychologists, economists, political scientists, sociologists, anthropologists, historians, jurists and educators'. What seemed needed was a method to 'present a series of fundamental questions concerning human behaviour, each of which has aspects of special interest to the several disciplines listed'.[4]

Others who responded included Walter F. Willcox, H. C. Taylor and Leon C. Marshall – all notable economists. Willcox, a Cornell University statistical economist known for his research on race discrimination, suggested that better development of statistical analysis, whether ultimately 'a science or a method', had been just 'adequately recognized in the Memorial's program'. To Taylor, renowned for his work in agricultural economics at the University of Wisconsin, great attention needed to be paid to agricultural economics and rural sociology, particularly to address the welfare of rural people. Marshall, the University of Chicago economist, summarized his agreeable understanding of the Memorial's position: 'Let us foster social science research, hoping thus to find generalizations from which may be derived rules of action in social technology. Research comes first; its technological applications come second'. Yet Marshall still struggled with whether or not 'the Memorial is going about its chosen task as wisely as it should'. Had too much emphasis gone to the fundamental development of the social sciences?[5]

Another group of respondents included officers and trustees at the Rockefeller philanthropies. Frank P. Bachman, of the General Education Board, observed how 'wide-flung' the 'field of social science and social technology' had become. 'Is not the Memorial undertaking to cooperate with so many different agencies that nothing impressive or permanent will be accomplished?' Perhaps the Memorial had insufficiently distinguished between functions of universities and functions of other organizations? Bachman, who was particularly abraded by an explosion of research projects at Columbia University, wondered if 'social science research is not being overstimulated – whether problems are being studied, not because they are pressing and have far-reaching significance, but because money is now available for such work'. H. J. Thorkelson, also of the General Education Board, had the social sciences in mind when he believed that the Memorial 'is correct in its policy of contributing toward research in these fields, for the accumulation of human knowledge regarding any aspect of social welfare is of fundamental importance'. Thorkelson perceived the continuing value in maintaining a distinction between scientists doing research and technicians seeking applications, and he asked: 'Does not the first field represent the more important one for a board to consider'?[6]

In contrast, one person who evidently did not take the 'science first' approach, yet who still thought in terms of a distinction between science and applications, was Selskar M. Gunn, of the Rockefeller Foundation. Gunn interpreted the Memorial's support for 'social technology' as indicating some recognition that 'much that has to do with social science is incapable at the present time of true scientific analysis'. Such a broad concept as 'social science' seemed to include areas that 'probably will never be capable of complete scientific evaluation'. Gunn recommended initiating more applied experiments.[7]

Cleveland E. Dodge, chair of the Memorial's 'Committee on Review', also provided some ideas. Like Gunn, Dodge favoured more work on applying scientific knowledge. The question, he asked, was 'whether we should give more study to the helping out of practical demonstrations along social lines rather than giving so much to developing theoretical work in the universities?'[8]

George Vincent, the Foundation's president, participated with a lengthy letter. He expressed general agreement with Ruml's guiding principles, and said that it seemed to him that there might be something valid to the idea of pursuing more real-world experiments. The Memorial had created a sound strategy by financially supporting social scientists while separately supporting studies of applications and policies within the realm of social technology. 'The delegating to universities or other agencies of the actual work in administration of investigation has vindicated itself ', he said. 'The Memorial has done well to limit its support of individual projects and to work towards institutional responsibility'. Vincent added a word of admiration for the level of success attained in meeting a principle of 'independence of responsible agencies' – with the idea being 'to detach agencies of investigation so far as possible from sources of funds'. Vincent also asked about the future if Rockefeller philanthropy became more involved in real-world experiments: '[I]s there danger of too close contact which might be interpreted as supervision and is possibly unconscious but nevertheless a real influence being brought to bear upon institutions with respect to their policies and programs'?[9]

Many valuable ideas came through in these letters, and the committee compiled a digest. They identified 160 main points, and categorized them under four headings: 'General Objectives', 'Scope of Program', 'Agencies or Means of Making the Program Effective' and 'Internal Organization'. Finally the committee prepared a summary report that boiled down all thoughts into two overriding objectives: the need to advance 'social science' and the need to better achieve 'social control'. The committee particularly noted many inquiries about 'The necessity of a more careful definition of the field of social sciences'. Respondents generally agreed that Rockefeller philanthropy should 'not make reform its immediate objective'. Yet some persons believed that reform could be a more active objective, at least if social conditions warrant it. For the present time, however, the main objective remained clear: 'to increase the body of knowledge which in the hands of competent technicians may be expected in time to result in substantial social control'. The Committee on Review ultimately declared: 'The purpose of the program in social science and social technology is so to increase the knowledge and understanding of social phenomena as to assure a more purposeful, satisfying, and beneficent development of human society'.[10]

The conclusion was that it was not yet time to use accumulated knowledge in the social sciences to begin any pursuit of a major investment in building social technologies directed toward reform. The social sciences needed still to attain more knowledge.

## Last Days of the Memorial

As 1928 came to a close, the Memorial's leadership could take stock of some outstanding achievements. One measure of success could be monetary; for during the time of Ruml's leadership, which began in 1922, large-scale appropriations by the Memorial reached over $20 million distributed for social science and social technology. Beyond that, many millions of dollars went to a wide mix of projects in social science and social technology. The Memorial had used its money, and that is one measure of things.[11]

Ruml's personal view can provide a measure of success. In his 'Final Report', Ruml reflected on many accomplishments. The intensive monetary infusion into the social sciences had taken hold and promoted a noticeably accelerated rate of development across a wide range of fields. Ruml expressed great confidence that connections were tightened between fundamental and applied social science, as he wrote 'that through the social sciences might come more intelligent measures of social control that would reduce such irrationalities as are represented by poverty, class conflict, and war between nations'. Ruml hoped to see applications of social science continue. When the Memorial's days were done, in January 1929, Ruml left Rockefeller philanthropy and took a position as Dean of Social Sciences at the University of Chicago.[12]

Another fair measure of success can be the level of respect held for Ruml's guiding principles. Attention to articulating the guiding principles had been reinforced many times at the Memorial, and especially in 1927, when the Memorial's trustees approved the 'Principles Governing the Memorial's Program in the Social Science'. At the final meeting of the Memorial, in December 1928, the trustees transmitted these principles to the Foundation's new Division of Social Sciences. Tacked on as well were two overriding objectives: to promote an appreciation of scientific methods; and to increase useful knowledge. Leadership at the new division soon also confirmed that applied social science had an important role to play, in that 'The hypotheses of social science can only rarely, if ever, be proved or disproved by laboratory methods'. Because tests of social science through practical applications were now seen as generally indispensable, 'the possibilities of social experimentation are to be kept constantly in mind; and opportunities for practical demonstrations may be utilized whenever they promise to throw light upon the validity of tentative social findings'.[13]

## The Division of Social Sciences

A plan was set. On 3 January 1929, the Rockefeller Foundation's Division of Social Sciences began operations. On that first day the transferred statement of guiding principles was approved by the Foundation's trustees, and Edmund E. Day began his work as director of the division. Day named Sydnor Walker as assistant director. The immediate plan for the division was to maintain the social sciences programme as it was. Existing financial commitments were to be met, and the process of evaluating grant proposals would be continued. A new phase was underway in the relationship between Rockefeller philanthropy and social science. And, a remarkable phase was completed.

# CONCLUSION

Did leaders in Rockefeller philanthropy promote preferred research agendas in the social sciences? Did their efforts conflict with an ideal of scientific objectivity?

Increasingly over a period from the late 1880s to the late 1920s, persons associated with Rockefeller philanthropy made genuine efforts to support social scientists while identifying ways in which personal biases could creep into their decision-making. Through a period of four decades, leaders at Rockefeller philanthropy established principles and mechanisms to protect against this. These principles and mechanisms proved relatively successful at neutralizing personal biases of at least most kinds. One overriding principle was an emphasis on supporting a range of projects diverse enough to neutralize any failures within Rockefeller philanthropy to restrain a personal, ideological or political bias. This book has made sense of this process, especially by considering sustained conversations between philanthropists and social scientists, episodic communications about grant proposals and awards, and occasional self-assessments within Rockefeller philanthropy. All evidence shows a process of learning about the principles of scientific neutrality.

The Rockefellers learned to keep informed about changing ideas concerning relationships between the business interest and the public interest. Within the context of these changing ideas, they increasingly favoured philanthropic support of social science. They appointed professional philanthropists and scientific experts to help ensure that there would be little evidence that Rockefeller philanthropy attempted to impose any particular direction on the social sciences.

The period covered in this book witnessed the creation of an experimental attitude toward finding new institutional arrangements to establish a modern, 'rationalized' society. This effort was supported by the Rockefellers. When it comes to specific interactions between Rockefeller philanthropy and the rise of modern social science, what comes through in the accumulative historical understanding is that for each step that John D. Rockefeller took that the public might decry or damn, he took a step that the public could declare as admirable or blessed. Sometimes a timeline is added so that we see Rockefeller being unkind in his earlier years, and kinder later on. Possibly there were always 'two

Rockefellers'. Or, just possibly everything can fit consistently into a single yet evolving view of the social responsibilities of business.

Rockefeller and his son, John D. Rockefeller, Jr, undoubtedly had complex and shifting motives from the late 1880s to the late 1920s. Evidence can be gathered that Rockefeller philanthropy may have supported 'power interests' – historian Donald Fisher has introduced some such evidence. Fisher tends to argue that Rockefeller philanthropy failed to avoid being at least somewhat controlling over the directions and uses of social science. Evidence can also fit with an idea that Rockefeller philanthropy intended to support the advancement of unbiased 'expertise' – historian Martin Bulmer has introduced some such evidence. Bulmer perceives that relatively neutral science and expertise emerged from social science supported with Rockefeller funds; that in effect, Rockefeller philanthropy managed to stay clear of any serious acts of manipulation over the directions and uses of social science. The first of these two lines of evidence and argument can lead one to be more critical of philanthropists by interpreting that the distribution of Rockefeller funds to social scientists was potentially manipulative and aimed to establish a capitalist cultural hegemony, and that any prospect of unfettered social science was incompatible with Rockefeller funding of social science. The second line of evidence and argument can produce an opposed tendency to see Rockefeller funding of social science as compatible with scientific freedom, and it interprets leaders within Rockefeller philanthropy as trying to ensure the maintenance of free inquiry. Potentially opposed frameworks for analysis thus emerge: 'power interests' versus 'detached expertise'.[1]

There can be a middle position too. To find any middle ground between persuasive uses and informative uses of social science was going to require, of persons within Rockefeller philanthropy, some constant vigilance in reassessing their own activities and points of view. As Rockefeller philanthropy supported social scientists, leaders within Rockefeller philanthropy never attained any absolute answer as to how best to support social science. They did, however, maintain a constant dialogue.

I have introduced evidence to establish a relative autonomy of social scientists who received Rockefeller support. I showed that the Rockefellers had a learning process with respect to the roles that social scientists should play in the modern world. I also showed the continual presence of an efficiency argument, as the Rockefellers identified how to distribute financial assistance to the greatest possible effect. While the Rockefellers were in the process of attaining great wealth within the business world, in part by adopting rather aggressive business tactics, they also engaged in a process of gathering their knowledge attained through experiential learning in the philanthropic world, so as to develop a business-like model for giving. My hope for *Rockefeller Philanthropy and Modern Social Science* is that it helps to explain an important phenomenon in the history of modern capitalism: the creation of the ideal of neutral, public-oriented social scientists.

# NOTES

## Introduction

1. Biographic episodes appear especially in the first few chapters. Unless otherwise noted, the information is drawn from one or more of the following works: J. Flynn, *God's Gold: The Story of Rockefeller and his Times* (New York: Harcourt, Brace and Co., 1932); A. Nevins, *A Study in Power: John D. Rockefeller, Industrialist and Philanthropist*, 2 vols (New York: Charles Scribner's Sons, 1953); G. Jonas, *The Circuit Riders: Rockefeller Money and the Rise of Modern Science* (New York and London: W. W. Norton & Company, 1989); R. Chernow, *Titan: The Life of John D. Rockefeller* (New York: Random House, 1998).

2. Important publications in this literature include M. Heald, *The Social Responsibilities of Business: Company and Community, 1900–1960* (Cleveland, OH: Case Western Reserve University, 1970); E. C. Kirkland, *Dream and Thought in the Business Community, 1860–1900* (Ithaca, NY: Cornell University Press, 1956); A. Tone, *The Business of Benevolence: Industrial Paternalism in Progressive America* (Ithaca, NY: Cornell University Press, 1997).

3. Religious arguments to support the philanthropic attitudes of Rockefeller and Rockefeller, Jr are in S. Hewa, 'The Protestant Ethic and Rockefeller Benevolence: The Religious Impulse in American Philanthropy', *Journal for the Theory of Social Behaviour*, 27:4 (1997), pp. 419–52; and C. E. Harvey, 'Religion and Industrial Relations: John D. Rockefeller Jr. and the Interchurch World Movement of 1919–1920', *Research in Political Economy*, 4 (1981), pp. 199–227.

4. H. D. Lloyd, *Wealth against Commonwealth* (New York: Harper & Row, 1894); see R. C. Kochersberger, Jr, 'Introduction', in R. C. Kockersberger, Jr (ed.), *More than a Muckraker: Ida Tarbell's Lifetime in Journalism* (Knoxville, TN: University of Tennessee Press, 1994), pp. 66–86; E. Morris, *Theodore Rex* (New York: Random House, 2001), pp. 205–7.

5. Chernow, *Titan*, pp. 432–5.

## 1 Business and Philanthropy

1. Biographic episodes appear especially in the first few chapters. Unless otherwise noted, the information is drawn from one or more of the following works: J. Flynn, *God's Gold: The Story of Rockefeller and His Times* (New York: Harcourt, Brace and Co., 1932); A. Nevins, *A Study in Power: John D. Rockefeller, Industrialist and Philanthropist*, 2 vols (New York: Charles Scribner's Sons, 1953); G. Jonas, *The Circuit Riders: Rockefeller*

*Money and the Rise of Modern Science* (New York and London: W. W. Norton & Company, 1989); R. Chernow, *Titan: The Life of John D. Rockefeller* (New York: Random House, 1998).

2.  Flynn, *God's Gold*, p. 271; Chernow, *Titan*, p. 237. Allan Nevins Papers (hereafter ANP), Special Collections, Columbia University, Butler Library, 112/24 (box 112, folder 24).
3.  Nevins, *Study in Power*, vol. 2, p. 177.
4.  ANP, 111/21. Underlined in the original document.
5.  Chernow, *Titan*, p. 302. ANP, 113/31.
6.  ANP, 110/15.
7.  Chernow, *Titan*, p. 300; ANP, 113/32.
8.  Chernow, *Titan*, pp. 315–6.
9.  ANP, 122/Colby.
10. ANP, 110/15.
11. K. W. Rose, 'Why Chicago and not Cleveland? The Religious Imperative behind John D. Rockefeller's Early Philanthropy, 1855–1900', Typescript, 1995, Rockefeller Archive Centre (hereafter RAC), Pocantico Hills, New York.
12. Rose, 'Why Chicago and not Cleveland?', p. 5.
13. Ibid., p. 4.
14. *Rockefeller Archive Centre Newsletter* (Fall 1999), p. 19.
15. K. W. Rose and D. H. Stapleton, 'Toward a "Universal Heritage": Education and the Development of Rockefeller Philanthropy, 1884–1913', *Teachers College Record*, 93:3 (1992), pp. 536–55, on pp. 539–42.
16. Ibid., pp. 539–42.
17. Ibid.
18. J. D. Rockefeller, *Random Reminiscences of Men and Events* (New York: Doubleday, Page & Co., 1909), p. 112.
19. C. H. Corey, *A History of the Richmond Theological Seminary* (Richmond, VA: J. W. Randolph Company, 1895), pp. 101–3.
20. Ibid., pp. 102–3.
21. Ibid., pp. 127–8.
22. Ibid., pp. 128–9.
23. Ibid., pp. 104, 183, 231; R. Hylton, 'University History', Virginia Union University, at http://www.vuu.edu/about_vuu/history.aspx [accessed 15 August 2012].
24. Rose, 'Why Chicago and not Cleveland?', p. 10.
25. Ibid., p. 11.
26. Ibid., p. 10.
27. Chernow, *Titan*, p. 240; ANP, 110/15.
28. Jonas, *Circuit Riders*, pp. 33–4.
29. ANP, 110/15.
30. C. S. Smith, *The American University, Annual Oration, Columbia College Library, June 2, 1887* (New York: Printed for the Chapter, 1887).
31. T. W. Goodspeed, *A History of the University of Chicago: The First Quarter Century* (Chicago, IL: The University of Chicago Press, 1916), pp. 12–44; Rose, 'Why Chicago and not Cleveland?', p. 8.
32. Goodspeed, *A History*, pp. 12–44.
33. Nevins, *Study in Power*, vol. 2, p. 163.
34. Ibid., p. 165.
35. Goodspeed, *A History*, p. 35.
36. Nevins, *Study in Power*, vol. 2, pp. 165–6.

37. Chernow, *Titan*, p. 310.
38. F. T. Gates, *Chapters in My Life* (New York: The Free Press, 1977), p. 96.
39. K. Rose, 'John D. Rockefeller, The American Baptist Education Society, and the Growth of Baptist Higher Education in the Midwest', Typescript, 1998, RAC.
40. ANP, 130/1. Underlined in the original document.
41. Chernow, *Titan*, p. 365; ANP, 130/Gates.
42. Gates, *Chapters in My Life*, pp. 84–8; J. Ganfield, 'Minnesota Academy through Pillsbury Military Academy, 1877–1957', Steele County Historical Society (Owatonna, MN, Typescript, 2001).
43. Chernow, *Titan*, p. 313.
44. A. Carnegie, *The Gospel of Wealth and Other Timely Essays* (New York: The Century Co., 1900), pp. 1–44, on pp. 15–6, 36.
45. Ibid., pp. 15–6, 36. See also O. Zunz, *Philanthropy in America: A History* (Princeton, NJ: Princeton University Press, 2012), p. 18.
46. Chernow, *Titan*, p. 313.
47. F. W. Shepardson, *Denison University 1831–1931: A Centennial History* (Granville, OH: Granville Times and Publishing Co., 1931), pp. 151–5, 163; Personal communication with Mary Prophet, Interim Director, Denison University Libraries, 12 June 2012.
48. Shepardson, *Denison University*, pp. 151–5, 163, 215.
49. Ibid., p. 215.
50. Chernow, *Titan*, p. 302.
51. S. A. Sandage, *Born Losers: A History of Failure in American Culture* (Cambridge, MA: Harvard University Press, 2005), p. 209; Chernow, *Titan*, pp. 299–300, 338.
52. Ibid., pp. 368–70.
53. B. W. Westfall, 'The William Rainey Harper/John D. Rockefeller Correspondence: Religion and Economic Control at the University of Chicago, 1889–1905', *Vitae Scholasticae*, 4:1–2 (1985), pp. 109–23, on p. 112.
54. Ibid.
55. Ibid., p. 113.
56. D. L. Seim, 'Objectivity vs. Advocacy: Newspaper Rhetoric during the "Bemis Affair" and the "Oleomargarine Controversy"', in J. Goodwin (ed.), *Between Scientists & Citizens* (Ames, IA: Great Plains Society for the Study of Argumentation, 2012), pp. 334–44.
57. See citations in ibid., p. 344; M. O. Furner, *Advocacy and Objectivity: A Crisis in the Professionalization of American Social Science* (Lexington, KY: University of Kentucky Press, 1975); H. E. Bergquist, Jr, 'The Edward W. Bemis Controversy at the University of Chicago', *AAUP Bulletin*, 58:4 (1972), pp. 384–93.
58. Clippings from the 'University of Chicago Scrapbook #1'; located in Special Collections, University of Chicago Libraries, Chicago, Illinois. In a few cases the cited articles are not in the scrapbook, and the citation herein is the name and date of the newspaper as listed.
59. A. Small, 'Free Investigation', *American Journal of Sociology*, 1:2 (1895), pp. 210–4.
60. Westfall, 'Harper/Rockefeller Correspondence', pp. 114–5.
61. Ibid., pp. 115–6.
62. Ibid.
63. 'Prof. Triggs's Comparison of Rockefeller and Shakespeare', *New York Times*, 21 October 1900, p. 15.
64. Ibid.
65. Ibid.
66. 'Must Not Talk of Rockefeller', *New York Herald*, 1 November 1900, p. 22.

## 2 Two Rockfellers

1. Biographic episodes appear especially in the first few chapters. Unless otherwise noted, the information is drawn from one or more of the following works: J. Flynn, *God's Gold: The Story of Rockefeller and His Times* (New York: Harcourt, Brace and Co., 1932); A. Nevins, *A Study in Power: John D. Rockefeller, Industrialist and Philanthropist* 2 vols (New York: Charles Scribner's Sons, 1953); G. Jonas, *The Circuit Riders: Rockefeller Money and the Rise of Modern Science* (New York and London: W. W. Norton & Company, 1989); R. Chernow, *Titan: The Life of John D. Rockefeller* (New York: Random House, 1998).

2. Chernow, *Titan*, p. 339.

3. Ibid., p. 341. I correct the quote by referring to C. A. Lloyd, *Henry Demarest Lloyd, 1847–1903, A Biography* (New York and London: G. P. Putnam's Sons, 1912), p. 197.

4. R. Sherman, 'The Standard Oil Trust: The Gospel of Greed', *Forum* (New York), 13:7 (1892), pp. 602–15.

5. R. J. Storr, *Harper's University: The Beginnings* (Chicago, IL: University of Chicago Press, 1966), p. 268.

6. Chernow, *Titan*, pp. 325–6.

7. Flynn, *God's Gold*, pp. 305–6.

8. Goodspeed, *A History*, p. 497; Chernow, *Titan*, p. 496.

9. Goodspeed, *A History*, p. 497.

10. Ibid., p. 292. See also J. E. Harr and P. J. Johnson, *The Rockefeller Century* (New York: Scribner's Sons, 1988), p. 28.

11. J. W. Ernst (ed.), *'Dear Father'/'Dear Son': Correspondence of John D. Rockefeller and John D. Rockefeller, Jr.* (New York: Fordham University Press, 1994), pp. 14–15.

12. E. R. Brown, *Rockefeller Medicine Men: Medicine and Capitalism in America* (Berkeley and Los Angeles, CA, and London: University of California Press, 1979), pp. 105–9, 111–3, 132–3.

13. Storr, *Harper's University*, p. 144; 'Starr J. Murphy Dies in Florida', *New York Times*, 5 April 1921, p. 19.

14. ANP, 116/58.

15. R. B. Fosdick, *John D. Rockefeller, Jr.: A Portrait* (New York: Harper & Row, 1956), p. 421.

16. R. B. Fosdick, *Chronicle of a Generation: An Autobiography* (New York: Harper & Brothers, 1958), p. 218. G. W. Corner, *A History of the Rockefeller Institute, 1901–1953: Origins and Growth* (New York: Rockefeller Institute Press, 1964), pp. 45–6.

17. Corner, *A History of the Rockefeller Institute*, pp. 1–55.

18. Flynn, *God's Gold*, p. 339; quote is from 'The Schools', *World*, 10 January 1900, p. 7.

19. 'Mr. Rockefeller and Standard Oil', *Engineering Magazine*, 20:1 (1901), pp. 761–4, on pp. 762–3.

20. Ibid., p. 763.

21. Ibid., p. 764.

22. 'John D. Rockefeller on the Witness Stand', *Paint, Oil and Drug Review*, 23:20 (1897), pp. 20–1.

23. Flynn, *God's Gold*, p. 340.

24. Ibid., p. 389.

25. Ibid., pp. 385, 387.

26. Morris, *Theodore Rex*, pp. 202–5.

27. S. Hubbard, *John D. Rockefeller and His Career* (New York: By the Author, 1904), p. 13; M. M. Brown, *A Study of John D. Rockefeller* (New York: n.p., 1905), p. 14; J. Spargo, *A Socialist View of Mr. Rockefeller* (Chicago, IL: C. H. Kerr & Co., 1905).

28. 'Rockefeller's Sermon', *Outlook*, 81 (7 October 1905), pp. 300–1.

29. 'How the Richest Man in the World Observes Christmas', *Woman's Home Companion*, 32:12 (1905), p. 14.

30. Quoted in J. Abels, *The Rockefeller Billions: The Story of the World's Most Stupendous Fortune* (New York: Macmillan, 1965), pp. 279–80.

31. Quoted in Chernow, *Titan*, p. 55.

32. 'Washington Gladden on the Rockefeller Gift', *Advance*, 49:13 (1905), p. 392.

33. Quoted in Flynn, *God's Gold*, p. 338.

34. 'Mr. Rockefeller and the American Board', *Outlook*, 79 (1 April 1905), pp. 767–9, on p. 769.

35. 'Tainted Money', *Independent*, 74 (6 April 1905), pp. 410–1.

36. 'The Tainted-Money Question', *Christian Work and the Evangelist*, 78:1991 (1905), p. 493.

37. 'God's Gold', *Missionary Review*, 28:5 (1905), pp. 379–80.

38. 'The Tainted Money Issue', *Congregationalist and Christian World*, 90:34 (1905), p. 276.

39. 'God's Gold', pp. 379–80.

40. Letter from F. T. Gates, n.d., RAC-FTG 2/48.

41. Gates, *Chapters in My Life*, p. 205.

42. Quoted in Chernow, *Titan*, pp. 497–8.

43. Quoted in ibid., p. 300.

44. G. T. White, *Formative Years in the Far West: A History of the Standard Oil Company of California and Its Predecessors through 1919* (New York: Appleton-Century-Crofts, 1962), pp. 277–80, 379.

45. Flynn, *God's Gold*, p. 394.

46. Ibid., p. 439.

47. S. E. Lederer, *Subjected to Science: Human Experimentation in America before the Second World War* (Baltimore, MD, and London: Johns Hopkins University Press, 1995), pp. 19, 77–85. Quote from B. Unti, '"The Doctors are so Sure That They Only are Right": The Rockefeller Institute and the Defeat of Vivisection Reform in New York, 1908–1914', in D. H. Stapleton (ed.), *Creating a Tradition of Biomedical Research: Contributions of the History of the Rockefeller University* (New York: The Rockefeller University Press, 2004), pp. 175–89, on p. 181.

48. J. D. Anderson, *The Education of Blacks in the South, 1860–1935* (Chapel Hill, NC: The University of North Carolina Press, 1988), pp. 86, 110–47, 153–9.

49. Fosdick, *John D. Rockefeller, Jr.*, p. 117.

50. Chernow, *Titan*, p. 482.

51. W. A. Link, *The Paradox of Southern Progressivism: 1880–1930* (Chapel Hill, NC: University of North Carolina Press, 1993), p. 27.

52. Gates, *Chapters in My Life*, p. 134.

53. R. B. Fosdick, *Adventure in Giving: The Story of the General Education Board* (New York: Harper & Row, 1962), p. 8.

54. Link, *The Paradox of Southern Progressivism*, p. 241.

55. A. Flexner, *I Remember: The Autobiography of Abraham Flexner* (New York: Simon and Schuster, 1940), p. 131.

56. E. Anderson and A. A. Moss, Jr, *Dangerous Donations: Northern Philanthropy and Southern Black Education, 1902–1930* (Columbia, MO, and London: University of Missouri Press, 1984), pp. 85–95.

57. Brown, *Rockefeller Medicine Men*, pp. 114–5; J. Ettling, *The Germ of Laziness: Rockefeller Philanthropy and Public Health in the New South* (Cambridge, MA: Harvard University Press, 1981), pp. 102–7.

58. Chernow, *Titan*, p. 490. Link, *The Paradox of Southern Progressivism*, pp. 151–3.

59. Rockefeller, *Random Reminiscences of Men and Events*, p. 119.

60. 'John D. Rockefeller at Play', *Harper's Weekly*, 53:2721 (1909), p. 17; A. P. Winston, *Public Opinion and the Standard Oil Company* (St Louis, MO: Nixon-Jones Printing Co., 1908); 'Simplicity of Rockefeller', *Current Literature*, 49:5 (1909), pp. 493–6; 'Impressions of Rockefeller', *World's Work*, 16:9 (1908), pp. 10703–15.

61. 'Two John D. Rockefellers', *Current Literature*, 45:11 (1908), pp. 503–6, on p. 503.

62. 'Religion and Conduct', *Living Age*, 262 (24 July 1909), pp. 249–252, on p. 249.

63. 'The Rockefeller Foundation', *Independent*, 68 (10 March 1910), pp. 535–6.

64. Chernow, *Titan*, p. 525.

65. Ibid., p. 443.

66. Ibid., p. 444.

67. Ibid., p. 556; Flynn, *God's Gold*, p. 447.

68. 'The Greatest Killing in Wall Street', *McClure's Magazine*, 39:4 (1912), pp. 409–20.

69. 'Uncle Sam's Present to John D. Rockefeller', *Current Literature*, 53:3 (September 1912), pp. 287–90.

70. See for example ibid, p. 288.

71. 'The Greatest Killing in Wall Street', pp. 409–20; 'Uncle Sam's Present to John D. Rockefeller', pp. 287–90.

72. Flynn, *God's Gold*, pp. 451–2. Harr and Johnson, *The Rockefeller Century*, pp. 9, 121. 'Charter of the Rockefeller Foundation', ch. 488, Laws of New York, 14 May 1913. See B. Howe, 'The Origins of the Rockefeller Foundation', in R. F. Arnove (ed.), *Philanthropy and Cultural Imperialism: The Foundation at Home and Abroad* (Boston, MA: G. K. Hall, 1980), pp. 1–25.

73. Brown, *Rockefeller Medicine Men*, p. 169.

## 3 Early Philanthropic Support of Social Science

1. An interesting early study is L. P. Ayres, *Seven Great Foundations* (New York: Russell Sage Foundation, 1911).

2. N. Reingold, 'National Science Policy in a Private Foundation: The Carnegie Institution of Washington', in A. Oleson and J. Voss (eds), *The Organization of Knowledge in Modern America, 1860–1920* (Baltimore, MD: Johns Hopkins University Press, 1979), pp. 190–223.

3. Carnegie Institution, *History of Labor in the United States* (New York: Macmillan Co., 1918).

4. R. Crocker, *Mrs. Russell Sage: Women's Activism and Philanthropy in Gilded Age and Progressive Era America* (Bloomington, IN: Indiana University Press, 2006).

5. J. M. Glenn, et al., *The Russell Sage Foundation, 1907–1946* (New York: Russell Sage Foundation, 1946).

6. M. C. Elmer, *Technique of Social Surveys* (Lawrence, KS: World Co., 1917); M. Gordon, 'The Social Survey Movement and Sociology in the United States', *Social Problems*, 21:3 (1973), pp. 284–98.

7. S. M. Harrison, *Social Conditions in an American City: A Summary of the Findings of the Springfield Survey* (New York: Russell Sage Foundation, 1920).

8. G. Alchon, 'Mary Van Kleeck and Social–Economic Planning', *Journal of Policy History*, 3:1 (1991), pp. 1–23.

9. P. U. Kellogg (ed.), *The Pittsburgh Survey: Findings in Six Volumes* (New York: Charities Publication Committee, 1910); D. C. Hammack and S. Wheeler, *Social Science in the Making: Essays on the Russell Sage Foundation, 1907–1972* (New York: Russell Sage Foundation, 1994).

10. B. D. McDonald III, 'The Bureau of Municipal Research and the Development of a Professional Public Service', *Administration & Society*, 42:7 (2010), pp. 815–35.

11. R. W. DeForest and L. Veiller (eds), *The Tenement House Problem* (New York: The Macmillan Co., 1903).

12. J. S. Dahlberg, *The New York Bureau of Municipal Research: Pioneer in Government Administration* (New York: New York University Press, 1966), p. v.

13. G. R. Taylor, *Satellite Cities: A Study of Industrial Suburbs* (New York and London: D. Appleton and Co., 1915), pp. 165–89, 224–9.

14. B. Selekman and M. Van Kleck, *Employee Representation in Coal Mines: A Study of the Industrial Representation Plan of the Colorado Fuel and Iron Company* (New York: Russell Sage Foundation, 1924).

15. J. Russell, 'The Coming of the Line: The Ford Highland Park Plant, 1910–1914', *Radical America*, 12:3 (1978), pp. 28–45.

16. G. M. Hooks and W. L. Flinn, 'The Country Life Commission and Early Rural Sociology', *Rural Sociologist*, 1:2 (1981), pp. 95–100. S. A. McReynolds, 'Eugenics and Rural Development: The Vermont Commission on Country Life's Program for the Future', *Agricultural History*, 71:3 (1997), pp. 300–29, esp. pp. 301–5.

17. A. F. Davis, 'The Social Workers and the Progressive Party, 1912–1916', *American Historical Review*, 69:2 (1964), pp. 671–88.

18. E. C. Lagemann, *The Politics of Knowledge: The Carnegie Corporation, Philanthropy, and Public Policy* (Middletown, CT: Wesleyan University Press, 1990).

19. G. G. Huebner, 'The Americanization of the Immigrant', *Annals of the American Academy of Political and Social Science*, 27:2 (1906), pp. 191–213, on p. 191.

20. J. M. Schwartz, 'Towards a History of the Melting Pot, or Why There is a Chicago School of Sociology but not a Detroit School', in M. Harbsmeier and M. T. Larson (eds), *The Humanities between Art and Science: Intellectual Developments, 1880–1914* (Copenhagen: Akademisk Forlag, 1989), pp. 59–78.

21. R. B. Fosdick, *The Story of the Rockefeller Foundation* (New York: Harper & Brothers, 1952), pp. 55–9.

22. R. E. Kohler, 'Science, Foundations, and American Universities in the 1920s', *OSIRIS*, 2nd ser., 3 (1987), pp. 135–64, on p. 140.

23. Fosdick, *The Story of the Rockefeller Foundation*, p. 59.

24. 'Memorandum Prepared on the Opportunities at Washington For Government Research', 17 March 1914, RAC, R.G. 1.1, ser. 200, 26/294. See also D. T. Critchlow, *The Brookings Institution, 1916–1952: Expertise and the Public Interest in a Democratic Society* (DeKalb, IL: Northern Illinois Press, 1985), pp. 9, 18, 32–3.

25. From a letter dated 13 June 1914; quoted in S. Agoratus, 'The Core of Progressivism: Research Institutions and Social Policy, 1907–1940' (PhD dissertation, Carnegie Mellon University, 1994), p. 134. See also J. A. Smith, *Idea Brokers: Think Tanks and the Rise of the New Policy Elite* (New York: The Free Press, 1991), pp. 52–8.

26. Handwritten notes onto a telegram, John D. Rockefeller, Jr to Jerome D. Greene, 11 November 1914, RAC, R.G. 1.1, ser. 200, 26/295.

27. Agoratus, 'The Core of Progressivism', p. 137.

28. W. F. Willoughby, 'The Institute for Government Research', *American Political Science Review*, 12:1 (1918), pp. 49–62.

29. Critchlow, *The Brookings Institution*, p. 57.

30. Ibid., p. 36–7.

31. J. D. Greene, 'Principles and Policies of Giving: Memorandum', Rockefeller Foundation Draft Report (1913), pp. 15–16, RAC-RF, R.G. 3, ser. 910, 10/10–11. D. M. Grossman, 'American Foundations and the Support of Economic Research, 1913–29', *Minerva*, 20:1–2 (1982), pp. 59–82, esp. pp. 59–62.

32. 'Rockefeller Foundation, History Source Material', RAC-History-Source Material, vol. 3, ser. 900, pp. 676–7. G. Adams, Jr, *The Age of Industrial Violence, 1910–1915: Activities and Findings of the United States Commission on Industrial Relations* (New York: Columbia University Press, 1966).

33. H. Heaton, *A Scholar in Action: Edwin F. Gay* (New York: Greenwood Press, 1968). J. E. Fell, Jr, 'Rockefeller's Right-hand Man: Frederick T. Gates and the Northwestern Mining Investments', *Business History Review*, 52:4 (1978), pp. 537–61.

34. Gates, *Chapters in My Life*, pp. 180–1, 186.

35. 'Information Furnished by the Rockefeller Foundation In Response to Supplementary Questionnaire Submitted by the United States Commission on Industrial Relations', 7 January 1915, p. 43. 'Memorandum Concerning a Proposed Economic Bureau', 21 January 1914, RAC-RF, R.G. 3, ser. 910, 2/10–11. See also S. Hewa, 'Toward the Well-Being of Mankind: Rockefeller Philanthropy and the Problem of Economic Research', *International Journal of Sociology and Social Policy*, 18:11–12 (1998), pp. 85–129.

36. E. F. Gay to J. D. Greene, 4 March 1914; E. F. Gay to J. L. Laughlin, 21 April 1914, RAC-RF, R.G.3, ser. 910, 2/10–11.

37. W. C. Mitchell, 'Memorandum', Rockefeller Foundation Draft Report, January 1914; also F. W. Taussig to J. D. Greene, 27 February 1914, RAC-RF, R.G.3, ser. 910, 2/10–11.

38. J. D. Greene, 'An Institute of Economic Research', Rockefeller Foundation Draft Report, January 1914, RAC-RF, R.G.3, ser. 910, 2/10–11.

39. 'Rockefeller Foundation, History Source Material', RAC-History-Source Material, vol. 3, ser. 900, pp. 676–7.

40. F. T. Gates, 'In Opposition to Endowment of Economic Research', 19 March 1914, RAC-RF, Gates Collection, 2/24, pp. 1–6. The direct words from the Rockefeller Foundation are from their description of goals submitted to Congress in January 1915. 'Information Furnished by the Rockefeller Foundation In Response to Supplementary Questionnaire Submitted by the United States Commission on Industrial Relations', 7 January 1915, p. 44.

41. 'Rockefeller Foundation, History Source Material', RAC-History-Source Material, vol. 3, ser. 900, pp. 679–80.

42. 'Rockefeller Foundation, History Source Material', RAC-History-Source Material, vol. 3, ser. 900, pp. 679–80. J. L. Laughlin, 'Memorandum', Rockefeller Foundation Draft

Report, undated, RAC-RF, R.G.3, ser. 910, 2/10–11; J. D. Greene, 'An Institute for Social and Economic Research', Rockefeller Foundation Draft Report, March 1914, RAC-RF, R.G.3, ser. 910, 2/10–11.

43. From the Rockefeller Foundation's description of their goals as submitted to Congress, in 'Information Furnished by the Rockefeller Foundation In Response to Supplementary Questionnaire Submitted by the United States Commission on Industrial Relations', 7 January 1915, p. 44.

44. F. T. Gates, 'In Opposition to Endowment of Economic Research', 19 March 1914, RAC-RF, Gates Collection, 2/24, pp. 1–6. See also F. T. Gates to J. D. Rockefeller, Jr, 19 March 1914, RAC-RF, Gates Collection, 2/24.

45. E. F. Gay to J. D. Greene, 17 April 1914, RAC-RF, R.G.3, ser. 910, 2/10–11; V. A. Morawetz and J. D. Rockefeller, Jr, letters from January 1914 to April 1914, RAC-RF, R.G.3, ser. 910, 2/10–11.

46. E. F. Gay, 'Report of Committee to the Rockefeller Foundation', Rockefeller Foundation Draft Report, 4 August 1914, 1–2, 4, RAC-RF, R.G.3, ser. 910, 2/10–11. V. A. Morawetz to J. D. Greene, 5 August 1914, RAC-RF, R.G.3, ser. 910, 2/10. See also 'Information Furnished by the Rockefeller Foundation In Response to Supplementary Questionnaire Submitted by the United States Commission on Industrial Relations', 7 January 1915, p. 45.

47. 'Information Furnished by the Rockefeller Foundation In Response to Supplementary Questionnaire Submitted by the United States Commission on Industrial Relations', 7 January 1915, p. 45; Gay, 'Report of Committee to the Rockefeller Foundation', ser. 910, 2/10–11.

48. V. A. Morawetz to J. D. Greene, 5 August 1914, RAC-RF, R.G.3, ser. 910, 2/10.

49. F. T. Gates to J. D. Rockefeller, Jr, 18 August 1914, RAC-RF, Gates Collection, 3/58.

50. J. D. Rockefeller, Jr to F. T. Gates, 24 August 1914, RAC-RF, Gates Collection, 3/58.

51. H. M. Gitelman, *Legacy of the Ludlow Massacre: A Chapter in American Industrial Relations* (Philadelphia, PA: University of Pennsylvania Press, 1988).

52. T. G. Andrews, *Killing for Coal: America's Deadliest Labour War* (Cambridge, MA: Harvard University Press, 2008), p. 245. G. S. McGovern and L. G. Guttridge, *The Great Coal-Field War* (Boston, MA: Houghton Mifflin, 1972).

53. 'Statement of John D. Rockefeller, Jr', US Congress, House Hearings, Subcommittee of the Committee on Mines and Mining, 63rd Congress, Second Session, *Conditions in the Coal Mines of Colorado* (Washington, DC: US Government Printing Office, 1914), vol. 2, pp. 2841–916.

54. Ibid., pp. 2851–2.

55. Ibid., p. 2852.

56. Quoted in B. Whitaker, *The Foundations: An Anatomy of Philanthropy and Society* (London: Eyre Methuen, 1974), p. 102.

57. Flynn, *God's Gold*, p. 459.

58. Adams, Jr, *The Age of Industrial Violence*, pp. 161–72, 211–2.

59. Flynn, *God's Gold*, p. 460; Grossman, 'American Foundations and the Support of Economic Research', p. 69; R. E. Hiebert, *Courtier to the Crowd: The Story of Ivy Lee and the Development of Public Relations* (Ames, IA: Iowa State University Press, 1966).

## 4 Early Rockefeller Support of Social Science

1. Correspondence between J. D. Greene and W. L. M. King, June 1914 to July 1914, RAC-RF, R.G.3, ser. 910, 2/10–11. See also 'Exhibit A. Summary of Mr. King's Experience With Labour Problems', in 'Information Furnished by the Rockefeller Foundation in Response to Questionnaires Submitted by United States Commission on Industrial Relations', submitted 25 January 1915, pp. 50–1.

2. F. A. McGregor, *The Fall and Rise of Mackenzie King: 1911–1919* (Toronto: Macmillan, 1962), p. 93; 'Rockefeller Foundation, History Source Material', RAC-History-Source Material, vol. 3, ser. 900, p. 703. See also J. D. Greene to W. L. M. King, 30 October 1914, RAC-RF, R.G.3, ser. 910, 2/10–11; 'Statement of John D. Rockefeller, Jr', before United States Commission on Industrial Relations, at Washington DC, 20–1 May 1915, pp. 5–6.

3. These quotations were provided to the United States Congress by the Rockefeller Foundation in December 1914; see 'Information Furnished by the Rockefeller Foundation in Response to Questionnaire Submitted by the United States Commission on Industrial Relations', 4 December 1914, pp. 10–11, 13; see also 'Information Furnished by the Rockefeller Foundation In Response to Supplementary Questionnaire Submitted by the United States Commission on Industrial Relations', 7 January 1915, pp. 37–8.

4. King described his research approach in a letter to E. F. Gay; see D. M. Grossman, 'American Foundations and the Support of Economic Research', pp. 59–82, esp. pp. 69–72.

5. 'Information Furnished by the Rockefeller Foundation In Response to Questionnaire Submitted by the United States Commission on Industrial Relations', 4 December 1914, pp. 11–12.

6. Ibid., 4 December 1914, pp. 11–3, 16–7.

7. 'Information Furnished by the Rockefeller Foundation In Response to Supplementary Questionnaire Submitted by the United States Commission on Industrial Relations', 7 January 1915, pp. 36–9.

8. 'Statement of John D. Rockefeller, Jr', before United States Commission on Industrial Relations, at New York City, 25 January 1915, pp. 1–3, 7–8.

9. 'Statement of John D. Rockefeller, Jr', before United States Commission on Industrial Relations, at Washington, DC, 20–1 May 1915, pp. 1–2, 5.

10. 'Statement of William H. Allen', before the United States Commission on Industrial Relations, Final Reports and Testimony, 8–9 (Washington, DC: US Government Printing Office, 1916), pp. 8327–42.

11. See Dahlberg, *The New York Bureaus of Municipal Research*.

12. United States Commission on Industrial Relations, Final Reports and Testimony, 8–9; 'Rockefeller Foundation, History Source Material', RAC-History-Source Material, vol. 3, ser. 900, p. 698.

13. J. D. Greene to E. F. Gay, 2 July 1914, RAC-RF, R.G.3, ser. 910, 2/10–11.

14. J. D. Greene to Members of the Executive Committee, 27 August 1914, RAC-RF, R.G.3, ser. 910, 2/10–11.

15. J. D. Greene to E. F. Gay, 10 August 1914 and 18 August 1914, RAC-RF, R.G.3, ser. 910, 2/10–11.

16. F. T. Gates to J. D. Rockefeller, Jr, 18 August 1914, RAC-RF, Gates Collection, 3/58; J. D. Rockefeller, Jr to F. T. Gates, 24 August 1914, RAC-RF, R.G.3, ser. 910, 2/10–11. See also W. L. M. King to J. D. Greene, 21 October 1914; J. D. Greene to E. F. Gay, 28 October 1914, RAC-RF, R.G.3, ser. 910, 2/10–11. 'Information Furnished by the

Rockefeller Foundation In Response to Supplementary Questionnaire Submitted by the United States Commission on Industrial Relations', 7 January 1915, p. 45.

17. McGregor, *The Fall and Rise of Mackenzie King*, p. 230.
18. Ibid., pp. 175–84, 223–6.
19. Ibid., pp. 175–84. See also R. M. Dawson, *William Lyon Mackenzie King: A Political Biography* (Toronto: Toronto University Press, 1958).
20. Rockefeller Foundation, 'Minutes', 27 October 1915, RAC-RF.
21. McGregor, *The Fall and Rise of Mackenzie King*, pp. 215–26, 247–8. W. L. M. King, *Industry and Humanity: A Study of the Principles Underlying Industrial Reconstruction* (Boston, MA, and New York: Houghton Mifflin, 1918).
22. King, *Industry and Humanity*, pp. 134, 178–9, 181–4, 204, 371–4.
23. C. E. Harvey, 'John D. Rockefeller, Jr., and the Social Sciences: An Introduction', *Journal of the History of Sociology*, 4:3 (1982), pp. 1–31.
24. J. Gunn, 'A Few Good Men: The Rockefeller Approach to Population, 1911–1936', in T. Richardson and D. Fisher (eds), *The Development of the Social Sciences in the United States and Canada: The Role of Philanthropy* (Stamford, CT: Ablex Publishing Corp., 1999), pp. 97–115, on pp. 102–3.
25. J. Shelley, et al., 'A Survey of Sources at the Rockefeller Archive Centre for the Study of Psychiatry and Related Areas', Typescript, 1985, RAC.
26. E. Black, *War Against the Weak: Eugenics and America's Campaign to Create a Master Race* (New York: Four Walls Eight Windows, 2003), p. 71; Zunz, *Philanthropy in America*, pp. 93–7.
27. H. Ellis, *The Task of Social Hygiene* (Boston, MA, and New York: Houghton Mifflin Co., 1912), p. 16.
28. Grossman, 'American Foundations and the Support of Economic Research', p. 75.
29. A. Franks, *Margaret Sanger's Eugenic Legacy: The Control of Female Fertility* (Jefferson, NC, and London: McFarland & Co., 2005), pp. 30–7.
30. J. D. Rockefeller, Jr, 'Introduction', in A. Flexner, *Prostitution in Europe* (New York: The Century Co., 1914), pp. vii–ix.
31. J. M. Jordan (ed.), '"To Educate Public Opinion": John D. Rockefeller, Jr. and the Origins of Social Scientific Fact-Finding', *New England Quarterly*, 64:2 (1991), pp. 292–7.
32. J. D. Rockefeller, Jr, 'Introduction', in G. J. Kneeland and K. B. Davis, *Commercialized Prostitution in New York City* (New York: The Century Co., 1913), pp. ii–iv.
33. Harr and Johnson, *The Rockefeller Century*, p. 158.
34. 'War Work of the Rockefeller Foundation', 1 March 1919, RAC-Rockefeller Family, R.G. 1.1, ser. 100, 57/567.
35. Fosdick, *Chronicle of a Generation*, p. 223; Fosdick, *John D. Rockefeller, Jr.*
36. D. M. Kennedy, *Over Here: The First World War and American Society* (Oxford and New York: Oxford University Press, 1980), pp. 45–92.
37. C. E. Harvey, 'John D. Rockefeller, Jr., Herbert Hoover, and President Wilson's Industrial Conferences of 1919–1920', in J. E. Brown and P. D. Reagan (eds), *Voluntarism, Planning, and the State: The American Planning Experience, 1914–1916* (Westport, CT: Greenwood Press, 1988), pp. 25–46.
38. R. L. Geiger, *To Advance Knowledge: The Growth of American Research Universities, 1900–1940* (New York: Oxford University Press, 1986).
39. J. D. Rockefeller, Jr., *Address by John D. Rockefeller Jr., Delivered at Pueblo, Colorado, October 1915* (Denver, CO: W. H. Kistler, 1915).
40. Ibid.

41. Selekman and Van Kleck, *Employee's Representation in Coal Mines*.
42. Kohler, 'Science, Foundations, and American Universities in the 1920s', p. 138; Jonas, *Circuit Riders*, pp. 84–8.
43. Kohler, 'Science, Foundations, and American Universities in the 1920s', p. 138; H. Plotkin, 'Edward C. Pickering and the Endowment of Scientific Research in America, 1877–1918', *Isis*, 69:2 (1978), pp. 44–57.
44. Kohler, 'Science, Foundations, and American Universities in the 1920s', p. 138.
45. Jonas, *Circuit Riders*, pp. 88–95.
46. N. Reingold, 'The Case of the Disappearing Laboratory', *American Quarterly*, 29:1 (1977), pp. 79–101.
47. R. C. Cochrane, *The National Academy of Sciences: The First Hundred Years, 1863–1963* (Washington, DC: National Academy of Sciences, 1978).
48. J. Farley, *To Cast Out Disease: A History of the International Health Division of the Rockefeller Foundation (1913–1951)* (New York and Oxford: Oxford University Press, 2004).
49. R. E. Kohler, 'Science and Philanthropy: Wickliffe Rose and the International Education Board', *Minerva*, 23 (1985), pp. 75–95.
50. Kohler, 'Science and Philanthropy'. See also General Education Board, *Annual Report, 1918/19* (New York: Rockefeller Foundation, General Education Board, 1919), pp. 68–9; General Education Board, *Annual Report, 1924/25* (New York: Rockefeller Foundation, General Education Board, 1925), pp. 7–8.
51. Kohler, 'Science, Foundations, and American Universities in the 1920s', pp. 136–8, 140, 148.
52. For more on Greene's views, see J. D. Greene, 'Memorandum on the Policy of the Rockefeller Foundation with Reference to the Concentration or Extension of its Field of Giving', 23 May 1916, RAC-RF.
53. Heaton, *A Scholar in Action*, p. 93.
54. Ibid., pp. 93–5, 97.
55. L. S. Mitchell, *Two Lives: The Story of Wesley Clair Mitchell and Myself* (New York: Simon and Schuster, 1953), pp. 349–62, on p. 351; Heaton, *A Scholar in Action*, p. 197.
56. Mitchell, *Two Lives*, pp. 350–1.
57. W. C. Mitchell, et al., *Income in the United States, its Amount and Distribution*, NBER Publication no. 1 and no. 2 (New York: Harcourt Brace, 1921–2). See also J. B. Judis, *The Paradox of American Democracy: Elites, Special Interests, and the Betrayal of Public Trust* (New York: Pantheon, 2000), pp. 19–20, 30.
58. National Bureau of Economic Research, *Business Cycles and Unemployment: Report and Recommendation of a Committee of the President's Conference on Unemployment*, 1921, NBER Publication no. 4 (New York: McGraw Hill, 1923).
59. Heaton, *A Scholar in Action*, pp. 197–8.
60. C. B. Saunders, Jr, *The Brookings Institution: A Fifty Year History* (Washington, DC: Brookings Institution, 1966), p. 29.
61. Grossman, 'American Foundations and the Support of Economic Research', p. 80.
62. Flynn, *God's Gold*, p. 479; I have fixed the quote from Flynn slightly.
63. Chernow, *Titan*, p. 314.
64. 'Rockefeller's View', *Farm & Fireside*, 41 (6 January 1917), n.p.
65. Chernow, *Titan*, p. xx.

## 5 The Laura Spelman Rockefeller Memorial

1.  I build upon M. Bulmer and J. Bulmer, 'Philanthropy and Social Science in the 1920s: Beardsley Ruml and the Laura Spelman Rockefeller Memorial, 1922–29', *Minerva*, 19:3 (1981), pp. 347–407.
2.  *Report* of the Laura Spelman Rockefeller Memorial, 1919–22, RAC-LSRM, ser. 2, 1/2, p. 7.
3.  *Report* ... 1919–22, p. 7. See also R. A. Meckel, *Save the Babies: American Public Health Reform and the Prevention of Infant Mortality, 1850–1929* (Baltimore, MD: Johns Hopkins University Press, 1990).
4.  'Rockefeller's Giant Gift', *Independent*, 104:51 (1920), pp. 399–400; L. Outhwaite, 'The Life and Times of the Laura Spelman Rockefeller Memorial', n.d., RAC-LSRM, ser. 1, 5/49, pp. 2–10.
5.  Bulmer and Bulmer, 'Philanthropy and Social Science', p. 353.
6.  *Report* ... 1919–22, p. 5.
7.  G. Alchon, *The Invisible Hand of Planning: Capitalism, Social Science, and the State in the 1920s* (Princeton, NJ: Princeton University Press, 1985), pp. 42–3. During his time at the NRC, James Angell published 'The Organization of Research', *Scientific Monthly*, 11 (1920), pp. 26–42. See also C. H. Grattan, 'Beardsley Ruml and his Ideas', *Harper's Magazine*, 204:5 (1952), pp. 72–86.
8.  A. Flexner to J. R. Angell, 28 November 1921; G. E. Vincent to R. B. Fosdick, 28 November 1921, RAC-RF, R.G.3, ser. 900, 2/19; R. B. Fosdick to J. D. Rockefeller, Jr, 3 December 1921, Raymond B. Fosdick Papers, Seeley G. Mudd Manuscript Library, Princeton University, box 7.
9.  Quotation from Bulmer and Bulmer, 'Philanthropy and Social Science', p. 368. E. Embree to R. B. Fosdick, 18 November 1921; Embree to Fosdick, 26 November 1921, RAC-LSRM, ser. 2, 2/31. R. B. Fosdick, 'Education, Food and Social Science', 2 October 1922; L. Outhwaite to B. Ruml, 16 June 1923, RACLSRM, ser. 2, 3/39.
10. Harr and Johnson, *The Rockefeller Century*, p. 190.
11. Later research shows how the mental test itself was biased against soldiers who lacked education. See N. K. Bristow, *Making Men Moral: Social Engineering during the Great War* (New York: New York University Press, 1996).
12. H. D. Lasswell, *Propaganda Techniques in the World War* (New York: A. A. Knopf, 1927); see also Kennedy, *Over Here*, pp. 45–92.
13. *Report* ... 1919–22, p. 7.
14. B. Ruml, 'General Memorandum by the Director', Laura Spelman Rockefeller Memorial (also titled: 'Memorial Policy in Social Science'), October 1922, RAC-LSRM, ser. 2, 2/31 (copy also located in ser. 3, 63/677).
15. Ibid. See also D. Fisher, *Fundamental Development of the Social Sciences: Rockefeller Philanthropy and the United States Social Science Research Council* (Ann Arbor, MI: University of Michigan Press, 1993), pp. 33–5.
16. Ruml, 'General Memorandum', pp. 8–9, 19–22.
17. Ibid., pp. 11–12.
18. W. F. Ogburn, *Social Change With Respect to Culture and Original Nature* (New York: B. W. Huebsch, 1922).
19. Ruml, 'General Memorandum', pp, 13–14.
20. Ibid., pp. 19–22, 30–31.

21. J. R. Angell to B. Ruml, 10 October 1922; see also B. Ruml to J. R. Angell, 6 October 1922, RAC-LSRM, ser. 3, 79/823. J. M. Glenn to B. Ruml, 29 October 1924; Ruml to Glenn, 1 December 1924, RAC-LSRM, ser. 3, 112/1114.

22. R. B. Fosdick, 'Rockefeller Foundation Biography', RAC-Biography File, Fosdick, ser. 2, 2/21. P. Collier and D. Horowitz, *The Rockefellers: An American Dynasty* (New York: Holt, Rinehart and Winston, 1976), pp. 138–44.

23. Outhwaite, 'The Life and Times of the Laura Spelman Rockefeller Memorial'.

24. Bulmer and Bulmer, 'Philanthropy and Social Science', p. 360. I make the generalization in regards to Ruml's interactions with the trustees based on my notes from the archives.

25. L. K. Frank, 'The Status of Social Science in the United States', March 1923, RAC-LSRM, ser. 3, 62/679, pp. 1, 6–7, 22, 24–25.

26. Ibid., pp. 10–12.

27. Ibid., pp. 6–8, 9–12, 17–8, 22, 25.

28. Ibid., pp. 20–2, 24–7.

29. B. Ruml to A. Woods, 26 May 1923, RAC-LSRM, ser. 2, 4/45.

30. Letter from University of Pennsylvania, 17 January 1923, RAC-LSRM, ser. 3, 75/790–1.

31. J. G. Morawski and G. A. Hornstein, 'Quandary of the Quacks: The Struggle for Expert Knowledge in American Psychology, 1890–1940', in J. Brown and D. K. Van Keuren (eds), *The Estate of Knowledge* (Baltimore, MD: Johns Hopkins University Press, 1991), pp. 106–33.

32. H. Cravens, *The Triumph of Evolution: American Scientists and the Heredity–Environment Controversy, 1900–1941* (Philadelphia, PA: University of Pennsylvania Press, 1978), pp. 78–86; see also H. Cravens, 'The Behavioural and Social Sciences', in M. K. Cayton and P. W. Williams (eds), *Encyclopedia of American Cultural & Intellectual History*, 3 vols (New York: Charles Scribner's Sons, 2001), vol. 1, pp. 669–77.

33. F. Samuelson, 'Struggle for Scientific Authority: The Reception of Watson's Behaviourism 1913–1920', *Journal of the History of the Behavioural Sciences*, 17:3 (1981), pp. 399–425; and F. Samuelson, 'Organizing for the Kingdom of Behaviour: Academic Battles and Organizational Policies in the Twenties', *Journal of the History of the Behavioural Sciences*, 21:1 (1983), pp. 33–47.

34. E. Heidbreder, *Seven Psychologies* (New York: Century Co., 1933).

35. 'University of Pennsylvania, Department of Industrial Research', 17 January 1923, RAC-LSRM, ser. 3, 75/790–791.

36. G. E. Mayo, Project Description, 1 March 1923, pp. 1–2, RAC-LSRM, ser. 3, 75/790–791.

37. R. C. S. Trahair, *The Humanist Temper: The Life and Work of Elton Mayo* (New Brunswick, NJ, and London: Transaction Books, 1984), pp. 83–5, 171–95.

38. B. Ruml to A. Woods, 20 May 1923, RAC-LSRM, ser. 3, 25/10.

39. 'Studies in Process in the Industrial Research Department', May 1923; see B. Ruml to J. Willits, 29 January 1923; Willits to Ruml, 14 May 1923; Willits to Ruml, 29 May 1923; Willits to Ruml, 1 October 1923; RAC-LSRM, ser. 3, 75/790–791.

40. J. Willits to B. Ruml, 25 April 1927, RAC-LSRM, ser. 3, 75/792.

41. Yale University File, RAC-LSRM, ser. 3, 79/823–828. See also J. Reed, 'Robert M. Yerkes and the Mental Testing Movement', in M. M. Sokal (ed.), *Psychological Testing and American Society, 1890–1930* (New Brunswick, NJ: Rutgers University Press, 1987 [1990]), pp. 234–60.

42. J. R. Angell to B. Ruml, 4 May 1923; B. Ruml to J. R. Angell, 8 February 1924; J. R. Angell to B. Ruml, 10 February 1923, RAC-LSRM, ser. 3, 79/823–8.

43. J. R. Angell to B. Ruml, 4 May 1923; Ruml to Angell, 8 February 1924; Angell to Ruml, 20 February 1923, RAC-LSRM, ser. 3, 79/823–8.

44. D. P. Crook, *Darwinism, War, and History: The Debate over the Biology of War from the* Origin of Species *to the First World War* (Cambridge: Cambridge University Press, 1994), p. 132.

45. 'Preliminary Formulation of Plan for Institute of Psycho-Biology at Yale University', attached with J. R. Angell to B. Ruml, March 1924, RAC-LSRM, ser. 3, 79/823–828. See also D. A. Dewsbury, 'Robert Yerkes, Sex Research, and the Problem of Data Simplification', *History of Psychology*, 1:1 (1998), pp. 116–29.

46. J. H. Capshew, 'The Yale Connection in American Psychology: Philanthropy, War, and the Emergence of an Academic Elite', in T. Richardson and D. Fisher (eds), *The Development of the Social Sciences in the United States and Canada: The Role of Philanthropy* (Stamford, CT: Ablex Publishing Corp., 1999), pp. 143–54; M. A. May, 'A Retrospective View of the Institute of Human Relations at Yale', *Behaviour Science Notes*, 6 (1971), pp. 141–72.

47. C. E. Seashore to B. Ruml, 10 April 1922; also Seashore to Ruml, 31 March 1922. L. Meriam to G. F. Willoughby, 20 April 1922, RAC-LSRM, ser. 3, 49/519.

48. C. S. Myers to B. Ruml, 20 November 1923; Ruml to Myers, 21 December 1923; Myers to Ruml, 25 January 1924. The statement of willingness to undertake projects for industrial and commercial firms is in the opening statement in the organization's journal, the *Journal of the National Institute of Industrial Psychology*, begun in January 1922. See also 'National Institute of Industrial Psychology: Statement Prepared for the Information of the Trustees of the Laura Spelman Rockefeller Memorial', 1924, RAC–LSRM, ser. 3, 56/610.

49. M. M. Sokal, 'James McKeen Cattell and American Psychology in the 1920s', in J. Brožek (ed.), *Explorations in the History of Psychology in the United States* (Lewisburg, PA: Bucknell University Press, 1984), pp. 273–323. See also L. Baritz, *The Servants of Power: A History of the Use of the Social Sciences in American Industry* (Westport, CT: Greenwood Press, 1960).

50. R. P. Gillespie, *Manufacturing Knowledge: A History of the Hawthorne Experiments* (New York: Cambridge University Press, 1991).

# 6 Research Centres

1. A. F. Bentley, *The Process of Government: A Study of Social Pressures* (Evanston, IL: Principia Press of Illinois, 1949 [1908]), p. 162; C. A. Beard, 'Political Science in the Crucible', *New Republic*, 13:46 (17 November 1917), pp. 3–4. See also A. Somit and J. Tanenhaus, *The Development of American Political Science: From Burgess to Behaviouralism* (New York: Irvington Publishers, 1982).

2. A fine study in which all of these figures appear in meaningful ways is R. Smith, *The Human Sciences* (New York: W. W. Norton and Company, 1997).

3. T. L. Haskell, *Emergence of a Professional Social Science: The American Social Science Association and the Nineteenth-Century Crisis of Authority* (Urbana, IL: University of Illinois Press, 1977).

4. J. W. Burrow, 'Coherence and Specialization in the Social Sciences in the Early Twentieth Century', in M. Harbsmeier and M. T. Larson (eds), *The Humanities between Art and Science: Intellectual Developments, 1880–1914* (Copenhagen: Akademisk Forlag, 1989), pp. 17–32.

5.  M. J. Deegan, *Jane Addams and the Men of the Chicago School, 1892–1918* (New Brunswick, NJ, and Oxford: Transaction Books, 1990), esp. pp. 33–69.
6.  P. M. Lengerman, 'The Founding of the American Sociological Review: The Anatomy of a Rebellion', *American Sociological Review*, 44:1 (1979), pp. 185–98. See also Furner, *Advocacy and Objectivity*; D. Ross, *The Origins of American Social Science* (Cambridge: Cambridge University Press, 1991).
7.  A. W. Small, 'The Present Outlook of Social Science', *American Journal of Sociology*, 18:4 (1913), pp. 433–69, on p. 456.
8.  R. L. Church, 'Economists as Experts: The Rise of an Academic Profession in the United States, 1879–1920', in L. Stone (ed.), *The University in Society*, 2 vols (Princeton, NJ: Princeton University Press, 1974), vol. 2, pp. 571–610.
9.  'Promotion of Economic Research', 21 September 1923, RAC-LSRM, ser. 3, 55/592. D. Fisher, 'American Philanthropy and the Social Sciences in Great Britain, 1919–1939: Reproduction of a Conservative Ideology', *Sociological Review*, 28:2 (May 1980), pp. 277–315. See also M. Bulmer, 'Beardsley Ruml and the School between the Wars: An Unsung Benefactor', *LSE Magazine*, 64:11 (1982), pp. 5–6; R. Dahrendorf, *LSE: A History of the London School of Economics and Political Science, 1895–1995* (New York: Oxford University Press, 1995).
10. Ibid., pp. 159–69.
11. LSE materials are in RAC-LSRM, ser. 1, 1/5 and 2/16; also in ser. 3, 55/592–595 and 56/599.
12. 'Memorandum from the London School of Economics and Political Science', July 1925, pp. 1–2; 'The Natural Bases of the Social Sciences', undated, RAC-LSRM, ser. 3, 55/594.
13. Ruml invited Malinowski to visit the United States in November 1925; B. Ruml to B. Malinowski, 12 November 1925, LSRM minutes, pages 25060–1. Also C. Merriam to B. Ruml, 24 April 1926. Malinowski's words are from his report at the end of his travels, as submitted to the Memorial in 1926; RAC-LSRM, ser. 3, 55/592–599.
14. R. Thornton, 'Malinowski and the Birth of Functionalism, or, Zarathustra in the London School of Economics', in J. T. Fraser and M. P Soulsby (eds), *Dimensions of Time and Life: The Study of Time* (Madison, CT: International Universities Press, 1996), pp. 251–66.
15. Fisher, 'American Philanthropy and the Social Sciences in Britain', 1919–1939: The Reproduction of a Conservative Ideology', in R. F. Arnove (ed.), *Philanthropy and Cultural Imperialism: The Foundations at Home and Abroad* (Boston, MA: G. K. Hall & Co., 1980), pp. 233–67, p. 295.
16. L. T. Hobhouse, *Social Development: Its Nature and Conditions* (New York: Holt, 1924).
17. L. Robbins, *The Nature and Significance of Economic Science* (London: Macmillan, 1932), p. 94. K. Bales, 'Charles Booth's "Survey of Life and Labour of the People in London, 1889–1903"', in M. Bulmer, K. Bales and K. K. Sklar (eds), *The Social Survey in Historical Perspective, 1880–1940* (Cambridge: Cambridge University Press, 1991), pp. 66–110.
18. F. A. von Hayek, 'The London School of Economics, 1895–1945', *Economica*, 13:49 (1946), pp. 1–31, on p. 25.
19. Smith, *The Human Sciences*, pp. 562–70.
20. Deegan, *Jane Addams and the Men of the Chicago School*, pp. 75–83.
21. It was Park who translated Simmel's two essays; contrasts between sociological ideas in Europe and in the United States are presented in H. Schwendinger and J. R. Schwend-

inger, *Sociologists of the Chair: A Radical Analysis of the Formative Years of North American Sociology (1883–1922)* (New York: Basic Books, 1974).

22. R. K. Haerle, Jr, 'William Isaac Thomas and the Helen Culver Fund for Race Psychology: The Beginnings of Scientific Sociology at the University of Chicago, 1910–1913', *Journal of the History of the Behavioural Sciences*, 27 (1991), pp. 21–41.

23. The term 'ecology' originated in German thought of the 1870s. See D. Breslave, 'The Scientific Appropriation of Social Research: Robert Park's Human Ecology and American Sociology', *Theory and Society*, 19 (1990), pp. 417–46; E. Gaziano, 'Ecological Metaphors as Scientific Boundary Work: Innovation and Authority in Interwar Sociology and Biology', *American Journal of Sociology*, 101 (1996), pp. 874–907.

24. R. E. Park, 'The City: Suggestions for the Investigation of Human Behaviour in the City Environment', *American Journal of Sociology*, 20:5 (March 1915), pp. 577–612. R. E. Park and E. W. Burgess, *Introduction to the Science of Sociology* (Chicago, IL: University of Chicago Press, 1921), p. 785. The mantra 'social control' was introduced during the 1890s by sociologist E. A. Ross; on the history of ideas about social control, beginning about 1920, see M. Janowitz, *The Last Half-Century: Social Change and Politics in America* (Chicago, IL, and London: University of Chicago Press, 1978), pp. 27–42.

25. M. Bulmer, *The Chicago School of Sociology: Institutionalization, Diversity, and the Rise of Sociological Research* (Chicago, IL: University of Chicago Press, 1984).

26. C. S. Johnson and Chicago Commission on Race Relations, *The Negro in Chicago: A Study of Race Relations and a Race Riot in 1919* (Chicago, IL: University of Chicago Press, 1922). For the Memorial's view, see 'Race Relations and Negro Work, 1926–27', RAC-LSRM, ser. 3, 98/996. See also N. Farber, 'Charles S. Johnson's *The Negro in Chicago*', *American Sociologist*, 26:3 (1995), pp. 78–88.

27. Interaction between the Memorial and the University of Chicago has been studied by M. Bulmer, 'The Early Institutional Establishment of Social Science Research: The Local Community Research Committee at the University of Chicago, 1923–30', *Minerva*, 18:1 (Spring 1980), pp. 51–100. L. C. Marshall to B. Ruml, 23 August 1923; C. E. Merriam to B. Ruml, 30 October 1923; Merriam to Ruml, 27 November 1923. In his October correspondence, Merriam presented a list of 'Suggested Topics for Long Time Survey'.

28. L. C. Marshall to B. Ruml, 7 March 1924; 'Memorandum' to L. K. Frank, 9 March 1925, RAC-LSRM, ser. 3, 70/744.

29. W. I. Thomas (in collaboration with R. Park and H. A. Miller), *Old World Traits Transplanted* (Chicago, IL: University of Chicago Press, 1921). See also R. E. L. Faris, *Chicago Sociology, 1920–1932* (San Francisco, CA: Chandler Publishing Co., 1967).

30. F. M. Thrasher, *The Gang: A Study of 1,313 Gangs in Chicago* (Chicago, IL, and London: University of Chicago Press, 1927), p. xi.

31. L. Wirth, *The Ghetto* (Chicago, IL: University of Chicago Press, 1928), p. xi.

32. L. Wirth, 'Urbanism as a Way of Life', *American Journal of Sociology*, 44:1 (1938), pp. 1–24, on p. 3.

33. On the work of Marshall with the NCSS, see E. Dawson, 'The Social Studies', *Journal of Social Forces*, 1:1 (1922), pp. 22–4; also, M. Lybarger, 'Origins of the Modern Social Studies, 1900–1916', *History of Education Quarterly*, 23:4 (1993), pp. 455–68. See also C. E. Merriam, 'Suggested Topics for Long Time Survey', 30 October 1923; Merriam to B. Ruml, 27 November 1923, RAC-LSRM, ser. 3, 70/744.

34. Early in his communications with the Memorial, Marshall sent Ruml multiple copies of his pamphlet titled 'Introduction to Social Studies'. Ruml evidently distributed a number

of these copies. Marshall then provided the requested memorandum on social science for engineers in February 1924; see L. C. Marshall to B. Ruml, 5 February 1924, RAC-LSRM, ser. 3, 70/744.

35. 'Report of S. P. E. E. Committee on Economic Content of Engineering Education', L. C. Marshall, November 1925, RAC-LSRM, ser. 3, 70/744.

36. B. Malinowski to B. Ruml, 1926 travel report, RAC-LSRM, ser. 3, 56/599. Chicago's department of anthropology carried on its own interaction over many years with the Memorial; RAC-LSRM, ser. 3, 70/746.

37. R. S. Lynd and H. M. Lynd, *Middletown* (New York: Harcourt Brace, 1929); C. E. Harvey, 'Robert S. Lynd, John D. Rockefeller Jr., and Middletown', *Indiana Magazine of History*, 79:4 (1983), pp. 330–54.

38. M. Mason to B. Ruml, 23 April 1927; B. Ruml to M. Mason, 10 May 1927, RAC-LSRM, ser. 3, 70/744–745.

39. L. C. Marshall, 'University Work in Economics and Business', 23 February 1928, RAC-LSRM, ser. 3, 70/744–745. See also L. C. Marshall, 'How May We Foster or Facilitate the Development of the Social Sciences?', *Journal of Political Economy*, 35:2 (1927), pp. 292–8.

40. L. C. Marshall to Beardsley Ruml, March 28, 1928, RAC–LSRM, ser. 3, 70/744–5.

41. RAC-Spelman Fund, ser. 5, 6/806.

42. H. D. Lasswell, 'The Cross-Disciplinary Manifold: The Chicago Prototype', in A. Lepawsky, E. Beuring and H. D. Lasswell (eds), *Search for World Order: Studies by Students of Quincy Wright* (New York: Appleton-Century-Crofts, 1971), pp. 416–28.

43. H. W. Odum to B. Ruml, 15 April 1924, RAC-LSRM, ser. 3, 74/776. H. W. Odum, *Social and Mental Traits of the Negro* (New York: Longman, 1910).

44. See also R. B. Vance and K. Jocher, 'Howard W. Odum', *Journal of Social Forces*, 33:2 (1955), pp. 203–17; G. B. Johnson and G. G. Johnson, *Research in Service to Society: The First Fifty Years of the Institute for Research in Social Science of the University of North Carolina* (Chapel Hill, NC: University of North Carolina Press, 1980).

45. See L. K. Frank to H. W. Odum, 5 June 1924, RAC-LSRM, ser. 3, 74/776.

46. H. W. Odum, 'A Southern Promise, n.d.; H. W. Odum to B. Ruml, 1 December 1924 RAC-LSRM, ser. 3, 74/776, pp. 4–7, 23.

47. B. Ruml to A. Woods, 12 May 1924, RAC-LSRM, ser. 2, 3/39. Correspondence between Ruml and Chase is in RAC–LSRM, ser. 3, SS6, 74/781.

48. H. W. Odum to L. Outhwaite, 12 May 1925, RAC-LSRM, ser. 3, 103/1039.

49. L. Outhwaite to H. Odum, 19 September 1925, RAC-LSRM, ser. 3, 103/1039.

50. H. W. Odum to L. Outhwaite, 19 September 1925; 'Preliminary Suggestions for Studies of Concrete Negro Problems', 23 September 1925; B. Ruml to H. W. Chase, 7 October 1925, RAC-LSRM, ser. 3, 103/1039–1042, esp. 1039.

51. H. Odum (ed.), *American Masters of Social Science* (New York: Holt, 1927).

52. The UNC research programme on black crime is noted in Leonard Outhwaite's 1926 memorandum, RAC-LSRM, ser. 3, 100/1015, p. 5. The Memorial's high impression of UNC's music studies is cited, for example, in the Memorial's memorandum of 1927, RAC-LSRM, ser. 3, 98/996, p. 7. See also Johnson and Johnson, *Research in Service to Society*.

53. H. Odum to B. Ruml, 26 September 1924; H. W. Chase to B. Ruml, 3 March 1925; H. Odum to B. Ruml, 26 March 1925, RAC-LSRM, ser. 3, 74/776.

54. L. Outhwaite to H. Odum, 18 February 1925; Odum to Outhwaite, 24 February 1925, RAC-LSRM, ser. 3, 103/1039–1042, esp. 1039.

55. G. B. Johnson to L. Outhwaite, 12 May 1925, RAC-LSRM, ser. 3, 103/1039.
56. The undated news clipping seems likely (based on other file contents) to be from 1928; it is from the *News and Observer*, Raleigh, North Carolina, RAC–LSRM, ser. 3, 74/788.
57. 'Columbia University – Social Science, 25 February 1925', RAC-LSRM, ser. 3, 50/526.
58. S. P. Turner, 'The World of Academic Quantifiers: The Columbia University Family and Its Connections', in M. Bulmer, K. Bales and K. K. Sklar (eds), *The Social Survey in Historical Perspective, 1880–1940* (Cambridge: Cambridge University Press, 1991), pp. 269–90.
59. See R. W. Wallace, 'Starting a Department and Getting it under Way: Sociology at Columbia University, 1891–1914', *Minerva*, 30:4 (1992), pp. 497–512; R. W. Wallace, 'The Struggle of a Department: Columbia Sociology in the 1920s', *Journal of the History of the Behavioural Sciences*, 27:3 (1991), pp. 323–40.
60. The February proposal and subsequent letters provided detailed description of the thirteen projects. The project to do research in the economics of the business corporation is described in a letter dated 21 March 1925, RAC-LSRM, ser. 3, 50/526.
61. UNC obtained a five-year grant on 28 May 1925. R. G. Hoxie, et al., *A History of the Faculty of Political Science, Columbia University* (New York: Columbia University Press, 1955), p. 109.
62. Ibid., pp. 123, 275.
63. Columbia University's Council for Research in the Social Science undertook the study of contemporary France; C. Hayes to B. Ruml, 26 December 1925. Council for Research in the Social Sciences to N. M. Butler, 18 February 1926; Council for Research in the Social Sciences to N. M. Butler, 23 November 1926. 'Report of the Council for Research in the Social Sciences to the University Council, October 15, 1929 – Columbia University'. RAC-LSRM, ser. 3, 50/527–8.
64. J. Parascandola, 'L. J. Henderson and the Mutual Dependence of Variables: From Physical Chemistry to Pareto', in C. A. Elliot and M. W. Rossiter (eds), *Science at Harvard University: Historical Perspectives* (Bethlehem, PA: Lehigh University Press, 1992), pp. 167–90, on pp. 181–4.
65. P. Buck (ed), *The Social Sciences at Harvard, 1860–1920: From Inculcation to the Open Mind* (Cambridge, MA: Harvard University Press, 1965); L. T. Nichols, 'The Establishment of Sociology at Harvard: A Case of Organizational Ambivalence and Scientific Vulnerability', in C. A. Elliot and M. W. Rossiter (eds), *Science at Harvard University: Historical Perspectives* (Bethlehem, PA: Lehigh University Press, 1992), pp. 191–222.
66. Nichols, 'The Establishment of Sociology at Harvard', p. 217.
67. Nichols, 'The Establishment of Sociology at Harvard', p. 192. See also Buck (ed.), *The Social Sciences at Harvard*.
68. J. Curtis to R. B. Fosdick, 17 February 1926; L. Outhwaite to B. Ruml, 29 April 1926. See also B. Ruml to E. Mayo, 15 March 1924, RAC-LSRM, ser. 3, 53/572.
69. Harvard's Fatigue Laboratory was directed by Lawrence J. Henderson, and was based in the business school.
70. Anon., 'Report of Committee on Handbooks in Psychology', *Psychological Bulletin*, 24 (1927), pp. 150–2. See also J. C. Burnham, 'The New Psychology: From Narcissism to Social Control', in J. Braeman, R. H. Bremner and D. Brody (eds), *Change and Continuity in Twentieth-Century America: The 1920s* (Columbus, OH: Ohio State University Press, 1968), pp. 351–98.

71. Parascandola, 'L. J. Henderson and the Mutual Dependence and the Mutual Dependence of Variables', p. 184; Nichols, 'The Establishment of Sociology at Harvard', pp. 193, 226–8, 235.

72. One specific appropriation of $155,000 came in May 1927 to cover a four-year period for the study of industrial efficiency.

# 7 Research Fields

1. J. H. Stanfield, *Philanthropy and Jim Crow in American Social Science* (Westport, CT: Greenwood Press, 1985).

2. B. B. Wessel to G. S. Ford, 29 April 1925. The interview that found the Memorial was 'favorably impressed with Mrs. Wessel's personality' was G. S. Ford and L. K. Frank, 'Interview with Bessie Bloom Wessel', 21 May 1925; J. Q. Dealey to G. S. Ford, 25 May 1925, RAC-LSRM, ser. 3, subser. 8.

3. B. B. Wessel to E. E. Day, 16 April 1928; B. B. Wessel, 'Memorandum for Dr. Day', 1928; see also B. Marshall to E. E. Day, 6 June 1928, RAC-LSRM, ser. 3, 51/533. The Connecticut project produced an article, B. B. Wessel, 'Ethnic Factors in the Population of New London, Connecticut', *American Journal of Sociology*, 35:2 (1929), pp. 263–70.

4. 'A Review of the Aims and Methods of the School of Applied Social Sciences', November 1925. M. Morlock to L. K. Frank, 3 February 1925; M. Morlock to L. K. Frank, 4 April 1925, RAC-LSRM, ser. 3, 62/666.

5. 'Proposed Department of Social Science, Fisk University', RAC-LSRM, ser. 3, 52/550.

6. 'Race Relations and Negro Work, 1926–2', p. 6.

7. P. J. Gilpin and M. Gasman, *Charles S. Johnson: Leadership beyond the Veil in the Age of Jim Crow* (New York: State University of New York Press, 2000), pp. 93–107.

8. J. W. C. Dougall to G. S. Ford, 18 May 1925; J. W. C. Dougall, 'A Memorandum of Some Observations Made in Connection with Negro Education During a Tour of the Southern States', 28 January 1925, RAC-LSRM, ser. 3, subser. 8, 100/1016, pp. 3, 12.

9. L. Outhwaite, 'Summary Letter' and 'Memorandum: The Negro in America', 1926, RAC-LSRM, ser. 3, 100/1015, pp. 1–4. See also J. H. Stanfield, 'Leonard Outhwaite's Advocacy of Scientific Research on Blacks in the 1920s', *Knowledge and Society*, 4:3 (1987), pp. 87–101.

10. Outhwaite, 'The Negro in America', pp. 3, 6–9.

11. Ibid., p. 5.

12. 'Race Relations and Negro Work, 1926–27', 1927, RAC-LSRM, ser. 3, 98/996, pp. 1–2.

13. Ibid.

14. K. R. Manning, *Black Apollo of Science: The Life of Ernest Everett Just* (New York and Oxford: Oxford University Press, 1983), p. 156.

15. RAC-LSRM, ser. 3, 98/998–1001. Another group supported by Memorial funds was the National Urban League, which had interests in working for race equality; RAC–LSRM, ser. 3, 100/1011–14.

16. V. N. Gamble, *Making a Place for Ourselves: The Black Hospital Movement, 1920–1945* (Oxford and New York: Oxford University Press, 1995), p. 123.

17. J. H. Kirkland to B. Ruml, 19 January 1925; J. H. Kirkland, 'The Social Sciences in Vanderbilt University, Resources and Plans', March 1925; 'Report on Provisions for Training in Social Technology', 1925, RAC-LSRM, ser. 3, 78/815.

18. Beardsley Ruml interview with J. H. Kirkland, 17 November 1925, RAC–LSRM, ser. 3, 78/815.

19. B. Ruml to W. L. Fleming, 30 January 1926, RAC-LSRM, ser. 3, 78/815.
20. W. L. Fleming to B. Ruml, 10 April 1926; B. Ruml to W. L. Fleming, 12 April 1926; W. L. Fleming to B. Ruml, 19 April 1926; the award granted in B. Ruml to W. L. Fleming, 3 May 1926, RAC-LSRM, ser. 3, 78/815.
21. E. A. Alderman to B. Ruml, 24 March 1925; E. A. Alderman to W. Rose, 3 April 1925, RAC-LSRM, ser. 3, 78/813–14.
22. H. W. Odum to B. Ruml, 28 January 1926; E. A. Alderman to B. Ruml, 8 February 1926, RAC-LSRM, ser. 3, 78/813–14.
23. W. Gee to B. Ruml, 23 March 1926; E. A. Alderman to B. Ruml, 30 March 1926. E. A. Alderman to B. Ruml, 22 April 1926. RAC-LSRM, ser. 3, 78/813–14.
24. Letter dated 4 June 1926; see also 'Memorandum of Interview' with W. Gee, n.d., RAC-LSRM, ser. 3, 78/813–14.
25. W. M. W. Splawn to B. Ruml, 18 January 1926; B. Ruml to W. M. W. Splawn, 26 January 1926, RAC-LSRM, ser. 3, 77/805; W. M. W. Splawn to B. Ruml, 13 May 1926, RAC-LSRM, ser. 3, 77/805.
26. W. M. W. Splawn, 'Grant Proposal', 25 January 1927, RAC-LSRM, ser. 3, 77/805, pp. 18–9, 25.
27. C. D. Simmons to B. Ruml, 26 August 1927, RAC-LSRM, ser. 3, 77/805.
28. 'Letter of inquiry' from M. M. Jones to A. Woods, 15 April 1925, RAC-LSRM, ser. 3, 73/768.
29. 'Research Program', April 1925, RAC-LSRM, ser. 3, 73/768, pp. 1–2.
30. A. Woods to B. Ruml, 16 April 1925, RAC-LSRM, ser. 3, 73/768.
31. President R. L. Wilber to B. Ruml, 6 May 1926; B. Ruml to President R. L. Wilber, 11 May 1926, RAC-LSRM, ser. 3, 69/724.
32. President Wilber to B. Ruml, 21 January 1927, RAC-LSRM, ser. 3, 69/724.
33. F. Ninkovich, 'The Rockefeller Foundation, China, and Cultural Change', *Journal of American History*, 70:2 (1984), pp. 799–820, on p. 801.
34. Ibid., pp. 803–4. M. B. Bullock, *An American Transplant: The Rockefeller Foundation and Peking Union Medical College* (Berkeley and Los Angeles, CA: University of California Press, 1980); T. Rosenbaum, 'A Survey of Sources at the Rockefeller Archive Centre for the Study of The Transfer of Western Science, Medicine, and Technology to China. The Archives of the China Medical Board and the Peking Union Medical College', Typescript, 1989, RAC.
35. P. B. Trescott, 'Institutional Economics in China: Yenching University, 1917–1941', *Journal of Economic Issues*, 26:4 (1992), pp. 1221–55.
36. Trescott, 'Institutional Economics in China', p. 1256.
37. O. D. Wannamaker, 'Grant Proposal', 1 March 1928, RAC-LSRM, ser. 3, 80/834–37, pp. 1–2.
38. P. B. Trescott, 'American Philanthropy and the Development of Academic Economics in China before 1949', in S. Hewa and P. Hove (eds), *Philanthropy and Cultural Context: Western Philanthropy in South, East, and Southeast Asia in the Twentieth Century* (Lanham, MD: University Press of America, 1997), pp. 157–81, on pp. 157, 159.
39. See M. B. Bullock, *The Oil Prince's Legacy: Rockefeller Philanthropy in China* (Washington, DC: Woodrow Wilson Centre Press, 2011), pp. 65–79.
40. T. N. Perkins to A. Woods, 26 January 1923; B. Ruml to N. H. Davis, 9 April 1923; N. H. Davis to B. Ruml, 21 April 1923; F. B. Stubbs to F. L. Polk, 14 September 1923, RAC-LSRM, ser. 3, subser. 8, 106/1081.

41. F. A. Golder to G. S. Ford, 17 March 1925; F. A. Golder, 'A Plan for the Study of the Russian Revolution', 1925. See also F. A. Golder to G. S. Ford, 16 March 1925, which further discusses the 'Economic Basis for the Territorial Division of European Russia', RAC-LSRM, ser. 3, 69/723.

42. Golder, 'A Plan for the Study of the Russian Revolution'.

43. RAC–LSRM, ser. 3, 49/512–13.

44. K. W. Rose, 'Survey of Sources at the Rockefeller Archive Centre for the Study of Twentieth-Century Africa', Typescript, 2003, RAC.

45. 'Negro Survey Africa, 1925–1926', RAC-LSRM, ser. 3, 102/1025.

46. 'University of South Africa, 1927', RAC-LSRM, ser. 3, 77/803.

47. J. M. Glenn to B. Ruml, 16 September 1924, RAC-LSRM, ser. 3, 77/804.

48. G. Bagge to B. Ruml, 20 September 1924, RAC-LSRM, ser. 3, 77/804. E. Craver, 'Gösta Bagge, the Rockefeller Foundation, and Empirical Social Science Research in Sweden, 1924–1940', in L. Jonung (ed), *The Stockholm School of Economics Revisited* (Cambridge: Cambridge University Press, 1991), pp. 79–97.

49. G. Cassel to W. Beveridge, 14 November 1924; G. Bagge to Memorial Trustees, 30 June 1925, RAC-LSRM, ser. 3, 77/804.

50. D. H. Stapleton, 'The Past and the Future of Research in the History of Science, Medicine and Technology at the Rockefeller Archive Centre', Typescript, n.d., RAC; Anon., 'Human Migration as a Field of Research', *Social Service Review*, 1:2 (1927), pp. 258–69. L. R. Kurtz, *Evaluating Chicago Sociology: A Guide to the Literature, with an Annotated Bibliography* (Chicago, IL, and London: University of Chicago Press, 1984), pp. 67–70.

51. 'Institute for Research in Land Economics and Public Utilities, Remarks on a tentative budget', December 1922, RAC-LSRM, ser. 3, 60/648–53.

52. A. Shaw to B. Ruml, 31 January 1923, RAC-LSRM, ser. 3, 60/648–53.

53. R. Ely to B. Ruml, 6 February 1923, RAC-LSRM, ser. 3, 60/648–53.

54. R. Ely to B. Ruml, 2 June 1923; B. Ruml to R. Ely, 12 November 1923; R. Ely to B. Ruml, 13 November 1923, RAC-LSRM, ser. 3, 60/648–53. Kept in the Memorial's files are articles titled 'Prof. Richard T. Ely Exposed!' and 'A Shameless Attack', both of which were critical of Ely.

55. C. L. Alsberg to B. Ruml, 27 May 1922; B. Ruml to C. L. Alsberg, 6 June 1922, RAC-LSRM, ser. 3, 69/722.

56. V. Kellogg to B. Ruml, 28 June 1922, RAC-LSRM, ser. 3, 57/617–23.

57. G. E. Hale to B. Ruml, 3 July 1922; G. E. Hale, 'A National Focus of Science and Research', June 1922, p. 1, RAC-LSRM, ser. 3, 57/617–23. See also R. M. Yerkes, 'The Work of [the] Committee on Scientific Problems of Human Migration, National Research Council', *Journal of Personnel Research*, 3:3 (1924), pp. 189–96.

58. 'Proposed Project for Research in the Agricultural Problem', 1924, p. 1, RAC-LSRM, ser. 3, 59/642.

59. Ibid., pp. 1–2.

60. Ibid., pp. 1–3, 9.

61. 'Research Program of the New School', RAC-LSRM, ser. 3, 59/642.

62. E. G. Nourse, 'What is Agricultural Economics?', *Journal of Political Economy*, 24:4 (1916), pp. 363–81.

63. Interview with E. G. Nourse, 20 January 1925, RAC–LSRM, ser. 3, 63/676.

64. B. Ruml, 'Director's Report – Social Sciences', 23 November 1926, RAC-LSRM, ser. 3, 63/676, p. 1. 'Report ... 1926–27', RAC-LSRM, ser. 3, 63/677.

65. Project Proposal, 1927, RAC-LSRM, ser. 3, 56/607.

66. E. E. Day to J. D. Black, 21 June 1928; J. D. Black to B. Ruml, 17 October 1928. RAC-LSRM, ser. 3, 48/495. T. Saloutos and J. D. Hicks, *Agricultural Discontent in the Middle West 1900–1939* (Madison, WI: University of Wisconsin Press, 1951), pp. 452–4. See also T. DeJager, 'Pure Science and Practical Interests: The Origins of the Agricultural Research Council', *Minerva*, 31:2 (1993), pp. 129–50.

67. *Helena Independent* (31 December 1924), p. 6. H. C. Wallace to B. Ruml, 17 November 1923, RAC-LSRM, ser. 3, 56/605; B. Ruml to R. T. Ely, 14 February 1924; R. T. Ely to B. Ruml, 12 April 1924, RAC–LSRM, ser. 3, 60/649. See also M. L. Wilson, 'The Fairway Farms Project', *The Journal of Land and Public Utility Economics*, 2:2 (1926), pp. 156–71.

68. H. F. Perkins, *First Annual Report of the Eugenics Survey of Vermont* (Burlington, VT: Eugenics Survey of Vermont, 1927), pp. 10–11.

69. Cravens, *Triumph of Evolution*, pp. 3–4, 48.

70. H. F. Perkins, *Second Annual Report of the Eugenics Survey of Vermont* (Burlington, VT: Eugenics Survey of Vermont, 1928), pp. 13–14; Perkins, *Fourth Annual Report of the Eugenics Survey of Vermont* (Burlington, VT: Eugenics Survey of Vermont, 1930), pp. 75–6.

71. H. F. Perkins, 'Plan for a Comprehensive Survey of Rural Areas in Vermont', March 1928, pp. 34, 37; H. F. Perkins to E. E. Day, 21 March 1928; H. F. Perkins to E. E. Day, 2 May 1928, RAC–LSRM, ser. 3, 77/810.

72. The proposal was approved in June 1928, RAC-LSRM, ser. 3, 77/810. See N. L. Gallagher, *Breeding Better Vermonters: The Eugenics Project in the Green Mountains* (Hanover, PA: University Press of New England, 1999), pp. 127–77.

73. H. C. Taylor, 'The Vermont Commission on Country Life', 11 October 1929, p. 2, RAC-LSRM, ser. 3, 77/810.

74. International Institute of Agriculture, grant application, RAC-LSRM, ser. 3, 39/407.

75. A. Friis to J. Shotwell, 18 September 1926; 'Memorandum, Institute of Economic History', September 1926, RAC-LSRM, ser. 3, 52/581.

76. M. Borell, 'Biologists and the Promotion of Birth Control Research, 1918–1938', *Journal of the History of Biology*, 20:1 (1987), pp. 51–87; Gunn, 'A Few Good Men, pp. 97–115.

77. Franks, *Margaret Sanger's Eugenic Legacy*, p. 38.

78. Franks, *Margaret Sanger's Eugenic Legacy*, pp. 32–3, 37. The word 'eugenists' was Rockefeller, Jr's word.

79. Jonas, *Circuit Riders*, p. 135; E. Barkan, *The Retreat of Scientific Racism: Changing Concepts of Race in Britain and the United States between the Two World Wars* (Cambridge: Cambridge University Press, 1992), pp. 41, 68.

80. Jonas, *Circuit Riders*, pp. 143–4, 157–9, 176–7.

81. Jonas, *Circuit Riders*, pp. 130–1; Barkan, *Retreat of Scientific Racism*, pp. 210–1.

82. E. R. Embree to R. B. Fosdick, 26 August 1925, RAC-RF, R.G.3, ser. 915, 4/33. 'Conversation with Flexner', RAC–RF, R.G.12.1, Series Diaries (Embree), 14/1925. Kohler, 'Science, Foundations, and American Universities in the 1920s', pp. 158–9.

83. F. T. Gates, 'Thoughts on the Rockefeller Public and Private Benefactions', 31 December 1926, RAC-Gates Collection, 2/47, p. 1.

84. Barkan, *Retreat of Scientific Racism*, pp. 111–2.

85. H. Odum to B. Ruml, 25 February 1925; H. Odum to G. S. Ford, 27 February 1925. *Greensboro Daily News*, RAC-LSRM, ser. 3, 74/776.

86. B. Ruml to A. Woods, 12 May 1924, RAC–LSRM, ser. 2, 63/39.

87. Dahrendorf, *LSE*, pp. 249–59.
88. Ibid., p. 256.
89. Barkan, *Retreat of Scientific Racism*, pp. 230–1.
90. Black, *War Against the Weak*; Franks, *Margaret Sanger's Eugenic Legacy*, p. 38.
91. E. Lomax, 'The Laura Spelman Rockefeller Memorial: Some of its Contributions to Early Research on Child Development', *Journal of the History of the Behavioural Sciences*, 13:3 (1977), pp. 283–93.
92. L. K. Frank, 'The Beginnings of Child Development and Family Life Education in the Twentieth Century', *Merrill-Palmer Quarterly*, 8:3 (1962), pp. 207–27; D. Bryson, 'Lawrence K. Frank, Knowledge, and the Production of the "Social"', *Poetics Today*, 19:3 (1998), pp. 401–21.
93. H. Pols, 'The World as Laboratory: Strategies of Field Research Developed by Mental Hygiene Psychologists in Toronto, 1920–1940', in T. Richardson and D. Fisher (eds), *The Development of the Social Sciences in the United States and Canada: The Role of Philanthropy* (Stamford, CT: Ablex Publishing Corp., 1999), pp. 115–42; H. Pols, 'Between the Laboratory and Life: Child Development Research in Toronto, 1919–1956', *History of Psychology*, 5:2 (2002), pp. 135–62.
94. M. A. Smith, et al., 'A Survey of Sources at the Rockefeller Archive Centre for the History of Child Studies', Typescript, 1988, RAC.
95. 'Board of Trustees Meeting', 26 February 1924, p. 15, RAC-LSRM, ser. 3, 63/677. J. Grant, 'Constructing the Normal Child: The Rockefeller Philanthropies and the Science of Child Development, 1918–1940', in E. C. Lagemann (ed.), *Philanthropic Foundations: New Scholarship, New Possibilities* (Bloomington and Indianapolis, IN: Indiana University Press, 1999), pp. 131–50, on p. 132. See also S. L. Schlossman, 'Philanthropy and the Gospel of Child Development', *History of Education Quarterly*, 21:3 (1981), pp. 275–99.
96. 'Parent Training', 26 March 1924, RAC-LSRM, ser. 3.5, 30/315; 'Parent Training', 3 September 1924, RAC-LSRM, ser. 3.5, 30/315; 'Child Welfare', 17 September 1925, RAC-LSRM, ser. 3.5, 30/315; 'Child Study and Parent Education', n.d., RAC-LSRM, ser. 3.5, 30/316.
97. L. K. Frank, 'Child Training', 1926, RAC-LSRM, ser. 3, 26/270.
98. RAC-LSRM, L. K. Frank, memo of interview with A. E. Richardson, Dean of School of Home Economics, Iowa State College, 2 March 1925; L. K. Frank to A. E. Richardson, 31 March 1925, RAC-LSRM, ser. 3, 32/341–2; L. K. Frank to A. E. Richardson, 26 March 1927, RAC–LSRM, ser. 3, 26/274. Frank to Richardson, 31 March 1925, RAC-LSRM, ser. 3, 32/341–2. See also Richardson to Frank, 18 January 1929, RAC-LSRM, ser. 3, 26/270.
99. M. Birk, 'Playing House: Training Modern Mothers at Iowa State College Home Management Houses, 1925–1958', *Annals of Iowa*, 64:1 (2005), pp. 37–66.
100. RAC-LSRM, ser. 3, 41/416–31, p. 430; see also an article in the file from *Time Magazine* (7 November 1938). H. Cravens, 'Child Saving in the Age of Professionalism, 1915–1930', in J. M. Hawes and N. R. Hiner (eds), *American Childhood* (Westport, CT: Greenwood Press, 1985), pp. 415–88; H. Cravens, *Before Head Start: America's Children and the Iowa Child Welfare Research Station* (Chapel Hill, NC, and London: University of North Carolina Press, 1993).
101. N. K. Berlage, 'The Establishment of an Applied Social Science: Home Economics, Science, and Reform at Cornell University, 1870–1930', in H. Silverberg (ed.), *Gender and*

*American Social Science: The Formative Years* (Princeton, NJ: Princeton University Press, 1998), pp. 185–232, on pp. 205–6.

102. A. P. Dinwiddie to B. Ruml, 10 February 1928, RAC-LSRM, ser. 3, 70/740. The grant was eventually awarded in 1929 through the Rockefeller Foundation.

103. RAC-LSRM, ser. 3, 63/675.

104. RAC–LSRM, ser. 3, 78/819. See also A. J. Todd, *The Scientific Spirit and Social Work* (New York: Macmillan Co., 1919); J. L. Gillin, 'The Tufts Report on Education and Training for Social Work', *Journal of Social Forces*, 1:3 (1923), pp. 383–90.

105. 'Memorandum of Interview', S. H. Walker, 23 May 1928; S. H. Walker to B. Ruml, 22 May 1928, RAC-LSRM, ser. 3, 73/772–3.

106. D. C. Jones and C. G. Clark, 'Housing in Liverpool: A Survey by Sample of Present Conditions', Read before the Royal Statistical Society, 29 May 1930; published in *Journal of Royal Statistical Society*, 93:4 (1930), pp. 489–537; D. C. Jones, et al., *The Social Survey of Merseyside*, 3 vols (Liverpool: University Press of Liverpool, 1934). For information about Booth's early survey, see Bales, 'Charles Booth's "Survey of Life and Labour of the People in London 1889–1903"', pp. 66–70.

107. Cravens, *Triumph of Evolution*, pp. 78–86; H. Cravens, 'The Wandering I.Q.: Mental Testing and American Culture', *Human Development*, 28:2 (1985), pp. 113–30.

108. 'Professional and Technical Schools', RAC-LSRM, ser. 3, 63/677.

109. Lasswell, 'The Cross-Disciplinary Manifold', pp. 416–9.

110. K. Rietzler, 'Research Report: The Rockefeller Foundation and the Search for International Order', Typescript, 2008, RAC, pp. 4–5, 27. See also K. Rietzler, 'Experts for Peace: Structures and Motivations of Philanthropic Internationalism in the United States and Europe', in D. Laqua (ed.), *Internationalism Reconfigured: Transnational Ideas and Movements between the World Wars* (London: I. B. Tauris, 2011), pp. 45–65.

111. A. Flexner to R. B. Fosdick and B. Ruml, 13 January 1926, RAC-LSRM, ser. 3, 52/551.

112. B. Ruml to A. Flexner, 9 March 1926; Ruml to Flexner, 9 December 1925, RAC-LSRM, ser. 3, 52/551.

113. During 1926 and 1927 Memorial trustees put together a Committee on Reorganization to evaluate their strategy in Europe; see 'Memorandum for the Committee on Reorganization by the Memorial's Representative for Great Britain and Ireland', J. R. M. Butler, December 1926, RAC-LSRM, ser. 3, 50/529–31.

114. H. Gilchrist to B. Ruml, 18 March 1925; A. Oltramare to B. Ruml, 21 September 1925, RAC-LSRM, ser. 3, 105/1061.

115. B. Ruml to A. Mendelssohn-Bartholdy,16 November 1925; A. Mendelssohn-Bartholdy to B. Ruml, 15 December 1925, LSRM, ser. 3, 52/561.

116. Radcliffe College submitted its initial inquiry on 10 November 1923. Their refined application was 'Radcliffe College. A Proposal for a Bureau of International Research', 1 February 1924, RAC-LSRM, ser. 3, 54/573. A. C. Coolidge, Harvard Library to A. Lawrence Lowell, 3 May 1924; A. A. Young to A. L. Lowell, 30 April 1924; A. L. Lowell to B. Ruml, 5 May 1924, RAC–LSRM, ser. 3, 54/573.

117. Rietzler, 'Experts for Peace'.

118. Rietzler, 'Research Report'.

119. F. L. Polk to B. Ruml, 9 April 1926, RAC-LSRM, ser. 3, 56/613. See also C. A. Beard, *The Advancement of Municipal Science* (New York: National Institute of Public Administration, 1910); C. E. Merriam, 'The Next Step in the Organization of Municipal Research', *National Municipal Review*, 11:3 (1922), pp. 274–81.

120. H. M. Pollack to B. Ruml, 24 January 1928, RAC-LSRM, ser. 3, 49/511.

121. L. Rosen, 'The Creation of the Uniform Crime Report: The Role of Social Science', *Social Science History*, 19:2 (1995), pp. 215–38.

122. A. Woods to K. Chorley, 25 October 1924, RAC-LSRM, ser. 3, 109/1102–3. The Memorial supported the University of Chicago Press from 1924 to 1931 and the University of North Carolina Press from 1924 to 1928. RAC-LSRM, ser. 3, 109/1106–7, 110/1108–10.

123. 'Memorandum on the Projected "Encyclopedia of the Social Sciences"', 21 February 1927, pp. 8–9, RAC-LSRM, ser. 3, 51/540.

124. W. F. Ogburn and A. Goldenweiser (eds), *The Social Sciences and their Interrelations* (Boston, MA, and New York: Houghton Mifflin Co., 1927), p. iii. P. M. Rutkoff and W. B. Scott, *New School: A History of the New School for Social Research* (New York and London: The Free Press, 1986), pp. 65–7.

125. Rutkoff and Scott, *New School*, pp. 65–7.

## 8 Research Organizations and Research Boundaries

1. F. Aydelotte, 'Educational Foundations with Special Reference to International Fellowships', *School and Society*, 22:52 (1925), pp. 799–803.

2. B. Ruml to Arthur Woods, 12 May 1924, RAC-LSRM, ser. 3, 3/39. 'Memorandum: Fellowship in the Social Sciences', 15 April 1924, RAC-LSRM, ser. 3, 63/678, p. 2. Prospective recipients were contacted in Europe during the years 1925–7; RAC-LSRM, ser. 3, 51/541–2.

3. E. E. Day and E. G. Nourse, 15 May 1929; 5 June 1929, RAC-LSRM, ser. 3, 52/549. Beardsley Ruml to Arthur Woods, April 22, 1924, RAC-LSRM, ser. 2, 3/39. S. Coben, 'Foundation Officials and Fellowships: Innovation in the Patronage of Science', *Minerva*, 14:2 (1976), pp. 225–40.

4. It appears to me that 81 out of 168 persons had either research preparation or a stated interest in economics; see 'Foreign Fellowships – Yellow Sheets', RAC-LSRM, ser. 3, 51/547.

5. B. Ruml to J. Rosenwald, 28 January 1925, RAC-LSRM, ser. 3, 52/549.

6. B. Ruml, 'Memorandum', 14 November 1923, RAC-LSRM, ser. 3, 60/647, p. 26. See also C. E. McGuire to B. Ruml, 16 December 1926, RAC-LSRM, ser. 3, 60/647.

7. RAC-LSRM, ser. 3, 49/517–18.

8. R. Brookings to W. Rose, 13 November 1923. See also the 1923 correspondences between R. Brookings and W. H. Hamilton, in RAC-LSRM, ser. 3, 49/517–18. Anon., 'A University Center for Research in Washington, DC', *Educational Record*, 3:1 (1922), pp. 50–8.

9. Mitchell, et al., *Income in the United States, its Amount and Distribution*. See also A. F. Burns (ed.), *Wesley Clair Mitchell: The Economic Scientist* (New York: National Bureau of Economic Research, 1972), pp. 31–43.

10. 'The Economic Foundation, Deed of Trust, February 2, 1923', RAC–LSRM, ser. 3, 51/538.

11. 'Memorandum', 22 October 1922; M. C. Rorty to B. Ruml, 4 November 1922, RAC-LSRM, ser. 3, 51/538. See Bulmer and Bulmer, 'Philanthropy and Social Science', p. 393.

12. Ruml shared ideas with George Vincent, Wickliffe Rose, Arthur Woods and Abraham Flexner; see for example B. Ruml to A. Woods, 13 August 1924, RAC-LSRM, ser. 2, 2/31. 'Conditions Affecting the Memorial's Participation in Projects in Social Science',

3 July 1924, RAC-LSRM, ser. 1, 1/9; also in RAC–LSRM, ser. 2, 2/31. Ruml presented the principles to the trustees on 10 July 1924; note in RAC-LSRM, ser. 1, 1/9.

13. C. E. Merriam, 'The Present State of the Study of Politics', *American Political Science Review*, 15:2 (May 1921), pp. 173–85, on p. 185. See also Alchon, *The Invisible Hand of Planning*, pp. 118–22.

14. Cited in B. Karl, *Charles E. Merriam and the Study of Politics* (Chicago, IL: University of Chicago Press, 1974), p. 145. Ross, *The Origins of American Social Science*, p. 401; E. Sibley, *Social Science Research Council: The First Fifty Years* (New York: Social Science Research Council, 1974), ch. 2. 'Memorandum from Director to Trustees', 26 February 1924, RAC-LSRM, ser. 1, 1/5, pp. 16–8.

15. C. E. Merriam, *New Aspects of Politics* (Chicago, IL: University of Chicago Press, 1925), pp. 184–219, on p. 189.

16. C. E. Merriam, 'Progress in Political Research', *American Political Science Review*, 20:1 (1926), pp. 1–13.

17. Merriam's views and Ruml's views are expressed in B. Ruml to R. B. Fosdick, 16 July 1923, RAC-LSRM, ser. 2, 3/39, RAC-LSRM, ser. 3, 63/677.

18. W. C. Mitchell, 'The Research Fellowships of the Social Science Research Council', *Political Science Quarterly*, 41:4 (1926), pp. 604–7, on pp. 605–6; Fisher, *Fundamental Development of the Social Science*, pp. 27–66; K. W. Worcester, *Social Science Research Council, 1923–1998* (New York: Social Science Research Council, 2001), p. 15.

19. Social Science Research Council, *Decennial Report, 1923–1933* (New York: Social Science Research Council, 1934).

20. Merriam, 'The Present State of the Study of Politics', p. 74.

21. Alchon, *The Invisible Hand of Planning*, pp. 57–60, 116–8, 167–9; M. C. Smith, *Social Science in the Crucible: The American Debate over Objectivity and Purpose, 1918–1941* (Durham, NC: Duke University Press, 1994), ch. 2.

22. N. Smith, *American Empire* (Berkeley and Los Angeles, CA: University of California Press, 2003), pp. 216–22; B. D. Karl, 'Foreword', in C. E. Merriam, *New Aspects of Politics*, pp. 1–32.

23. 'Tentative Agenda. Dartmouth Conference, Informal Summer Conference of Social Scientists and Allied Groups, August 24th to September 5th', 1925, RAC-LSRM, ser. 3, 52/563. Ruml sent initial letters to psychologists on 26 February 1925, RAC-LSRM, ser. 3, 53/563 and 53a/565.

24. W. C. Mitchell to G. S. Ford, 3 June 1925; C. Merriam to G. S. Ford, 5 June 1925, RAC-LSRM, ser. 3, 52/562. See Fisher, *Fundamental Development of the Social Sciences*, pp. 59–64.

25. 'Tentative Agenda. Dartmouth Conference, Informal Summer Conference of Social Scientists and Allied Groups, August 24th to September 5th', RAC-LSRM, ser. 3, 52/563. Produced at the first meeting were: 'Report of the "Committee on Problems and Policy, Social Science Research Council"', 127 pages; 'Report of Joint Conference of the Committee on Problems and Policy of the Social Sciences Research Council Meeting with Other Representatives of the Social Sciences in Attendance upon the Dartmouth Conference of Social Scientists and Allied Groups', 192 pages, quotation from p. 186; RAC-LSRM, ser. 3, 52/569.

26. RAC-LSRM, ser. 3, 52/562. See also Hanover Conference Minutes, 9–10 August 1926, RAC-SSRC, accession 1, ser. 6, subser. 9, 329/1892, p. 492. C. Beard to R. Crane, 25 September 1934, RAC-SSRC, accession 2, ser. 4, subser. 1, 704/8465. Outhwaite, 'The Life and Times of the Laura Spelman Rockefeller Memorial', pp. 134–8.

27. B. Ruml, 'Introductory Remarks', Hanover Conference 1927 Proceedings, RAC-LSRM, ser. 3, 52/569.

28. 'Hanover Economic Conference, September 3–8, 1928. Dartmouth College', RAC-LSRM, ser. 3, 67/702–4.

29. Social Science Research Council, *Decennial Report, 1923–1933* (New York: Social Science Research Council, 1933), p. 13.

30. See the Social Science Research Council's series of *Annual Reports*, as well as Social Science Research Council, *Decennial Report, 1923–1933*. See also A. F. Kuhlman, 'Social Science Research Council: Its Origin and Objectives', *Journal of Social Forces*, 6:3 (1928), pp. 583–8.

31. Quoted in D. L. Sills, '50th Anniversary of the 1930 Hanover Conference: The Letters of Robert Redfield to his Wife Keep the Past Alive', *Items: Social Science Research Council*, 34:2 (1980), p. 36.

32. D. L. Sills, 'A Requiem for P&P: Notes on the Council's Late Committee on Problems and Policy', *Items: Social Science Research Council*, 50:4 (1996), pp. 94–7, on p. 94.

33. 'Confidential Report to Colonial Woods on Activities of Seven Organizations Assisted by the Laura Spelman Rockefeller Memorial', 1926, RAC-LSRM, ser. 3, 63/678.

34. Ibid.

35. W. F. Ogburn to L. Frank, 4 September 1928, RAC-LSRM, ser. 3, 64/682–90. See also B. Laslett, 'Gender and the Rhetoric of Social Science: William Fielding Ogburn and Early Twentieth-Century Sociology in the United States', in J. Cox and S. Stromquist (eds), *Contesting the Master Narrative: Essays in Social History* (Iowa City, IA: University of Iowa Press, 1998), pp. 19–49; and V. L. Bullough, 'The Rockefellers and Sex Research', *Journal of Sex Research*, 21:2 (1985), pp. 113–25.

36. L. K. Frank to C. E. Wissler, 20 August 1928; W. F. Ogburn to L. K. Frank, 4 September 1928, RAC-LSRM, ser. 3, 64/682–90.

37. RF, R.G. 1, ser. 205A, 4/53–64.

38. See H. Hoover, 'Foreword', in W. C. Mitchell (ed.), *Recent Social Trends in the United States: Report of the President's Research Committee on Social Trends* (New York and London: McGraw Hill Book Co., 1933), p. 111. See also N. J. Smelser and D. R. Gerstein (eds), *Behavioural and Social Sciences: Fifty Years of Discovery, in Commemoration of the Fiftieth Anniversary of the 'Ogburn Report', Recent Social Trends in the United States* (Washington, DC: National Academy Press, 1986); M. Bulmer, 'The Decline of the Social Survey Movement and the Rise of American Empirical Sociology', in M. Bulmer, K. Bales and K. K. Sklar (eds), *The Social Survey in Historical Perspective, 1880–1940* (Cambridge: Cambridge University Press, 1991), pp. 291–315, on p. 309.

39. No detailed study seems to exist of the SSRC's relationship to Franklin D. Roosevelt and the New Deal. Worcester, *Social Science Research Council*, p. 23, cites a few sources doing work in this direction. Rockefeller, Jr's views were shared in an August 1933 radio broadcast praising the President's National Recovery Act; see Harvey, 'John D. Rockefeller, Jr., and the Social Sciences', p. 14.

40. 'Definition of Council Objectives', 1928, RAC-SSRC, accession 2, ser. 4, subser. 1, 704/8465, p. 1.

41. 'Development of Present Council Policy', RAC-SSRC, accession 2, ser. 4, subser. 1, 704/8465, p. 1. Quotation is from R. Frank, '"Interdisciplinary": The First Half Century', *Items: Social Science Research Council*, 42:3 (1988), p. 73. See also D. L. Sills, 'A Note on the Origin of "Interdisciplinary"', *Items: Social Science Research Council*, 40:1 (1986), pp. 17–18.

42. C. Rist, 'The Present State of Teaching and Research in Economics and Social Sciences in France, Proposals for Its Improvement', 1923, RAC-LSRM, ser. 3, 63/680. B. Ruml to C. Rist, 20 July 1926, RAC-LSRM, ser. 3, 63/680. Another letter supporting the value of Rist's survey came from E. R. A. Seligman (as Ruml cited it in his 20 July letter).

43. B. Ruml to A. Flexner, 9 January 1925, RAC-LSRM, ser. 3, 63/676.

44. J. C. Cobb, 'The Social Sciences', September 1925, RAC-LSRM, ser. 3, 63/676. Personal communication with Nat Cobb, descendent of John Candler Cobb, 8 October 2012.

45. 'Memorandum on the Needs of the International Committee of Historical Sciences', 26 March 1925, RAC-LSRM, ser. 3, 48/498, p. 1. American Council of Learned Societies, RAC-LSRM, ser. 3, 48/496. For the ACLS's report, see F. A. Ogg, *Research in the Humanistic and Social Sciences: Report of a Survey Conducted for the American Council of Learned Societies* (New York and London: The Century Co., 1928).

46. A. Woods to B. Ruml, 2 August 1925, RACLSRM, ser. 3, 105/1064; 'Study of the Humanities', n.d., RAC-LSRM, ser. 3, 105/1064.

47. B. Ruml to G. W. Young, 3 October 1925; Memorandum to Colonial Woods, 16 September 1926, RAC-LSRM, ser. 3, 105/1064–5.

48. G. W. Young, 'A Summary of Impressions Received during an Inquiry Made on Behalf of the Laura Spelman Rockefeller Memorial with a Recommendation', October 1926, RAC-LSRM, ser. 3, 105/1064–5, pp. 1–3.

49. R. Eisler to A. Flexner, 28 April 1926, RAC-LSRM, ser. 3, 105/1064.

50. A. C. Seward to B. Ruml, 28 May 1926, RAC-LSRM, ser. 2, 50/521. Fisher, 'American Philanthropy and the Social Sciences in Britain', p. 291; M. Bulmer, 'Sociology and Political Science at Cambridge in the 1920s: An Opportunity Missed and an Opportunity Taken', *Cambridge Review*, 102:29 (1981), pp. 156–9.

51. Fisher, 'American Philanthropy and the Social Sciences in Britain'; Bulmer, 'Sociology and Political Science at Cambridge in the 1920s'; D. Fisher, 'Philanthropic Foundations and the Social Sciences: A Response to Martin Bulmer', *Sociology*, 18:4 (1984), pp. 580–7, on p. 480; M. Bulmer, 'Philanthropic Foundations and the Development of the Social Sciences in the Early Twentieth Century: A Reply to Donald Fisher', *Sociology*, 18:3 (1984), pp. 572–9.

52. The words of Coss to Ruml are quoted in E. Craver, 'Patronage and the Directions of Research in Economics: The Rockefeller Foundation in Europe, 1924–1938', *Minerva*, 24:2–3 (1986), pp. 204–22, on p. 206; see J. J. Coss to B. Ruml, 28 February 1924, RAC-LSRM, ser. 3, 51.

53. B. Ruml to E. M. Hopkins, 10 August 1926, RAC-LSRM, ser. 2, 4/45. S. Ahmad, 'American Foundations and the Development of the Social Sciences between the Wars: Comment on the Debate between Martin Bulmer and Donald Fisher', *Sociology*, 25:3 (1991), pp. 511–20, on p. 515.

54. L. K. Frank to B. Ruml, 6 April 1927, RAC-LSRM, ser. 3, 105/1064.

55. 'Report ... 1925–26', RAC-LSRM, ser. 3, 63/677.

56. 'Memorandum of Interview', Dean H. W. Jervey interviewed by L. K. Frank, 29 January 1927, RAC-LSRM, ser. 3, 50/525. See W. J. Samuels, 'Law and Economics: Some Early Journal Contributions', in W. J. Samuels, J. Biddle and T. W. Patchak-Schuster (eds), *Economic Thought and Discourse in the 20th Century* (Aldershot: Edward Elgar, 1993), pp. 217–86.

57. H. W. Jervey to L. K. Frank, 3 February 1927, RAC-LSRM, ser. 3, 50/525.

58. Yale Law School, 'Program of Research in the Administration of the Law', 1927, RAC-LSRM, ser. 3, 78/830, pp. 1–2, 7.

59. L. K. Frank to R. M. Hutchins, 2 March 1927, RAC–LSRM, ser. 3, 78/830.
60. J. R. Angell to B. Ruml, 8 December 1927, RAC-LSRM, ser. 3, 78/830.
61. R. M. Hutchins to E. E. Day, 9 December 1927, RAC-LSRM, ser. 3, 78/830. See also J. R. Angell, 'The University and the School of Law', *American Bar Association* (April 1928), p. 1.
62. B. Ruml to J. R. Angell, 16 December 1927, E. E. Day to R. M. Hutchins, 22 December 1927, RAC-LSRM, ser. 3, 78/830.

## 9 Preparing for the Merger with the Rockefeller Foundation

1. 'Principles Governing the Memorial's Program in the Social Sciences', 22 November 1927, RAC-LSRM, ser. 3, 63/678.
2. RAC–LSRM, ser. 3, 50/529–31.
3. H. S. Pritchett to R. B. Fosdick, 5 January 1928, RAC-LSRM, ser. 3, 50/530.
4. One memorandum dealing with the Committee on Review lists twenty-five letters received from 'outsiders'; W. C. Mitchell to R. Fosdick, 20 January 1928, RAC-LSRM, ser. 3, 50/530.
5. W. F. Willcox to R. Fosdick, 8 January 1928; H. C. Taylor to R. Fosdick, 17 January 1928; L. C. Marshall to R. Fosdick, 30 January 1928, RAC-LSRM, ser. 3, 50/530.
6. F. P. Bachman to R. B. Fosdick, 21 December 1927; H. J. Thorkelson to R. B. Fosdick, 30 December 1927, RAC-LSRM, ser. 3, 50/529.
7. S. M. Gunn to R. B. Fosdick, 20 December 1927, RAC-LSRM, ser. 3, 50/529.
8. C. E. Dodge to R. B. Fosdick, 5 January 1928, RAC-LSRM, ser. 3, 50/530.
9. G. E. Vincent to R. B. Fosdick, 5 January 1928, RAC-LSRM, ser. 3, 50/530.
10. There were four groupings of recommendations. The section on 'General Objectives of the Laura Spelman Rockefeller Memorial' contained fifty-six points gathered from the letters. 'Scope of Program of the Laura Spelman Rockefeller Memorial' consisted of forty-eight points, 'Agencies or Means of Making the Program Effective' consisted of forty-eight points, and 'Internal Organization or Machinery of Operation' consisted of eight points. RAC-LSRM, ser. 3, 50/530. 'Report of Trustees Committee on Review', RAC-LSRM, ser. 3, 50/530, pp. 1–2.
11. Principal appropriations for social science for the years 1923 through 1928 are summarized, in table form, in Bulmer and Bulmer, 'Philanthropy and Social Science', pp. 386–7.
12. Ruml, 'Final Report', pp. 10–11.
13. 'Principles Governing the Memorial's Program in the Social Sciences', presented at the Rockefeller Foundation meeting, 31 December 1928, RAC-RF, R.G.3, ser. 910, 2/11.

## Conclusion

1. One example of a 'middle position' on this topic is Ahmad, 'American Foundations and the Development of Social Sciences between the Wars', pp. 511–20.

# WORKS CITED

## Primary Sources

### *Manuscript Collections*

Allan Nevins Papers, Special Collections, Columbia University Libraries, New York, New York.

Laura Spelman Rockefeller Memorial, Rockefeller Philanthropy Collections, Rockefeller Archive Centre, North Tarrytown, New York.

Rockefeller Foundation, Rockefeller Philanthropy Collections, Rockefeller Archive Centre, North Tarrytown, New York.

University of Chicago Scrapbooks, Special Collections Department, Joseph Regenstein Library, University of Chicago, Chicago, Illinois.

### *Unpublished Sources from the Rockefeller Archive Centre*

Rietzler, K., 'Research Report: The Rockefeller Foundation and the Search for International Order', Typescript, 2008, Rockefeller Archive Centre (hereafter RAC), North Tarrytown, New York.

Rose, K. W., 'Why Chicago and Not Cleveland? The Religious Imperative behind John D. Rockefeller's Early Philanthropy, 1855–1900', Typescript, 1995, RAC.

—, 'John D. Rockefeller, The American Baptist Higher Education Society, and the Growth of Baptist Higher Education in the Midwest', Typescript, 1998, RAC.

—, 'Survey of Sources at the Rockefeller Archive Centre for the Study of Twentieth-Century Africa', Typescript, 2003, RAC.

Rosenbaum, T., 'A Survey of Sources at the Rockefeller Archive Centre for the Study of The Transfer of Western Science, Medicine, and Technology to China. The Archives of the China Medical Board and the Peking Union Medical College', Typescript, 1989, RAC.

Shelley, J., et al., 'A Survey of Sources at the Rockefeller Archive Centre for the Study of Psychiatry and Related Areas', Typescript, 1985, RAC.

Smith, M. A., et al., 'A Survey of Sources at the Rockefeller Archive Centre for the History of Child Studies', Typescript, 1988, RAC.

Stapleton, D. H., 'The Past and the Future of Research in the History of Science, Medicine and Technology at the Rockefeller Archive Centre', Typescript, n.d., RAC.

Wilkie, J. S., 'Discipline and the Body of the Well-Child', Typescript, 2005, RAC.

# Published Primary Sources

## *Government Documents*

'Charter of the Rockefeller Foundation', ch. 488, Laws of New York, 14 May 1913. Reprinted as 'Schedule A', in 'Information Provided by the Rockefeller Foundation in Response to Questionnaires Submitted by United States Commission of Industrial Relations', submitted 25 January 1915.

'Exhibit A. Summary of Mr. King's Experience With Labor Problems', in 'Information Provided by the Rockefeller Foundation in Response to Questionnaires Submitted by United States Commission of Industrial Relations', submitted 25 January 1915.

'Information Furnished by the Rockefeller Foundation in Response to Questionnaire Submitted by the United States Commission on Industrial Relations', 4 December 1914.

'Information Furnished by the Rockefeller Foundation in Response to Supplementary Questionnaire Submitted by the United States Commission on Industrial Relations', 7 January 1915.

'Statement of John D. Rockefeller, Jr', US Congress, House Hearings, Subcommittee of the Committee on Mines and Mining, 63rd Congress, Second Session, *Conditions in the Coal Mines of Colorado* (Washington, DC: US Government Printing Office, 1914), vol. 2, pp. 2841–916.

'Statement of John D. Rockefeller, Jr', before United States Commission on Industrial Relations, at New York City, 25 January 1915.

'Statement of John D. Rockefeller, Jr', before United States Commission on Industrial Relations, at Washington, DC, 20 and 21 May 1915.

'Statement of William H. Allen', before United States Commission on Industrial Relations, Final Reports and Testimony, 8–9 (Washington, DC: US Government Printing Office, 1916), pp. 8327–42.

'Testimony of John D. Rockefeller', US Industrial Commission, Preliminary Report on Trusts and Industrial Combinations, 56th Congress, First Session, 30 December 1899, Document no. 476, part 1, pp. 794–7.

## *Newspapers and Journals*

*Advance*, 1905

*Christian Work and the Evangelist*, 1905

*Congregationalist and Christian World*, 1905

*Current Literature*, 1908–12

*Engineering Magazine*, 1901

*Farm & Fireside*, 1917

*Forum*, 1892

*Harper's Weekly*, 1909

*Helena Independent*, 1924

*Independent*, 1905, 1910, 1920

*Living Age*, 1909

*McClure's Magazine*, 1912

*Missionary Review*, 1905

*New York Herald*, 1900

*New York Times*, 1900, 1921

*Outlook*, 1905

*Paint, Oil and Drug Review*, 1897

*Time Magazine*, 1938

*Woman's Home Companion*, 1905

*World*, 1900

*World's Work*, 1908

## Other

Personal Communication, Mary Prophet, 12 June 2012.

Personal Communication, Nat Cobb, 8 October 2012.

# Secondary Sources

Abels, J., *The Rockefeller Billions: The Story of the World's Most Stupendous Fortune* (New York: Macmillan, 1965).

Adams, G., Jr, *The Age of Industrial Violence, 1910–1915: The Activities and Findings of the United States Commission on Industrial Relations* (New York: Columbia University Press, 1966).

Agoratus, S. A., 'The Core of Progressivism: Research Institutions and Social Policy, 1907–1940' (PhD dissertation, Carnegie Mellon University, 1994).

Ahmad, S., 'American Foundations and the Development of the Social Sciences between the Wars: Comment on the Debate between Martin Bulmer and Donald Fisher', *Sociology*, 25:3 (1991), pp. 511–20.

Alchon, G., *The Invisible Hand of Planning: Capitalism, Social Science, and the State in the 1920s* (Princeton, NJ: Princeton University Press, 1985).

—, 'Mary Van Kleeck and Social–Economic Planning', *Journal of Policy History*, 3:1 (1991), pp. 1–23.

Anderson, E. and A. A. Moss, Jr, *Dangerous Donations: Northern Philanthropy and Southern Black Education, 1902–1930* (Columbia, MO, and London: University of Missouri Press, 1984).

—, *Dangerous Donations: Northern Philanthropy and Southern Black Education, 1902–1930* (Columbia, MO: University of Missouri Press, 1999).

Anderson, J. D., *The Education of Blacks in the South, 1860–1935* (Chapel Hill, NC: University of North Carolina Press, 1988).

Andrews, T. G., *Killing for Coal: America's Deadliest Labor War* (Cambridge, MA: Harvard University Press, 2008).

Angell, J. R., 'The Organization of Research', *Scientific Monthly*, 11 (1920), pp. 26–42.

—, 'The University and the School of Law', *American Bar Association Journal* (April 1928), p. 1.

Anon., 'A University Center for Research in Washington, DC', *Educational Record*, 3:1 (1922), pp 50–8.

Anon., 'Human Migration as a Field of Research', *Social Service Review*, 1:2 (1927), pp. 258–69.

Anon., 'Report of Committee on Handbooks in Psychology', *Psychological Bulletin*, 24 (1927), pp. 150–2.

Aydelotte, F., 'Educational Foundations with Special Reference to International Fellowships', *School and Society*, 22:52 (1925), pp. 799–803.

Ayres, L. P., *Seven Great Foundations* (New York: Russell Sage Foundation, 1911).

Bales, K., 'Charles Booth's "Survey of Life and Labour of the People in London 1889–1903"', in M. Bulmer, K. Bales and K. K. Sklar (eds), *The Social Survey in Historical Perspective, 1880–1940* (Cambridge: Cambridge University Press, 1991), pp. 66–110.

Baritz, L., *The Servants of Power: A History of the Use of the Social Sciences in American Industry* (Westport, CT: Greenwood Press, 1960).

Barkan, E., *The Retreat of Scientific Racism: Changing Concepts of Race in Britain and the United States between the Two World Wars* (Cambridge: Cambridge University Press, 1992).

Beard, C. A., *The Advancement of Municipal Science* (New York: National Institute of Public Administration, 1910).

—, 'Political Science in the Crucible', *New Republic*, 13:46 (17 November 1917), pp. 3–4.

Bentley, A. F., *The Process of Government: A Study of Social Pressures* (Evanston, IL: Principia Press of Illinois, 1949 [1908]).

Bergquist, H. E., Jr, 'The Edward W. Bemis Controversy at the University of Chicago', *AAUP Bulletin*, 58:4 (1972), pp. 384–93.

Berlage, N. K., 'The Establishment of an Applied Social Science: Home Economics, Science, and Reform at Cornell University, 1870–1930', in H. Silverberg (ed.), *Gender and American Social Science: The Formative Years* (Princeton, NJ: Princeton University Press, 1998).

Birk, M., 'Playing House: Training Modern Mothers at Iowa State College Home Management Houses, 1925–1958', *Annals of Iowa*, 64:1 (2005), pp. 37–66.

Black, E., *War Against the Weak: Eugenics and America's Campaign to Create a Master Race* (New York: Four Walls Eight Windows, 2003).

Borell, M., 'Biologists and the Promotion of Birth Control Research, 1918–1938', *Journal of the History of Biology*, 20:1 (1987), pp. 51–87.

Breslave, D., 'The Scientific Appropriation of Social Research: Robert Park's Human Ecology and American Sociology', *Theory and Society*, 19 (1990), pp. 417–46.

Bristow, N. K., *Making Men Moral: Social Engineering during the Great War* (New York: New York University Press, 1996).

Brown, M. M., *A Study of John D. Rockefeller* (New York: n.p., 1905).

Brown, E. R., *Rockefeller Medicine Men: Medicine and Capitalism in America* (Berkeley and Los Angeles, CA: University of California Press, 1979).

Bryson, D., 'Lawrence K. Frank, Knowledge, and the Production of the "Social"', *Poetics Today*, 19:3 (1998), pp. 401–21.

Buck, P. (ed.), *The Social Sciences at Harvard, 1860–1920: From Inculcation to the Open Mind* (Cambridge, MA: Harvard University Press, 1965).

Bullock, M. B., *An American Transplant: The Rockefeller Foundation and Peking Union Medical College* (Berkeley and Los Angeles, CA: University of California Press, 1980).

—, *The Oil Prince's Legacy: Rockefeller Philanthropy in China* (Washington, DC: Woodrow Wilson Center Press, 2011).

Bullough, V. L., 'The Rockefellers and Sex Research', *Journal of Sex Research*, 21:2 (1985), pp. 113–25.

Bulmer, M., 'The Early Institutional Establishment of Social Science Research: The Local Community Research Committee at the University of Chicago, 1923–30', *Minerva*, 18:1 (Spring 1980), pp. 51–100.

—, 'Sociology and Political Science at Cambridge in the 1920s: An Opportunity Missed and an Opportunity Taken', *Cambridge Review*, 102:29 (1981), pp. 156–9.

—, 'Beardsley Ruml and the School between the Wars: An Unsung Benefactor', *LSE Magazine*, 64:11 (1982), pp. 5–6.

—, 'Philanthropic Foundations and the Development of the Social Sciences in the Early Twentieth Century: A Reply to Donald Fisher', *Sociology*, 18:3 (1984), pp. 572–9.

—, *The Chicago School of Sociology: Institutionalization, Diversity, and the Rise of Sociological Research* (Chicago, IL: University of Chicago Press, 1984).

—, 'The Decline of the Social Survey Movement and the Rise of American Empirical Sociology', in M. Bulmer, K. Bales and K. K. Sklar (eds), *The Social Survey in Historical Perspective, 1880–1940* (Cambridge: Cambridge University Press, 1991), pp. 291–315.

Bulmer, M. and J. Bulmer, 'Philanthropy and Social Science in the 1920s: Beardsley Ruml and the Laura Spelman Rockefeller Memorial, 1922–29', *Minerva*, 19:3 (1981), pp. 347–407.

Burnham, J. C., 'The New Psychology: From Narcissism to Social Control', in J. Braeman, R. H. Bremner and D. Brody (eds), *Change and Continuity in Twentieth-Century America: The 1920s* (Columbus, OH: Ohio State University Press, 1968), pp. 351–98.

Burns, A. F. (ed.), *Wesley Clair Mitchell: The Economic Scientist* (New York: National Bureau of Economic Research, 1972).

Burrow, J. W., 'Coherence and Specialization in the Social Sciences in the Early Twentieth Century', in M. Harbsmeier and M. L. Larson (eds), *The Humanities between Art and Science: Intellectual Developments, 1880–1914* (Copenhagen: Akademisk Forlag, 1989), pp. 17–31.

Capshew, J. H., 'The Yale Connection in American Psychology: Philanthropy, War, and the Emergence of an Academic Elite', in T. Richardson and D. Fisher (eds), *The Development of the Social Sciences in the United States and Canada: The Role of Philanthropy* (Stamford, CT: Ablex Publishing Corp., 1999), pp. 143–54.

Carnegie, A., *The Gospel of Wealth and Other Timely Essays* (New York: The Century Co., 1900), pp. 1–44.

Carnegie Institution, *History of Labor in the United States* (New York: Macmillan Company, 1918).

Chernow, R., *Titan: The Life of John D. Rockefeller* (New York: Random House, 1998).

Church, R. L., 'Economists as Experts: The Rise of an Academic Profession in the United States, 1879–1920', in L. Stone (ed.), *The University in Society*, 2 vols (Princeton, NJ: Princeton University Press, 1974), vol. 2, pp. 571–610.

Coben, S., 'Foundation Officials and Fellowships: Innovation in the Patronage of Science', *Minerva*, 14:2 (1976), pp. 225–40.

Cochrane, R. C., *The National Academy of Sciences: The First Hundred Years, 1863–1963* (Washington, DC: National Academy of Sciences, 1978).

Collier, P. and D. Horowitz, *The Rockefellers: An American Dynasty* (New York: Holt, Rinehart and Winston, 1976).

Corey, C. H., *A History of the Richmond Theological Seminary* (Richmond, VA: J. W. Randolph Company, 1895).

Corner, G. W., *A History of the Rockefeller Institute, 1901–1953: Origins and Growth* (New York: The Rockefeller Institute Press, 1964).

Cravens, H., *The Triumph of Evolution: American Scientists and the Heredity–Environment Controversy, 1900–1941* (Philadelphia, PA: University of Pennsylvania Press, 1978).

—, 'Child Saving in the Age of Professionalism, 1915–1930', in J. M. Hawes and N. R. Hiner (eds), *American Childhood* (Westport, CT: Greenwood Press, 1985), pp. 415–88.

—, 'The Wandering I.Q.: Mental Testing and American Culture', *Human Development*, 28:2 (1985), pp. 113–30.

—, *Before Head Start: America's Children and the Iowa Child Welfare Research Station* (Chapel Hill, NC, and London: University of North Carolina Press, 1993).

—, 'The Behavioural and Social Sciences', in M. K. Cayton and P. W. Williams (eds), *Encyclopedia of American Cultural & Intellectual History*, 3 vols (New York: Charles Scribner's Sons, 2001), vol. 1, pp. 669–77.

Craver, E., 'Patronage and the Directions of Research in Economics: The Rockefeller Foundation in Europe, 1924–1938', *Minerva*, 24:2–3 (1986), pp. 204–22.

—, 'Gösta Bagge, the Rockefeller Foundation, and Empirical Social Science Research in Sweden, 1924–1940', in L. Jonung (ed.), *The Stockholm School of Economics Revisited* (Cambridge: Cambridge University Press, 1991), pp. 79–97.

Critchlow, D. T., *The Brookings Institution, 1916–1952: Expertise and the Public Interest in a Democratic Society* (DeKalb, IL: Northern Illinois University Press, 1985).

Crocker, R., *Mrs. Russell Sage: Women's Activism and Philanthropy in Gilded Age and Progressive Era America* (Bloomington, IN: Indiana University Press, 2006).

Crook, D. P., *Darwinism, War, and History: The Debate over the Biology of War from the Origin of Species to the First World War* (Cambridge: Cambridge University Press, 1994).

Dahlberg, J. S., *The New York Bureau of Municipal Research: Pioneer in Government Administration* (New York: New York University Press, 1966).

Dahrendorf, R., *LSE: A History of the London School of Economics and Political Science, 1895–1995* (New York: Oxford University Press, 1995).

Davis, A. F., 'The Social Workers and the Progressive Party, 1912–1916', *American Historical Review*, 69:2 (1964), pp. 671–88.

Dawson, E., 'The Social Studies', *Journal of Social Forces*, 1:1 (1922), pp. 22–4.

Dawson, R. M., *William Lyon Mackenzie King: A Political Biography, 1874–1923* (Toronto: Toronto University Press, 1958).

Deegan, M. J., *Jane Addams and the Men of the Chicago School, 1892–1918* (New Brunswick, NJ, and Oxford: Transaction Books, 1990).

DeForest, R. W. and L. Veiller (eds), *The Tenement House Problem* (New York: The Macmillan Co., 1903).

DeJager, T., 'Pure Science and Practical Interests: The Origins of the Agricultural Research Council', *Minerva*, 31:2 (1993), pp. 129–50.

Dewsbury, D. A., 'Robert Yerkes, Sex Research, and the Problem of Data Simplification', *History of Psychology*, 1:1 (1998), pp. 116–29.

Ellis, H., *The Task of Social Hygiene* (Boston, MA, and New York: Houghton Mifflin Co., 1912).

Elmer, M. C., *Technique of Social Surveys* (Lawrence, KS: The World Co., 1917).

Ernst, J. W. (ed.), *'Dear Father'/'Dear Son': Correspondence of John D. Rockefeller and John D. Rockefeller, Jr.* (New York: Fordham University Press, 1994).

Ettling, J., *The Germ of Laziness: Rockefeller Philanthropy and Public Health in the New South* (Cambridge, MA: Harvard University Press, 1981).

Farber, N., 'Charles S. Johnson's *The Negro in Chicago*', *American Sociologist*, 26:3 (1995), pp. 78–88.

Faris, R. E. L., *Chicago Sociology, 1920–1932* (San Francisco, CA: Chandler Publishing Co., 1967).

Farley, J., *To Cast Out Disease: A History of the International Health Division of the Rockefeller Foundation (1913–1951)* (New York and Oxford: Oxford University Press, 2004).

Fell, J. E., Jr, 'Rockefeller's Right-hand Man: Frederick T. Gates and the Northwestern Mining Investments', *Business History Review*, 52:4 (1978), pp. 537–61.

Fisher, D., 'American Philanthropy and the Social Sciences in Great Britain, 1919–1939: The Reproduction of a Conservative Ideology', *Sociological Review*, 28:2 (May 1980), pp. 277–315.

—, 'American Philanthropy and the Social Sciences in Britain, 1919–1939: The Reproduction of a Conservative Ideology', in R. F. Arnove (ed.), *Philanthropy and Cultural Imperialism: The Foundations at Home and Abroad* (Boston, MA: G. K. Hall & Co., 1980), pp. 233–67.

—, 'Philanthropic Foundations and the Social Sciences: A Response to Martin Bulmer', *Sociology*, 18:4 (1984), pp. 580–7.

—, *Fundamental Development of the Social Sciences: Rockefeller Philanthropy and the United States Social Science Research Council* (Ann Arbor, MI: University of Michigan Press, 1993).

Flexner, A., *I Remember: The Autobiography of Abraham Flexner* (New York: Simon and Schuster, 1940).

Flynn, J., *God's Gold: The Story of Rockefeller and his Times* (New York: Harcourt, Brace and Co., 1932).

Fosdick, R. B., *The Story of the Rockefeller Foundation* (New York: Harper & Brothers, 1952).

—, *John D. Rockefeller Jr.: A Portrait* (New York: Harper & Row, 1956).

—, *Chronicle of a Generation: An Autobiography* (New York: Harper & Brothers, 1958).

—, *Adventure in Giving: The Story of the General Education Board* (New York: Harper & Row, 1962).

Frank, L. K., 'The Beginnings of Child Development and Family Life Education in the Twentieth Century', *Merrill-Palmer Quarterly*, 8:3 (1962), pp. 207–27.

Frank, R., '"Interdisciplinary": The First Half Century', *Items: Social Science Research Council*, 42:3 (1988), p. 73.

Franks, A., *Margaret Sanger's Eugenic Legacy: The Control of Female Fertility* (Jefferson, NC, and London: McFarland & Co., 2005).

Furner, M. O., *Advocacy and Objectivity: A Crisis in the Professionalization of American Social Science* (Lexington, KY: University of Kentucky Press, 1975).

Gallagher, N. L., *Breeding Better Vermonters: The Eugenics Project in the Green Mountains* (Hanover, PA: University Press of New England, 1999).

Gamble, V. N., *Making a Place for Ourselves: The Black Hospital Movement, 1920–1945* (Oxford and New York: Oxford University Press, 1995).

Ganfield, J., 'Minnesota Academy through Pillsbury Military Academy, 1877–1957', Steele County Historical Society (Owatonna, MN, Typescript, 2001).

Gates, F. T., *Chapters in My Life* (New York: Free Press, 1977).

Gaziano, E., 'Ecological Metaphors as Scientific Boundary Work: Innovation and Authority in Interwar Sociology and Biology', *American Journal of Sociology*, 101 (1996), pp. 874–907.

Geiger, R. L., *To Advance Knowledge: The Growth of American Research Universities, 1900–1940* (New York: Oxford University Press, 1986).

General Education Board, *Annual Report, 1918/19* (New York: Rockefeller Foundation, General Education Board, 1919).

—, *Annual Report, 1924/25* (New York: Rockefeller Foundation, General Education Board, 1925).

Gillespie, R. P., *Manufacturing Knowledge: A History of the Hawthorne Experiments* (New York: Cambridge University Press, 1991).

Gillin, J. L., 'The Tufts Report on Education and Training for Social Work', *Journal of Social Forces*, 1:3 (1923), pp. 383–90.

Gilpin, P. J. and M. Gasman, *Charles S. Johnson: Leadership beyond the Veil in the Age of Jim Crow* (New York: State University of New York Press, 2000).

Gitelman, H. M., *Legacy of the Ludlow Massacre: A Chapter in American Industrial Relations* (Philadelphia, PA: University of Pennsylvania Press, 1988).

Glenn, J. M., et al., *The Russell Sage Foundation, 1907–1946* (New York: Russell Sage Foundation, 1946).

Goodspeed, T. W., *A History of the University of Chicago: The First Quarter Century* (Chicago, IL: The University of Chicago Press, 1916).

Gordon, M., 'The Social Survey Movement and Sociology in the United States', *Social Problems*, 21:3 (1973), pp. 284–98.

Grant, J., 'Constructing the Normal Child: The Rockefeller Philanthropies and the Science of Child Development, 1918–1940', in E. C. Lagemann (ed.), *Philanthropic Foundations: New Scholarship, New Possibilities* (Bloomington and Indianapolis, IN: Indiana University Press, 1999), pp. 131–50.

Grattan, C. H., 'Beardsley Ruml and his Ideas', *Harper's Magazine*, 204:5 (1952), pp. 72–86.

Grossman, D. M., 'American Foundations and the Support of Economic Research, 1913–29', *Minerva*, 20:1–2 (1982), pp. 59–82.

Gunn, J., 'A Few Good Men: The Rockefeller Approach to Population, 1911–1936', in T. Richardson and D. Fisher (eds), *The Development of the Social Sciences in the United States and Canada: The Role of Philanthropy* (Stamford, CT: Ablex Publishing Corp., 1999), pp. 97–115.

Haerle, R. K., Jr, 'William Isaac Thomas and the Helen Culver Fund for Race Psychology: The Beginnings of Scientific Sociology at the University of Chicago, 1910–1913', *Journal of the History of the Behavioural Sciences*, 27 (1991), pp. 21–41.

Hammack, D. C. and S. Wheeler, *Social Science in the Making: Essay on the Russell Sage Foundation, 1907–1972* (New York: Russell Sage Foundation, 1994).

Harr, J. E. and P. J. Johnson, *The Rockefeller Century* (New York: Scribner's Sons, 1988).

Harrison, S. M., *Social Conditions in an American City: A Summary of the Findings of the Springfield Survey* (New York: Russell Sage Foundation, 1920).

Harvey, C. E., 'Religion and Industrial Relations: John D. Rockefeller Jr. and the Interchurch World Movement of 1919–1920', *Research in Political Economy*, 4 (1981), pp. 199–227.

—, 'John D. Rockefeller, Jr., and the Social Sciences: An Introduction', *Journal of the History of Sociology*, 4:3 (1982), pp. 1–31.

—, 'Robert S. Lynd, John D. Rockefeller Jr., and Middletown', *Indiana Magazine of History*, 79:4 (1983), pp. 330–54.

—, 'John D. Rockefeller, Jr., Herbert Hoover, and President Wilson's Industrial Conferences of 1919–1920', in J. E. Brown and P. D. Reagan (eds), *Voluntarism, Planning, and the*

*State: The American Planning Experience, 1914–1916* (Westport, CT: Greenwood Press, 1988), pp. 25–46.

Haskell, T. L., *Emergence of a Professional Social Science: The American Social Science Association and the Nineteenth-Century Crisis of Authority* (Urbana, IL: University of Illinois Press, 1977).

Heald, M., *The Social Responsibilities of Business: Company and Community, 1900–1960* (Cleveland, OH: Case Western Reserve University, 1970).

Heaton, H., *A Scholar in Action: Edwin F. Gay* (Cambridge, MA: Harvard University Press, 1952).

—, *A Scholar in Action: Edwin F. Gay* (New York: Greenwood Press, 1968).

Heidbreder, E., *Seven Psychologies* (New York: Century Co., 1933).

Hewa, S., 'The Protestant Ethic and Rockefeller Benevolence: The Religious Impulse in American Philanthropy', *Journal for the Theory of Social Behaviour*, 27:4 (1997), pp. 419–52.

—, 'Toward the Well-Being of Mankind: Rockefeller Philanthropy and the Problem of Economic Research', *International Journal of Sociology and Social Policy*, 18:11–12 (1998), pp. 85–129.

Hiebert, R. E., *Courtier to the Crowd: The Story of Ivy Lee and the Development of Public Relations* (Ames, IA: Iowa State University Press, 1966).

Hobhouse, L. T., *Social Development: Its Nature and Conditions* (New York: Holt, 1924).

Hooks, G. M. and W. L. Flinn, 'The Country Life Commission and Early Rural Sociology', *Rural Sociologist*, 1:2 (1981), pp. 95–100.

Hoover, H., 'Foreword', in W. C. Mitchell (ed.), *Recent Social Trends in the United States: Report of the President's Research Committee on Social Trends* (New York and London: McGraw Hill Book Co., 1933), p. 111.

Howe, B., 'The Origins of The Rockefeller Foundation', in R. F. Arnove (ed.), *Philanthropy and Cultural Imperialism: The Foundations at Home and Abroad* (Boston, MA: G. K. Hall, 1980), pp. 1–25.

Hoxie, R. G., et al., *A History of the Faculty of Political Science, Columbia University* (New York: Columbia University Press, 1955).

Hubbard S., *John D. Rockefeller and His Career* (New York: By the Author, 1904).

Huebner, G. G., 'The Americanization of the Immigrant', *Annals of the American Academy of Political and Social Science*, 27:2 (1906), pp. 191–213.

Hylton, R., 'University History', Virginia Union University, at http://www.vuu.edu/about_vuu/history.aspx [accessed 15 August 2012].

Janowitz, M., *The Last Half-Century: Social Change and Politics in America* (Chicago, IL, and London: University of Chicago Press, 1978).

Johnson, C. S. and Chicago Commission on Race Relations, *The Negro in Chicago: A Study of Race Relations and a Race Riot in 1919* (Chicago, IL: University of Chicago Press, 1922).

Johnson, G. B. and G. G. Johnson, *Research in Service to Society: The First Fifty Years of the Institute for Research in Social Science of the University of North Carolina* (Chapel Hill, NC: University of North Carolina Press, 1980).

Jonas, G., *The Circuit Riders: Rockefeller Money and the Rise of Modern Science* (New York and London: W. W. Norton & Company, 1989).

Jones, D. C. and C. G. Clark, 'Housing in Liverpool: A Survey by Sample of Present Conditions', *Journal of the Royal Statistical Society*, 93:4 (1930), pp. 489–537.

Jones, D. C., et al., *The Social Survey of Merseyside*, 3 vols (Liverpool: University Press of Liverpool, 1934).

Jordan, J. M. (ed.), '"To Educate Public Opinion": John D. Rockefeller, Jr. and the Origins of Social Scientific Fact-Finding', *New England Quarterly*, 64:2 (1991), pp. 292–7.

Judis, J. B., *The Paradox of American Democracy: Elites, Special Interests, and the Betrayal of Public Trust* (New York: Pantheon, 2000).

Karl, B. D., 'Foreword', in C. E. Merriam, *New Aspects of Politics* (Chicago, IL: University of Chicago Press, 1925 [1970]).

—, *Charles E. Merriam and the Study of Politics* (Chicago, IL: University of Chicago Press, 1974).

Kellogg, P. U. (ed.), *The Pittsburgh Survey: Findings in Six Volumes* (New York: Charities Publication Committee, 1909–14).

Kennedy, D. M., *Over Here: The First World War and American Society* (Oxford and New York: Oxford University Press, 1980).

King, W. L. M., *Industry and Humanity: A Study of the Principles Underlying Industrial Reconstruction* (Boston, MA, and New York: Houghton Mifflin Co., 1918).

Kirkland, E. C., *Dream and Thought in the Business Community, 1860–1900* (Ithaca, NY: Cornell University Press, 1956).

Kochersberger, R. C., Jr, 'Introduction', in R. C. Kockersberger, Jr (ed.), *More than a Muckraker: Ida Tarbell's Lifetime in Journalism* (Knoxville, TN: University of Tennessee Press, 1994), pp. xxiv–xxv, 66–86.

Kohler, R. E., 'Science and Philanthropy: Wickliffe Rose and the International Education Board', *Minerva*, 23 (1985), pp. 75–95.

—, 'Science, Foundations, and American Universities in the 1920s', *OSIRIS*, 2nd ser., 3 (1987), pp. 135–64.

Kuhlman, A. F., 'Social Science Research Council: Its Origin and Objectives', *Journal of Social Forces*, 6:3 (1928), pp. 583–8.

Kurtz, L. R., *Evaluating Chicago Sociology: A Guide to the Literature, with an Annotated Bibliography* (Chicago, IL, and London: University of Chicago Press, 1984).

Lagemann, E. C., *The Politics of Knowledge: The Carnegie Corporation, Philanthropy, and Public Policy* (Middletown, CT: Wesleyan University Press, 1990).

Laslett, B., 'Gender and the Rhetoric of Social Science: William Fielding Ogburn and Early Twentieth-Century Sociology in the United States', in J. Cox and S. Stromquist (eds), *Contesting the Master Narrative: Essays in Social History* (Iowa City, IA: University of Iowa Press, 1998), pp. 19–49.

Lasswell, H. D., *Propaganda Techniques in the World War* (New York: A. A. Knopf, 1927).

—, 'The Cross-Disciplinary Manifold: The Chicago Prototype', in A. Lepawsky, E. Beuring and H. D. Lasswell (eds), *Search for World Order: Studies by Students of Quincy Wright* (New York: Appleton-Century-Crofts, 1971), pp. 416–28.

Lederer, S. E., *Subjected to Science: Human Experimentation in America before the Second World War* (Baltimore, MD, and London: The Johns Hopkins University Press, 1995).

Lengerman, P. M., 'The Founding of the American Sociological Review: The Anatomy of a Rebellion', *American Sociological Review*, 44:2 (1979), pp. 185–98.

Link, W. A., *The Paradox of Southern Progressivism: 1880–1930* (Chapel Hill, NC: University of North Carolina Press, 1993).

Lloyd, C. A., *Henry Demarest Lloyd, 1847–1903, A Biography* (New York and London: G. P. Putnam's Sons, 1912).

Lloyd, H. D., *Wealth against Commonwealth* (New York: Harper & Row, 1894).

Lomax, E., 'The Laura Spelman Rockefeller Memorial: Some of its Contributions to Early Research in Child Development', *Journal of the History of the Behavioural Sciences*, 13:3 (1977), pp. 283–93.

Lybarger, M., 'Origins of the Modern Social Studies, 1900–1916', *History of Education Quarterly*, 23:4 (1983), pp. 455–68.

Lynd, R. S. and H. M. Lynd, *Middletown* (New York: Harcourt Brace, 1929).

McDonald, B. D., III, 'The Bureau of Municipal Research and the Development of a Professional Public Service', *Administration & Society*, 42:7 (2010), pp. 815–35.

McGovern, G. S. and L. G. Guttridge, *The Great Coal-Field War* (Boston, MA: Houghton Mifflin, 1972).

McGregor, F. A., *The Fall and Rise of Mackenzie King: 1911–1919* (Toronto: Macmillan, 1962).

McReynolds, S. A., 'Eugenics and Rural Development: The Vermont Commission on Country Life's Program for the Future', *Agricultural History*, 71:3 (1997), pp. 300–29.

Manning, K. R., *Black Apollo of Science: The Life of Ernest Everett Just* (New York and Oxford: Oxford University Press, 1983).

Marshall, L. C., 'How May We Foster or Facilitate the Development of the Social Sciences?', *Journal of Political Economy*, 35:2 (1927), pp. 292–8.

May, M. A., 'A Retrospective View of the Institute of Human Relations at Yale', *Behaviour Science Notes*, 6 (1971), pp. 141–72.

Meckel, R. A., *Save the Babies: American Public Health Reform and the Prevention of Infant Mortality, 1850–1929* (Baltimore, MD: Johns Hopkins University Press, 1990).

Merriam, C. E., 'The Present State of the Study of Politics', *American Political Science Review*, 15:2 (May 1921), pp. 173–85.

—, 'The Next Step in the Organization of Municipal Research', *National Municipal Review*, 11:3 (1922), pp. 274–81.

—, *New Aspects of Politics* (Chicago, IL: University of Chicago Press, 1925 [1970]).

—, 'Progress in Political Research', *American Political Science Review*, 20:1 (1926), pp. 1–13.

Mitchell, L. S., *Two Lives: The Story of Wesley Clair Mitchell and Myself* (New York: Simon and Schuster, 1953).

Mitchell, W. C., et al., *Income in the United States, its Amount and Distribution*, NBER Publication no. 1 and no. 2 (New York: Harcourt Brace, 1921–2).

—, 'The Research Fellowships of the Social Science Research Council', *Political Science Quarterly*, 41:4 (1926), pp. 604–7.

Morawski, J. G. and G. A. Hornstein, 'Quandary of the Quacks: The Struggle for Expert Knowledge in American Psychology, 1890–1940', in J. Brown and D. K. Van Keuren (eds), *The Estate of Social Knowledge* (Baltimore, MD: Johns Hopkins University Press, 1991), pp. 106–33.

Morris, E., *Theodore Rex* (New York: Random House, 2001).

National Bureau of Economic Research, *Business Cycles and Unemployment: Report and Recommendation of a Committee of the President's Conference on Unemployment*, 1921, NBER Publication no. 4 (New York: McGraw Hill, 1923).

Nevins, A., *A Study in Power: John D. Rockefeller, Industrialist and Philanthropist*, 2 vols (New York: Charles Scribner's Sons, 1953).

Nichols, L. T., 'The Establishment of Sociology at Harvard: A Case of Organizational Ambivalence and Scientific Vulnerability', in C. A. Elliot and M. W. Rossiter (eds), *Science at Harvard University: Historical Perspectives* (Bethlehem, PA: Lehigh University Press, 1992), pp. 191–222.

Ninkovich, F., 'The Rockefeller Foundation, China, and Cultural Change', *Journal of American History*, 70:2 (1984), pp. 799–820.

Nourse, E. G., 'What Is Agricultural Economics?', *Journal of Political Economy*, 24:4 (1916), pp. 363–81.

Odum, H. W., *Social and Mental Traits of the Negro* (New York: Longman, 1910).

– (ed.), *American Masters of Social Science* (New York: Holt, 1927).

Ogburn, W. F., *Social Change With Respect to Culture and Original Nature* (New York: B. W. Huebsch, 1922).

Ogburn, W. F. and A. Goldenwieser (eds), *The Social Sciences and their Interrelations* (Boston, MA, and New York: Houghton Mifflin Co., 1927).

Ogg, F. A., *Research in the Humanistic and Social Sciences: Report of a Survey Conducted for the American Council of Learned Societies* (New York and London: The Century Co., 1928).

Parascandola, J., 'L. J. Henderson and the Mutual Dependence of Variables: From Physical Chemistry to Pareto', in C. A. Elliot and M. W. Rossiter (eds), *Science at Harvard University: Historical Perspectives* (Bethlehem, PA: Lehigh University Press, 1992), pp. 167–90.

Park, R. E., 'The City: Suggestions for the Investigation of Human Behaviour in the City Environment', *American Journal of Sociology*, 20:5 (1915), pp. 577–612.

—, 'The City as a Social Laboratory', in T. V. Smith and L. D. White (eds), *Chicago: An Experiment in Social Science Research* (Chicago, IL: University of Chicago Press, 1929).

Park, R. E. and E. W. Burgess, *Introduction to the Science of Sociology* (Chicago, IL: University of Chicago Press, 1921).

Perkins, H. F., *First Annual Report of the Eugenics Survey of Vermont* (Burlington, VT: Eugenics Survey of Vermont, 1927).

—, *Second Annual Report of the Eugenics Survey of Vermont* (Burlington, VT: Eugenics Survey of Vermont, 1928).

—, *Fourth Annual Report of the Eugenics Survey of Vermont* (Burlington, VT: Eugenics Survey of Vermont, 1930).

Plotkin, H., 'Edward C. Pickering and the Endowment of Scientific Research in America, 1877–1918', *Isis*, 69:1 (1978), pp. 44–57.

Pols, H., 'The World as Laboratory: Strategies of Field Research Developed by Mental Hygiene Psychologists in Toronto, 1920–1940', in T. Richardson and D. Fisher (eds), *The Development of the Social Sciences in the United States and Canada: The Role of Philanthropy* (Stamford, CT: Ablex Publishing Corp., 1999), pp. 115–42.

—, 'Between the Laboratory and Life: Child Development Research in Toronto, 1919–1956', *History of Psychology*, 5:2 (2002), pp. 135–62.

Reed, J., 'Robert M. Yerkes and the Mental Testing Movement' in M. M. Sokal (ed.), *Psychological Testing and American Society, 1890–1930* (New Brunswick, NJ: Rutgers University Press, 1987 [1990]), pp. 234–60.

Reingold, N., 'The Case of the Disappearing Laboratory', *American Quarterly*, 29:1 (1977), pp. 79–101.

—, 'National Science Policy in a Private Foundation: The Carnegie Institution of Washington', in A. Oleson and J. Voss (eds), *The Organization of Knowledge in Modern America, 1860–1920* (Baltimore, MD: Johns Hopkins University Press, 1979), pp. 190–223.

Rietzler, K., 'Experts for Peace: Structures and Motivations of Philanthropic Internationalism in the United States and Europe', in D. Laqua (ed.), *Internationalism Reconfigured: Transnational Ideas and Movements between the World Wars* (London: I. B. Tauris, 2011), pp. 45–65.

Robbins, L., *The Nature and Significance of Economic Science* (London: Macmillan, 1932).

Rockefeller, J. D., *Random Reminiscences of Men and Events* (New York: Doubleday, Page & Company, 1909).

Rockefeller, J. D., Jr, 'Introduction', in G. J. Kneeland and K. B. Davis, *Commercialized Prostitution in New York City* (New York: The Century Co., 1913), pp. ii–iv.

—, 'Introduction', in A. Flexner, *Prostitution in Europe* (New York: The Century Co., 1914), pp. vii–ix.

—, *Address by John D. Rockefeller, Jr., Delivered at Pueblo, Colorado, October 1915* (Denver, CO: W. H. Kistler, 1915).

Rockefeller Foundation, *President's Review and Annual Report for 1915* (New York: Rockefeller Foundation, 1915).

—, *Annual Reports, years 1929 through 1930* (New York: Rockefeller Foundation, 1929–30).

Rose, K. W. and D. H. Stapleton, 'Toward a "Universal Heritage": Education and the Development of Rockefeller Philanthropy, 1884–1913', *Teachers College Record*, 93:3 (1992), pp. 536–55.

Rosen, L., 'The Creation of the Uniform Crime Report: The Role of Social Science', *Social Science History*, 19:2 (1995), pp. 215–38.

Ross, D., *The Origins of American Social Science* (Cambridge: Cambridge University Press, 1991).

Russell, J., 'The Coming of the Line: The Ford Highland Park Plant, 1910–1914', *Radical America*, 12:3 (1978), pp. 28–45.

Rutkoff, P. M. and W. B. Scott, *New School: A History of the New School for Social Research* (New York and London: Free Press, 1986).

Saloutos, T. and J. D. Hicks, *Agricultural Discontent in the Middle West 1900–1939* (Madison, WI: University of Wisconsin Press, 1951).

Samuels, W. J., 'Law and Economics: Some Early Journal Contributions', in W. J. Samuels, J. Biddle and T. W. Patchak-Schuster (eds), *Economic Thought and Discourse in the 20th Century* (Aldershot: Edward Elgar, 1993), pp. 217–86.

Samuelson, F., 'Struggle for Scientific Authority: The Reception of Watson's Behaviourism 1913–1920', *Journal of the History of the Behavioural Sciences*, 17:3 (1981), pp. 399–425.

—, 'Organizing for the Kingdom of Behaviour: Academic Battles and Organizational Policies in the Twenties', *Journal of the History of the Behavioural Sciences*, 21:1 (1983), pp. 33–47.

Sandage, S. A., *Born Losers: A History of Failure in America* (Cambridge, MA: Harvard University Press, 2005).

Saunders, C. B., Jr, *The Brookings Institution: A Fifty Year History* (Washington, DC: Brookings Institution, 1966).

Schlossman, S. L., 'Philanthropy and the Gospel of Child Development', *History of Education Quarterly*, 21:3 (1981), pp. 275–99.

Schwendinger, H. and J. R. Schwendinger, *Sociologists of the Chair: A Radical Analysis of the Formative Years of North American Sociology (1883–1922)* (New York: Basic Books, 1974).

Schwartz J. M., 'Towards a History of the Melting Pot, or Why There is a Chicago School of Sociology but not a Detroit School', in M. Harbsmeier and M. T. Larson (eds), *The Humanities between Art and Science: Intellectual Developments, 1880–1914* (Copenhagen: Akademisk Forlag, 1989), pp. 59–78.

Seim, D. L., 'Objectivity vs. Advocacy: Newspaper Rhetoric during the "Bemis Affair" and the "Oleomargarine Controversy"', in J. Goodwin (ed.), *Between Scientists & Citizens* (Ames, IA: Great Plains Society for the Study of Argumentation, 2012), pp. 334–44.

Selekman B. and M. Van Kleck, *Employee Representation in Coal Mines: A Study of the Industrial Representation Plan of the Colorado Fuel and Iron Company* (New York: Russell Sage Foundation, 1924).

Shepardson, F. W., *Denison University 1831–1931: A Centennial History* (Granville, OH: Granville Times and Publishing Co., 1931).

Sherman, R., 'The Standard Oil Trust: The Gospel of Greed', *Forum* (New York), 13:7 (1892), pp. 602–15.

Sibley, E., *Social Science Research Council: The First Fifty Years* (New York: Social Science Research Center, 1974).

Sills, D. L., '50th Anniversary of the 1930 Hanover Conference: The Letters of Robert Redfield to his Wife Keep the Past Alive', *Items: Social Science Research Council*, 34:2 (1980),
p. 36.

—, 'A Note on the Origin of "Interdisciplinary"', *Items: Social Science Research Council*, 40:1
(1986), pp. 17–18.

—, 'A Requiem for P&P: Notes on the Council's Late Committee on Problems and Policy',
*Items: Social Science Research Council*, 50:4 (1996), pp. 94–7.

Small, A. W., 'Free Investigation', *American Journal of Sociology*, 1:2 (1895), pp. 210–4.

—, 'The Present Outlook of Social Science', *American Journal of Sociology*, 18:4 (1913), pp.
433–69.

Smelser, N. J. and D. R. Gerstein (eds), *Behavioural and Social Sciences: Fifty Years of Discovery, in Commemoration of the Fiftieth Anniversary of the 'Ogburn Report', Recent Social
Trends in the United States* (Washington, DC: National Academy Press, 1986).

Smith, C. S., *The American University, Annual Oration, Columbia College Library, June 2,
1887* (New York: Printed for the Chapter, 1887).

Smith, J. A., *The Idea Brokers: Think Tanks and the Rise of New Policy Elite* (New York: The
Free Press, 1991).

Smith, M. C., *Social Science in the Crucible: The American Debate over Objectivity and Purpose,
1918–1941* (Durham, NC: Duke University Press, 1994).

Smith, N., *American Empire* (Berkeley and Los Angeles, CA: University of California Press,
2003).

Smith, R., *The Human Sciences* (New York: W. W. Norton and Company, 1997).

Social Science Research Council, *Decennial Report, 1923–1933* (New York: Social Science
Research Council, 1934).

Sokal, M. M., 'James McKeen Cattell and American Psychology in the 1920s', in J. Brožek
(ed.), *Explorations in the History of Psychology in the United States* (Lewisburg, PA: Bucknell University Press, 1984), pp. 273–323.

Somit, A. and J. Tanenhaus, *The Development of American Political Science: From Burgess to
Behaviouralism* (New York: Irvington Publishers, 1982).

Spargo, J., *A Socialist View of Mr. Rockefeller* (Chicago, IL: C. H. Kerr & Co., 1905).

Stanfield, J. H., *Philanthropy and Jim Crow in American Social Science* (Westport, CT: Greenwood Press, 1985).

—, 'Leonard Outhwaite's Advocacy of Scientific Research on Blacks in the 1920s', *Knowledge
and Society*, 4:3 (1987), pp. 87–101.

Storr, R. J., *Harper's University: The Beginnings* (Chicago, IL: University of Chicago Press,
1966).

Taylor, G. R., *Satellite Cities: A Study of Industrial Suburbs* (New York and London: D. Appleton and Co., 1915).

Thomas, W. I., (in collaboration with R. Park and H. A. Miller), *Old World Traits Transplanted* (Chicago, IL: University of Chicago Press, 1921).

Thornton, R., 'Malinowski and the Birth of Functionalism, or, Zarathustra in the London
School of Economics', in J. T. Fraser and M. P. Soulsby (eds), *Dimensions of Time and*

*Life: The Study of Time* (Madison, CT: International Universities Press, 1996), pp. 251–66.

Thrasher, F. M., *The Gang: A Study of 1,313 Gangs in Chicago* (Chicago, IL, and London: University of Chicago Press, 1927).

Todd, A. J., *The Scientific Spirit and Social Work* (New York: Macmillan Co., 1919).

Tone, A., *The Business of Benevolence: Industrial Paternalism in Progressive America* (Ithaca, NY: Cornell University Press, 1997).

Trahair, R. C. S., *The Humanist Temper: The Life and Work of Elton Mayo* (New Brunswick, NJ, and London: Transaction Books, 1984).

Trescott, P. B., 'Institutional Economics in China: Yenching University, 1917–1941', *Journal of Economic Issues*, 26:4 (1992), pp. 1221–55.

—, 'American Philanthropy and the Development of Academic Economics in China before 1949', in S. Hewa and P. Hove (eds), *Philanthropy and Cultural Context: Western Philanthropy in South, East, and Southeast Asia in the Twentieth Century* (Lanham, MD: University Press of America, 1997), pp. 157–81.

Turner, S. P., 'The World of Academic Quantifiers: The Columbia University Family and Its Connections', in M. Bulmer, K. Bales and K. K. Sklar (eds), *The Social Survey in Historical Perspective, 1880–1940* (Cambridge: Cambridge University Press, 1991), pp. 269–90.

Unti, B., '"The Doctors are so Sure That They Only are Right": The Rockefeller Institute and the Defeat of Vivisection Reform in New York, 1908–1914', in D. H. Stapleton (ed.), *Creating a Tradition of Biomedical Research: Contributions to the History of The Rockefeller University* (New York: Rockefeller University Press, 2004), pp. 175–89.

Vance, R. B. and K. Jocher, 'Howard W. Odum', *Social Forces*, 33:2 (1955), pp. 203–17.

Von Hayek, F. A., 'The London School of Economics, 1895–1945', *Economica*, 13:49 (1946), pp. 1–31.

Wallace, R. W., 'The Struggle of a Department: Columbia Sociology in the 1920s', *Journal of the History of the Behavioural Sciences*, 27:3 (1991), pp. 323–40.

—, 'Starting a Department and Getting it under Way: Sociology at Columbia University, 1891–1914', *Minerva*, 30:4 (1992), pp. 497–512.

Wessel, B. B., 'Ethnic Factors in the Population of New London, Connecticut', *American Journal of Sociology*, 35:2 (1929), pp. 263–70.

Westfall, B. W., 'The William Rainey Harper/John D. Rockefeller Correspondence: Religion and Economic Control at the University of Chicago, 1889–1905', *Vitae Scholasticae*, 4:1–2 (1985), pp. 109–23.

Whitaker, B., *The Foundations: An Anatomy of Philanthropy and Society* (London: Eyre Methuen, 1974).

White, G. T., *Formative Years in the Far West: A History of Standard Oil Company of California and Its Predecessors through 1919* (New York: Appleton-Century-Crofts, 1962).

Willoughby, W. F., 'The Institute for Government Research', *American Political Science Review*, 12:1 (1918), pp. 49–62.

Winston, A. P., *Public Opinion and the Standard Oil Company* (St Louis, MO: Nixon-Jones Printing Co., 1908).

Wilson, M. L., 'The Fairway Farms Project', *Journal of Land and Public Utility Economics*, 2:2 (1926), pp. 156–71.

Wirth, L., *The Ghetto* (Chicago, IL: University of Chicago Press, 1928).

—, 'Urbanism as a Way of Life', *American Journal of Sociology*, 44:1 (1938), pp. 1–24.

Worcester, K. W., *Social Science Research Council, 1923–1998* (New York: Social Science Research Council, 2001).

Yerkes, R. M., 'The Work of [the] Committee on Scientific Problems of Human Migration, National Research Council', *Journal of Personnel Research*, 3:3 (1924), pp. 189–96.

Zunz, O., *Philanthropy in America: A History* (Princeton, NJ: Princeton University Press, 2012).

# INDEX

For Product Safety Concerns and Information please contact our EU
representative  GPSR@taylorandfrancis.com
Taylor & Francis Verlag GmbH, Kaufingerstraße 24, 80331 München, Germany

www.ingramcontent.com/pod-product-compliance
Ingram Content Group UK Ltd.
Pitfield, Milton Keynes, MK11 3LW, UK
UKHW021618240425
457818UK00018B/621